Blake

Congratulations on becoming
regional director for the new Louisville
area. I know the next 5 years will be
absolutely amazing. The gifting and
talents God has given you to express
His love and your love to others is a
pleasure for me to watch.

I hope you enjoy Tom's book
written in Pagosa, with other terrific
contributors, that God has brought about
for this time in church history.

I recommend reading chapter 7
and 13 to get a feel for the book.

Love you son. I am very proud
of you.

Dad.

Contagious Fire

Enflaming Hearts for God and Mission

R. Thomas Ashbrook

Contagious Fire

Enflaming Hearts for God and Mission

R. Thomas Ashbrook

FOREWORD BY Stephen A. Macchia

Published by R. Thomas Ashbrook

Unless otherwise noted, scripture is taken from the NEW AMERICAN STANDARD BIBLE© Copyright © 1960, 1962, 1963, 1968, 1971, 1972, 1973, 1975, 1977, 1995, by the Lockman Foundation.

Readers should be aware that Internet Web sites offered as citations and/or sources for further information may have changed or disappeared between the time this was written and when it is read.

Limit of Liability/Disclaimer of Warranty: While the publishers and authors have used their best efforts in preparing this book, they make no representations or warranties with respect to the accuracy or completeness of the contents of this book and specifically disclaim any implied warranties of representatives of written sales materials. The advice and strategies contained herein may not be suitable for your situation. You should consult with a professional where appropriate. Neither the publishers nor authors shall be liable for any loss of profit or any other commercial damages, including but not limited to special, incidental, consequential, or other damages.

Library of Congress Cataloguing-in-Publication Data

Ashbrook, R. Thomas

Contagious Fire: Enflaming Love for God and Mission / R. Thomas Ashbrook

Library of Congress Control Number: 2018900871

ISBN 978-0-9916368-5-3

Spiritual Formation. 2. Spirituality. 3. Missions. 4. Evangelism

Printed in the United States of America

First Edition

Contents

ACKNOWLEDGEMENTS   XI

FOREWORD XIII

PREFACE   XVII

CHAPTER 1...1
EMBERS CAN BE FANNED INTO FLAME - HOPE FOR THE
CHURCH

CHAPTER 2... 25
THE NATURE OF DIVINE FIRE – SPIRITUAL FORMATION
FROM A BIBLICAL PERSPECTIVE:

CHAPTER 3... 55
BECOMING CONTAGIOUS FIRE - ON THE JOURNEY
PERSONALLY AND INTENTIONALLY

CHAPTER 4... 79
IGNITING THE SPARK INTO FLAME - FOLLOWING JESUS

CHAPTER 5.. 105
SPARKING THE CHURCH - A VISION FOR CONTAGIOUS
CHRISTIANS

CHAPTER 6.. 133
HOW TO SPREAD THE FIRE - DISCOVERING THE WAY
FORWARD

CHAPTER 7.. 165
REVEALING THE FLAME AND DISPELLING THE FEAR -
TEACHING ABOUT SPIRITUAL FORMATION

CHAPTER 8.. 199
TOUCHING THE FIRE - OPPORTUNITIES FOR
EXPERIENTIAL DISCOVERY

CHAPTER 9...235
COMBATING THE FIRE EXTINGUISHERS - FACING THE
DRAGON TOGETHER

CHAPTER 10: 269
FANNING CONTAGIOUS FIRE - WORSHIP THAT MODELS
ABIDING IN LOVE

CHAPTER 11 295
BECOMING CONTAGIOUS BONFIRES - SPIRITUALLY
FORMING COMMUNITY

CHAPTER 12: 325
HEALING MINISTRY – REMOVING THE BLOCKS TO LOVE

CHAPTER 13 351
THE WINDS OF CONTAGIOUS FIRE - SPIRITUAL
FORMATION AS MISSIONAL MOMENTUM

CHAPTER 14 375
CONTAGIOUS FIRE – PULLING IT ALL TOGETHER

STORIES ABOUT CHURCHES PURSUING CONTAGIOUS
FIRE

RESOURCES FOR YOUR CONTAGIOUS FIRE

FOLLOWING JESUS INTO CONTAGIOUS FIRE

APPENDIX A...427
SPIRITUAL FORMATION DEFINITION FROM TRUE NORTH
PROJECT

APPENDIX B: 429
SHORTENED MODELS BASED ON TERESA OF AVILA'S SEVEN
MANSIONS WITH CURRICULUM SUGGESTIONS FOR EACH
STAGE

APPENDIX C 443
CONTEMPLATIVE DIALOGUE COVENANT

CONTRIBUTORS TO CONTAGIOUS FIRE.............................445

CHARLIE DODRILL

TAMMY LONG

CHRIS LYONS

STEVE MACCHIA

BILL O'BYRNE

CHUCK ORWILER

MELANIE SAINT JAMES

CHRIS SCHUTTE

DEBBIE SWINDOLL

TERRY TARLETON

STEVE THULSON

JD WARD

TED WUESTE

MARKUS HUGHES – COVER ARTIST

SPIRITUAL FORMATION RESOURCES 461
BY R. THOMAS ASHBROOK

ACKNOWLEDGEMENTS

As you will see as you get into *Contagious Fire*, this work emerged through the collaboration of a number of spiritual formation and missional church leaders from around the country. Through the use of a public website, www.contagiousfire.com, they helped develop the book flow, commented on the development of chapter content, and shared insights, stories, and illustrations that I have included in each chapter. Many others watched the development of *Contagious* Fire, using the material in their own settings and supported us in prayer for faithful completion of the project. For All these Contributors and Practitioners, I am deeply grateful. You can find information about our Contributors in the closing section of the book.

My wife, Charlotte's encouragement and support for the year that I have been chained to this project has made it all possible. Several of the Contributors also acted as Readers to try to head me off at the pass when I headed for the "too radical" cliff and brought me back out of webs of confusion. My deepest gratitude to Bill O'Byrne, Melanie Saint James, and Chris Lyons. Special thanks to Arlene Kampe, Patti Barton, and Becky Fluerry, who tracked down endless run-on sentences, typos, and grammar issues. My deep appreciation goes to Marcus Hughes, an impressionist artist here in Pagosa Springs, who designed the cover art for *Contagious Fire*, given as a gift for this project. My close friend, Martti Tulamo, a renowned Finnish architect, graciously created the chapter sketches. We owe a huge debt of gratitude to Carter Zimmerman who set up the Contagious Fire website that allowed our Collaborators to interact and our Practitioners to follow along with the development of the book.

Most of all, I want to honor our Lord Jesus Christ who calls us to accomplish the impossible and then provides the words, patience, and fortitude necessary for sinners to complete His assignment. Fun!

FOREWORD

Stephen A. Macchia

Generally when we hear the word "contagious" we immediately consider transmittable indications of a cold or the flu, or a disease not properly medicated or inoculated against. "Fire" has a similar visceral response: enjoy it if it's contained, but extinguish or flee from it when it wreaks havoc on everything in its pathway.

So why in the world would Tom Ashbrook title a book "Contagious Fire" when the words themselves suffer from such immediately disconcerting connotations?

Precisely because when they are flipped upside down the two words form a spiritually combustible combination...and something we pray will transpire among the people of God worldwide who take the time to read this remarkable text.

Those of us, who know the Lord, can attest to the fire deep within the belly of our souls...and we are confident that when Jesus takes residence in the center of our hearts, life is never the same again. As a result, there should follow a contagious joy that wells up from deep within us, in addition to prayers offered and actions taken for the spiritual vitality of all humankind.

The story of the two disciples on the road to Emmaus (Luke 24) is emblematic of the contagious fire of the soul. Just a few days after Jesus' crucifixion, they were on a seven-mile hike homeward. They were in disbelief, downcast, despondent and discouraged. They were doubting their own feelings and experiences; their hopes were crushed, and their faith was dashed upon the rock. Was anything they had previously come to believe about Jesus true?

But then Jesus joins them on their journey. He walks alongside them. He opens the Scriptures and speaks about the promises fulfilled in their midst. He joins them at the table, breaks bread with them, enjoys fellowship in their midst, and watches the eyes of their hearts become enlightened...like never before. He doesn't stay physically present with them for very long, but his luminous presence was undoubtedly spectacular. He made himself known to them in a powerful way, and their eventual discernment of his presence, power and peace is reflected in their singular comment to one another, "Were not our hearts burning within us?"

When a heart begins to burn for Jesus there is simply no turning back. Initially upon our conversion from darkness to light, this reality is vibrantly alive. Tending to the fire deep within the soul is the singular determination for how long the fire stays lit. We tend to our souls as individuals, we tend to the fire in communities, and we delight to observe how the Holy Spirit keeps the embers aflame by his loving initiatives of grace, mercy and peace. When the two disciples notice Jesus in their midst, they run immediately to share the good news: their souls are on fire and Jesus is alive!

In very positive terms, for indeed their fire became contagious, their joy was infectious. Instead of a contagious despondency and disheartened disbelief, their contagious life was one of love, grace and peace. And throughout history there are myriad numbers of those who have kept the flame of Christendom ablaze for each new generation.

Recently I was with a group of pastors, considering together the state of their soul, the effectiveness of their ministry life, and the quality of their local church experience. To a person there were stories of strife, discontent, confusion, exhaustion, and long-standing frustration. I was shocked how prevalent these concerns had become. Each of the leaders present shared how hard it had been to work toward resolution and embrace a new way of being together as a faith community.

Finally, one of the quiet ones in the group began to share her recent experiences as a pastoral leader in a small urban church. She began describing the hunger that exists in her setting, a small church struggling to maintain any sense of health and vitality. The finances were drying up as fast as the heaviness in the hearts of those in her neighborhood. The needs of families and the homeless were beyond the scope of their capabilities to help. But, slowly, over several laborious weeks and months, a small handful of congregants began meeting together in a brand new way.

Their gatherings began as an alternative Sunday evening worship service, in the form of a small group. From a handful of three to a substantial group of twelve, their covenant was very simple: gather for 90 minutes total. The first few minutes were for fellowship and a simple prayer, followed by a brief lectio on a passage of Scripture. This was followed by 20 minutes of silence, held sacred by all. After the silence concluded they shared what they had noticed. Subsequently, the group crafted a simple rule of life for their week: daily silence (bookended by Scripture and prayer), weekly fasting (from food as well as technology and other items), and a commitment to serve others sacrificially.

This small urban church in a rather unknown city in the northeast is experiencing a radical reformation. The fire within the souls of this small group is revolutionary...and contagious. Just listening to the story was infectious for the other pastors within earshot. It will be exciting to see where God leads this church in the future. They are becoming spiritually attentive, with a fire lit deeply within their souls that's increasingly more and more contagious, thanks be to God.

In the pages that follow, Tom and his team invite you to consider the biblical and historical text of your faith in light of your present realities. As you work through the chapters ahead of you, be mindful of the moments when your own heart is burning with joy and delight. Notice in this book the gifts God is giving for your own soul. Pray into the invitations herein for your church and your ministry community.

The work that's been done to collate and dispense the chapters you're about to read have been presented out of love...for God, for the Church, for spiritual leaders, and for disciples everywhere. May the words you read and the reflections you encounter ignite and transform the *contagious fire* welling up from the depth of your soul.

Stephen A. Macchia

Lexington, Massachusetts

PREFACE

Most of my life has been devoted to shepherding flocks of believers in the Church. I experienced great joys as people came to know the Lord and I saw lives changed, marriages and families healed, and love, hope, and joy explode in the hearts of followers of Jesus. I also felt great pain whenever the churches I served struggled with conflict, doubt, resistance to our Lord's leading, and provided a poor witness to our Lord's greatness and love to the community.

Seventeen years ago, the Lord called me to follow Him into the lives of Christian leaders with encouragement to know His love more deeply and to minister from that secret place of abiding. These leaders fell in love with Jesus in new and deeper ways. As leaders' hearts became formed more and more in the image of Christ, I again witnessed new life and vibrant ministry. Most of them shepherded flocks of believers stuck in shallow faith and religious institutionalism. These transformed leaders now longed to see their congregations flourish with the same abiding love that they had discovered and invited their members to explore a deeper relationship with Jesus. Unfortunately, the pastors' invitations were often ignored or thwarted.

I have longed to write something that could encourage and support these Christian leaders, both in their desire to see new and vibrant love for Jesus in their people who would then extend that love to the world. As I prayed about what to write, the Lord gave me two words that have defined this project: First, He told me to entitle the work, *Contagious Fire*, because that describes the nature of what He is doing in the Church. Second, He told me that I am not smart enough to write such a book. He wanted to speak not only through one pastor with experience in one niche of the Christian family, but through many leaders from many backgrounds, who experience both the successes and frustrations of enflaming the hearts of believers to love God and love their neighbors—from expressions of the Body of Christ.

I searched through my contacts, asking, "Who do I know working in the thick of a contagious fire type ministry that might be willing to collaborate with me in developing and contributing to *Contagious Fire*?" I wrote twenty leaders, hoping that four or five would be willing to invest the time and effort. To my amazement nineteen said they would pray about participating. Ultimately, thirteen amazing pastors and ministry professionals have contributed thoughts, examples, and stories to the pages that follow. On our interactive website, www.contagiousfire.com, we developed the flow of the book, the chapter outlines, and discussed potential content for each chapter. What amazing contributions!

Therefore, we invite you to read *Contagious Fire* as a participant in a discussion. Explore the topics with us; stop and pray; discuss what you're reading with others; ask Jesus what He wants you to do.

You'll find discussion questions for each chapter in Chapter 14 designed to help you reflect on your own readiness to proceed. The questions assume that you have been in the process of implementing *Contagious Fire*, but could be used in a personal or group reflection on each chapter, as you read.

Most of all, pray with us that Christian leaders all over the world would catch fire with the love of God and share that love to the ends of the earth!

Tom Ashbrook

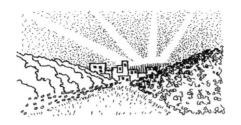

CHAPTER 1

EMBERS CAN BE FANNED INTO FLAME - HOPE FOR THE CHURCH

Have you ever wondered what it might be like to pastor a church or lead a ministry where your members lived so on fire with the love of Jesus that they couldn't help but reach out with love for those around them? Can you imagine the resulting exploding missional momentum, without ever uttering the term evangelism? What if the local church and its ministries focused exclusively on loving God and neighbor? What would it look like if every member intentionally followed Jesus into such a deep and abiding relationship with the Trinity that their hearts caught fire with contagious love? Could you keep up with a people for whom it became natural to live out contagious and inviting lives in their contexts in such a way that the Kingdom of God became blazingly evident?

A few years ago, I expressed my longing this way:

"Can we picture a church where loving God and taking that love to our neighbors is simply what church is about? What would it be like to have Sunday morning worship radiate our dynamic love for Jesus, and the preaching and teaching guide us to discover and live out that love more fully? Can we imagine a church of spiritual pilgrims, recognizing their unique journeys to the heart of God, dependent on one another for help and encouragement in that adventure? What if small groups and spiritual friendships were intentionally facilitated to focus on helping us grow

1

spiritually, and live out the love of Jesus in the world around us? What might happen if the leadership of the church was formed by a community of men and women whose intimacy with God was so deep that they were able to discern His specific leading for the body, rather than have to rely on canned programs and traditions? What if, one day, you were reading about Jesus and His disciples' overnight trip to the mountain to pray together, followed by their journey to the valley to work miracles among people who desperately needed God's love, and we were able to say, 'Of course; that's what happens every week at our church.'?" *Mansions of the Heart*, R. Thomas Ashbrook, pg. 233

I'm searching everywhere to find men and women who share that dream and will explore with me how to make it a reality! Maybe you're one of them. To that end, I'd like to invite you into a kind of community dialogue, around a virtual "campfire." As you've read in the Preface, Contagious Fire grew out of the dialogue of a number of men and women experienced in the spiritual formation movement and in missional outreach. If you haven't already, turn to the Contributors Section near the end of the book and read their bios. You'll hear great insights from them in the following pages about their experience with the kind of contagious life that sets the world on fire. This Contagious Fire Community represents Jesus' followers who exhibit a raging desire to see the Church, in all its forms, become like a forest fire of God's love. We long for God's loving presence to so inflame His followers that the world's dark night shines with love's brilliance and draws those who don't yet know Him, by its contagion.

We're daring to believe that this fire of Love goes way beyond glowing embers, subtle flickers, or kindly warmth. Jesus calls us to become part of the fire that He's casting across the earth—fire so intense and powerful that Christians rise to embrace His presence and surrender their hearts to His transformation. We're standing with the simple and foolish who first believed that God's love burned so intensely that Jesus surrendered His divine attributes to become one of us, to rescue us through His cross from the cold darkness of death. We're witnesses to the truth that the fire of His love has spread across time and space and ignited us with His amazing life. We've risked everything to become flame throwers of love to see the Church alive with the brilliance of a City set upon a hill, drawing all people to its love, life, and eternal redemption. We see this contagious community streaming into the streets of the world—to neighbors, coworkers, the poor, and the unreached with a love so attractive that God ignites hearts that secretly long for Him. We're absolutely convinced that it can happen today—to the Church and to us. Foolishness, some say! We'll see.

So, welcome to this dialogue about Jesus' Church. I know, it may feel challenging to dialogue with an author and Contributors whose thoughts have been printed on paper pages or encoded in eBook graphics. Our dialogue can happen, however, because the Holy Spirit resides within me as I write, within the Contributors as they comment, and within you as you read. He connects us all to Jesus and the Father as we share our dreams and visions for the Body of Christ. The Holy Spirit has called us together because this dialogue has to happen—it's not an option. The fact is, we have to talk about it; we'll explode if we don't at least try to put words to it! The Holy Spirit has been whispering visions and dreams within your heart and ours—visions that simultaneously cause us to gasp with joyous expectation and groan with gut-wrenching agony. As we look into our own hearts, we see, "as in a glass darkly," glimpses of the Church that Jesus commissioned, "The City Set Upon a Hill." We've become filled with a deep passion to live into its reality. At the same time, we all feel our own weariness in the shadow of a Church crippled with religion, rather than ablaze with love. We need a community of like-minded dreamers to help us maintain the courage to explore the vision.

Convergence of Two Movements of the Holy Spirit

Imago Christi, the ministry in which I serve, and the ministries of the Contagious Fire Project Contributors, agree that we see a new wind of the Holy Spirit blowing in many churches, worldwide. Two torches of the Holy

Spirit seem to be gaining brilliance among followers of Jesus around the globe: First, we see among many leaders a growing emphasis on deepening intimacy with Jesus and intentional Spiritual Formation as the focus of church life. Second, many leaders have begun to focus on the Missional Church imperatives to meet people where they live with the fire of God's love in practical ways.

In the first, Jesus calls us to return to our "first love," and to follow Him personally and specifically. In the most remote third-world villages and in first-world towns and urban metropolises, we see Christian leaders responding to the Holy Spirit's invitation to a new and deepening relationship of loving intimacy with the Trinity. Many of them tell us that this ever-growing abiding relationship clarifies and strengthens their identities as beloved followers of Jesus, and heals and transforms their personal brokenness. As they learn to truly abide with Christ in prayer and community, He attunes their attentiveness to the present reality of Jesus' shepherding. The Holy Spirit then creates increasing Christ-likeness in their own character and their relationships with others, and sets them free to live abundantly in the fellowship of the Trinity's dance of love.

At the same time, in the second, Jesus calls us to make His love for the world the very center of the life of the Church, not just one of its ministries. The Holy Spirit is igniting, in many leaders around the world, a more organically outward understanding of the Church. They see the Church as open and porous, living its life with Jesus among people who don't yet know Him. These leaders don't want to focus on maintaining an institution or organization designed to perpetuate the inner circle. They envision a church, not just open to or desirous of new "members," but a community of believers who live as an incarnational presence within the world, loving people where they need God's love and power. Missional churches desire to love first, then share why they love.

Both movements experience the struggles of countercultural change and the temptations to try to "capture" the Holy Spirit's work. Within the spiritual formation movement, some have sought the love of God for their own healing and renewal, focusing inwardly and losing sight of the lost and needy. Some missional leaders have attempted to program and legislate evangelistic outreach within their churches, missing the truth that human compassion or obligation can't adequately motivate sacrificial living. Only God's love, flaming within us, can provide the momentum to overcome our selfishness and send us into the world. "We love because God first loved us."

Leaders within both spiritual formation and the mission perspectives have expressed concerns that the other may be moving in the wrong direction, neglecting key elements of either the Great Commandment or the Great Commission. It is, however, by embracing both these biblical imperatives that we truly grasp the call of God in our time. As Love becomes perfected within us, we "leaders in transformation" discover a new passion to lead everyone in our ministry context into a new and profound intimacy with Jesus—one that empowers the Church to live out its call to both the Great Commandment and the Great Commission. We see these two torches of the Holy Spirit converging!

Within *Contagious Fire*, therefore, I want to invite you to explore your heart and the Holy Spirit's whispers; think about your own journey with Jesus and the road ahead. Read conversationally—talk to God; talk back to me; find a friend and listen to God together. Where does this kind of fire start? How does it spread? What does it mean to become ignited, as a leader and as a church, with love that becomes a Contagious Fire? To begin our conversation, let's explore a familiar story that sets the context for our exploration.

> And behold, two of them were going that very day to a village named Emmaus, which was about seven miles from Jerusalem. And they were talking with each other about all these things which had taken place. While they were talking and discussing, Jesus Himself approached and began traveling with them. But their eyes

were prevented from recognizing Him. ... and they approached the village where they were going, and He acted as though He were going farther. But they urged Him, saying, "Stay with us, for it is getting toward evening, and the day is now nearly over." So, He went in to stay with them. When He had reclined at the table with them, He took the bread and blessed it, and breaking it, He began giving it to them. Then their eyes were opened and they recognized Him; and He vanished from their sight. They said to one another, **"Were not our hearts burning within us while He was speaking to us on the road, while He was explaining the Scriptures to us?"** And they got up that very hour and returned to Jerusalem, and found gathered together the eleven and those who were with them.... (Luke 24:13-17, 28-33)

We see that Jesus ignited these three disciples' hearts through His presence. I'd guess that He had taught those scriptures to His followers many times before. Now, however, maybe because of their own desperation, they experienced far more than information—the Word of God touched their darkness personally. The fire of real love always starts in an encounter with Jesus.

Scripture often relates love and zeal for God with fire. Here are a few examples:

He makes the winds His messengers,

Flaming fire His ministers. Psalms 104:4

King David

•

"I have come to cast fire upon the earth; and how I wish it were already kindled! Luke 12:49

Jesus

Then I saw a new heaven and a new earth; for the first heaven and the first earth passed away, and there is no longer any sea. And I saw the holy city, new Jerusalem, coming down out of heaven from God, made ready as a bride adorned for her husband. And I heard a loud voice from the throne, saying, "Behold, the tabernacle of God is among men, and He will dwell among them, and they shall be His people, and God Himself will be among them, and He will wipe away every tear from their eyes; and there will no longer be any death; there will no longer be any mourning, or crying, or pain; the first things have passed away." And He who sits on the throne said, "Behold, I am making all things new." Revelation 21:1-5

Apostle John

"And as you go, preach, saying, 'The kingdom of heaven is at hand.' Matthew 10:7

Jesus

Men and women of God have carried this longing for fire for centuries.

The day will come when, after harnessing the ether, the winds, the tides, gravitation, we shall harness for God the energies of love. And, on that day, for the second time in the history of the world, man will have discovered fire.

– Pierre Teilhard de Chardin

As members of this historical community, let's dare to touch the fire ourselves and see where the Holy Spirit takes us. First however, a promise: I want to assure you, before we launch into this discussion, that neither I nor our Contributors intend to try to tell you what to do or to project some fix-it program for your ministry. In fact, our foundational principle won't even let us try—we're convinced that only Jesus can shepherd you through the complexities of your unique ministry context. We simply want to invite you to consider, with Him, some of the aspects that the Contributors and I have been learning about how God's love moves from warmth within a person's heart to Love's contagious fire—in a church that changes the world.

Fire

As you've already seen, we're using "fire" as a biblical metaphor for the dynamic movement of God's transforming love. Moses first met God in a burning bush and then received God's law in a fire that made His face glow. Moses even described God as a "Consuming Fire." God ordered that fire consume the offerings of love to God in the Tabernacle and then the Temple, and instructed that an ever-burning fire symbolize the Lord's eternal presence. Elijah went directly to heaven in a chariot of fire. Isaiah's sins were forgiven, and his ministry launched as God touched his lips with a burning coal taken from the altar fire. Isaiah foresaw Jesus as God's fire that would restore and redeem the world. John the Baptist introduced Jesus as the one who would baptize with the Holy Spirit and with fire. Jesus compared His followers as a city set upon a hill, lit with firelight that then enlightens everyone.

John the Baptist's statement reminds us that fire also represents God's judgment of sin and the destruction of everything that opposes Him. Seen from the perspective of a follower of Jesus, however, this same "fire" lovingly burns away the chaff and dead branches within us that hinder our ability to fully live in God's love and then love others as He loves us. Therefore, *Contagious Fire* speaks of God, who is Love, as He forgives, restores, redeems, enlightens, loves, and sets our hearts on fire with love for God and neighbor. Our Lord desires that the light of His redeeming love burn so brightly within the Church that no one need feel the heat of God's judgment!

Building on our fire metaphor, we'll picture our journey of love using what we know about how fire begins, builds, and spreads, letting these movements describe the process of moving from spiritual growth to missional impact, personally and corporately.

I'd like to share a bit of my story and stories from a few from our Contributors, to illustrate the movement of God's fire of love.

After receiving a degree in engineering and another in management, I sensed, in the midst of a career in the aerospace industry, God calling me to become a preacher. I entered ministry with two overriding passions—foci for my fire. My fire shown as a zeal for both evangelism and the experiential visibility of Jesus in the local church. Both hot spots emerged out of my own history. My religious upbringing reflected American culture rather than God's desire for the Church. "Work hard and do the best you can, and everything will work out OK." That doctrine's lie didn't make itself known to me until my junior year in college when I fled to a professor to find out why nothing in my life was working out "OK," at all. I hadn't seen this chalk-dust-covered English professor since Freshman Composition. An amazing and brilliant teacher, Dr. Lambert seemed to care about his students. In retrospect, I now recognize my attraction to his warmth and light, but I had no idea he was "religious." Dr. Lambert pointed me to the God that I was quite sure didn't exist. He suggested that I ask Him to help me and challenged me to "just see what happens." As an emerging scientist, up for an experiment, and in absolute desperation, I did. God did, too—and my life began. God planted a tiny ember of love within me that brought a noticeable warmth in the midst of my depression.

My passion for evangelism came from living twenty-two years on the dark side and never wanting anyone else to have to do that. My vision for the Church also came from what I didn't experience in churches I'd visited growing up—Jesus. I had attended several brands with friends over the years, reinforcing my belief that "religion" wasn't for me. In retrospect, I quite correctly came to that conclusion because religion was all that I experienced there. My heart longed, without knowing it, for Jesus, for my real identity in the creation, for love and belonging—for fire. Religion couldn't offer any of that; it was never intended to. Sitting here, writing to you, my eyes tear up just thinking about someone coming to a "Christian" church and finding only religion, not Jesus. I long for the Church to really live as the Body of Christ in discernible ways. I've spent some twenty odd years in those pursuits as a pastor and another fifteen as a missionary to pastors. Starting on my knees in my professor's living room, God set my heart on fire, first with His love, and then with love for others. Hardest of all, He has fanned those flames of love to the point where I could begin to love myself. While I saw sparks flicker in many others, I often wondered why the fire of God's love seemed to be kept largely hidden within people's hearts. What would it take for the flames to become contagious—to blaze forth to reveal what others, without knowing it, longed for—Jesus and the healing love of God.

To start, we'll build on our analog. Most of us have started a campfire or built a fire in a fireplace. Let's describe how we might build something much greater—a signal fire.

- We find an igniter, a flame.

- We let the igniter heat a small piece of wood until it starts to burn.

- We bring other small pieces of wood close enough to the burning piece to receive its heat, but not so close as to block the flow of air.

- As the fire among the small pieces becomes secure, we add larger pieces of wood, maintaining the correct spacing.

- As the fire becomes hot and bright, we add larger pieces of wood, piling them in a crisscross manner that allows us to build a tower where heat and air flow allow the flames to shoot upward into the sky.

- We ignite torches and run into the night to invite people stumbling in the dark to receive the light and invite them to the warmth of our bonfire.

- As our guests become warmed, we offer them a torch and take them with us into the night.

- Soon, signal fires emerge around the world.

Now to the conversation, and it's your turn: How did God call you to follow Him? What did the flames of your "first love" look like? What have you learned and what questions have caused aches in your heart?

Now it's my turn again. Several years into my pastorate, God snagged me again. He began to show me that Jesus was pursuing me with His love. I had believed in Jesus ever since college; would have told you that He was the most important person in my life; I even embraced near poverty to serve Him. Jesus, however, wanted more; He wanted me to abide in His love—actually, experientially. It felt as though I was like Andrew or Peter or James or John in Galilee and Jesus kept walking by saying, "Follow Me." I was following Him; what more did He want? He wanted to heal my unlovable vision of myself, to blow on my little spark of love, to make it flame until the heat and light and glory of it made my low self-esteem irrelevant. God showed me that He wanted to so consume and heal me that the flickers of love in my heart would burst forth into a consuming fire. I discovered that my parishioners' "heart hearths" contained only glowing embers not because of Jesus, but because of me, their spiritual leader. I realized that I had to discover how to lead others into the depths of God's love to the point where their holy fires became contagious!

Some months later, when serving a Lutheran church in Sandy, Utah, those flames began to singe our staff—some with warmth and curiosity and others with irritation and concern. Finally, three of our staff went with me on retreat at a local monastery to attempt to hear from God about how the Holy Spirit sets fire to a church. We vowed to continue in prayer and conversation until the Lord brought us to one mind. It took four agonizing days for Jesus to get through to us with a list of thirty-four instructions we were to obey ourselves and to take to the church. As soon as possible after we returned home, we called a meeting of our church elders, and shared what we felt the Lord had told us. All thirty-four points can be summarized in two simple statements: 1. "I, Jesus, am head of the church; follow Me in unity and peace." 2. Depend totally on the Holy Spirit to set fire to people's hearts. (Both points challenged the education and brilliance we had been depending on.)

To our amazement, the whole leadership became willing to fully submit to Jesus, to drop the sacred *Roberts' Rules of Order* and the traditional rule of committees, and stepped out in faith to learn how to actually follow Jesus—together. Obedience stretched and challenged us, to say the least, but the results proved truly amazing. As leaders and congregation, we learned with humility to understand ourselves and others with compassion and forgiveness. As we learned to let Jesus' love into the recesses of our hearts, congregational worship became vibrant and alive with our Lord's contagious love. Over time, a significant percentage of our congregation could tell stories of their exodus from Mormonism and their new life in Jesus, from dead forms to the brightness of an inviting fire.

God works in unique ways with each of us. Terry Tarleton, one of our Contributors and a Vineyard pastor shared a glimpse into his own story about this same discovery.

> *I came to a place in life and ministry where I hit a huge wall and was desperate for transformation. Funny thing is I thought I was transformed! Almost seven years ago, my wife and I looked at each other and said, 'The Church looks no different from the world.' We decided that we needed to deal with our own brokenness, and started down a path toward the inner journey of deepening intimacy with Jesus. Our own journeys brought us to a place where our church was able to see transformation in us which opened the door for many of our members to take a step toward their own transformation via abiding intimately in Christ.*

Terry's church became known for its presence in the community and its care and love for others—contagious fire! In both our lives, Jesus taught us again the simple truth we had preached on for years, "We love because He first loved us." Only when we experience the transforming love of God, will we have the motivation and the ability to love our neighbor. Only through the growing fire of our own spiritual formation can the Holy Spirit ignite the waiting hearts of others with our flickering love for them.

Taking the fire analogy further, let's list some basic insights about fire and Love:

- 1. Fire always comes from an external energy source.

- *The Holy Spirit*

- 2. Fire requires both combustible material and a supportive environment.

- *Our willing life and the winds of the Holy Spirit in community*

- 3. Fire changes matter into energy—heat and light.

- *Our response to God into dynamic love which blesses others*

- 4. Fire flourishes when the material and the environment relate in a way that enhances combustion.

- *We receive God's love in personal prayer and in spiritual community.*

- 5. Fire's heat and light support life when guided and controlled.

- *Love and insight in God's wisdom and guidance*

- 6. Fire's heat brings energy to the human body enhancing its function.

- *God's love sets us free from fear and emboldens our love for others.*

- 7. Fire's light enables the human body to see clearly and find its direction.

- *Love clarifies our motives and guides our actions.*

- 8. Fire attracts human beings when its heat and light nurture life.

- *Our innate need to be loved senses God's love in others and draws us to them.*

- 9. Fire spreads when the energy from one source heats another combustible material to an igniting temperature.

- *God's love for us creates love within us, both for God and for others.*

- 10. Fire becomes contagious when one sees its beneficial effects, causing the other to move close enough to receive that fire.

- *Our unconditional love for others causes them to seek God's love which ignites love within them*

God births our visions for His Church out of the contexts in which we live and the internal conditions of our own souls. God had to show me the difference between following Him and trying to program an evangelistic church with the engineering and management skills I'd learned. He had to show me that until I let him heal my own heart and fan the flames of my first love, it could never happen to my congregation. God gave Terry and his wife a good look at the secularity of their own church to show them that God wanted to heal their own hearts, first. Then, they could show others around them what wholeness looked like and be able to invite others into the abundant life of Jesus.

Now it's your turn: How has God birthed vision for His Bride in your heart? How do these "flaming" words connect with you right now?

Back to me: In our Contributor discussions, we agreed that leaders seem to develop a contagious fire type vision for the Church out of two seemingly opposite life situations. Some of us grew up knowing the deep love of Jesus and never lost sight of the centrality of that first love in the mission of the

Church. God's love relationship has sustained and guided ministry over the years. You may respond, "Yes! This is just the way my fire was first kindled!" For example, Bill O'Byrne, co-founder and team leader of *Imago Christi*, shares his story about growing up with his pastor father in a vibrant Christ-centered church. "

Many of us, maybe most, come to this discussion from a more difficult position. We've been wounded and even broken by the challenges of leading a church. We might respond to this contagious fire discussion with, "That might sound good if I weren't nursing burns from a different kind of fire—the kinds of institutional and political fire that scorches people and leaves them scarred for life." Some of us might feel, "Sure, I want my ministry to be on fire and contagious, but I'm so tired that there's not much spark left in me." Chris Lyons, pastor of Youth and Family Ministries, shares his perspective:

> We're on a journey with Jesus, but often too distracted by our own issues/struggles to even recognize that Jesus is traveling with us, wooing us to open up to Him about what is really going on with us... trying to steer our experiences into the deeper story of God's narrative where even our failures and disappointments can make sense. And somehow if we can return the favor – invite Jesus to "stay with us" – if we were to slow down and make space and time to be still – then our eyes can be opened, too! Then our missional momentum sends us out to share about that experience.

Wherever you find yourself, there's no denying that today's church has to be the hardest place on the planet to lead. Our rapidly changing culture and global mobility have left many churches with unclear identities and confused leadership expectations. Our culture seems increasingly hostile to what it sees as "Christian religion." While a few mega-churches, "something-for-everyone" giants, seem to flourish, most smaller churches find themselves struggling, both to survive and to prove their relevance in society. Once prominent and respected leaders in our communities, pastors now struggle with suspicion from non-Christians, criticism from members, and elusive markers for success to support their own self-esteem. Statistics about burnout for Christian leaders seem staggering! Interestingly, all this "bad news" could actually be the occasion for something fantastic. God has our attention, and He's up to something.

Now you: From which primary direction has your longing for the Church developed? What's tended to block your ability to move forward?

OK, I'm in: For many of us who've been in ministry for some time, skepticism has become a knee-jerk reaction to calls for renewal or revival; hope lost can be hard to regain. Movements and programs have come and gone and, from where many of us stand, conditions have only seemed to worsen. Maybe visions of a new kind of church serve only the very young who've not yet been beaten up by the church. Possibly, these dreams should be left to the old who remember the "good old days," deluded that it can happen again. It's possible that our retirement or the second coming might take us out of the game and, although we hate this status quo, just waiting it out might be the safest solution. Some feel called to martyrdom in the first place so we could just tell them to go for it. Or, maybe, Jesus intends for us to trust Him.

Your turn: What skepticisms lurk within your heart and what fuels them? Too tired? Too busy? Too wounded? Doing good enough? We've all got them, but it helps to bring them into the light. Reflect a bit and then I'll share.

I'm in: So, what do we do with our skepticism and low expectations that God will really do something? We've all looked for some switch that would produce greater faith or shut up the voices which discourage us. At the same time, we realize that some level of appropriate "caution" can save us from needless expenditure of energy and another disappointment. So many books; why should you keep reading this one? "God, are these guys on the right track, or is this just another rendition of 'old time religion' sung to a new tune? Even if I find myself interested, how do I move from the flame I'm nurturing to a contagious fire?"

I'd never presume to tell you to just jump on our bandwagon, but I do

16

invite you simply to consider, in your heart, your starting place with God. In *Imago Christi*, we call this our First Order Calling. Let's look at Matthew 22:36-38.

> "Teacher, which is the great commandment in the Law?" And He said to him, " 'you shall love the Lord your God with all your heart, and with all your soul, and with all your mind.' This is the great and foremost commandment."

Why love? Jesus connects our love for Him with our ability to follow Him. Three times Jesus asks Peter if he has moved from friendship to love.

> So, when they had finished breakfast, Jesus said to Simon Peter, "Simon, son of John, do you love (agape – unselfish love)) Me more than these?" He said to Him, "Yes, Lord; You know that I love (phileo – friendship) You." He said to him, "Tend My lambs." He said to him again a second time, "Simon, son of John, do you love (agape) Me?" He said to Him, "Yes, Lord; You know that I love (phileo) You." He said to him, "Shepherd My sheep." He said to him the third time, "Simon, son of John, do you love (phileo) Me?" Peter was grieved because He said to him the third time, "Do you love (phileo) Me?" And he said to Him, "Lord, You know all things; You know that I love (phileo) You." Jesus said to him, "Tend My sheep. John 21:15-17

The apostle Paul tells us that love trumps everything else. In the great love chapter,1 Corinthians 13, Paul describes the nature of true love, "[Love] bears all things, believes all things, hopes all things, endures all things. Love never fails." He concludes this amazing description by saying, "But now faith, hope, love, abide these three; but the greatest of these is love."

Again, we could ask, "Why love?" The apostle John explains why love stands at the heart of our relationship with God. In 1 John 4:15-17, he proclaims, "Whoever confesses that Jesus is the Son of God, God abides in him, and he in God. We have come to know and have believed the love which God has for us. God is love, and the one who abides in love abides in God, and God abides in him."

In *Imago Christi*, therefore, we call God's Greatest Commandment His "First Order Calling." It's where we all begin and just what we tell every seeker: God invites us into a personal relationship with Himself through faith in Jesus Christ. Our First Order Calling isn't fulfilled in a simple "decision for Christ," however. It takes time for us sin-sick and broken prodigals to learn to abide, to fully receive God's forgiveness and love, just the way we are. We have to learn to trust God to let His life-giving love restore us and transform our hearts of stone into hearts of flesh, to begin to love God the way Jesus does. It's in that abiding that the warmth of God's love in us becomes a flicker and then a flame. It's in the quiet place with Jesus that the Holy Spirit fans love's flames until they become bright and beautiful—contagious!

The second "Greatest" commandment undergirds our missional emphasis, and, interestingly, has to do with love as well. Returning to Matthew 22, we read, "The second is like it, 'You shall love your neighbor as yourself.' On these two commandments depend the whole Law and the Prophets." Jesus takes it even further. If loving our neighbor the same way we love ourselves isn't hard enough, Jesus then moves the bar a notch higher beyond this Old Covenant command to love our neighbor. In John 13:34-35, we read, "A new commandment I give to you, that you love one another, even as I have loved you, that you also love one another. By this all men will know that you are My disciples, if you have love for one another." In John 15:16, we read, "You did not choose Me but I chose you, and appointed you that you would go and bear fruit, and that your fruit would remain, so that whatever you ask of the Father in My name He may give to you. This I command you, that you love one another."

The command to love sets an incredibly high goal for us to attain, impossible in our own strength. Our ability to love others has to be God loving others through us. Fortunately, He's delighted to do that.

Finally, at the conclusion of Matthew's gospel, we hear Jesus' command in the words we have come to know as the Great Commission.

And Jesus came up and spoke to them, saying, "All authority has been given to Me in heaven and on earth. Go therefore and make disciples of all the nations, baptizing them in the name of the Father and the Son and the Holy Spirit, teaching them to observe all that I commanded you; and lo, I am with you always, even to the end of the age. Matthew 28:18-20

You guessed it; we call this second greatest commandment and the Great Commission, our "Second Order Calling." As we allow Jesus to draw us into deepening intimacy with the Trinity and grow in our love for Him, we realize, often to our surprise, that God's love begins to attract others to Jesus' love within us in the most natural ways. Then we long to love God in others. With new eyes, we see those around us as God's Beloved—valued as treasures in His heart. With this contagious fire blazing within us, we experience great joy when we love our neighbor as Jesus loves us—both for His sake and our neighbors'.

Life in our First Order Calling empowers our ability to follow Jesus in our Second Order Calling. Many of us, however, have inadvertently reversed the order and find ourselves ministering uphill, without much fire, until we're stuck and burned out. We all at least started out in the First Order Calling. In my case, making the First Order first came easily because I felt so needy for love and healing, and God's love flickering within me truly sustained me. But, I became impatient. It didn't take long for me to recognize that my low self-esteem could be bolstered by Second Order Calling success. Without realizing it, I decided that I had learned to abide well enough. With only a few glowing embers, I launched out to serve God. Before long, I became so busy serving that I had little time to abide, to simply be with Jesus and let Him make me more alive—more on fire. Without the intimacy of my First Order Calling, I soon found that trusting Jesus in the Second Order Calling became harder than I thought. Finally, after a few trips through the valley of the shadow, I let my Shepherd reorient me again. It's still a challenge for me to keep both callings balanced.

So, we see that the fires of love for God in our spiritual formation and the contagion of that fire in missional love for others lies at the heart of Jesus' ministry and His call to us since the beginning. At the same time, Jesus' challenge to the church in Ephesus might find some other targets in many of our churches today. After commending the church for hard work, theological integrity, and resistance to heresy, He states,

> But I have this against you, that you have left your first love. Therefore, remember from where you have fallen, and repent and do the deeds you did at first; or else I am coming to you and will remove your lampstand out of its place — unless you repent. Revelation 2:4-5

While we all may affirm the Great Commandment and the Great Commission, these imperatives may also feel like heavy chains in our already busy, tired, and discouraged hearts. So, we need to accept Jesus' invitation to come to Him, to answer His First Order Calling of love, allow Him to fan love's smoldering embers until we can say with Isaiah, "Here am I; send me." It's not up to us to redeem the world or even to bring others to Christ; we need simply to trust Him, let Him love us, and then step out.

Your Turn: How do you respond at a gut level, as we discuss how Jesus connects our wholehearted love for God to our ability to love our neighbor, igniting His fire of love within us until it becomes contagious to others? It's not a new concept to you, I know, but how does it make you feel—right now? Do you find that you need encouragement from God to live it out, or are you ready to go?

My Turn: We can trust our Lord's invitations and commands even though we've been significantly tested in our attempts to provide spiritual leadership in our churches and ministries. Yet trust does not come easily for most of us. We repeat our early childhood mantra, "I want to do it myself!" So, we try brains, brawn, influence, control, pleasing, appeasing, until despair and defeat grip our hearts. Then anger, blame, doubt and rationalization usually follow. Finally, if we can, we surrender to God and hear His invitation to trust Him. When we've done everything to make God's plan work, He asks us, simply and often without consolation, "Are you going to trust me?" Every day we face that decision again, to strive or abide. For most of us, our call to trust Jesus comes not so much in the throes of some grand venture, but in simply daring to dream dreams and see visions amidst everyday life. That's all I am asking you to do here. Just dream with me about the Bride of Christ.

So, my friend, I am suggesting that we dare to envision a church where people intentionally respond to God's First Order Calling to abide in His love, becoming light and salt, and then in glorious blaze—a loving fire so contagious that the world comes to know His love through us. I'm not offering some magic program. Contagion happens organically, naturally. Yet, fire and love spread best when the environmental conditions support the flames. Although the Holy Spirit will guide each one of us uniquely, consistent with our situations, our Contributors and I have discovered several important dimensions of our journey with God that need to be considered by us all. Here's our journey map.

CHAPTER 1: EMBERS CAN BE FANNED INTO FLAME - HOPE FOR THE CHURCH

CHAPTER 2: THE NATURE OF DIVINE FIRE – SPIRITUAL FORMATION FROM A PERSPECTIVE:

CHAPTER 3: BECOMING CONTAGIOUS FIRE - ON THE JOURNEY PERSONALLY AND INTENTIONALLY

CHAPTER 4: IGNITING THE SPARK INTO FLAME - FOLLOWING JESUS TOGETHER IN AN INTERNAL LEADERSHIP COMMUNITY

CHAPTER 5: SPARKING THE CHURCH - A VISION FOR CONTAGIOUS CHRISTIANS

CHAPTER 6: HOW TO SPREAD THE FIRE - DISCOVERING THE WAY FORWARD

CHAPTER 7: REVEALING THE FLAME AND DISPELLING THE FEAR - TEACHING ABOUT SPIRITUAL FORMATION

CHAPTER 8: TOUCHING THE FIRE - OPPORTUNITIES FOR EXPERIENTIAL DISCOVERY

CHAPTER 9: COMBATTING THE FIRE EXTINGUISHERS - FACING THE DRAGON TOGETHER

CHAPTER 10: FANNING CONTAGIOUS FIRE - WORSHIP THAT MODELS ABIDING IN LOVE

CHAPTER 11: BECOMING CONTAGIOUS BONFIRES - SPIRITUALLY FORMING COMMUNITY

CHAPTER 12: FREED TO BURN BRIGHTLY - HEALING MINISTRY THAT REMOVES THE BLOCKS TO LOVE

CHAPTER 13: THE WINDS OF CONTAGIOUS FIRE - SPIRITUAL FORMATION AS MISSIONAL MOMENTUM

CHAPTER 14: CONTAGIOUS FIRE – PULLING IT ALL TOGETHER

Thanks for the discussion, my friend. This may feel really exciting to you, or it may feel way too much for weary bones. Nothing you can do about either. I'd love for you to consider, between now and our next meeting, the longing of your heart—for Jesus and for His church. If you've read this far, I know you have some powerful longings. Your longings may show themselves in the form of positive visions and desires, or they might manifest as deep pains and frustrations. Either way, let's explore Contagious Fire, together!

Now, It's Your Turn.

CHAPTER 2

THE NATURE OF DIVINE FIRE – SPIRITUAL FORMATION FROM A BIBLICAL PERSPECTIVE:

Great to see you're still with me! In our previous discussion, we agreed that Jesus desires to set our hearts on fire with His love in a way that recreates us. Through our Lord's suffering, death, and resurrection—and our response of faith—God brings us into a restored relationship of forgiveness and love. The Holy Spirit's flame of transformation slowly restores us to Himself in a relationship of love. Ultimately, that transformation restores the image and likeness of God that were originally created within us. Our hearts ignite with love for God. As the radiance of abundant life in Christ shines more and more fully through us, we become contagious—others see glimpses of the very thing their hearts long for. Sparks of God's love ignite their hearts and the process continues until the contagious fire of God's love spreads beyond the Church into the world for which Jesus died.

Jesus said that when He is lifted up that He would draw all people to Himself. (cf. John 12:32) Despite the struggles we have experienced in our own lives and churches, we want—more than anything else in the world— to believe that Jesus' words are true and that His call on our lives will not be given in vain. We want our own lives to become transformed in a way that not only keeps our hearts ablaze, but ignites the hearts of others in and beyond our own ministries.

However, before we can cooperate with God's transforming work in our own lives, or lead a ministry into a life of "blazing spiritual maturity," we need to understand what the journey looks like. What's God really after – character, behavior, ministry, love? Do we grow spiritually by learning or experiencing? What actually produces change in us – is it through practicing spiritual disciplines or in prayer and contemplation? Is spiritual formation an inward or an outward journey? Good questions with not-so-easy answers. Simply tossing together and serving up a concoction of a few Lectio Divinas, sermons on love, rules of life, and prayer just won't do. If we and our people are to become convinced to let Jesus set our hearts on fire and to follow Him, we need to clearly understand the dynamics of God's invitation to deepening intimacy with Him. Jesus is the Fire. He enlightens the journey of transformation that sets us free to live abundantly as sons and daughters of God.

Our understanding of Christian spiritual formation must come from the clear teaching of Scripture. While many of us have learned from various Christian traditions about spiritual disciplines and experiences, for our understanding to be truly Christian, it must be fundamentally biblical. We must be able to see our own spiritual growth in the context of both the teaching and the experience of Jesus and the Apostles. The contributors and I will suggest passages we feel lie at the heart of becoming Christ-like, that guide us to practically love our neighbors. However, every person who desires to know Jesus more fully, follow Him more closely, and lead others to do the same, must come to their own understanding of the goal and process of spiritual growth and be able to communicate it consistently within their context.

Let's continue, then, by looking at some foundational Scriptures that discuss the transformational process of our sanctification. Then we can draw some conclusions about the nature of God's work within us. Of course, we can truthfully say that the whole of the Bible speaks of God's transformation in our lives, both with historical models and with injunctions for our lives today. I'll suggest a few here that we feel represent a general picture within a New Testament/New Covenant context. I know that you already know all this, but laying it out might help get us on the same page and provide a resource for those you lead.

Scriptural Foundations for Spiritual Formation: Let's focus our exploration of Scripture by focusing on some key questions. Can we find clear teaching in Scripture about God's GOAL in our spiritual growth? What PROCESS does God use to accomplish His goal within us? What kind of JOURNEY and time-line does Scripture describe for our transformation into Christ-likeness? Scripture ties these three elements together as it pictures Jesus as our Shepherd.

The Lord is my shepherd,

I shall not want.

He makes me lie down in green pastures;

He leads me beside quiet waters.

He restores my soul;

He guides me in the paths of righteousness

For His name's sake.

Even though I walk through the valley of the shadow of death,

I fear no evil, for You are with me;

Your rod and Your staff, they comfort me.

You prepare a table before me in the presence of my enemies;

You have anointed my head with oil;

My cup overflows.

Surely goodness and lovingkindness will follow me all the days of my life,

And I will dwell in the house of the Lord forever. Psalms 23

Let's explore the goal, the process and the journey of spiritual formation. What is the fire of God's love intended to accomplish? How do our initial embers of love grow into a contagious blaze? What can we expect to experience as God's love transforms us?

The Goal: Where Is Jesus Shepherding Us?

In my previous book, *Mansions of the Heart*, I address the various alternative goals for our spiritual growth. Some of them turned out to be "dead ends" if we're looking for God's ultimate goal for us. For example, while God certainly desires us to grow in holiness, we found that we never reach perfection. The more we grow, the more we discover how far we have yet to mature. We also explored the possibility that God primarily desires that we become a better worker in the Kingdom. We saw, however, that just trying to become more productive makes our relationship with God simply a means to a "greater" end, and reflects more of our cultural values than it does the heart of God. A focus on continually working harder ultimately ends in frustration and exhaustion. Another potential goal, personal wholeness and health, could be what God wants most for us. Unfortunately, we saw again that this goal represents an endless process of introspection which itself undermines what it seeks. Finally, we explored the foundational promises of the Christian message and found LOVE central to everything God wants for us, even the key to growth in holiness, work, and wholeness.

Let's review a few key Scriptures to see love's centrality. In John 3:16, we find that love motivated all that God intended by coming to us in Jesus.

For God so loved the world, that He gave His only begotten Son, that whoever believes in Him shall not perish, but have eternal life. For God did not send the Son into the world to judge the world, but

28

that the world might be saved through Him. John 3:16-17

In Matthew 22: 37-38, Jesus puts our love relationship with God at the center of all that God has done in salvation history.

> One of them, a lawyer, asked Him a question, testing Him, "Teacher, which is the great commandment in the Law?" And He said to him, "you shall love the Lord your God with all your heart, and with all your soul, and with all your mind. This is the great and foremost commandment. The second is like it, you shall love your neighbor as yourself. On these two commandments depend the whole law and the prophets. Matthew 22:35-40

John 15:9-11 tells us that abiding in this love relationship with God results in our ability to follow Jesus faithfully and in joy. Jesus says,

> Just as the Father has loved Me, I have also loved you; abide in My love. If you keep My commandments, you will abide in My love; just as I have kept My Father's commandments and abide in His love. These things I have spoken to you so that My joy may be in you, and that your joy may be made full. John 15:9-11

Finally, Paul states that love stands as the most important element in our relationship with God and our service to Him. After listing all the spiritual gifts, He states that without love each one becomes useless and concludes with:

> But now faith, hope, love, abide these three; but the greatest of these is love. 1 Corinthians 13:13

It's clear from these key passages, and from hundreds of others, that it's our Lord's primary goal to establish a relationship of love between God and every person—a life-giving relationship that brings us forgiveness, salvation, redemption, and eternal life. Let's sample some Scriptures that show us how He shepherds us there.

The Process: How Does Jesus Shepherd Us into the Transformation of His Likeness?

From the very beginning, God's followers have longed for a heart that could be faithful to His ways. The Psalmist wrote:

> Create in me a clean heart, O God, and renew a steadfast spirit within me. Psalm 51:10

God told the prophet Ezekiel that to restore humanity's place with God, lost in the disaster of the fall, He would have to actually recreate our hearts.

> And I will give them one heart, and put a new spirit within them. And I will take the heart of stone out of their flesh and give them a heart of flesh, that they may walk in My statutes and keep My ordinances and do them. Then they will be My people, and I shall be their God. Ezekiel 11:19-21

This transformational "heart transplant" begins as we receive Jesus as Lord.

> The word is near you, in your mouth and in your heart — that is, the word of faith which we are preaching, that if you confess with your mouth Jesus as Lord, and believe in your heart that God raised Him from the dead, you will be saved; for with the heart a person believes, resulting in righteousness, and with the mouth he confesses, resulting in salvation. Romans 10:8-10

The apostle John explains that what God begins in faith and baptism continues in an ongoing process that perfects our love relationship with Him and sustains and develops our new heart.

> Whoever confesses that Jesus is the Son of God, God abides in him, and he in God. We have come to know and have believed the love which God has for us. God is love, and the one who abides in love abides in God, and God abides in him. By this, love is perfected with us, so that we may have confidence in the day of judgment; because as He is, so also are we in this world. There is no fear in love; but perfect love casts out fear, because fear involves punishment, and the one who fears is not perfected in love. We love, because He first loved us. 1 John 4:15-19

To enable this perfection of love within us, Jesus gives us His Holy Spirit and invites us into a life-giving intimacy with Him out of which our transformation and our discipleship emerge.

It will come about after this

That I will pour out My Spirit on all mankind;

And your sons and daughters will prophesy,

Your old men will dream dreams,

Your young men will see visions.

"Even on the male and female servants

I will pour out My Spirit in those days.

…and it will come about that whoever calls on the name of the Lord

Will be delivered; Joel 2:28-30, 32

The apostle Paul explains that our perfection in love transforms us, over time, into the very image of Christ.

But we all, with unveiled face, beholding as in a mirror the glory of the Lord, are being transformed into the same image from glory to glory, just as from the Lord, the Spirit. 2 Corinthians 3:18

Jesus invites us into a life-giving symbiotic relationship analogous to how branches relate to a vine, exchanging life-giving substance—in our relationship with God, it's love. Within this abiding relationship, we grow and mature into the likeness of the Vine.

I am the true vine, and My Father is the vinedresser. Every branch in Me that does not bear fruit, He takes away; and every branch that bears fruit, He prunes it so that it may bear more fruit. You are already clean because of the word which I have spoken to you. Abide in Me, and I in you. As the branch cannot bear fruit of itself unless it abides in the vine, so neither can you unless you abide in Me. I am the vine, you are the branches; he who abides in Me and I in him, he bears much fruit, for apart from Me you can do nothing… Just as the Father has loved Me, I have also loved you; abide in My love. If you keep My commandments, you will abide in My love; just as I have kept My Father's commandments and abide in His love. These things I have spoken to you so that My joy may be in you, and that your joy may be made full. John 15:1-6, 9-11

Paul prays for our ongoing discovery of God in love, the key to our transformation.

For this reason I bow my knees before the Father, from whom every family in heaven and on earth derives its name, that He would grant you, according to the riches of His glory, to be strengthened with power through His Spirit in the inner man, so that Christ may dwell in your hearts through faith; and that you, being rooted and grounded in love, may be able to comprehend with all the saints what is the breadth and length and height and depth, and to know the love of Christ which surpasses knowledge, that you may be filled up to all the fullness of God. Ephesians 3:14-19

Paul makes it clear that our spiritual formation, our transformation, continues over time, and requires our ongoing cooperation.

Therefore, I urge you, brethren, by the mercies of God, to present your bodies a living and holy sacrifice, acceptable to God, which is your spiritual service of worship. And do not be conformed to this world, but be transformed by the renewing of your mind, so that you may prove what the will of God is, that which is good and acceptable and perfect. Romans 12:1-2

The apostles teach us that God uses even the difficulties we face to grow and mature us.

And not only this, but we also exult in our tribulations, knowing that tribulation brings about perseverance; and perseverance, proven character; and proven character, hope; and hope does not disappoint, because the love of God has been poured out within our hearts through the Holy Spirit who was given to us. Romans 5:3-5

Consider it all joy, my brethren, when you encounter various trials, knowing that the testing of your faith produces endurance. And let endurance have its perfect result, so that you may be perfect and complete, lacking in nothing. James 1:2-4

Scripture tells us that our transformation happens in the heart, where mind, body, and spirit meet. Therefore, our whole person becomes involved in this transformational process.

> And you shall love the Lord your God with all your <u>heart</u>, and with all your <u>soul</u>, and with all your <u>mind</u>, and with all your <u>strength</u>. Mark 12:30

> Now may the God of peace Himself sanctify you entirely; and may your spirit and soul and body be preserved complete, without blame at the coming of our Lord Jesus Christ. Faithful is He who calls you, and He also will bring it to pass. 1 Thessalonians 5:23-24

We see that God transforms us into the image of Christ. He accomplishes this formation through in the depth of intimacy with the Trinity, lived out through abiding in God—in a life of mutuality and life-giving love. As His love becomes perfected within us, we come to manifest the very nature of Jesus. We see this process paralleled within our own embryonic development. Within the deep intimacy of our mother's womb, we receive the very elements of our form and personality through our loving connectedness with her.

The Journey: What Might We Expect to Experience as Our Shepherd Leads Us Into Christ-likeness?

While our redemption through the Cross (our conception, to use our previous example) happens in an instant, our sanctification—our transformation, takes not just nine months but a lifetime. Jesus, our Good Shepherd invites us forward, but we can either cooperate and follow, or we can resist. Our resistance may be unintentional because we have not yet learned to hear His voice. It all takes time. The apostles have learned that each person progresses on their journey of spiritual formation at different paces and stages. Let's look at some example passages.

> Therefore, we do not lose heart, but though our outer man is decaying, yet our inner man is being renewed day by day. For momentary, light affliction is producing for us an eternal weight of glory far beyond all comparison, while we look not at the things which are seen, but at the things which are not seen; for the things which are seen are temporal, but the things which are not seen are eternal.   2 Corinthians 4:16-18

But grow in the grace and knowledge of our Lord and Savior Jesus Christ. 2 Peter 3:18

For though by this time you ought to be teachers, you have need again for someone to teach you the elementary principles of the oracles of God, and you have come to need milk and not solid food. For everyone who partakes only of milk is not accustomed to the word of righteousness, for he is an infant. But solid food is for the mature, who because of practice have their senses trained to discern good and evil. Hebrews 5:12-14

I have written to you, children, because you know the Father. I have written to you, fathers, because you know Him who has been from the beginning. I have written to you, young men, because you are strong, and the word of God abides in you, and you have overcome the evil one. 1 John 2:14

Now for this very reason also, applying all diligence, in your faith supply moral excellence, and in your moral excellence, knowledge, and in your knowledge, self-control, and in your self-control, perseverance, and in your perseverance, godliness, and in your godliness, brotherly kindness, and in your brotherly kindness, love. For if these qualities are yours and are increasing, they render you neither useless nor unfruitful in the true knowledge of our Lord Jesus Christ. 2 Peter 1:5-8

We've learned that this journey into Christ-likeness takes a lifetime and requires our intentional cooperation, empowered by the Holy Spirit. Jesus shepherds us through life situations, inviting us to learn to know His heart and follow His leading, leaving behind our attachments to the world's strategies and schemes, learning to think, feel, walk in the Spirit.

The Destination: Where is Our Shepherd Taking Us?

God's spiritual formation within us is profoundly personal; it's also profoundly about our neighbor and the world. Most profoundly, however, God transforms us because of the destiny of all creation—the Kingdom of God and the new heaven and earth.

In all wisdom and insight, He made known to us the mystery of His will, according to His kind intention which He purposed in Him with a view to an administration suitable to the fullness of the times, that is, the summing up of all things in Christ, things in the heavens and things on the earth. Ephesians 1:8-10

Therefore, if anyone is in Christ, he is a new creature; the old things passed away; behold, new things have come. Now all these things are from God, who reconciled us to Himself through Christ and gave us the ministry of reconciliation, namely, that God was in Christ reconciling the world to Himself, not counting their trespasses against them, and He has committed to us the word of reconciliation. 2 Corinthians 5:17-19

Wow!

Chris Schutte, Senior Pastor of Christ Church Anglican, shares the impact in his life of this Kingdom nature of our transformation:

In considering, "What is God after?" I immediately thought, "a new creation." It seems important that we understand our own individual journeys with God in the context of God's global / historical work of redeeming and renewing all of creation. Paul's words in 2 Cor 5 seem so relevant here: "The love of Christ urges us on," and "'If anyone is in Christ, there is a new creation." (Note the translation here, which many scholars prefer to, "If anyone is in Christ, he (or she) is a new creation"), "God was in Christ reconciling the world to himself," "he has given us the ministry of reconciliation," etc. I think that being a part of God's cosmic work is exciting, and often our focus on individual transformation can be reduced to self-help if not understood first and foremost as a part of God's overarching work.

Steve Thulson, Lead Pastor at Centennial Covenant Church, underscores this kingdom perspective.

For me, such a vision of formation offsets the instinct merely to get something from God for MY little self-managed life as if Jesus is simply a great resource, rather than being drawn more and more into HIS life in His new creation. It seems like our growth through the stages/ mansions moves increasingly from accepting Christ "in us" toward practically realizing we are "in Christ."

We've discovered that Jesus shepherds us into the very Kingdom of God on earth. Along the way, He recreates us into His own image and likeness so that we can fully live the abundant life in this world, yet with the victory of our King. To help us grasp this amazing and mysterious process, Scripture used many metaphors and analogies to describe a formation that's so grand that we cannot comprehend it with our senses. The apostle Paul expresses the mystery this way. "For now, we see in a mirror dimly, but then face to face; now I know in part, but then I will know fully just as I also have been fully known. 1 Corinthians 13:12.

Let's pull together what we've learned about Jesus' shepherding us through what we have called "Spiritual Formation."

Definitions

How, then, might we define "Spiritual Formation?" While we use the terms, "spiritual formation" and "discipleship" to refer to the process of spiritual growth, the modern understanding of discipleship makes it akin to "milk" for new believers. By discipleship, most churches mean basic training in knowledge of the Scriptures, prayer, etc. We use the words "spiritual formation" to include the whole growth process, from milk to solid food, both in understanding and in experience. A number of authors and teachers have offered good definitions of spiritual formation. In *Mansions of the Heart*, I suggested this one:

> [Spiritual Formation is] The process that takes place in us, as the life of the Spirit of God transforms our life through deepening love and intimacy with Father, Son, and Holy Spirit, remaking us in the likeness of Jesus Christ, in His love for the Father and the world.

Several years ago, I had the opportunity to serve as a "Drafter" and compiler of a collaborative work on a spiritual formation definition through the work of the Spiritual Formation Alliance, called True North. Spiritual formation writers, educators, and practitioners, from around the country, spent several months writing and redacting a definition that we hoped would provide a kind of consensus. Although the definition ended up much longer than the one I wrote in *Mansions*, I like it for both its depth and scope. Eventually, the final draft was approved in a meeting of both the "Drafter" and "Crafter" groups at the International Renovaré Conference in San Antonio in 2009. This "Call to Spiritual Formation" has since been translated into a number of languages and signed by hundreds of spiritual formation leaders around the globe. As the full text is fairly lengthy, I'll share the main headings here. See the full document in Appendix A.

> Christian spiritual formation is the process of being shaped by the Spirit into the likeness of Christ, filled with love for God and the world.
>
> God calls us all to become like Jesus.
>
> Our engagement with God's transforming grace is vital.
>
> Spiritual formation happens in community.
>
> Spiritual formation is, by its very nature, missional.

Love as the Life and Substance of God:

I'd like to say a few more words about love and why it's so vital to our transformation and destiny. "Love," it seems to me, is often trivialized into a warm feeling or kindly action. People love food, love sports, love their favorite entertainer, etc. The whole of spiritual formation can be summed up in one of the most misunderstood words in the Bible—LOVE. Yet, I think that I'm not alone in missing the point most of my life. Jesus teaches us that the greatest possible response to God, our supreme act of obedience to His commandments, is to love Him. But why "love"? Wouldn't obedience or honor or respect or trust or... be good enough? Does God somehow need us to feel kindly about Him, even adore Him? Why love?

We can ask the same question about the second greatest response to God—loving our neighbor. Again, we must ask "Why should we be expected to love our neighbor?" Loving our family and close friends would certainly seem appropriate, but why our neighbor (or enemy)? Wouldn't kindness, help, respect, and so forth be adequate?

The apostle Paul takes the word "love" even further. In 1 Corinthians 13, he concludes his famous list of the attributes of love with the words, "But now faith, hope, love abide—these three; but the greatest of these is love." Again, we can only stand mystified! <u>Faith</u> in Jesus as Lord and Savior saves us for eternity. <u>Hope</u> in the Lordship of Jesus, the truth of His promises, and the power of His presence keeps us going between now and eternity. So, again we must ask: "Why would affection toward God and neighbor be the greatest?" God's goodness toward us certainly deserves our greatest gratitude which surely produces feelings of warmth, endearment, and even affection—at least when He does what we want. Our neighbor's behavior, on the other hand, may produce none of those responses. How do we stir up love when that affection may be neither invited or warranted? What's the big deal about love? Tina Turner sings: "What's love got to do with it? What's love but a secondhand emotion?"

While everyone might affirm love as a desirable thing, most of us have experienced that love seldom measures up to our expectations. Surrounded by imperfect parents, siblings, friends, etc., our experience of love is, at best, imperfect. People may "feel good" about us, but their behavior doesn't make us feel good. Many of us can say that we'd rather people love us than not; but in the end, it really may not make a lot of difference. With this idea and experience of love, we can quickly blow past Scripture's words about love to get to the "really important" stuff. We have to stop and rethink "love" from a biblical perspective before we can ever trust it.

Ted Wueste, a pastor and founder of the Spiritual Formation Society of Arizona, comments about the critical nature of this question.

I'm convinced that "love" is a non-starter for most people because they have a fairly faulty view of the love of God. Love is, in most theological descriptions and teachings, transactional and cold. God is viewed as demanding and harsh—you better do what He says, and love is seen as an obligation on His part toward His poor, destitute creation.

I think that the apostle Paul had the same concern for the people of his time. Let's listen to his passion as he describes the nature of love.

Love is patient, love is kind and is not jealous; love does not brag and is not arrogant, does not act unbecomingly; it does not seek its own, is not provoked, does not take into account a wrong suffered, does not rejoice in unrighteousness, but rejoices with the truth; bears all things, believes all things, hopes all things, endures all things. Love never fails.... 1 Corinthians 13:4-8

Paul further describes love in his list of the fruit of the Spirit, the result of God's presence within us.

But the fruit of the Spirit is love—joy, peace, patience, kindness, goodness, faithfulness, gentleness, self-control.... Galatians 5:22-23

God's love for us is also described like the passionate desire of lovers. Jesus calls Himself the "Bridegroom" and us, His "Bride." We can also see this heart desire expressed in Song of Songs, in its imagery of love.

[God speaking to us] How beautiful and how delightful you are, My love, with all your charms! [We, the object of His love respond] "I am my beloved's, and his desire is for me. Song of Solomon 7:6, 10

History's most beautiful love poetry and songs might better portray God's love for us than most of our theological books.

Another apostle homes in on the importance and interrelationship of love. John, in his first letter makes some amazing statements. I've listed the text previously, but let's look at it again here.

Beloved, let us love one another, for love is from God; and everyone who loves is born of God and knows God. The one who does not love does not know God, for God is love. 1 John 4:7-8

John shows us that love far transcends a feeling; LOVE is the very nature and essence of God. He equates knowing God with the reality of God's life—LOVE, within us. While love can generate a number of emotional responses, true LOVE is God Himself. John repeats his famous equation and goes on to tell us about the heart of our transformation into Christ-likeness.

> Whoever confesses that Jesus is the Son of God, God abides in him, and he in God. We have come to know and have believed the love which God has for us. God is love, and the one who abides in love abides in God, and God abides in him. By this, love is perfected with us, so that we may have confidence in the day of judgment; because as He is, so also are we in this world. There is no fear in love; but perfect love casts out fear, because fear involves punishment, and the one who fears is not perfected in love. We love, because He first loved us. 1 John 4:15-19

We can summarize the passage by using John' equational style:

Faith in Jesus as the Son of God results in abiding in God—living in the same space. Thus...

The space or existence we share with God is called LOVE—God Himself. Thus...

This abiding in God's life—Perfect Love—perfects His nature within us. Therefore...

As God's nature—LOVE—Is perfected within us, fear ceases to rule our lives. Therefore...

In the LOVE of God, in the absence of fear, we are able to fully live in faith and hope. Therefore...

Abiding in LOVE makes us like Jesus. Alas...

The greatest of these is LOVE!

How might we picture this amazing truth that the Holy Spirit has revealed to us so simply? Jesus uses another analogy about His nature. He said, "I am the Light of the world; he who follows Me will not walk in the darkness, but will have the Light of life." (cf. John 8:12) Seeing these passages about love and about light together, we recognize that God, as LOVE acts like LIGHT. Just as Jesus does not speak about emotion when He talks about love, His use of the word "light" does not refer to photons. Both terms refer to Life, itself.

So, let's use light and love synonymously. Imagine how a plant responds to the light of the sun. The leaves, receiving the life-giving energy, produces photosynthesis, which in turn gives life to the whole plant. Some plants, such as the sunflower, even turn toward the sun to cooperate with its gift of life. As beautiful a picture as sunlight and plants might portray, our human reception of God-Love-Light shows a beauty of spectacular proportions. God-Love-Light shines on us, envelopes us, fills us, and brings life to our whole being. God doesn't stop here, however. He enables us to become light ourselves; he transforms us into light, as well. Jesus tells us:

> You are the light of the world. A city set on a hill cannot be hidden; nor does anyone light a lamp and put it under a basket, but on the lampstand, and it gives light to all who are in the house. Let your light shine before men in such a way that they may see your good works, and glorify your Father who is in heaven. Matthew 5:14-16

Using the metaphor of abiding—living in and with, let's imagine the scene again. God-Love-Light shines upon us, fills us, and transforms us. As we abide in Christ, we, become aglow with God-Love-Light. We shine that same light upon one another, as believers who abide in Jesus. No wonder Jesus says, "For where two or three have gathered together in My name, I am there in their midst." (cf. Matthew 18:20) Then together, Jesus compares us to a beautifully lit city upon a hill!

God does not command us to love Him because it's the right thing to do, but because it is the natural thing to do. He does not command us to love our neighbor because we should, but because it is all we can do when Jesus lives within our hearts and we are transformed into His likeness! Love stands greater than faith and hope because God-Love produces faith and hope! Of course, we don't love God or our neighbor perfectly—we're still in process. Perfection doesn't happen for us until we're raised in perfection. (cf. 1 Corinthians 15:50-52)

The centrality of love returns us again to our understanding of First and Second Order Callings. It is only to the extent that we learn to follow Jesus into the heart of God's love that we will ever be able to love our neighbor through sharing the Gospel and caring for the poor and needy.

Bill O'Byrne, co-founder of *Imago Christi*, shares about the impact of this realization of love in his life.

> *As an illustration of the centrality of love in the journey, I was personally struck early on in my spiritual formation by the Parable of the Prodigal Son, and an article which called it the Parable of the Pursuing Father. The article points out the counter-cultural love of the father, running out to save his son from the village stoning him. The focus of the article helped me shift my focus of understanding the parable, and then shifted my experience of the parable, from the brothers' problems, to the Father and his goal for them. I saw my own mixed motives in coming to God in the Prodigal's desperate attempt to somehow get food from someone who might pity him, even if it meant humiliating himself before his father. But then as I experienced the Father running out to meet me, I realized that the Prodigal never finished his rehearsed speech. Why? I, like the boy, was undone by the Father's love, and my motives were transformed. I could no longer settle for a mere, manipulative "transaction," when I was being offered radical love. Coming to God, whether it is for the first time in conversion, or the thousandth time in prayer, is about much more than just a formula of repentance and return. I was counting on pity, I got a restorative love that had more healing and relationship than I ever bargained for!*

Chuck Orwiler, a Friends Church pastor, reflects about the fundamental nature of love:

> *I was quite taken by a comment from Dallas Willard many years ago (I don't remember if I read it or heard him.). I believe it was in*

reference to 1 John 4:16. Willard said that if we viewed smaller and smaller increments of the substance of the universe until we got to the most basic stuff of what is (Trust me, Willard said this better!), that the most basic stuff of what is - is Love. It is Love because God is Love and He is the most elemental substance of all that is. All of this is so breathtaking to me!

We've seen that Scripture understands Jesus' use of the word "love" to refer to the very life and presence of God—IN RELATIONSHIP. Our transformation comes more from our life IN His love than through the work of His power. We abide in Love/God both in our personal relationship with Jesus and in our relationships with others. God's divine Light and Love radiate upon us through others in whom He dwells. We experience Love when we care for others who may not know the Lord but who are deeply loved by Him. Understanding love as the nature and life of God helps us realize why our life together in community becomes so essential. One day, possibly, the Light of Christ alone will be enough for us. However, on the journey to Perfect Love, God intends that we flourish in His light, both in communion with Him personally and in community with the radiance of our glowing brothers and sisters in Christ.

First and Second Order Calling

God calls us first to grow in a loving relationship with Him and then, out of that relationship, to let that love flow to others through ministry. If we launch into the Second Order Calling without the fire produced in the First, we find that we don't have the wisdom or stamina to sustain missional momentum in the Great Commission. While we've discussed First and Second Order Callings in Chapter 1, our Contributors expressed the need to return again to this vital perspective for two reasons: First, we ministry leaders often overlook the centrality of our own love relationship with God. Tammy Long, Pastor of Spiritual Formation in a large multi-ethnic congregation, expresses her concerns this way:

First, I think we have to really underscore and triple score First

43

Order Call, even for those familiar with the concept. There can be the tendency to assume this as a given and keep moving to the Second Order, where I think most people focus and reside. Truly understanding and embracing our First Order Call from the very beginning, is crucial, essential, and the place from which everything else flows. Although we hope pastors would be right with us on this, I don't think we can assume this is true. They are on their spiritual journey, as well. The Second Order Calling—doing for God, fulfilling the Great Commission, etc., is so deeply ingrained in us that we speak of the Great Commandment almost as a "drive-by" without really parking there. EVERYTHING we will discuss hinges on pastors really embracing and understanding the meaning of the First Order Call. I'm not sure what it will take for this to move from head to heart, (as the Spirit moves and leads) but my prayer is that First Order Call will be a huge "aha" and/or re-centering.

Jesus connects the vitality of His relationship with the Father to His ability to do ministry.

Truly, truly, I say to you, the Son can do nothing of Himself, unless it is something He sees the Father doing; for whatever the Father does, these things the Son also does in like manner. John 5:19

Tammy's concerns for us certainly proved true of me, as I shared in Chapter 1. Recapturing and living into our "first love" will prove to be both the most vital and yet the most difficult dimension of our own spiritual growth and of our ability to lead others spiritually. While God ignites our fire in our response to His First Order calling, so many of us have become addicted to productivity and performance that we're blinded to our own "absence" in the most fundamental truth that we believe and teach. As Tammy says, we need to be continually reminded where to start and where to return when we get distracted.

The second reason we want to address First and Second Order Callings again relates to their integrative nature. While we can fully say, "First Things First," the reality is that God doesn't call us to stay locked up in some monastery until we're mature enough to hit the streets. Loving God and loving neighbor go together. We grow in both dimensions along the whole spiritual formation journey path. Leave out the First to jump to the Second will prove deadly; forgetting the Second to turn inward will stunt our growth and thwart our ministry. Let's look again at Scripture to see how this plays out.

> I am the vine, you are the branches; he who abides in Me and I in him, he bears much fruit, for apart from Me you can do nothing... This is My commandment, that you love one another, just as I have loved you. John 15:5-6, 12

The "fruit" that Jesus speaks about refers both to the "fruit of the Spirit" (cf. Galatians 5:22) within us as well as the fruit of good works. (cf. Colossians 1:10)

A Model for the Spiritual Formation Journey

Encouraging people to respond to God where they are in their journey with Him means that we need to have some idea about the nature of the journey—where it starts, where it ends up, and the experience of the terrain in-between. I cannot overstate how many times I've met and ministered to Christian leaders who were on the brink of leaving formal ministry because they misunderstood where God had them in the transformation process. When we think of this lifelong transformation from the developmental perspectives of maturing, growing up, building relationships, etc., we realize that change is always essential to growing. As we mature, our abilities change; we meet new obstacles and opportunities; and we experience our Heavenly Father parenting us differently. When we know what to expect and recognize changes as a normal, we can cooperate with the Lord in the process.

What might such a model of spiritual growth look like? While we would expect to experience certain aspects of our growth to happen over and over and to greater and lesser degrees, we would also expect there to be a progression. We would want a model based on Scripture, simple enough to understand, but detailed enough to find signposts or markers from which to relate our relative position. The roadmap should be tested by time and the experiences of those who have traveled it over the years.

Wouldn't it be wonderful if we could find one single passage of Scripture that accomplished all this for us? Unsurprisingly, however, God's word comes to us across centuries of biblical history and through the inspiration and experience of Jesus' followers ever since. The Holy Spirit continued to enlighten the Church to the depths of these truths as well as guide believers in the experience of their reality for our lives. Whatever model we choose should be faithful to these clear teachings.

As we look both at Scripture and the spiritual fathers and mothers in the Church, one might expect to find dozens of spiritual growth models. Interestingly, there are very few.

The early Desert Fathers talked about our spiritual journey in three phases: purgation, illumination, and union. They saw believers grow spiritually through seasons of dealing with sin and brokenness. Gradually Christians moved into years of coming to really know God in Christ personally and seeing themselves as they really are. Finally, believers came to live their remaining years in deep intimacy with God. These three phases have formed the basic foundation for how the Church has viewed spiritual growth. We can also find some discussions of the progression of Christian virtues, most of which are quite complex and use language in a way unfamiliar to the modern world.

As you may have guessed, I've found Teresa of Avila and John of the Cross the most helpful in developing a model which describes the spiritual developmental process. Teresa's model of the seven mansions of growth proves to be easy to understand and faithful to the clear teachings of Scripture. These seven mansions described by Teresa in the seventeenth century remain the historical model most read and used today.

There have been a number of attempts to develop other models, as the spiritual formation movement has progressed into our own time. For example, Hagberg and Guelich, in their book *Critical Journey*, describe a six-stage progression, not unlike Teresa, but focusing on the development of faith rather than love, and based on their own experience with leaders that they counseled. Bruce Demarest in his book, *Seasons of the Soul: Stages of Spiritual Development* uses Brueggemann's pattern of beginnings (orientation), spiritual trials (disorientation), and spiritual renewal (reorientation) to describe elements or seasons in our spiritual journey.[1] Despite the word "stages" in the title, we find that orientation, disorientation, and reorientation describe circular seasons of experience which happen over and over throughout our walk with God. While a helpful read, it does not describe the progressive journey description we are looking for. Personally, I think that Teresa provides the best description upon which we can build.

Because Scripture does not provide one model of spiritual growth, we are free, and possibly obligated, to describe a spiritual formation model that our people can understand in their own context. For example, Steve Thulson and Centennial Covenant Church's Journey Team felt that the seven mansions or stages described by Teresa might be too detailed for members of the congregation. Therefore, they grouped some of the Teresian stages together to form four. See Appendix A.

Of course, I would encourage you to read *Mansions of the Heart* if you have not already. But for an overview, I'll summarize the phases of growth for you here. Teresa of Avila, a Spanish reformer within the Catholic Church during the Reformation, was asked by her leaders to describe the fantastic spiritual growth in the renewal movement which she led. She prayed that God would give her a picture of the spiritual growth process which would speak to the people of her time in ways they could personally relate. Teresa reports that God gave her a picture of our heart as a crystal-clear castle in which we

1. Bruce Demarest, Seasons of the Soul: Stages of Spiritual Development (Downers Grove, IL, Intervarsity Press, 2009)

journey through inwardly spiraling rooms, as a visual symbol of our spiritual growth. Each group of rooms, called mansions, represents phases of growth, from becoming a Christian to finally living in full union with God. These phases of growth follow the pattern of the everyday experiences of growing up physically and falling in love and marrying as experiential analogies.

Teresa drew from Jesus' use of similar analogies when he taught about "cities set upon a hill" and described His relationship with His followers as "Bridegroom and Bride." He encouraged His disciples to move from bond servant to friend to beloved. John the apostle, uses the analogy of maturing physically when he addressed his letter figuratively to children, young men, and fathers. Teresa pictures our life with God as a progressive journey through mansions, or seasons of life of the castle of our hearts—where God abides with us, drawn forward by the Light of Christ emanating from the center. We enter the "castle" when we become Christians and move more and more toward intimacy with God in Christ over our lifetime. While the stages are progressive, they overlap. Rather than moving linearly from one to another, we explore our life with God more as pilgrims. Gradually, we journey forward and back, exploring here and there, as we are wooed onward by our Lord. While we move generally toward the center, we can become stuck along the way. Teresa says, in fact, that she believes that most really devoted followers of Jesus explore as far as the fifth mansion, but many flee back to more familiar territory because they have no one to explain the wonders that God has for them. Here's a short summary of the seven Teresian Mansions.

Teresian Mansion Descriptions

FIRST MANSION - New Beginnings

In the First Mansion, as new Christians we're just beginning to learn what it means to be "in the world, but not of it." Our love relationship focuses largely on getting God's help to obtain the worldly pleasures we've not been able to get for ourselves. We generally understand God's love as His willingness to do good things for us. God continues to call us to Himself by responding to our calls for help.

SECOND MANSION - Between a Rock and a Hard Place

In the Second Mansion, we have come to realize that God's way is best and have earnestly determined to live a moral life. But the world, with its false pleasures and gratifications, still attracts us. This Mansion is marked by internal struggle and significantly mixed motives. While we may have come to love God in gratitude, our love for the world remains still strong, pulling at our affections. Although this conflict doesn't feel like spiritual growth to the believer, it can draw us more deeply into prayer where God touches our hearts with His love and calls us onward into a deeper relationship of love and trust.

THIRD MANSION - Following Jesus

By the time we reach the Third Mansion, we have developed a relatively balanced life of discipleship. Love for God has matured from one-sided receiving to the sense of mutual friendship, and a desire to love others. Regular church attendance and ministry, consistent prayer, concerted effort to live the Christian life, and a genuine desire to please and honor God provide signs of spiritual growth. Prayer in the Third Mansion still focuses mainly on requests for help.

FOURTH MANSION - Discovering the Love of Jesus

In the Fourth Mansion, God turns our attention turns more and more to Jesus. God begins to reveal His presence through profound touches of His love and presence. We're given the beginnings of grace to "see" and "feel" God in prayer and in life. Our attention shifts more toward the Giver than the gifts, and our love for God takes on new importance. God's love transforms our hearts to enable a longing for deeper intimacy with the Lord.

FIFTH MANSION - Longing for Oneness with God

As we explore the Fifth Mansion, God calls us to begin to live into the

High Priestly Prayer of Jesus in John 17—the call to union with God. Love deepens to the point that, like a man and woman contemplating marriage, we desire to live with God as the center of life. Deepening intimacy also draws us into deeper loving communication. Contemplation becomes a regular part of our prayer experience, with times of deep and adoring silence, times of just being with God. Hunger for God deepens and intensifies, and our motives become increasingly purified. We often feel dissatisfied with our ability to really serve God in ways that adequately reflect our love for Him. This longing to serve God more purely, reveals a greater awareness of our own depth of wounding and creates a yearning for healing that will give us freedom to fully love and to be loved.

SIXTH MANSION - The Passion of God's Love

In the Sixth Mansion we experience deeper levels of God's transforming love. We now have a desire to live with God alone, to sense His presence continually, and to express our love for Him in utter responsiveness and obedience. Times of prayer become intense experiences of the fire and passion of the love of God and love for Him. In these last mansions, we may also experience the Dark Nights. Despite these seasons without "experiencing" God, our passion and depth of love for God becomes ablaze to the point that we long to be consumed by His fire.

SEVENTH MANSION - A Life of Love in the Trinity

The Seventh Mansion represents the season of living into the deepest intimacy with God that one can experience in this life. It is marked by a complete integration of mind, body, and spirit, in the life of Christ—a full abiding in Love. At its best, it is the completion of the statement of the apostle Paul, "It is no longer I who live, but Christ lives in me" (Galatians 2:20). Within this season, fear has been cast out through our union with God and the perfection of Love within us.[2]

---

2. Complete descriptions of the Teresian Mansion descriptions can be found in *Mansions of the Heart: Exploring the Seven Stages of Spiritual Growth*, R. Thomas

This lifetime journey of deepening intimacy and love with the Trinity combines God's calling, our response, and God's power to move forward. Neither God nor we accomplish this transformation within us alone; God initiates, we cooperate both in our desire and in our will to grow, and God empowers us to move forward. Like any relationship, for love to emerge and grow, we must become intentional about the process.

Intentionality

Let's discuss our role in this process of transformation into the likeness of Christ. How do we respond to God's love—both in our personal relationship with Him and in our care for others? We have seen, in the Scriptures we've cited, that the Holy Spirit both initiates and empowers our transformation; we simply cannot work hard enough to be like Jesus or imitate Him, to make it happen. Yet in most of the Scriptures we have reviewed, we find exhortation, command, and even pleading. God does not overpower and drag us into the Kingdom or into the Seventh Mansion. The Gospel reveals God's loving invitation, not a dominating force. Jesus loves, beckons, calls, and invites us. Faith, even though empowered by the Holy Spirit, forms our response of love. Although Jesus invites us to abide, we must choose to make ourselves available. While God produces love within us, we choose to exercise that love. Like a man and woman who find themselves falling in love, we must reorganize our daily lives to provide space for intimacy where that love can mature. In the freedom God has given us, we intentionally cooperate with Him in our personal transformation and in our missional outreach. Let's discuss one of the significant ways God encourages us to deepen in our love—intentionally.

Spiritual Community

While new birth happens within each one of us personally, God's birthing process always involves other followers of Jesus. When God's love in us becomes connected to God's love in others, we experience greater degrees of

Ashbrook, Published by Jossey-Bass, 2009

God's glory and our growth in Love accelerates. God loves, speaks, teaches, and encourages us through His other followers, as well as in our personal prayer. Jesus prays that we might live in this kind of community of love with Him and with others, and the apostles describe the power that we discover with one another in spiritual community.

> I do not ask on behalf of these alone, but for those also who believe in Me through their word; that they may all be one; even as You, Father, are in Me and I in You, that they also may be in Us, so that the world may believe that You sent Me. John 17:20-21

> For where two or three have gathered together in My name, I am there in their midst. Matthew 18:20

> Therefore, confess your sins to one another, and pray for one another so that you may be healed. James 5:16

> ...to the building up of the body of Christ; until we all attain to the unity of the faith, and of the knowledge of the Son of God, to a mature man, to the measure of the stature which belongs to the fullness of Christ. Ephesians 4:12-13

Returning to the Interior Castle analogy, we see that we are not the only ones in the Castle, or on the journey. Jesus calls into a mutually supportive community that provides encouragement, help, teaching, coaching, and modeling. Jesus journeys with us personally, within us, as well as through others. We're never intended to go it alone.

Where Do We Go From Here?

We've overviewed the nature of our spiritual growth and key elements that help us follow Jesus as He shepherds us. We've seen that, as we yield to God's amazing love, He sets our hearts on fire with His love, emblazons us in the very image of Christ, and makes us so contagious that sparks of love ignite the longing and passion of those around us.

Where do you go from here? Should you buy copies of *Contagious Fire* for your whole church or ministry team? Is it time to launch the sermon series already forming in your head? As eager as you might be to move forward, we'd suggest that you take it slow, listen to God for a bit, and then start at the beginning. God loves you so profoundly that He longs to lead you personally in the most exciting journey of your life. He wants to so build and strengthen you into His image that your leadership will reflect His presence and glory. Jesus wants to bless your ministry and the world by devoting Himself first, to you!

CHAPTER 3

BECOMING CONTAGIOUS FIRE - ON THE JOURNEY PERSONALLY AND INTENTIONALLY

Well, my friend, I'm excited that you're still with me in this discussion! Awesome! I can assume, therefore, that the Holy Spirit has spoken to you about spiritual formation and missional church, at both a personal and a corporate level—God has sparked your fire. Like me, you want more. We long to live in a more intimate relationship with Jesus and reach out more powerfully to the world with the Gospel message. We pray that our churches can do the same thing. We long for the day when our loving intimacy with God results in the outpouring of His love to everyone around us, as we partner with Him in bringing His Kingdom. We want to become a contagious fire!

You may have come to this conclusion from a variety of perspectives and situations. But how you got here isn't the point; what's important—you're here and God brought you here. Let's discuss how to proceed. As I've said before, it started with God, and now it continues with you. Let me share a story about one of my starts.

I climbed Mt. Whitney during my senior year in High School. After reading about the tallest mountain in the 48 states and the trail that led all the way to the top, the adventure possessed me. Having backpacked a lot in the Sierras, I felt confident in my ability to make the climb. I convinced a friend to join me, assuring him that I could get him to the top in an easy two-day hike. Equipped with our cheap leather boots, backpacks filled with supplies and canned goods, we set out from Southern California, drove to Lone Pine, and headed up this 14,995-foot mountain.

We did get to the top, just as I had promised. However, altitude sickness, bloody feet, and hunger (We buried the canned goods, permanently, about a third of the way up.) turned the would-be adventure into a nightmare—one we didn't want to talk about—much less repeat. My friend found it hard to trust me for the next adventure that I suggested. Many years later, I received a picture from my son, Stephen. It showed him sitting on the top of Mt. Whitney with a big grin and a little sign which read, "I love you, Dad." An experienced backpacker and climber, using all the right gear and supplies, Stephen led his group up the mountain, past the ninety-five switchbacks, to the top where they were enjoying the spectacular beauty. Stephen had learned that he could only lead others on a journey for which he had prepared and traversed himself. The picture still sits on my desk to remind me that the same truth applies to our journey of spiritual formation.

While it's possible for a group to explore places for the first time together, aware that the venture may not turn out as planned, our churches expect leadership, not exploration, from their pastors. We cannot lead where we have never been; we can't give away what we don't have. "Spiritual leadership" comes from the flame within us that burns white hot in deep intimacy with the Trinity. Glowing embers, tucked way down inside us, can't ignite fires within others. In the realm of spiritual formation, however, attempts seem to be made all the time.

I can't overstate the number of times I've talked to pastors who, after reading a book about spiritual formation or attending a conference, announced that they planned to take their congregational discipleship to a new level. If only their members would grow up spiritually, all sorts of problems could be solved. Many of these leaders had read *Mansions of the Heart* or *Presence* and commented how meaningful the books had been for them. However, when I asked if I or *Imago Christi* might be of some assistance with their new church venture, they often assured me that they had the situation well in hand. The sermon series had already been written, the small group devotional prepared, and so forth. They felt confident that, through this new fall program, the resulting spiritual growth would prove really important for those that needed it. The next year, many of these same leaders had found another new program which they hoped would solve all sorts of problems.

Terry Tarleton commented about underestimating his own readiness to lead people deeper in the quote I used in the previous chapter, when he said, "I thought I was already transformed." He understood the concept of transformation into Christ-likeness, but still needed more experience with his own growth before leading his congregation into new territory.

A little "spiritual" experience can have the same effect. Too many times we see leaders get a taste of a deeper relationship with Jesus and suddenly consider themselves spiritually advanced. Maybe a silent retreat or an exposure to Lectio Divina, or while reading some famous book (like *Mansions of the Heart* - smile), Jesus touched us with His love in a new way and we suddenly longed for more   both for ourselves and more for others. Thats a wonderful gift! We can be tempted, however, to simply try to duplicate our new rendezvous with Jesus and then talk other people into going for the same experience. Whether we overestimate our progress or simply want to hurry, we may need to slow down and more fully enter the journey ourselves. Were all beginners in this process of transformation into the image of Jesus; it takes more than one night on the mountain.

Where to Start

While we don't have to live fully in the Seventh Mansion before we can invite others into a transforming relationship with Jesus, we need to be living intentionally on the journey, far enough along for those close to us to spot the difference. Without the humility gained through discovering our own brokenness, revealed in our deepening intimacy with God, we can easily trivialize the struggles others face. The fire of our love relationship with Jesus, while always in process of growing, can become contagious only when others see the radiance and warmth of its flames—flames of love for God and love for those we want to lead.

Our Collaborators and I have seen a progression in our own lives that we feel you can discuss with the Lord regarding your own way forward. If you're already "climbing the mountain," to return to that analogy, our suggestions may help you with preparation and your process in continuing your journey with God. Hopefully, they'll help you become a great guide for others to follow.

Discerning First and Second Order Calling – What's Driving Your Life and Ministry?

Several of the considerations we'll suggest may prove diagnostic—particularly the first. In the previous chapters, we've discussed the two levels or natures of God's call on our lives. We've agreed that the First Order Call, representing the Great Commandment to love God with everything in us, forms our foundational relationship with God in Christ and empowers our Second Order Call to follow Him in whatever way He leads us, including the Great Commission. Theologically, I don't get much push back about this concept. Practically, however, I find that we tend to live primarily in one calling, only making "necessary" visits to the other. For us to understand how to cooperate with God's work in us going forward, we need self-knowledge about our place in both First and Second Order Callings.

In my own journey, God rescued me as an adult in the throes of grief and dismay that I could not produce abundant life myself. The amazing, and at first hard to believe, truth that God loves me just the way I am has been life-changing. I had viewed myself, for a variety of reasons, as unlovable. To cope with my self-condemnation, I learned to work hard to make myself useful to others so that they would affirm me and I could feel loved. I equated usefulness with "worthy to be loved." Serving God provided me the ultimate usefulness, so I worked really hard at it. If you'd asked me about calling, I'd have told you that God's love was absolutely the most important thing in my life—definitely my First Order Calling.

Some ten years into ministry, God snagged me for the second time. I began to realize that I'd been kidding myself for years. When Jesus invited me into deeper intimacy, I wholeheartedly agreed. To my dismay, however, I found spending quality prayer time almost impossible. While I had blocked time off to be with my family, I worked the rest of the time. I filled my schedule to the brim with people and programs, spurred on by outward success in ministry—and thus, the feelings of being lovable. As I shared earlier, I felt passionate about helping people experience Jesus in my church, inviting them to know Him as Lord and Savior. What better way to be useful than bringing new life to people and providing a growing and vibrant church to our community!

Sure, I prayed. I prayed all the time. I told God what to do and when to do it. I asked Him for direction and power, which He often gave them to me. But sit with Him, wait on Him, take time for Him? Not so much. I spent the vast majority of my time and energy following my Second Order Calling. If I had treated my wife the way I treated God, my marriage would never have survived. I don't think I'd "lost" my first love, but it had certainly gone underground. It took a monastery, a mystic monk, and some radical in-your-face encounters with God to begin to refocus my life on my First Order Calling.

Some years later, while pursuing my Doctor of Ministry degree in Spiritual Formation and Leadership at George Fox Evangelical Seminary, I met Chuck Orwiler, a fellow student. Chuck pastored a small Friends church in Denver,

Colorado. Our shared passions for Jesus and the church made friendship easy. Working together with Chuck in a class group, I discovered that we differed greatly, however, in the ways we followed Jesus. I poured out my Type-A driven genius to get things rolling. Chuck, annoyingly, often responded to my ideas with something like, "It's certainly worth thinking about, Tom; I'll have to ponder it a bit." I wrote his hesitancy off to the difference between my extroverted style and his introverted reflective nature. Consistently, however, when Chuck responded later, he'd share the most profound insights, ones that not only spoke wisely into the topic, but invited deeper thoughts. As Chuck and I became good friends, I learned more about his prayer-life. He just liked being with God, intentionally and undistracted, spending quality time each day. A look at his schedule revealed personal retreats, with little or no agenda other than being with God. Chuck's First Order Calling (I didn't understand the concept then.) didn't take long to spot. Several years later, after I moved to Denver, I saw how this deep intimacy with God enabled Chuck to listen attentively to his people and patiently encourage them to see God more fully. His parishioners understood his First Order Calling because they could see it happening in him. I'm not sure I've met anyone with greater spiritual authority in his Second Order calling.

I have to admit, however, that I find Chuck an exception to the rule with the many pastors I have come to know. While the majority of pastors describe themselves as introverts, most of us start out chasing a great cause, building a great ministry, pouring our lives into our work. We focus almost entirely on our Second Order Calling. Even when we discover spiritual formation, we may easily see the speck in our church members' eyes and congratulate ourselves for our great vision. Many times, it takes hitting a wall of some sort, a significant frustration or failure, to enable us to see the log in our own eye and ask God to take it out. But it doesn't have to be that way.

Ted Wueste describes his own early movements into spiritual formation and the things that proved helpful to him.

It all began with reading and then meeting with a counselor, but God took me to the next level with a couple of intensive retreats/ conferences in which I met with a group of like-minded seekers. I had to get off the grid and into a community where I could explore. Regular silent retreats became significant and I began to engage formation practices and experiences outside of daily ministry. They became something I owned rather than just a part of my current ministry/job. Meeting with a spiritual director and a formation group outside my church proved important, as well. Getting First Order/Second Order priorities in line … discovering my desire for God and intimacy with Him was vital. Growth included learning contemplative practices and shifting my lifestyle with a rule of life.

Before one moves beyond personal spiritual growth, a couple of things should be considered. We need to have grown just far enough that we have actually experienced and processed what we are leading others into; if counseling or healing is a part – enough time needs to have passed to ensure that change is actually happening and not just "insights" into the need for healing. Often leaders stop with "insights" and never push through to transformation; finally, spiritual formation needs to be a lifestyle, so the leaders continue to grow and move forward.

If you're like me, you may find Ted's admonitions challenging. However, his insights reflect my own experience as well as those of our Contributors. God will call us to the leadership part soon enough. While He's at work in us, Jesus may well be preparing the hearts of our congregation for their next steps.

Learning About Spiritual Growth/Formation

To my surprise, I found out that I'd been taught almost nothing about spiritual formation in seminary. I learned a little bit about what was called discipleship, but had to learn most of that from other pastors and books. I spent my first years in ministry assuming that what I had learned about discipling new believers in their spiritual growth was all there was to spiritual growth. Years later—now a pastor, I began asking myself what discipleship looked like for my own life. I realized that I'd never really heard anyone talk about "discipleship" for maturing believers before. Of course, I knew that neither my faith nor my life represented total purity or perfection. Knowing that I'd never become perfect in this world, I didn't worry about "growth" unless one of my flaws started causing problems. Looking back, however, I realize that I'd tried not to let people see my flaws and didn't invite them to point out the ones they did see. My "success" in ministry adequately assured me that my personal discipleship would suffice. I prayed for what I needed and studied the Bible and theology so that I could teach and preach well. I lived morally and accountably with peers and worked hard at being a good husband and father. I repented when I messed up. My level of spiritual maturity seemed "good enough."

When I began to long for a more intimate relationship with Jesus, however, I found that I had no idea how to find it. I also discovered that none of my pastor friends did either, apart from cranking the same shallow discipleship list. Some inferred that if I longed for a deeper relationship with God it must mean that some sin lurked within me that had to be located and expunged. After a lot of expunging, I felt just as hungry. I'd been a Christian and a pastor long enough to have arrived safely at the "good enough" stage. A year earlier I would have been willing to settle for good enough, but now God relentlessly tugged at my heart. Jesus whispered to me in the strangest ways and places. I felt as though He stood physically near me, but hidden in the shadows. Glimpses of His nearness made me starve and thirst for more of Him.

I remember talking to Brother Boniface, a monk at Holy Trinity Abbey who became my spiritual mentor. The monastery guesthouse had become a place to get away to work on sermon series and teaching curriculum. One day we walked together through the lush pastures that provided the monks' support. These 1600 acres basked in the beauty of the surrounding snow-capped mountains. As we strolled along, I complained about how hard it felt to really know God. I expressed frustration with only seeing Him work silently and invisibly in the ministry of my church, but not really feeling His presence or hearing Him speak to me. Bon stopped instantly on the path and pointed to a wild flower. "See that blue flower?" "Yes, I stammered." "There's more of God in that wildflower than you could experience in a lifetime." Walking on, he then expounded for the next hour about God's presence within us and in everything around us—always communicating to us in every moment. Waving his arms, he quoted Scripture after Scripture driving his case home with the eloquence of a Martin Luther or a Billy Graham.

Later that evening, I walked alone in the monastery orchard reflecting. I stopped and said aloud to God, "If You are always here and always communicating, why do I hear You so seldomly? And, when I do, why so cryptically?" God replied to me instantly in my mind, "Tom, I'm shouting at you all the time!" "Then why don't I hear you?" I almost yelled. Immediately the passage from Ezekiel came to mind, "I will remove from you the heart of stone and replace it with a heart of flesh." (Ezekiel 36:26) I understood what He meant—I needed to be recreated. Sin had hardened and deformed my ability to "walk with God in the cool of the Garden." The Holy Spirit would have to enable my heart to know Him, to hear Him, to discern His presence and love. At that moment, I realized that I had absolutely no idea how such a thing happened.

On another visit, Boniface suggested that I read *The Way of a Pilgrim*, the anonymous account of a disabled Russian pilgrim who wandered from village to village teaching people the Jesus Prayer. I'd never heard of this "oldest Christian prayer since the Lord's Prayer." It goes, "Lord Jesus Christ, Son of God, have mercy on me, a sinner." (Cf. Luke 18:13) I later learned that the Jesus Prayer had been passed down from the Desert Fathers who lived in the wastelands of Egypt and who Christianized most of the country. The Desert Fathers taught that the whole of the Christian message was contained in this simple prayer. Lord – who is my lord? Jesus – who is Jesus? The Messiah, the Son of God. What has He done for me? Had mercy upon me. Who am I? A sinner. The Desert Fathers prayed this prayer repeatedly, first in time with their walking, then synchronized with their breathing, and finally, with their heart beat. They took seriously the biblical invocation to "pray without ceasing," (cf. 1 Thess 5:17) and taught their autonomic nervous systems to keep the prayer going even when busy with other things. I read with skepticism, cautious of rote prayers which could lose their meaning through mindless repetition—skepticism until I tried it. I'd also never heard of the Desert Fathers—pre-Reformation, you know. That prayer still resonates through my being, always reminding me of His presence and love which floods my soul.

My next visit to the Monastery presented me with a stack of books—the Philokalia, the writings of the Desert Fathers. Wow! These hermits taught not only about what God does within us, but how it actually happens and ways we can cooperate. I'd never read writers who so intricately interwove Scripture into their thought. Those mind-blowing discoveries led me to study the Church Fathers and Mothers. My seminary education had taught me little about them, except where some had strayed into some "heresy." Bernard of Clairvaux, Teresa of Avila, John of the Cross—truly amazing!

Not only did these Christian mystics from other times and cultures open doors that I'd never even knocked on, but they reframed my experience of God from different perspectives. Knowing and loving God meant everything to them. Yet their lives resulted in amazing missional impact. I "met" men and women who were so on fire for God and so in love with Him that they sacrificed everything. History records their contagious love and the wildfires of renewal and evangelism. Did my theology become Eastern Orthodox or Romans Catholic? No, of course not. But I found their perspectives refreshing and the ways they experienced and taught about loving intimacy with God were exhilarating.

About this same time, I discovered Richard Foster and Dallas Willard and attended Renovare' Conferences. I realized that I wasn't the only Protestant Evangelical catching fire. So much to be learned; so much to be experimented with; so much to be integrated—I had no idea! Years later, when I asked an editor what he thought of my book draft, he candidly replied, "You don't know what you don't know about writing. Let me put you in touch with someone who can show you." When I started this spiritual formation journey, I had no idea about what I didn't know—about God, about spiritual formation, and about myself. I'm a slow reader and "much too busy" to spend a lot of time at it, so it is taking me a long time. But until I learned what I didn't know, I was in no shape to lead my congregation into deeper waters and new fire.

Locating One's Self on a Journey Paradigm

When we're off on a journey, a map usually proves helpful. Locating ourselves in a framework that describes the spiritual formation journey provides a vital element in our preparation for authentic spiritual leadership. After reading and digesting Teresa of Avila, I recognized my place in the Third Mansion as well as God's invitation to explore the Fourth. For many years, I'd grown in my relationship with the Lord through working alongside Him. In my early years, He taught me in youth and small group ministry in my local church. Later, He taught me to follow Him building airplanes in the aerospace industry. Still later, full-time pastoral ministry provided many opportunities to see Jesus at work in real time. He taught me what He's like in practice, and led me to discover how to cooperate with Him in daily life. During my earlier conversion phase, I thought relationship with God focused on me because God's grace within me proved truly life-changing. Later, I discovered that our life together could also be about others as I experienced how God's love and power motivated and guided me into peoples' lives in life-changing ways. Dallas Willard used the word, "apprentice" for this Third Mansion phase of getting to know Jesus, learning how He thinks and works.

Later, still, I realized that God had begun to show me more of Jesus, not just how to get our work done, but to come to experientially know Jesus. While I had loved Him at some level for many years, I was now falling in love with Him. I learned from reading Teresa of Avila and John of the Cross that God was leading me into a transition season, discovering new territory and experience that I would find confusing, frustrating, exhilarating, and saddening. While the day would come when my life would be totally centered in my Lord, I saw that I was nowhere close.

Thomas Dubay, in his book *Fire Within*, written about Teresa and John, says that "Most significant spiritual growth is discerned by the believer as backsliding."[1] After spending so many years as an "expert" about the Bible, theology, and church growth, this deeper experience of Jesus opened my eyes to His unimaginable mystery. I now had to learn to cope with living as a total novice—expert about nothing. While I don't think that I'd been prideful before, this new humbling proved more than uncomfortable. Before I could lead my people forward in their own journeys, I had to learn to let this new love and humility fan the flames of my love for God. I had to become a contagious fire. I also learned that my first priority would be to develop a consistent life of abiding prayer, to spend time each day to be with God in an attentive, listening, loving way. Abiding prayer proved the hardest spiritual discipline I have faced so far—until I became addicted to prayer. My spiritual leadership had to emerge from the prayer closet.

Tammy Long shares her insights about the relationship between our own spiritual growth and our ability to lead others spiritually.

> I think it is key to gain some clarity as to why a leader wants to move the church into spiritual growth and missional momentum. This relates to the idea that a leader cannot lead where he or she has not been (and is seeking to go). If they are seeking a program or movement for numerical growth or perceived church health or success, or because a church is supposed to be growing, their efforts will be limited.
>
> I believe such a movement only catches fire when leaders themselves are on the journey personally, not "professionally." Ideally,

---

1. Thomas Dubay, *Fire Within: St. Teresa of Avila, St. John of the Cross and the Gospel-On Prayer.* Ignatius Press, 1989. Pg.4

it is the lead pastor who catches this vision because it is amazing what happens when the lead pastor becomes a catalyst, supporter, and champion. But I have observed that it can also come from other leaders who fan the fire and it catches in a grassroots way. I personally was very encouraged and affirmed by a book called A Quiet Pentecost, by Dwight Judy, which speaks to how a little leaven can impact the entire body.

All God needs from us is a little leaven, glowing embers. However, He doesn't want to leave us there; He wants to fan our flames until we become a very fire of love. God doesn't drag us along in our spiritual formation boot camp; He invites us to cooperate with Him. Understanding a journey roadmap, such as Teresa's Seven Mansions, and our relative place in the process can help us better understand what we're experiencing, and discover how to cooperate. A Mapping Tool for the Teresian Mansions can be found on the Resource page of *Imago Christi's* website. This coaching tool provides a "score" in each of the seven phases of growth, with coaching to help us interpret what that region of spiritual experience means for our formation. *Imago Christi's* Spiritual Formation Discovery for Leaders retreat provides a three-day process of self-discovery and encouragement related to the Teresian Mansions.

Cooperating with God's Transforming Process

Through these Discoveries and personal coaching, I've been privileged to encounter the spiritual lives of hundreds of Christian leaders. I find many of them in the beginning explorations of the Fifth Mansion—the growing desire to experience the unity with God that Jesus prays for in John 17:21, "...that they may all be one; even as You, Father, are in Me and I in You, <u>that they may also be in US</u>, so that the world may believe that You sent Me." In this stage, we experience more than ever before the reality of "Christ in you, the hope of glory." (Colossians 1:27) Our experience of His presence reveals His glory, which can be both frightening and exhilarating. His presence can also reveal our own "lack of glory" which can horrify us. Teresa believes most serious Christians at least touch the Fifth Mansion, but many quickly flee back because the terrain feels so strange and they have no mentors to help them navigate.

I remember the first time I met James, the lead pastor of a large Bible church, in one of *Imago Christi's* Discoveries. He agreed to attend at the last minute and often ducked out of sessions to take calls that he thought might demand his presence elsewhere. During the sessions, James didn't smile and kept pretty much to himself. Later in the Discovery, as we presented the Teresian Mansions, he began to show more interest. He even leaned forward in his chair, seemingly engrossed in both the presentations and the table sharing. After the Discovery, I visited with James at his church. He explained how discouraged he had felt about his faith. He expressed particular guilt about how little he sensed God's presence in his practice of the four-step discipleship process he taught his church. James had wondered if his "weak faith" disqualified him for ministry, and considered seeking another profession. Now, as we talked, James leaned across his desk and virtually glowed with excitement. He'd misinterpreted spiritual growth as backsliding. His frustration with himself, God, and his church, when put in context, revealed a new movement of the Holy Spirit within him. Jesus had been, in fact, inviting him to live more deeply in His love and to show His church how to live there too. No wonder he felt so dissatisfied. Once James began cooperating with Jesus' shepherding, in light of this new season in his journey, depression turned into joy and adventure returned to his ministry.

As activist leaders, most of us need to learn how to become attentive to God and discern His leading. Words of knowledge, wisdom, and prophesy prove powerful gifts for ministry, but our Shepherd matures us personally with quiet whispers and gentle blowings which can only be discerned when the wind, fire, and earthquakes have been stilled. This need to discern leads me to the next two considerations.

Abiding Prayer – Both Diagnostic and Transforming

I've mentioned abiding prayer several times in this chapter because it's been so hard for me and yet so central to my life with God. I find, however, that most Christian leaders I meet struggle with it as well and stagnate in their growth because they don't pursue it. We say we love God, but let's face it—we're pragmatic. We're in ministry to get things done; we need to spend our efforts in real accomplishments that our people can see. Prayer is important to us only to the extent that it gets things done. We'll fast and pray for days to get God to reveal the right strategy or to provide the resources for some great project. But when Jesus calls us to go up to the mountain with Him and pray, we either ignore the invitation, suggest that later would be better for us, or go up for a few minutes—rather than for the night. We may even tell ourselves that we're not contemplatively wired.

Scripture and Christian history demonstrate that women and men who become great evangelists, missionaries, and founders of movements also become great women and men of prayer. Their prayer becomes more like communing with God than talking to Him, more listening than asking. Jesus invites us into a relationship of abiding, like branches with the vine. In this abiding, prayer becomes connectedness—the sharing of life, an intimacy out of which Jesus could say, "I do what I see the Father doing." (John 5:19)

We might rightly say that we abide with Christ all the time. However, we also recognize that, in the hustle and bustle of daily life, it's impossible to actually discern our abiding, to be attentive to Him, aware of His transforming love, and able to hear His word to us. We're called to the prayer closet, not just to learn something, hear something, get something done, but to simply BE with God, to sit with him in His love, to let Him create a new heart within us. Over time, we dare to put down the devotional book, to close the Bible for a bit and just let Him love on us and maybe even love Him in return. For us missional types, however, abiding prayer can feel almost impossible.

For me, God used the Ignatian Exercises and the monastery to kick start me. James Wakefield, then a Baptist pastor, introduced me to the 19th

Annotation of the Spiritual Exercises of St. Ignatius. The "Exercises" present
a 24 to 26-week daily prayer experience. Each day, one spends about an hour
with a passage of Scripture, usually a New Testament gospel story. After
reading the passage slowly several times, we enter it imaginatively, watching
what the Holy Spirit points out that relates to us. We let God interact with
us about our experience in the story and in our lives, and then journal about
our prayer experience. James drafted a Protestant version of the Exercises
(He said to me one day, "It's just the Four Spiritual Laws!") and talked me
into trying it out on our staff and elders. Each week we'd do the exercise and
then meet with another person to debrief our journal. I was trapped! If I
welched, I'd be found out to be the charlatan, for sure. Yet, the Exercises gave
me a general process to follow that wasn't too restrictive, and I found, to my
surprise, that God did meet me in these prayer times—in amazing ways.
At the end of the year, the Exercises had carved a "groove for prayer" in my
heart—I had become addicted! I spent the next two years using the same
process with the Psalms. Again, amazing!

The Monastery provided another important tool for God in breaking
my addiction to work and productivity. Boniface said to me once, "There's
a monk in all of us, but some of us need to get off the scene to discover
him." I started going on retreat at Holy Trinity Abbey for three or four days
a month. After we moved from the area to pastor in another church, I went
for a week, four times a year. Each day I would attend the seven worship
services, called offices. The monks graciously let me sit with them as they
chanted the Psalms, sang hymns, and prayed. While I did take people with
me at times, I spent most of the time alone, taking meals in my room. Every
few days, a walk with Brother Boniface challenged and enriched my retreat.
Eventually, I began to discern Jesus carrying on conversations with me,
ones He initiated—not me. Gradually, I learned to become still and listen,
to love and be loved. Over time, I learned that the "real me" was, in fact, the
monk. Friends would ask my wife, Charlotte, how she could let me leave
her and our three kids that often. Once she responded, "He comes home a

better husband." However, it works best for you—whether or not you need a monastery, abiding prayer can never be just an option. Unless we spend quality time with God on the mountain, we will never be able to follow Him on the plain.

Facing Issues of Control – Jesus is Lord

We leaders can become masters of control. It might also be said that we become leaders because we have mastered control. Control can be a good thing and certainly out-of-control—when it comes to leadership, isn't good at all. We need self-control, the fruit of the Spirit, to be able to plan and organize. We need to be able to provide an environment without chaos for people to move together toward a worthy goal. However, as you know, control has a dark side.

Having grown up in an environment that felt more like chaos than stability, I soon equated control with safety and security, and I learned skills intended to provide just that. Not long into marriage, management, and then the pastorate, I learned that trying to control others usually backfired. It proved to be oppressive and produced resistance rather than cooperation and productivity—people just don't like being controlled. Without giving in to a "what-ever" leadership style, I had to learn how to lead in a way that brought consensus and group commitment to goals. This new style of leadership became even more imperative as I learned that the Holy Spirit gifts and empowers each person. Only as I encouraged and listened to the work of the Spirit in the leadership team and then the church, could we truly discover God's leading. I hadn't yet discovered, however, that trying to control God didn't work either.

This horrifying realization became clear for me in this agonizing process of learning to abide with God in prayer. As I tried and failed over and over again to "be still and know that I am God," I began to see my relationship with God in a new light. In the beginning, my prayer life had been totally about me—about control. I told God when we would talk and what we would talk about. I prescribed what Scripture He could use to speak to me. I gave Him an allotted time in which to make Himself heard, and then I'd walk away—on to more important things. God demonstrated amazing patience!

As I learned about contemplative prayer and began to try it, I realized that I had somehow missed the teaching that abiding prayer is a gift from God. I tried all the techniques I'd read about to try to get God to do what He was supposed to do. I withdrew to a quiet place alone, stilled my mind (to the extent that was ever possible), focused on a passage of Scripture or just focused on Him. God was supposed to produce warm feelings within me and enlighten me with deep spiritual truths. God, in His mercy, did give me a few tastes here and there, but nowhere near what I thought He should do— what I "deserved." Time and again, after prayer times filled with frustration, the Lord would whisper, "You mean that I'm not enough for you, Tom? You need feelings and insights, too?" Each time, those words broke my heart— He was exactly right. I wanted more than God and I wanted it my way!

I've discovered that Jesus meant it when He said, "Follow Me." He didn't say, "What would you like to do and how may I help you." Countless exasperating experiences have resulted in countless new surrenders until I finally dumped my illusions of control. Of course, the temptation still returns and sometimes I yield to it. I find the sin of Adam and Eve still lurks in me. If I learn enough and become wise enough, I can run my life myself; with the right "spiritual maturity," I can provide for myself the control that will give me safety and stability—and, of course, make God proud.

In the early days after the founding of *Imago Christi*, Endi Kovacs introduced a new word to me— "followership." Endi, one of my first real brothers in spiritual formation ministry, grew up and still lives and ministers as a spiritual formation missionary in Budapest, Hungary. He understood that authentic Christian leadership results only as we follow Jesus. We can only lead because we follow Jesus, not simply on principles of belief or religion, but specifically, intentionally, and obediently. People won't long for, and shouldn't follow, a great vision or ideal. Real Christians want to follow Jesus. They will follow us only to the extent that they discern that we, and they, follow Jesus. We might try to project spiritual authority based on some new theme and program every year or a great new book for a sermon series or by imitating some great church. Our people, however, would soon discover that we're not leading at all, but floundering in the sea of ecclesiology, tossed by the lure of success, or sinking with the fear of failure. We learn followership in the prayer closet.

Spiritual Direction

Spiritual direction, almost unheard of in Protestant circles a decade or so ago, is becoming more and more popular. "Spiritual Direction" describes a specific type of mentoring that focuses on one's spiritual life, helping the directee develop the ability to listen to God and discern His leading. Once only the ministry of pastors or possibly church deacons and elders (or monks and nuns for those brave enough to seek them out), spiritual direction is now practiced by "ordinary" people who walk deeply with Jesus. Christian colleges and seminaries and even some churches train people to listen to God with others as spiritual directors. The biblical injunctions to comfort others with the same comfort we have received has always been there, but often not the training (cf. 2 Corinthians 1:4).

The term, spiritual "direction," can be, in many ways, a misnomer. Spiritual directors learn to listen to God, to know themselves, to understand the journey of faith, to listen to others, and to help their directees listen to God. God directs; the spiritual director and directee both attempt to follow. While some of us may be naturally attuned to walking with others, we all need to learn the skills that can enable us to do so effectively. We've all had the experience of trying to share a struggle only to be interrupted with the other person's story, followed by their best advice. However, that person probably does really care and with the right training might make an excellent spiritual director.

Spiritual direction proves a particularly helpful resource for Christian leaders, for a number of reasons. First, we tend to become isolated. Many studies find pastors among the most isolated of professionals. People can expect us to have it altogether, so they don't ask, and we don't tell, about our struggles. In fact, in many cases, parishioners simply don't want to know. Second, peers often feel unavailable. Measures of success prove so elusive in the church that we secretly compete with other churches. "How can I trust someone that's just waiting to find out what a failure I am or to steal my members?" We need, therefore, people to listen who aren't threatening.

Thirdly, we can easily confuse knowledge about God and knowledge of God. A medical doctor, in contrast, doesn't share quite the same challenge. He or she may know everything about heart surgery, for example, but if their head can't properly guide their hands, the patient dies. We can preach and teach with such eloquence that we may begin to believe that we actually experience what we're talking about. We need someone safe enough to share our fears and struggles, to listen to our wonderings and reflections, to ask us to say more, and to encourage us. God uses others to remind us about what we sometimes forget—that God still loves us. Whether a paid spiritual director or a trusted friend who can truly listen, we need someone who has traveled a bit further, learned the terrain a bit more, to walk with us. Remember when people only went to a doctor when they got really sick? Now we've learned that these medical professionals can help keep us healthy, too. In the same way, we don't have to be "in trouble" to seek out a spiritual friend and guide. As new believers, seeking out a discipler was considered a wise thing to do. Why should it be different now?

Transparency and Vulnerability

While we can find it really helpful to become transparent and vulnerable with a trusted spiritual director or friend, an appropriate level of those same attributes proves essential both for fanning the flames of our personal love for God and the flames of others. For all the same reasons that pastors and ministry professionals can hide, our people can become isolated as well. When we leaders act, even unintentionally, as though we have it altogether, our parishioners can feel that we expect near perfection of them. Many people feel that in any journey of faith, most of them should have pretty well arrived by now. Questions and obstacles can be perceived as weakness and failure to be hidden safely away, at least until troubles reach crisis proportions. When this happens more people leave the church than seek out the pastor to talk about their issues.

One of the signs that Christianity isn't some contrived myth about super heroes to be worshiped can be seen in the fact that Scripture describes believers' faults and failures, often in vivid detail. Only the Trinity comes through clean. Abraham, Isaac, Jacob, Moses, the prophets, and the disciples of Jesus all struggled to follow God, all failed at various levels, and ALL told the truth about it. If we asked our congregations if they could follow the leadership of one of these men or women of God, they would stand and applaud. Why do we wonder why it's so hard for them to follow leaders who hide?

Chris Schutte shares his thoughts about our self-knowledge and our willingness to be open about it.

> Who might be ready to lead this kind of a process? It seems important to me that he or she is able to embrace brokenness and seek healing. The kind of humility and generosity that usually results from engaging with the dark and wounded places in our souls is essential to lead others well on this journey.

When we share appropriately about our own journey of discovery, both in its struggles and victories, people become encouraged to join us and to explore their own journey more fully. On the other hand, when we lead from a position of strength and exhort our people to shape up and get it right, to grow up spiritually, etc., they feel criticized and judged, burdened with more work. The greatest acts of leadership we can ever provide our people reveals our own humanity and foibles in the light of our deepening love for God and the freedom to be ourselves in His love. We're not called to be the fire for our people, but to become contagious with God's fire. Only in our true earthen vessels can the fire of God's love shine through in an inviting way. Only in vulnerably and honestly in our journey can we become contagious fire for others.

Melanie Saint James comments about our need for growing spiritually together.

> We need guides and the presence of community to walk with us along the way. At my current church we like to say, "No one walks alone". Anyone who is serious about spiritual growth needs a companion or two. All of us need people who are a little farther along on the journey to help us understand some of the seasons of spiritual growth and who can hold our feet to the fire when things become difficult and uncertain. Much of the time, spiritual growth doesn't look like growth at all, and so we need mentors and companions who can assure us that we are right where God wants us to be, even when our spiritual life actually looks like it is falling apart.

Becoming Contagious

In summary, we encourage you not to jump into a programmatic spiritual formation ministry prematurely. Let this chapter form a kind of prayerful assessment about your own walk with Jesus. Are you learning to discern His heart? To what extent do you live deeply in His love with your First Order Calling actually first in your life? What is your progress in discovering your own wounds and blocks that inhibit the depth of your relationship with God? How well do you understand the journey of transformation and your place in it?

Ask the Lord to increase the flames of love within your heart to the point where you and others can recognize real spiritual growth—not just in your rhetoric, but in your relationships. Let Jesus love you where you find yourself in process, cooperate with Him in your becoming like Him, and listen for His clear direction to take the next step. Jesus excels in patience and invites us to trust Him with the timing.

Chuck Orwiler discusses our readiness to move forward.

> *As I reviewed Christ's life in Luke's Gospel, I've noticed, in chapters 13-19, a number of hard sayings of Jesus – the kinds of things that make us wonder if we have what it takes to be a disciple. At the same time Jesus lingered with sinners, and people who were eager to hear Him. Sometimes the disciples were just plain stumped by what Jesus said to them. This is the raw material Jesus is pleased to work with. So, I want to be careful at this point of defining at what point a leader needs to have journeyed. In a metaphor of our journey with God, George MacDonald (The Princess and Curdie) observed that how far up the mountainside one is, isn't the issue. What matters more is whether one is on the way up or on the way down. The leader on the way up the mountain can gather a flock to join in the upward journey. That's our story.*

Whether you have felt on the way up the mountain of God or drifting downward, our Great Shepherd beckons us to His side, offers us His hand, and lovingly motions upward. In response to our concerns about our disabilities and wounds and fears, Jesus smiles and says, "Take up that cross—I've got you; you're not alone. Others wait just ahead who need you." (cf. Matthew 11:28 and Mark 8:34)

In Chapter 4, we'll discuss those waiting to journey with you and Jesus— those who need you, and who you can't lead without.

CHAPTER 4

IGNITING THE SPARK INTO FLAME - FOLLOWING JESUS

Once Jesus has set fire to our own leader hearts, we long to share the fire of that love with others. We particularly long to empower our congregational members to experience the kind of contagious fire that launches them into personal abundant life. We know that once they're set free by the touch of God's fire, they'll naturally and intentionally reach out to others with the love of Jesus. Motivated by that desire for our people, we ask ourselves, "What kind of leadership will enable this kind of fire to become contagious?"

Let's return to our fire analogy and the process that God designed for fire to spread. We saw that a piece of combustible material becomes ignited from some external energy source. In our case, our love for God began with His great torch of love for us. Through our life experience, He drew us just close enough that a spark of love struck a place in our hearts that longed for real love. His closeness continued to heat that place within us until a glowing ember of love flickered, and finally became a flame. In our fire analogy, we saw that one log cannot sustain a healthy fire, but needs to be brought close enough to other logs that both heat and oxygen can increase the mutual energy of the "group" fire—a campfire. Now we have a fire that has become sustainable and useful. In Chapter 4, we will discuss the process of creating this "campfire" of men and women within a ministry. Together, they can increase their own flames of love, support the spiritual growth of others in the group, and finally become a blazing hearth from which the whole congregation can catch fire.

In Chapter 3, we discussed the importance of a spiritual community of honesty and vulnerability where we can listen to the voice of our Shepherd together, learn from one another, and share mutual encouragement. Jesus invites us all to "abide in Him," all branches on the single Vine, in clusters or communities, living interdependently and supportively. While we experience God alone in prayer, we also experience Him in one another. It takes both connections with God to truly come to know Jesus. So, let's explore this vital part of spiritual community that forms our next step—how our leadership sparks others to long for more of Jesus in and through a "spiritual leadership community."

Jesus spread the fire of God's transforming love across the earth in a simple yet profound way—He called together a group of disciples. He loved them and exposed them to the Love that is God to the point that their love became so contagious and life-giving that their names have been given, over the centuries, to grand mountain ranges, beautiful cathedrals, and newborn babies. Peter, James, John, Mary, Martha, Thomas, identify women and men around the globe. Talk about contagious fire!

Jesus built a spiritual leadership community at the core of His ministry to proclaim the Good News and demonstrate God's love through healing and miracles. Jesus formed a leadership community to spread the good news of the coming Kingdom of God for at least four reasons.

Jesus needed the love and support of others. Of course, Jesus called the disciples together for strategic purposes. We also see Him call them onto the mountain to pray with Him and to the Garden of Gethsemane to support Him in His anguish about His coming suffering and death. Jesus relied upon His disciples and the women that followed Him to handle the logistical details of His housing, food, and travel to free Him to minister with the Twelve. He needed them to go ahead of His coming visits to prepare the hearts of the people that would become open to Him.

Jesus knew that others would have to become God's contagious love for the world after His death and resurrection. Early in His ministry, we see the contagious fire in Andrew draw Peter to Jesus. Jesus invested significant time fanning the flames of love in these twelve disciples so that He could trust them to extend His voice and loving power throughout the world.

Jesus modeled the kind of communal lifestyle that reflects the Trinitarian love of God and sustains God's love in His Beloveds.

Jesus did not minister alone because He understood how His skeptical culture, and ours, would respond. One man or woman who seems to be on fire with love for God and neighbor can be (and usually is) easily dismissed as an anomaly—someone who's either an exception to the rule or on a different journey. Hundreds and thousands aren't so easily ignored. The disciples' testimonies drew crowds, filled with expectation. As crowds encountered more crowds, expectation grew into hope and faith—ready to receive Jesus and His message of love. Fire spread contagiously.

So, Jesus leads in a community of many stories and testimonies of men and women whose hearts have been ignited with the love of Jesus, and now share that love contagiously with everyone they meet. Jesus aimed, from the beginning, to spread a bonfire of contagious love across the earth, but He started with a small group of twelve men.

People of faith change when their hearts become captivated by a shared God-given vision—one most often embodied and communicated by a leader. Churches and ministries don't change because the leader simply gets some new obsession. It's hard for people to embrace any new vision, much less one that challenges every member to mature in a loving relationship with God with an intimacy that results in contagious love for neighbor. That vision requires a momentous cultural shift for a majority of churches because most of our visions have narrowly focused on our own well-being or the growth of the institution. Contagious fire can feel frightening for those not yet aflame, so it's easy to stay hunkered down.

We know, from Scripture and experience, that no lasting change can happen in a group or organization unless it first happens in its leaders. No one leader, whether Senior Pastor, Elder, or staff member, no matter how influential or loved, can lead such a countercultural change alone; it takes a broad-based leadership team working under the direct guidance of the Holy Spirit. Only Jesus knows how to accomplish the transformations necessary in our unique communities, in the right way with the right timing —first in leadership and then in the congregation. Ultimately, people will follow and discover for themselves when they see the reality of Christ-likeness in respected leaders who encourage them to know the love of God more personally.

This spiritual leadership community, therefore, has the same fourfold purpose that we saw in Jesus:

Support - First, it provides the community support and interaction essential to the leader's own spiritual growth. Jesus shared a unique relationship with the Father and the Holy Spirit for His own growth. Luke tells us, "And Jesus kept increasing in wisdom and stature, and in favor with God and men." Luke 2:52-3:1 We, however, need the mutual support, encouragement, perspectives, and spiritual gifts of the Body of Christ to support our spiritual growth. Smoldering logs become a campfire.

Empowerment - Second, such a leadership community provides a context in which the senior leader, shepherding from a position of personal discovery and vulnerability, affirms, blesses, and empowers the other leaders, inviting them into a shared spiritual discovery journey. The campfire builds and grows in heat and brilliance.

Truth - Third, the loving relationships developed within the spiritual leadership community reveal God's love, modeling the Kingdom life of abiding together in God's love. The brilliance of this leadership campfire becomes a contagious beacon, inviting others to consider a more intense and bright relationship with Jesus and others.

Send - Fourthly, the contagious fire of the leadership team becomes the two's and the seventies that Jesus sends out into the life of the congregation. Whether a senior leader in the congregation or a member of the staff responsible for "spiritual formation," no one person can ultimately connect effectively with enough people to precipitate such a major cultural shift in any congregation. Logs from the blazing campfire can now be taken as torches to ignite and build fires of God's love inside individuals and groups within the congregation.

Within the Spiritual Leadership Community, God SETS fire to their own lives and eventually to the church and beyond. What kind of leadership can build and nurture a team that SETS this kind of radical change into motion?

Leadership largely determines the extent to which the flames of a congregation's growing love relationship with God becomes contagious. We all have personal leadership styles which have emerged from our personalities, experiences, and the models we've worked under. We must ask, however, what kind of leadership style helps kindle the fire in our own hearts and sparks the embers in those around us? Let's look more deeply at Jesus' leadership style. We might be surprised to discover how "contemporary" it really is.

Significant advances in human history can be traced back to Jesus. Christianity's willingness to embrace all creation as "good" inspired science, industry, exploration, and the arts. In recent years, even the science of management has recognized that Jesus modeled a leadership style that changed the world—a leadership style that works. Before Jesus, leadership could be defined simply as the exercise of power. A person could be considered a "leader" only when he or she possessed power over other people. Leaders had the ability to reward obedience and punish disobedience. Some leaders could be described as benevolent and others vicious and cruel. Either way, it all boiled down to power and authority. Even God's followers, described in the Old Testament era, used power as the basis of their leadership.

Jesus led in a different way—one that modern leadership textbooks have begun to teach, whether they admit it is based on Jesus or not. While Jesus possessed "all power in heaven and earth," His leadership did not draw on that power, but on love—He led authentically out of His own character. Let's look at some of the attributes of Jesus' leadership style.

> **Jesus Led as a Follower**—He openly expressed that, in mutual love with the Father, He only did what He saw the Father doing and that He could only accomplish what He did by the Father's leading (cf. John 5:19).

> **Jesus Led in Humility**—He always deferred to His Father's will, in love for the Father and for others (cf. Matthew 11:28-30).

> **Jesus Led in Service**—His actions were always driven by His love for others and their needs (cf. Mark 10:45).

> **Jesus Led by Example**—He lived out the values embodied in God's love and encouraged and demonstrated the reality of the Kingdom through loving interaction with others (cf. John 13:15).

> **Jesus Led in and Through Community**—He invited others to abide with Him in love, taught and empowered them, and then sent them out with the mission of love in the Kingdom of God (cf. John 17:18).

> **Jesus Led in Vulnerability**—He honored and loved His followers by revealing both His strengths and His weaknesses. For example, He told them about His encounter with the devil in the desert, that the

attack was so vicious and painful that it took angels to care for Him. He shared the pain and tears He felt about God's people in their suffering and rebellion. Jesus asked His disciples to pray with Him and for Him as He struggled in the Garden (cf. 2 Corinthians 13:4).

Jesus Led by Giving His Leadership Away—He delegated the entire Kingdom venture—the contagious fire of God's transforming love—into the hands of His followers. (cf. Matthew 28:18).

Jesus' leadership proved historically remarkable because He never used power to coerce, intimidate, or manipulate others to follow Him. He demonstrated that a Good Shepherd creates a flock bound together by love and leads from within its midst. He draws others into an interdependent relationship, like the human body. As Head of the Body, He invites His followers to participate rather than overpowers them to submit. Jesus' followers came to lead just like Him because they longed to BE like Him. We could call Jesus' leadership style CONTAGIOUS LEADERSHIP.

Leaders in management theory today might not use the word "love" to describe best leadership practice. They have learned, however, that a participative care for team members honors and equips them. It releases their creativity, motivates their full investment, and empowers them as leaders. Jesus' followers became so motivated, invested, and empowered that they gave their very lives for the cause of the Kingdom.

Many great leaders today find that this kind of relationally contagious leadership motivates similar devotion to a common cause. They're discovering the apostle Paul's wisdom when he said, "the law (power) kills, but the Spirit brings life" (cf. Romans 8:1). We can foolishly pile logs together and then demand that they become fire. It will never happen. Our pile of logs only catches fire when they become ignited by another fire. In the case of the Church, God is both the other Fire and the Leader, where the "senior" leader, or any leader tasked with a mission, follows Him with the torch.

Why so many Christian leaders today attempt power-based leadership amazes me. We accumulate the power of knowledge; we build power into pastoral job descriptions; we skillfully craft the power of winsome personality, articulation, and persuasion; we cultivate the power of group approval and influence; and, if possible, we relish in the power of success by building big churches, attracting large crowds, and touting "international" outreach. Eventually, when power no longer works (and it ultimately fails), many of us give up leading. Instead, we teach or counsel. We may decide to cheerlead, or provide group entertainment, or…. When our Old Testament leadership style lets us down, we may simply find another church or ministry, or leave ministry altogether.

Chris Schutte, comments about the complexity of dealing with the subject of "power" in different leadership situations.

> *Since we come from different polities, applying the spiritual community paradigm will look differently. We often lapse into a "power-based" leadership model, because that is what we see around us, and the Contagious Leadership vision takes a lot of work! I do think that the issue of "power" is often misunderstood. Andy Crouch's book "Playing God," and his latest, "Weak and Strong," have great insights into the use of power within the Church. As a pastor, I find that day-to-day leadership is often entirely pragmatic–what do we need to get done? The vision of a community listening to the Lord together is countercultural in most churches.*

Jesus promised to work with us—and work with us He does, despite how difficult we make it for Him. He invites us, however, to do it His way. How could Jesus honor, particularly in the leadership of spiritual formation, a secular leadership style that contradicts the very life we want others to discover? This journey of deepening intimacy with Jesus can become the place to let Him lead our leading.

Steve Macchia, founder and leader of Leadership Transformations commented about power-based leadership.

> *This issue is vital to the contagious fire experience. Unless there is a shared leadership vision and accompanying values among the*

leadership team, the fire will quickly extinguish…or, worse yet, slowly extinguish! I've seen this, over and over again, and believe firmly that "it's all about leadership." When there is a shared conviction that we must lead completely differently from the "power" and "top down" approach, there is healthy synergy for the way forward. Unfortunately, due to the "power" leadership motifs in the corporate world, and even in business and education, as well as in many churches, this can be like pushing a rock uphill. I've been a part of teams where "body" matters more than "power," and I've been sideswiped by the "power" mongers too. The natural default is to "power," and the "body" analogy will only be lived out if those involved have a heart for Jesus and his model of leadership. This chapter is what I would describe as the "turnkey" to effectively proceeding or not…unless the fire is within the context of the leadership team, lone rangers will be left to defend and protect the way of spiritual formation and will most likely be consumed by those who "power" their way forward.

Charlie Dodrill commented about resistance to the contagious leadership style and the openness and vulnerability it requires for both the leader and the team.

I have found a reluctance among staff to be open about personal and vulnerable areas of their own lives…particularly with lead pastors. I think there can be an insecurity about where we are spiritually and in life circumstances…particularly if we believe others on our staff are more advanced or "spiritual" than we are. I find lead pastors reluctant to enter vulnerable, spiritual community with their staff because they still must look at it organizationally (as much as we hate to use that term). There are some–especially in the lead leadership role–who find it difficult to have such discussions amongst the staff because it feels strange to be so intimately involved with those we may have to fire.

Many of our Contributors expressed similar sentiments about the difficulties we face when we're challenged to use a contagious leadership style. I'm trusting that you, however, have moved in that direction already or find its potential rewards worth the risk of trying. In my own move toward a contagious leadership style, I found that my spiritual leadership team helped me learn, through their honest feedback and encouragement.

Terry Tarleton commented about the importance of his own journey of transformation in facilitating a spiritual leadership team.

> We planted our church almost 16 years ago. For the first 12 years or so I led from a power position. I tend to be a strong leadership type, so that worked for me. I was in charge and people knew it. Over those years, I had more than one person in our church come to me and say that I was "intimidating and unapproachable." It was easy for me to dismiss those comments because they were so infrequent and "obviously" didn't represent the views of the majority of our church.

> In about 2012 or so, as I was well on my journey of knowing Jesus, not just knowing about Him, and developing a deeper inner life with Jesus, I began to shift. Our monthly leadership "business" meetings became more relational. I began to care more about getting to know my leaders in a deeply personal way, than I cared about educating them from my great wisdom and knowledge. Gradually, people began to open up and share their hurts, their passions, and their fears. The entire team has grown in intimacy with Jesus and each other. Several years later I would now say we have a "Contagious" leadership style; one where no one person has to have all the right answers or be the "go to person." We do learn from each other through our stories. Through choosing to intimately follow Jesus, my leadership style changed simply because I changed.

Terry's experience highlights the leader's own spiritual growth as part of a leadership community.

Choosing a Spiritual Leadership Team

Let's think about some of the factors related to building a spiritual leadership team. I realize that no two churches have identically formed leadership teams. Senior leaders must consider the uniqueness of their own group and choose wisely. The polities of our church structures often determine how leadership should work. Some churches and ministries form around a senior leader who is held responsible for the life and welfare of the congregation and the accomplishment of its vision. In such a church, the "board" may not represent the "spiritual" leadership within the congregation.

The senior leader must form the spiritual leadership team from scratch.

Other churches function quite differently, with committees and boards for almost every function, with *Roberts' Rules of Order* defining the decision-making process, and the senior leader given little room to make change. Often such a church's committees and boards are made up by people with the secular expertise akin to the committee function—finance, education, youth ministry, etc. Large churches often use skilled multiple staffs who may or may not represent "spiritual leadership" in the congregation. Smaller churches may have only one paid leader, with volunteers filling the key ministry functions. Again, these volunteers may or may not represent the real spiritual leaders and influencers in the congregation.

In any case, the senior leader's decision to follow Jesus into his or her own spiritual formation forms the most important and essential step to fan the flames of God's love in the congregation. Then, choosing the right spiritual leadership team to accompany the leader will be the second. Many factors must be considered. For example, who's responsible for key aspects of congregational life and therefore needs to be part of any change? Who may not have any organizational titles or responsibilities, but wields influential power to support or stop change? Who can the senior leader trust? While considering these potential members, it's essential that we ask Jesus. He's demonstrated an amazing ability to pick the most unlikely characters, turn them into saints, and accomplish great things!

For example, God led me into the Lutheran clan, whose foundations have been built upon the concept of "the priesthood of all believers." Lutherans have historically been so afraid of somehow birthing another pope, they appoint committees for almost everything, leaving no one person able to overly rock the boat or lead the flock off a cliff. Even relatively small church constitutions have defined lists delineating who "must" be involved in any "change" (the word is only spoken softly).

In the church in which I first began learning to let the Lord deepen my love for Jesus, He led me to cautiously form a core group with only three of our staff members as our spiritual leadership team. Only when God got this small group on the same page, did the Lord lead us to expand the group to include our elders. A larger church I served some years later employed about fifteen full-time ministry staff who had developed a real love and trust for one another. That group provided a great group to form a spiritual leadership team. Whatever your situation, the spiritual leadership team should eventually be made up of the people who will be responsible for initiating change and encouraging people to embrace it. These men and women may or may not appear to be the most "spiritual" people in the congregation. Let Jesus show you who He wants you to invite.

Inviting Leaders into a Personal Adventure Rather Than a Church Program

Now that we've assembled the "kindling" for our campfire, let's reflect some about nurturing its fire. Some suggest that becoming part of something greater than ourselves produces motivation. More than we might like to admit, this can be code language for becoming part of someone else's vision or becoming a pawn to be used and later discarded for that something greater. Now that I am a member of a church, not its pastor, I quickly discern the difference. I grieve over the number of times I have asked others to become my pawns without realizing it. The heart of this spiritual leadership team cannot be about the leader, or the church; it has to be about the group members, including the leader, and their relationship with Jesus.

The ways we form our spiritual leadership team and develop its process may say more about program versus adventure than our words. While we always need to start with a plan or process in mind, we must remember that Jesus leads as He chooses. So, we need to leave lots of room for change. How many times have we seen a leader design a program for the congregation and then invite people into a "field test" to work the bugs out, but not to contribute in any meaningful way? There's no adventure in that.

Once, I asked a colleague in CRM, (Church Resource Ministries), for a critique of a class I had designed. He responded, "You've stolen their discovery; you told them what Jesus wanted to reveal within them personally." Through our work with leaders in *Imago Christi*, we've learned that what we teach can prove helpful; what people discover from Jesus, however, proves life-changing—an adventure with Jesus. When we over-lead or try to control the group process too tightly, however, we often get in God's way—we steal the discovery. Jesus will lead the way forward, often through the insights and suggestions of the group members.

Our goal within the spiritual leadership team should help to create a "First Order Community." By definition, we have "leaders" in the room—women and men who like to get things done, who may hurry to implement change in the congregation or ministry. While the time will come for leading change, the primary purpose now is to facilitate the spiritual growth of the members of the group. As we have discussed earlier, we not only experience Jesus directly in solitude and prayer, we also experience Him in and through His other followers. The spiritual leadership team must devote itself to following Jesus as He teaches them to seek, ask, wait, abide, and listen. Through open, honest, and vulnerable interaction, members of the group share their own discoveries and struggles and support other members in their journeys of discovery.

Some "study" can certainly facilitate this process. Depending on the spiritual maturity and biblical literacy of the group, books on prayer and other spiritual disciplines will prove really helpful. The group facilitator may also discern that the group needs more basic studies to build a theological foundation on which to enter into deeper intimacy with God. For example, if members of the group hold a legalistic, harsh, judgmental view of God, "intimacy" might feel frightening. Study and reflection about God's loving nature and His intentions for our good in the Kingdom may be a prerequisite to more "formational" topics. A study of the biblical foundations for spiritual formation found in Chapter 2 might provide material for such a study.

Whatever study or resource we choose, it's important that the fundamental purpose of the group is not to gain "information," but formation. We're together to know the Trinity more personally, not just know more "about" the Trinity. Therefore, the study and discussion process should focus primarily on how the group members respond personally to the material and how it addresses their own personal walk with the Lord. For this to happen, we must create an atmosphere of trust, safety, and confidentiality, without judgment. We must respect one another's place in this journey of discovery and provide an open place to struggle with our growth, without fear of criticism. Therefore, our initial "curriculum" in the spiritual leadership community may need to focus on group process and the ways we work together to build this supportive environment. As we've discussed before, the leader's ability to model this openness and vulnerability will prove essential for the group members to establish safe relationships. Many church members have found their church to be the last place they'd want to expose their weaknesses, doubts, and fears. Sometimes our "prayer chains" violate confidentiality and destroy trust. The first and most important mission of the spiritual leadership community will be to build and maintain this environment of trust, truth, and clear expectations. Only in such an atmosphere will people have the courage to risk and grow.

Consider forming a Spiritual Leadership Community Covenant to which each person would commit. Such a covenant might include:

I'll make our meetings first priority and show up unless there is an emergency.

I will read and reflect on the material assigned for group discussion.

I will share openly and honestly, honoring the time allotted, and listen to others without interruption, advice, or judgment.

I will keep confidential everything shared within our group meetings, even from my spouse or close spiritual friends.

I will pray for members of our group daily between meetings.

One of the significant "products" of our First Order community comes through the development of "language" to describe our spiritual experience. Probably for most of us, faith-conversations have previously focused primarily on biblical and doctrinal truths and ministry activities. For example, we have not often been asked how we experienced God in prayer, or to describe what happened within us during worship. We struggle to find words to describe our relationship with God generally and in particular situations.

A defined "Group Process" can help members focus on the interpersonal nature of their time together and not stray off into theological rabbit holes or ministry implications. Essential elements might include:

Opening Prayer: We ask for Jesus' guidance in the group time

Context Sharing: Each person briefly shares the life events since the last meeting that provide the context for their life with God. It's vital that each person be given opportunity to share personally. If the spiritual leadership group is too large, given time constraints, consider using smaller groups for sharing.

Reflections: The leader invites reflections on the reading, study and prayer assigned for this meeting.

Personal Experience: Group members share struggles and/or blessings relating to God since the last meeting.

Prayer Requests: How can we pray for your relationship with God this coming week? (We find it much easier to ask for prayers for medical or life issues, but shy away from asking for prayer for our spiritual life.)

When choosing discussion materials, I find it helpful to use some "independent" resource, rather than one developed by the leader, which gives group members the freedom to discover, agree or disagree, without fear of offending the group leader. Many spiritual formation groups as well as spiritual leadership teams have used my two previous books, *Mansions of the Heart* and its *Study Guide,* and *Presence* and its study guide, *Discovering Christ's Presence.* Both resources provide sections for personal reflection outside the group and questions for discussion together. The novel, *Presence,* might be a safer place to begin with a group not overly familiar with spiritual formation. A group, which wants to spark a longing for deeper intimacy with Jesus, might start with *Presence* and then move to *Mansions,* which describes the process for living into that longing.

Tammy Long, describes her success in using *Mansions.*

If the leader is open to going beyond a program mindset, and grasps that such a movement starts with him or her, then I feel the place to start is with an understanding of the spiritual growth path. Mansions of the Heart has had a tremendous impact on our church vision and focus for spiritual growth. Mansions casts the vision that there is "more" in our relationship with God and speaks to the hunger that many leaders feel, but don't know what's missing. It fans their hunger with spiritual practices that create space for experiencing God's incredible love. We found that it served to launch our journey with language, a roadmap, and next steps to go deeper. I think that the momentum can generate on its own.

I also agree with the comments about grasping the love of God; that we say it, but don't know it in our gut, and deep down have trouble believing it. As I note below for my own story, I agree that it is experiencing that love that compels us to draw near.

Because leaders themselves are in different places on the journey, I think the first place to start is to help them understand there is a journey and to fan a hunger for more of a love relationship with God with the pragmatics of what that means and what the journey looks like.

Why Leaders Say "Yes" To Spiritual Formation but Don't Really Mean It

Let's assume that we've chosen a spiritual leadership team. Let's further assume that the facilitator (hopefully the senior leader) has personally visited with each one, shared his own journey and sense of calling. Let's also assume that the leader has wisely shared that he cannot follow God's leading alone and needs this trusted companion to journey and learn with him. Let's assume that the potential team member has accepted the invitation. The campfire has been laid, the fire has been added through prayer, study, and discussion. Some of the logs, however, just don't seem to ignite. What's wrong?

Many times, we'll discover that we have wet kindling—some of our "yes" responders really meant "no." Why would anyone do that, we ask? I'm sure you're thinking of all kinds of reasons, recalling all the times that people—maybe even you, have nodded their heads in a "yes" response, when time proved that's not at all what they wanted to do.

It can be hard to say "no" for many reasons. In some leadership cultures, staff members simply do not say "no" to their boss. Some people find it almost impossible to say no to someone they love or respect. Who dares to say "no" to spiritual growth or discipleship? It would sound like rejecting Jesus Himself! It's the same with missions, outreach, and evangelism; people either says "yes" or remain silent. Most of them find themselves terrified of the words and of the potential expectations and opportunities for failure they represent. For our spiritual leadership group, we can say for sure that none of them, including the leader, knows what they are getting into. Therefore, expectations need to be made as clear as possible, even though the Covenant may not have been formed. As much as we may want a particular person on our team, it's important to ask them to pray about it and then give them an easy out.

There's just no way around it; no amount of vetting will assure the success of your spiritual leadership team. But then, when have you ever been assured of success? There may be some ways to respect the frailty of your team members and give them an opportunity to opt out. For example, one might form the team on a trial basis for a limited time with the knowledge that at some not too distant date one could opt to stay in or step out. The team formation could, and probably should, be cast as an experiment, with no fixed expectations or outcomes implied. If, however, members of the group authentically experience Jesus in the midst of a community of honesty, trust, and safety, nothing could keep them away. Damp logs can dry and ignite, given time and loving attention. While we have to admit that not every member of the team will be able to remain committed and might need to excuse themselves, the nature of the departure will dramatically affect the team and its perception by the congregation. The same ground rules for life in the community must govern the process of leaving. A person who leaves the community, feeling loved, respected, and accepted where they are on the journey—without judgment may well carry the spiritual growth torch into the congregation in unexpected and helpful ways.

Forming the Team That Can Burn

Let's review some of the principles that help the spiritual leadership team to function in a contagious way. Drawing again from our fire-building knowledge, we remember that logs have to be placed with the right distance and configuration that will allow the heat of one log to lie close enough to ignite and support the fire of others, but with enough distance to allow for airflow to provide the necessary oxygen. In our spiritual leadership team, we similarly need the right level of intimacy among members and the freedom to encounter the Holy Spirit uniquely. Contagious leadership approaches, modeled by Jesus, can help create this balance.

Lead from Weakness

One of the challenges we face when we invite people to pursue spiritual growth or formation can be an implication that others are spiritually inferior. No one responds well to that message. We all know we have room to mature, but we'd hate it if someone, particularly a leader, came up to us and told us so. If we go to a gym and seek out a fitness trainer and that person gives us some pointers, we'd consider it helpful. If that same trainer walked up to us when we entered the gym and pointed out our flabby abdomen or weak biceps, we'd feel insulted. On the other hand, if that trainer spotted us and said something like, "You'd make a great athlete," or "I would love for you to join our rowing team," we'd be honored, whether or not we accepted the invitation.

How we lead our spiritual formation leadership team can either shut members down or free them for discovery. We can give them the freedom to recognize their own growing edges and then take them to the Lord, or we can make people feel ashamed and want to hide. Saying something like, "Oh don't worry, I used to have problems like that" won't cut it. A leader's current, real-time struggle, shared in openness and vulnerability becomes the greatest way to encourage and free others to trust Jesus and grow. Admittedly, we need to be wise about appropriate levels of vulnerability and discern when our story may prove helpful to another. We also need to honor the ability of others to share and give them time to trust the group. Many, if not all, members of the group may have experienced unsafe church environments where judgment made pretending the norm. It takes time to unlearn and relearn. Our loving patience and personal and humble vulnerability can become a new doorway for others to learn to honestly explore and discover God's love.

Charlie Dodrill comments about the challenge that vulnerability may pose for many leaders.

> *Sharing where we are on our spiritual journey with peers and other leaders within the church and in other ministry contexts, requires a substantial amount of vulnerability. We have to be willing to step out of the "leadership" role, and view ourselves and those with whom we are meeting as other brothers and sisters in the Body of Christ. There is no hierarchy when we talk about spiritual journeys. All of us are equal under the eyes and the presence of a loving Lord. Being willing to admit our faults, our addictions, temptations, as*

well as the joys and the successes is really, really hard for almost all of us, but especially when we are sharing these things with people who have the power to both hire and fire us. Many of us are used to working under a job title that assumes we are spending regular time with the Lord, but sometimes, this is just not the case and we fear being exposed. However, authenticity, vulnerability, the willingness to talk about temptation and weakness in a leader's life are the very hallmarks of what millennials are searching for in the Church today. They long for leaders who are honest and know how to walk their talk. So in many ways, all of this is crucial for the continuing health and life of most churches as they look to the future.

Speaking from my experience as a Lead Pastor for many years, I can agree with Charlie that sharing openly with my staff proved challenging. As much as I wanted to be accepted as "just a brother in Christ" who needs honesty and affirmation, I have sometimes seen others become hesitant to share openly. Maybe they're thinking, "How can the leader of our church and team be struggling with this issue? What if he crashes and burns? We'll all go down in flames." I also sense their reluctance to share honestly. "I do want a deeper relationship with Jesus, but what if it doesn't happen? What if our leadership team and the Lead Pastor interpret my struggle as professional incompetence?" It's true that the fire of God's love reveals the branches that need to be pruned. The fire can feel hot and uncomfortable. We all have to continually ask ourselves the extent to which we really want to live and grow in God's refining fire; whether it's important enough to us to risk. Inside each of us dwells an insecure little girl or boy who shudders with fears of rejection. If the senior leader of the spiritual leadership community (whether lead pastor or another staff member responsible for the group) hides, the rest of the group needs to lovingly invite them to come out and play.

The kind of community lived out by the leadership team will be reproduced in the congregation, no matter what we say or teach. If we lead from strength, the congregation will hide their weaknesses and resist the journey of spiritual growth. If we lead from openness and vulnerability, the congregation will recognize that life with God always invites us on a journey of discovery and that our fellow travelers will support us in the process.

Ted Wueste shares his insights about the way God uses our spiritual leadership communities.

> *If shepherding people into deepening intimacy with the Trinity is the goal, then there has to be trust and vulnerability so that people can let down their guards with God. This is "practiced" in our human relationships to engender openness to God, and vice versa. It is not easy with a staff team. Often, staff members will tell you whatever you want to hear in order to stay in good standing. Or, they might resist, having never experienced something like it before. It is important to create an environment where life with God is paramount. As strange as that sounds, many church leadership cultures focus on results and efficiency, etc.—not God. I've experienced staff members saying, "I appreciate you asking me about my life but I need help in practical ministry." Understanding how to cultivate an environment for community and how to navigate the landmines seems vital. At the end of the day, the slow, hard work of this task must have modeling at the base — for a senior leader to simply talk about spiritual intimacy and not live it, won't get things very far. It seems to me that it can be difficult to have a leadership team (elder and/or staff) on the same page initially – it can take a lot of time unless it is a really small team. A leader needs to be extremely patient. I think of Jesus with his disciples – He poured into them daily for three years and many of them were still "knuckleheads" right up to the crucifixion. Building a leadership team must not be idealized but pursued patiently, knowing that much of the work is dealing with resistances to the deeper work of the Spirit in our lives (e.g., "get behind me Satan").*

Learn From One Another

Scripture reveals Jesus as a great teacher. He spent significant time with His disciples, revealing His own heart and the truths of His mission. The biblical accounts also show us that many of the lessons the disciples learned were learned from one another. The Holy Spirit taught each of the disciples in their daily experiences. Jesus sent them out in two's not only to proclaim the Kingdom, but to create opportunities for the Spirit to teach them. Jesus provided the space as well as the intimacy. For example, Peter learned about Jesus through Andrew's zeal and excitement. The disciples discovered the truth about greatness as they watched James and John struggle with projecting earthly power into heavenly realms. They learned about human frailty as they watched one another flee and hide at Jesus' crucifixion. They learned about courage from Stephen.

Jesus leads and teaches us in the context of a spiritual community as we observe one another. Each of the disciples responded to Jesus differently. Some cried out in fear while Peter stepped out of the boat and walked on water. Peter denied Jesus openly while John stood with His mother at the foot of the cross. In the same way, each member of our group will respond to Jesus in different ways, unique to one's own personality, experience with God, place in the journey, and so forth. Therefore, it's important not to judge one another, but to gain greater insight into our own lives as we recognize our own potential for the same reaction, be it courage or fear.

Don't Give Advice

God provides many ways to touch our lives with His loving fire. Consequently, we need to be wary of normalizing behaviors and experiences that a few have found helpful. For example, those who find a rule of life meaningful can be tempted to recommend it for everyone. Someone who met Jesus profoundly in a silent retreat may think that silent retreats are a must for everyone. We need to invite our people to share their spiritual experiences in ways that are descriptive rather than prescriptive. As group members, including the leader, learn to trust the safety of the group, they'll begin to share their real-time experiences about their growth and struggle. When each person listens with hearts tuned to Jesus' guidance, He shepherds us into the spiritual practices that He knows will provide discovery.

Focus on Experience Rather than Information

Many ministry teams and spiritual leaders, however, find it very difficult to share openly and vulnerably about their own spiritual experience. We theologians, teachers, and preachers can become so enamored with ideas and concepts that we fail to recognize when we've become focused on ourselves rather than others. Sometimes we inadvertently hide behind our theological or biblical expertise to avoid our more "subjective" experiences. Ideas can fill our time rather than the practical matters of living with God that enable us to discover more about Him and ourselves. Many of us confuse thinking creatively about God with experiencing Him. We can get so elated with some profound insight that we forget about God altogether.

The Desert Fathers teach that the devil uses a very subtle tactic to distract us. To divert us from true prayer and communion with God, a demon reveals some biblical or theological truth that we may not have thought of before. Elated with this new insight, it then tempts to focus on the concept rather than on God. Excited about this new revelation, we don't realize that we have turned from God Himself to cherish this prized possession instead. Then, if possible, the demon tempts us to become prideful in our discovery, convinced that we have become much more spiritual than most.

Let People Struggle How to Describe Their Experiences

People can also find it hard to talk about spiritual experience, because they have never learned language to describe it. For example, Brother Boniface, my mentor-monk, told me once that his vocation of prayer depended on his ability to "intuit God's heart." I had occasionally felt or sensed God's desire in some matter, but struggled to describe it to others. Did God "speak" to me? No, not exactly. Did I experience some "vision" or "emotion?" No. Without the language to share my experience, I would often simply keep it to myself. Boniface taught me new language—intuit God's heart, that expressed my subjective and mysterious encounter with my Lord. Later I discovered additional language through historical writers who focused primarily on experience of God rather than our more modern authors who often focus more on productivity than relationship. When we recognize our tendencies to focus on ideas or struggle with our inability to put words to our experiences, we can watch for it, admit it to one another, and call ourselves back to discovery—back to Jesus.

Learning to Follow Jesus Together

Eventually, the spiritual leadership team must decide how and when to lead the congregation forward. While the following chapters will discuss some common elements such as teaching, worship, experiences, etc., each congregation and leadership team must seek the Lord's guidance uniquely. We can learn from other ministries and churches; however, we must resist the temptation to resort to some plug-and-play program. Jesus wants to lead every ministry personally, specifically, uniquely suited to who they are, their cultural context, and their needs. When your spiritual leadership group becomes ready, "Where do we go from here?" will have to become the subject of their discernment. While I encouraged you that one didn't have to reach the Seventh Mansion before they could coach and lead others, I implore you not to move from the First Order nature of the group to the Second Order planning too soon. No, we can't wait until everyone in the group has accomplished everything they need to do—that takes a lifetime. We must, however, have gone further than look at the map, guess at what the journey might feel like, and sample a few spiritual disciplines. Once God has accomplished in us, the spiritual leadership team, what we want Him to accomplish in the congregation, we're ready to begin asking questions about how and when and with whom we take spiritual formation and missional momentum into the congregation. Jesus sent the disciples out two by two only when they were ready, and we must not only follow His example, we must do what we see Him doing.

In the following chapters, we'll discuss developing vision, mission, and strategy and suggest some basic categories for planning such as teaching, worship, etc. We're looking at a long-term investment; it won't be ready to roll out next fall. We're talking about the lifetime movement of the Holy Spirit in us as leaders, in our congregation for decades to come, and in our community and world until the Lord returns. We're fanning the embers that God will turn into flames of love that will spread a contagious fire across the earth. Jesus has chosen each one of us to play a vital role—today. Ask Him where He wants to lead you—today, so that contagious fire can enflame your church tomorrow.

In Chapter 5, we'll talk about Vision. Rather than jumping to form some spell-binding vision for the congregation, we'll discuss the fiery vision for intimacy with God that's been growing in your own heart and the hearts of the spiritual leadership community. Expanding that vision, we'll discuss how it extends beyond ourselves into the lives of others and the world. Get ready to consider turning the whole church "visioning process" 180 degrees around—from leader-down to people-up!

CHAPTER 5

SPARKING THE CHURCH - A VISION FOR CONTAGIOUS CHRISTIANS

If you're reading Contagious Fire for general interest and overview, let's continue our discussion of a vision of a church or ministry whose members so reflect a love relationship with God that their love for God and others radiates in a contagious way. These followers of Jesus, simply by being themselves, will attract others to get to know them better and discover the fire they've been longing for. The Holy Spirit uses this contagious fire to ignite a deep desire for "more"—more life, more hope, more joy, more freedom, more love.

If, on the other hand, you are using Contagious Fire as a guide for bringing that vision into reality within a church or ministry, we need to clarify some prerequisites for continuing with Chapter 5. So, here's a **STOP** sign. It reads:

Danger! Obstacles Ahead -

Before Proceeding, Be Prepared!

Do you understand the Spiritual Formation Journey?

Are you well along on this journey yourself?

Are you traveling with leadership companions?

If you can honestly answer "yes" to these questions, then may the gates to Chapter 5 open wide to you and bid you safe journey. If you're taking shortcuts, however, concerned that there isn't enough time or that it just couldn't be that hard, I urge you to STOP. I suggest that you return to the previous chapters and ask the Lord to help you dig in for real. Bring your real spiritual growth and preparation into reality in your own experience and in the life of your spiritual leadership community. It's worth your investment in your own relationship with God and in the future of your church. Our enemy loves shortcuts; don't let him wreck what you know God wants for you and your ministry.

JD Ward, leads a Church Resource Ministries team called ReWire. He works with churches to build missional communities which experience personal spiritual formation in the midst of ministering to the poor. JD comments about our readiness to move from our focus on our personal transformation to congregational transformation.

> *I think we might want to give our leaders a way to assess where they are on the journey and if they should lead out or wait. Examples might include: talking to a spiritual director, completing some formal formation program, and becoming conversant with different practices and traditions in formation. And still we admit there is no real measure. God's work can happen outside these things. But we all need some way to self-evaluate. I think one of the most powerful tests of progress is a leader's ability to embrace their shadow side and see transformation there.*

Bill O'Byrne has coached many church and missionary leaders through their own discovery of God's transforming love. He suggests another way a leader can discern readiness to move forward.

> *Probably the most common "mistake" happens when a leader experiences something significant in their own spiritual life. Immediately, the leader wants to build the church's new mission/ vision strategy around "spiritual formation." They need to let their*

personal experience sufficiently "marinate," so that it bears consistent, lasting fruit in their life, and isn't just the "latest kick" that they are on. ...One of the most consistent signals that I have seen that a leader is ready to bring others along is that the leader's spouse has given unsolicited feedback that the leader is a new person now. "Most significant spiritual growth is discerned by the believer as backsliding." — Thomas Dubay. We're not necessarily very good at seeing our own readiness.

Agreeably, none of us can ever be "completely ready" in the sense of having arrived. By definition, our spiritual growth happens over a lifetime journey. The question we have to assess, personally and with the feedback of others, asks, "Am I living and growing in the dimensions of deeper relationship with God that I want for others to experience? Do I see new fire in my belly for Jesus and new love for others? Can my people see the reality of what I want to talk to them about—in me? While not claiming to be an expert, if you can respond affirmatively and God has given you and your leadership community a peace about moving forward at the congregational level, then let's proceed.

So, let's talk about vision. Vision represents a picture of the preferred future. One's vision could be one of disaster, doom, and gloom. Hopefully, your vision is a wonderful new reality that attracts us, energizes us, and motivates us to action. God had a fantastic vision when He created the universe, the Earth, and the human race. He envisioned an eternal partnership with beautiful beings who have a soul, a spirit, and a free will—beings who would live with Him in His life-giving love, respond in love, and experience the joy of sharing in His creative activity and care for the Earth. After the fall seemed to shatter God's vision, we see His new vision of a redeemed humanity and a new heaven and earth where we would realize His heart's desire for us. When Jesus looked into the future, He envisioned people who would receive Him as King. In this new kingdom, we would accept Jesus' invitation for a renewed relationship in love, forgiveness, eternal life, and partnership. As daughters and sons of our King, we would be so united with

His life and love that the reign of His love would flow through us into this world. God delighted in His promise to give us power through the Holy Spirit, and eternal destiny in His loving presence. As the Apostle Paul came to know the heart of God, he recognized that His vision spread beyond the Israelites to all the people of the world.

Steve Macchia, has worked with hundreds of church leaders attempting to cast vision and comments on the nature of our vision.

> *Many leaders don't know the difference between vision (preferred future) and mission (what we're doing today to help us get there). Having spiritual formation at the center of both vision and mission requires that leadership "gets it" in the core of their being and then invites others into that hope-filled future together.*

In the following Chapter we'll begin to discuss mission—"the how to get there" phase. For now, however, we need to stick to the picture of the future that God has given us, our vision. Then we'll discuss calling forth visions in our people and finally, the collective vision of the Body.

Discovering Our Own Vision

To illustrate vision development, I'll share about my own vision journey. Following my conversion, my emerging "vision" focused mostly on the solution to my own problems and my ability to live happily ever after. The fire of God's love for me slowly ignited my own fire of love for myself, giving me the confidence to let Jesus shepherd me through daily life. As my relationship with Jesus matured, His love brightened the flames of love to the point that I could see beyond my own needs to those of others. His light increasingly revealed His love for those around me, and I began to see His desire to use me to become a loving presence for them. At that point, I could say that my vision for my preferred future focused primarily on what we have called Second Order Calling—to serve Him more faithfully by loving and helping others.

Several years later, my vision, for my relationship with God and for my ministry, took a radical turn as Jesus began to woo me into the Fourth Mansion of spiritual growth, where He revealed more of Himself to the point that He captured my heart in love. The Lord brought me into contact with Brother Boniface, a Cistercian monk at Holy Trinity Abbey, whose love for God and for me blazed with a fire that I hadn't encountered before. Boniface had given his whole life to serve God in prayer and worship. His intimacy with God radiated with the very beauty of Jesus so contagiously that I longed to be like him. He lived a contagious abiding peace that I yearned for myself. He also related to me with a loving and profound wisdom that continually opened my eyes to new dimensions of my Lord and of myself. Not only did I appreciate his love and ministry to me, but I wanted to live out the fire of God's love that I saw in him.

I knew that I was not called to become a monk, for which my wife and kids were deeply grateful! My vision had to be formed to my own calling and context—a Lutheran pastor. I realized that the contagious fire I saw in Boniface came from his deep abiding relationship with Jesus—birthed in contemplative prayer. Whenever I talked with Bon, I felt as though I was drawn into his prayer closet and given access to Jesus' presence in a profound way. I began to pray for and envision those qualities of intimacy and loving wisdom to shine forth in my own life and ministry. As this new vision of myself took root in my heart, I gained new strength to carve out more time for prayer and to let God draw me into deeper dimensions of listening and abiding prayer. In this process, I realized that my vision had to be grounded in my First Order Calling. Boniface's ability to be God's person for me stemmed from his abiding relationship with Jesus. Slowly, my First Order vision began to take shape: a man profoundly connected to Jesus and filled with His love. From that image, the Second Order dimension of my vision could come into focus. I longed to become a better listener—to Jesus and to others. I pictured sermons and teaching that reflected what Jesus had said to me and told me to share. I longed to husband Charlotte and father my children the way God husbands and fathers me. Instead of dreading the beggars that so often stole my precious time, I dreamed that Jesus would draw needy folk to my door so that I might let them meet Him. While I had been satisfied with our church's calling to reach out to our Mormon community, I now wondered what it might look like to reach out beyond our city and country with the love of Jesus. My heart burned with this amazing invitation from Jesus! Slowly I not only saw the vision—I came to believe it would become a reality!

At some point, my dear reader, your vision expanded beyond your own happiness to embrace God's vision. You began to envision what your life might be like if you really walked with Jesus at a heart level, communed with the Father as Jesus does, and lived fully in the freedom and joy of abundant life, given by the Holy Spirit—the First Order dimension. Now, your vision has expanded into the Second Order—to include your ministry or church, and the world. It's that vision, no matter how hazy it may feel, that has you reading this book, daring to learn and grow and risk everything. Your vision has been ignited from the flames of God's love and has created a fire within you that gives you no rest until you become its torch for others.

> If I say, "I will not remember Him
>
> Or speak anymore in His name,"
>
> Then in my heart it becomes like a burning fire
>
> Shut up in my bones;
>
> And I am weary of holding it in,
>
> And I cannot endure it. Jeremiah 20:9

Let's talk, therefore, about what we do with this implanted vision and what it means to carry the torch of God's contagious fire in a way that spawns vision in others, particularly your spiritual leadership community. Although we discussed spiritual leadership community in Chapter 4, your contagious fire vision has probably been forming before that community was formed and taking further shape through its community life. If we're to become torchbearers, we need to recognize the terrain through which we have to journey and the obstacles and barriers that can divert us from our path or hide the firelight we carry.

"Vision" is not a new word to us. Unfortunately, it often rings a dull thud in our hearts rather than an exciting clarion call. Most of our churches have crafted vision statements that somehow embrace the Great Commission and ministry to the poor, disadvantaged, etc. A few vision statements include the Great Commandment—as well, although often omitting the word, "love." We leaders embrace these bold visions, however, with the full knowledge that many, if not most, of our congregational members don't—they simply don't care.

Why the lethargic response? It's simple—the vision statement represents an institutional preferred future rather than a personal one. Even though we put slogans in our advertising, hang banners as visual reminders, and preach challenging sermons to somehow imprint our missional vision, it seldom receives much more than polite nods or lip service. There may have been a real fire behind the vision statement—at least in the leader, but its heat has been diverted and its light deflected. Our members hold visions that focus much more personally—inside ourselves, for ourselves. Seldom, however, do our personal visions include God's contagious fire for the Kingdom of God.

A pastor of twenty-six years and six churches, I've spent countless hours with vision committees (Lutherans have lots of committees!), crafting vision statements that we hoped would lift our congregants' focus beyond their own struggles, raise their sights to God and to the hurting world around us. We endlessly wordsmithed catchy phrases and long whitepapers that we hoped might focus and inspire our people. I can't remember how many dozens of books I've read that insisted that without "Tom's" vision, the people would perish.

It felt good to have a vision statement and all its trappings. When people asked me what the church was about, I could point proudly to the banner on the wall. Inwardly, however, I wondered why that person didn't seem impressed. I have to admit that I've seldom, maybe never, seen MY vision inspire anyone—at least not for long and not for very far. Why? My vision inspires and motivates me because I believe it's God's vision for me. Why has it been so hard to realize that only God's vision for others motivates them? I've taken my vision and projected it upon the church and then wondered why it didn't result in lasting change. I had been inadvertently projecting MY fire rather than God's.

Even when we attempt to cast God's bright vision and invite people to interpret it for themselves, we may find our audience donning dark sunglasses. Members can hear their leaders' call to new horizons with a kind of deadweight lethargy. They're busy, overcommitted, and tired. While everyone wants to attend a successful church, new horizons usually come with new work. Most of us feel that our personal Christian walk is "good enough." We're forgiven, saved, somewhat biblically literate, give some money to the church, attend when we can, and maybe help out a bit—good enough. Sure, we know other people who need to get off their duffs, so we'll sing the theme song with gusto, hoping that others will get it. Now and again, as the song or sermon drones on, the pastor or elder wonders, "What would it really take to motivate every member to care enough about others to live missional lives in the church and in their life contexts?" That's exactly the question we're pursuing in *Contagious Fire*. But to cast motivational vision, we need to learn to "vision" differently. A person's fire must be ignited from within.

Fear of Survival Blocks Vision

To do vision differently, we need to first consider our context—our churches, primarily in America—in the time in which we live. I'm writing in the year 2017, but you may need to update the picture to fit the context in which you're reading. We need to look at the culture, the church, and the folks who call themselves Christians. People's vision often starts within their present situation and extends only as far as the next hill. To help people vision in a Kingdom perspective, therefore, we need to take seriously our church's present circumstance. What's the condition of the kindling we want to catch fire?

There isn't room here to detail all the prevailing church statistics; besides, your church is unique. Having said that, we can see issues facing most of our churches that can make visioning difficult. Our increasingly mobile and global society, connected to instant information and opinion, diminishes the degrees of "uniqueness" in any segment of society, particularly our churches. While we may have our denominational or non-denominational distinctives, church size differences, and geographic peculiarities, church leaders readily admit that most of their congregants no longer fit the "mold" that their institutions were designed to serve. Institutional allegiances have weakened in every sector of our society. Now churches often take the brand/denomination out of their name because they find that their membership comes from a wide variety of backgrounds. Unlike past decades, people pick a church they like rather than one associated with their background. Increasingly, people choose not to go to church at all. One doesn't have to look far to get a feel for the trends. My first click on an internet search for church trends found the following titles:

> 7 Startling Facts: An Up-Close Look at Church Attendance in America
>
> The Number One Reason for the Decline in Church Attendance
>
> ...
>
> Why Nobody Wants to go to Church Anymore
>
> Study Finds Megachurches Seeing Drop in Weekly Attendance
>
> A New Documentary Looks at Declining Church Attendance

A denominational leader in the Pacific Northwest recently emailed his pastors asking for prayer for the twenty or so churches in his state that could no longer afford a full-time pastor and the additional twenty that were only a one-member-death away from being unable to afford a part-time pastor. He admitted that there were some strong congregations (he didn't say growing) in his district, but it was clear that the overall attendance trend leaned dangerously downward. I have heard, as I am sure you have, many similar accounts. While we can certainly find growing churches around the country, we also find that much of that growth comes from the dying churches that can't provide the "one-stop-shopping" for all ages and interests possible for larger churches. For many churches today, vision focuses no further than survival.

Another cultural context that influences our ability to cast vision in the church comes from the crisis of many of our church leaders. Dr. Stacy Rinehart, founder of MentorLink International, provides leadership coaching for missionaries around the world. He shared some concerning statistics. His data suggests that about 30% of full-time missionaries leave ministry after five years and that 50% leave after 10 years. He also referenced a website that reports statistics about church staff. The statistics were dated in 2009, but probably don't look much different today. Let me list just a few.[1]

Of pastors interviewed,

> 90% report working between 55 to 75 hours per week.

> 90% feel they are inadequately trained to cope with the ministry demands.
> 50% feel unable to meet the demands of the job.
> 70% say they have a lower self-image now than when they first started.
> 70% do not have someone they consider a close friend.

> 50% have considered leaving the ministry in the last months.
> 50% of the ministers starting out will not last 5 years.

1. http://freebelievers.com/article/why-pastors-leave-the-ministry. Statistics dated 2009

Only 1 out of every 10 ministers will actually retire as a minister in some form.

Over 1,700 pastors left the ministry every month in the previous year.

Over 1,300 pastors were terminated by the local church each month, many without cause.

We could delve into speculations about reasons for church decline and pastoral crisis, but the issue that I'd like to address here relates to many of our churches and their visional mindset—mistrust of their leaders and fear for church survival.

Abraham Maslow, a renowned psychologist, in his publication "A Theory of Human Motivation," identified what he called a "hierarchy of needs" that determines what motivates us.[2] His now widely accepted view holds that we can only be motivated at a given level when needs at the more fundamental levels have been adequately met. The hierarchy lists the needs from the most basic need at the bottom of the pyramid.

Self-transcendence

Self-actualization

Belonging and Love

Esteem

Safety

Physiological Health

Safety and survival certainly rank in the lower half of this need hierarchy.

---

2. Abraham *Maslow (Motivation and Personality. New York, NY: Harper. 1954)*

Interestingly, the Gospel offers to meet each need level through the Lordship of Jesus. However, when our faith consists more of knowing about God rather than knowing Him, and about religion rather than relationship, many churchgoers find themselves in church survival mode. When Jesus talks about abundant life, He invites us to live in the highest category of human fulfillment—living beyond a "self" focus, living in love with God and with our neighbor as an integral part of the coming Kingdom of God. Survival mode blinds our vision of God's best. It doesn't attract us; it's never contagious. When we talk vision, we have to begin where people live.

People find it difficult to see visions and dream their dreams of becoming alive with God's love and sharing that love when they fear for their own survival as a church. We're called to lift their heads to see their destinies in the light of the Kingdom of God where they're not only safe, but dwell in the victory of the King of Kings. God called Elisha to that same task when the Israelites, surrounded by the Armenians, were sure they would not live to see the morning. God had to open their eyes.

> Now when the attendant of the man of God had risen early and gone out, behold, an army with horses and chariots was circling the city. And his servant said to him, "Alas, my master! What shall we do?" So, he answered, "Do not fear, for those who are with us are more than those who are with them." Then Elisha prayed and said, "O Lord, I pray, open his eyes that he may see." And the Lord opened the servant's eyes and he saw; and behold, the mountain was full of horses and chariots of fire all around Elisha. 2 Kings 6:15-17

When the fire of God's love within church leadership grows so bright that the people see and experience true Love in their midst, they will dare to believe that God can ignite that same fire within them. In the light of God's glory and "perfect love," fear gives way to faith and hope—and eventually to vision—personal vision for their own preferred future, in Christ.

Structures and Traditions That Block Vision

We're called to invite our membership to discern God's vision for their growing relationship with Him. However, the church "buildings" they live in often block their view. Sometimes the polity, structures, traditions, and leadership style within our ministries can inadvertently establish opposing visions or distort people's ability to "lift their eyes unto the hills." (cf. Psalm 121) Let me mention a few that I've encountered. The following categories certainly overlap, but can provide some places to watch for personal vision "flame retardant." You'll recognize the ones that exist in your own context and spot others that I haven't mentioned.

Preset Institutional Visions

As we've discussed above, many, if not most, churches have identified institutional vision statements intended to guide the personal visions of its members. The institutional vision, however, may not connect with its members. These "visions" usually contain three or four key words, often ones that sound alike or start with the same first letter. Examples might be "Know, Grow, Go." Or, how about "Seek, Surrender, Serve"? The list can be almost endless.

While some of these vision acronyms may seem trite, others may reflect the unique calling of the congregation and help focus the trajectory of the congregation. For example, Centennial Covenant, where Steve Thulson serves as lead pastor, developed an excellent vision statement that combines spiritual formation and missional outreach.

Our Vision: We are a growing congregation

of friendly people seeking to be Christ-centered and people-caring.

Our Mission: To glorify God by following Jesus
on a shared journey of transformation
in His mission to our broken world.

I love that vision of mission and identity. We must ask, however, whose vision is it? Without judging Centennial Covenant, we often lift up the vision of church leaders for the institution or tell our people how their personal vision should read. Our people become motivated by their vision for their own lives, not for the institution. God's fire within each person's heart projects the vibrant picture that draws them into God's future for them. How might we invite our members to envision their personal life in ways that include Christ-centered, friendly, and caring lives, following Jesus in a shared journey of transformation, and a mission to our broken world? That might sound simple, but the code language, well understood by the leadership, might confuse people or miss them altogether. What does it really mean to live a Christ-centered life? How does one follow Jesus? What is a shared journey of transformation? How does one deal with a broken world—isn't that more the concern of the UN? Caring and friendly, we get. I happen to know that Centennial Covenant has gone to great lengths to unpack those words, but you get the idea how an institutional vision statement can radiate from banners and websites without really motivating people to seek God for their own vision. God motivates vision through the fire of His love, witnessed in the contagious blaze in others, and experienced within one's own heart.

Different churches highlight various Scriptural injunctions or congregational objectives that can limit our ability to vision. Examples might include evangelism, teaching, signs and wonders, healing, community service, foreign missions, church growth, justice advocacy, warm and friendly community life, etc. These church emphases each imply a vision for the future, not only for the church, but for the church member. For many, the seeming call to conformity can form a roadblock for members' discovery of God's vision for them personally. Members might believe that their personal relationship with God should include one or more of the core objectives of the church. Why should they even explore a personal vision when the church has already given them one? If the banner in front of the church reads, "Go Make Disciples," yet my inner urging focuses on ministry to the poor, I may feel out of step. For many, the church vision can create guilt rather than excitement for their future with Jesus. What they may hear is, "This is where you're supposed to be, so get to work!"

Core Values in the Church

Every person and group form core values that, to some degree, define them. Core values represent our basic beliefs about ourselves and the world around us. They're formed in our own personal development and imported into the group by its leaders, either formally or informally. For example, *Imago Christi* highly values the importance of a love relationship with God and with one another for its members. While we also value our ministry objectives, we constantly call ourselves back to this core value as the foundation from which our ministry emerges. Imagine the struggle one of our community members would have if called by God to become a hermit.

Institutional vision statements often represent many of those core values. Every group, however, has additional core values that may be less obvious. Examples might include conformity or self-expression, freedom or control, openness and vulnerability or presenting a good witness, tradition or creativity, security or risk, obedience or self-determination, community or individuality, survival or growth, and so on. Most people settle and stay in a church because they share most of the core values of the larger group. Sometimes, group core values can make it difficult for individuals to listen openly to God for His vision for their lives. We can inadvertently project these core values as conditions for our relationship with the community and with God. We may think we are inviting our members to listen to God and envision His preferred future for them without realizing that our core values have become so powerful that they block our people's ability to even try to hear God.

I served as an associate pastor in a large suburban church which prided itself on its new evangelism program. All the staff were expected to take the Kennedy Evangelism Training which focused on cold-call, door-to-door encounters. We were to memorize and share our elevator speech testimony and push for a decision for Christ. Ultimately, the program failed and the word "evangelism" became negative for most of the congregation. Leadership had failed to recognize a core value within its upper-class membership. One member put it bluntly. "We don't invade people's privacy unannounced; we don't discuss personal issues until meaningful relationships have been formed; we form relationships slowly and cautiously. 'Evangelism' isn't even polite." Perhaps, a different style of evangelism that embraced the congregation's core values might have worked.

Church Decision-making Structures

I've already poked fun at the Lutherans, my church family during my pastoring years, for its reliance on committees and boards to guide and direct the church. In contrast, I recently met with a pastor in a different church tradition that commented, "As pastor, I make the rules and guide the life of the church. If people don't like it, they can find another church." Many churches place importance on membership and rely on approval by the majority for decisions. Others view their constituency simply as people who "fellowship" with that church, looking only to senior leadership to make decisions. Many churches form combinations and variations of these styles. We need to understand the incredible influence organizational leadership structure exerts on our members and their sense of personal responsibility, particularly when we think about individual vision. Why should I consider listening to God personally if I expect to be told what to do by another person or to conform to the majority? While we can't easily change our church structures, we can recognize how they affect our people. We can then explore how we might free them to listen personally to God's heart and trust Him to give them dreams and visions. In both cases, the open, honest, and vulnerable sharing of the leader's personal discovery—as personal discovery rather than prophetic proclamation—can set others free to seek God in their own way and discover the fire the Holy Spirit has ignited within them.

Institutional Identity

We've discussed the various aspects that affect the ability to discern personal vision related to the differences in the institutional structures and values of various churches. We want to focus here on the extent to which members of the church identify with and even define themselves with the institution. How many times have we heard or said statements like, "I'm a Baptist or Methodist, or...?" These identity labels can form core values and corresponding practices so strongly entrenched that we find it difficult to envision beyond them. For example, a person may have had a long history in churches that emphasize the vital importance of biblical literacy, but finds it uncomfortable to talk about personal relationship with God. Another person, raised in a church that focuses only on feel-good theology but with poor biblical teaching, may envision a grand relationship with God that simply doesn't square with the Kingdom promises of Scripture. In some groups, members may only hear about a personal relationship with God in Jesus Christ as an invitation to conversion, and seldom even think about it after they become members. Other churches may emphasize the importance of moral purity to the extent that its members would find it hard to imagine a close relationship with God at all, because they don't feel worthy. When we consider spiritual growth as a lifelong deepening intimacy with the Trinity, we must recognize the individual context in which that message is being sent. People may never have been invited to freely imagine their own relationship with God and may find the thought frightening or disturbing. We have to start with people in their present place on the journey and then literally "SEE" their unfolding life of love with God. Chapter 7 addresses ways that teaching supports our members' spiritual growth. We may find that our teaching must begin with the basics of God's loving character, His forgiveness and redemption, and His desire to shepherd us as we are.

Prevalent Leadership Style

We've discussed the importance of a Contagious Leadership style in Chapter 3, and its impact on personal vision. Contagious leaders model a journey with Jesus through open and honest vulnerability, leading from weakness. Jesus said, "Let your light shine before men in such a way that

they may see your good works, and glorify your Father who is in heaven."
(Matthew 5:16) Unfortunately, when leaders project an "I've got it made
with God" persona or hide themselves with "I keep my problems to myself"
relationships, people will be hesitant to envision themselves on any growing
journey with Jesus that feels uncertain or mysterious. When leadership
imposes its own vision on others, it often feels like insubordination for
members to envision for themselves, no matter what may be said from the
pulpit.

A Contagious Leadership style, modeled by Jesus, invites people into a
personal relationship with God in which they expect Him to show them
the vision He has put upon their hearts. Then He draws them into groups/
churches where they're invited to share their collective visions and establish
a group vision based on what God has put within the members of the
Body. The group vision, however, doesn't override the personal vision,
but encourages and embraces it. Now people not only have permission to
envision and hear from God, they know that their personal vision depicts
what God has asked them to become and to do. They become committed
to their personal vision because it's God's Word to them. They're committed
to the group vision because it contains their own heart's desire. They realize
that the fulfillment of their personal vision depends on the realization of the
visions of the group members. People own what they help to create, and they
will invest in what they own.

Melanie Saint James, shares her perspective about vision and leadership.

*This chapter really begins to turn the whole understanding of
leadership on its head. This is quite revolutionary thinking – but
learning how to midwife the First and Second Orders call for the
members of one's church seems radically life giving and the place
where I would love to be!*

Chris Lyons builds on Melanie's insight.

*Midwife is such a rich image! God is growing something that is
naturally and miraculously being shaped and formed within us—a*

life filled with the fire of His love. For this vision to really live, it must come out of us. Sometimes this can be a painful process, but that's what birth is all about!

Discerning Vision

As you can see, I'm suggesting that we "inspire vision" in a way that may be new for most of us—180 degrees from the way I've worked on vision for years and the way you may well have cast vision, as well. I'm suggesting that the organic nature of the Church as the Body of Christ demands that corporate vision emerge from the visions of its members who have received those visions from the Head—Jesus.

Casting vision from the bottom up can be fraught with many difficulties for leaders and for the members of our ministries. However, that's the way Contagious Life leadership works—it's how Jesus works. While the barriers and roadblocks we face are real, they're not closed doors for the Holy Spirit. He is already casting visions within our people, giving them hopes and dreams for new relationship with Him. Those visions may be deeply buried or unrecognized, but they are there. Jesus calls leaders to help His people listen to what He has put in their hearts, to dare to trust Him there, and then to own their responsibility to abide in Christ until His blazing fire of love consumes them and becomes contagious to all.

Although some of you may be loving the idea of this 180-degree change in visioning process, Melanie Saint James expresses the concern that you and many of your members may have.

> *The concept of pastors and their leadership teams not only seeking to know and understand God's will for THEM as well as helping the individual members of their church discover and discern God's vision for their lives - is so radical that I'm wondering if this might actually happen in the contemporary church. Institutional vision has become a contemporary idol in many of our churches. Our pastors and elder boards spend hours and hours and large sums of money to determine the institutional vision, and letting go of that in exchange for helping to midwife the vision of the individual members of the*

church seems like a bridge too far for many.

I thank Melanie for her honesty. In many churches and leadership teams, the bridge to this Contagious Leadership way of casting vision may prove too long and frightening to even consider. I'm praying that YOU, however, may be willing to follow Jesus' way of casting fire upon the earth—through setting individual hearts on fire with His love and letting those fires make the church a blazing City Set Upon a Hill!

If you're a leader in a Christian ministry or church, you will have to decide, in your own context, how the Lord is leading you to move forward in your setting, how to motivate, encourage, and enable your people to dare to vision. Hopefully, you're seeking the Lord as part of a spiritual leadership community where you discern together. Your process will be unique to some degree because each of us are different people in different situations. God will lead us uniquely to accomplish His desires for us and our people-if we hear His voice and let Him lead. Having said that, I would like to suggest that you consider some basic movements that, at some level, should be common to us all.

Pray and Listen.

This whole endeavor of the Kingdom was started by God and only God can set His Church on fire. Pray and listen personally and with your spiritual leadership group. Expect Jesus to guide you, not just bless what you have decided to do. These words from the song, "Build Your Kingdom Here" by Rend Collective, express the heart of our prayer.

> Come set Your rule and reign
> In our hearts again
> Increase in us we pray
> Unveil why we're made
> Come set our hearts ablaze with hope
> Like wildfire in our very souls

Recognize Your Own Vision For Yourself, Not Just Your Church.

As you consider your own place on your journey with God, what longing has He put within you that pictures your heart's desire for the most perfect relationship with the Trinity that you could imagine this side of heaven? Focus on your First Order Calling to love God; leave the Second Order ministry vision for later. Picture it, feel it, put words and images to your vision for your relationship with God. Identify honestly the struggles and challenges that you face in your life and intimacy with Jesus. How would this vision address these issues? Don't just imagine them gone, but envision how your new relationship with Jesus would walk you through these issues. Craft a statement which clearly describes your God-relationship vision. In *Imago Christi*, we call them "Longing Statements."

Now go to your Second Order Calling to love your neighbor. Who among God's beloved has He laid upon your heart? How has He gifted you? How does love flow through you naturally? Picture yourself so free in the love of Jesus that nothing intimidates you. What would it look like for you to embody Jesus with those people in the ways natural to you? What would you do if you knew that you couldn't fail?

Charlie Dodrill comments about the importance of looking at vision from both a First Order and a Second Order perspective.

> *I think we've all seen a lot of assuming that the two are the same. First Order, "primarily relational" vision, is a tough thing to find in many churches. It seems the visions that grow quickly are led by (mostly) men who cast Second Order vision strongly and clearly and gather a following ready to do the work. These visions have to do with "doing" and don't deal with the relationship with Jesus that motivates and empowers change. I've not heard many preachers/leaders separate First and Second Order visions.*

How might you craft a vision statement that will be helpful to you as well as contagious to others? Without trivializing what God has given us into a trite limerick, or an "elevator speech," how can we capture and communicate the preferable future God has for us? If we observe how God's prophets have called people to vision, we see a consistent tool—story.

> In the year of King Uzziah's death, I saw the Lord sitting on a throne, lofty and exalted, with the train of His robe filling the temple. Seraphim stood above Him, each having six wings: with two he covered his face, and with two he covered his feet, and with two he flew. And one called out to another and said, "Holy, Holy, Holy, is the Lord of hosts, the whole earth is full of His glory." And the foundations of the thresholds trembled at the voice of him who called out, while the temple was filling with smoke... Then I said... (cf. Isaiah 6:1-5).

Everyone understood Isaiah's passion to follow God and his mission. They understood that Isaiah's life had been changed by God's action with the burning coal that touched his lips. They understood that he now embodied God's great love for His people, as well as His grief over their disobedience. When the Israelites heard him speak, they could see and feel the fire out of which he had been sent. Your story and my story may not sound as dramatic, but they represent no less a profound experience of God—it IS the same Fire! How do we tell our stories in a way that both shares our fire and invites others to discover theirs?

We might think of our vision story in three categories.

1) What circumstance did God use to get my attention?

2) What did He reveal about me and His desire to transform me? What would my relationship with God look like if His desire and my desire became a reality? (First Order Calling)

3) How does God desire to flow His love through me to others? (Second Order Calling)

Our vision statement needs to paint a picture rather than just give information. If what we write enflames our hearts, it can become contagious to others.

Chris Schutte, shares about the importance of the relational nature of our vision.

> *The emphasis on vision being primarily, relationship is essential. So many of us tend to look at our relationship with God as transactional, and then our obedience to God, in serving others, in much the same way. But a vision that emerges from a love relationship with God and loving our neighbor, opens the door to so much creativity. The pastor and the leadership team need to be on board with this paradigm, and learn the skill of discernment together. The image of empowering our people to share how it is they love God and neighbor, then blessing and celebrating this together, is powerful and compelling.*

Opening the door to creativity speaks to the whole purpose of vision. God makes His loving purposes clear to us in a picture we can embrace and live into. Once we see the creativity God is releasing within us, we can shine that light of a heart on fire to spark the visions of others.

Share Your Vision.

A real struggle related to vision for me took place in the Salt Lake City area where I served as a relatively new senior pastor in a medium-sized Lutheran church. As I grew to understand both the Mormon and Christian cultures in the area, I realized that a "fortress" mentality held most of the Christian churches in a deadly grip. Rather than reaching out to the majority population with the love of Jesus, our churches clustered into safe groups to preserve their identity and ideals against a hostile culture. We read books about the doctrines of the Latter Day Saints. Sometimes, we were filled with pride that we held the true biblical theology and judged our neighbors for their misguided, if not demonic doctrines. We saw ourselves as mission outposts, martyrs for God, locked securely behind our church doors.

One day I had an opportunity to meet a Mormon couple in their home. A Christian TV show they had watched raised some questions that they had verbalized to neighbors who were members of our church. Our member family arranged the meeting, warning me that this couple held tightly to their Mormon upbringing. After initial introductions, sharing a coke (no coffee allowed), they expressed their interest in knowing what "other churches" believed. I suggested that they might begin by describing their own beliefs about God and their relationship with Him. Their story would give me a feel for how I might share my own similar and different beliefs in ways that could be helpful.

To my amazement, both the husband and wife described a deeply personal relationship with God and a faith that "somehow" Jesus lived in their hearts as Savior. They knew little about the Bible and nothing about the classical Christian creeds. They both feared that they might not measure up or actually go to even the lowest of the three heavens. While regular attenders at the local Ward (the name for what we might call a church), the couple felt bored with the legalistic teachings and irritated with the pressure to conform. With a tone of exasperation, they finished with, "Where can we go to find out more about the love of God?" I shared my own faith story, pointed them to some key Scripture verses, and invited them to visit our church.

Driving back to church, I felt struck by my own pervasive judgments and assumptions about "Mormons." Not only was this couple fearful about going to hell, but before this conversation, I was quite sure they would. I longed to find a way that our own congregation could not only break down the drawbridge that protected our fortress, but actually extend the love of Jesus into our community.

However, most of the members of our church had been raised in this fortress mentality and thought that any "evangelism" into the Mormon community would prove hopeless. I had to share my vision, but I had no idea about what sharing the love of Jesus in a hostile culture might look like.

I began to plead with God, "How do we break down our walls of judgment against those around us so that we could begin to love in a contagious way?" Should I write a whitepaper for our church? Would a sermon series be the place to start? I tried both with no results. People just thought me naive, quite sure I'd eventually grasp the reality of the strength of the pagan culture in which we lived. Our church wasn't ready for "my vision for them," but it turned out that they would listen to my vision—for me. I shared this statement in our newsletter.

I see myself so connected to Jesus that His love frees me from my needs for success and approval and emboldens me to trust Him with my own destiny to live in the abundance of His love and beauty.

Freed from my prejudices toward, atheists, Mormons, people who don't attend church, or those who don't fit our church norms, I see myself as a channel of God's love and healing to my community of faith and to God's beloved outside our church. I see myself as a part of a loving, discerning, and supportive fellowship of believers who meet people at their point of need and invited them into the family of Jesus.

I asked my leadership community to help me realize the vision God set aflame within me. I told them I had no idea about where to start or how to reach out to the Mormons around us. I shared that this vision frightened me and that I needed their prayers, guidance, and support. The Elders immediately surrounded me, laying on hands in prayer. Soon, some asked, "How can I help?" Eventually, all I needed to do was give them a little help. As people saw the fire of my own vision, they responded with compassion and began to think about how they could help me. Some warned that such a path would be fraught with danger and even demonic reprisal. Others advised me to just keep care of my flock. Many, however, tried to be more helpful and think creatively with me. The fire in my own heart began to ignite the embers in others and the Holy Spirit fanned the flames. Before too long, others began to dream dreams and see visions. In the coming years, converted Mormons represented a significant percentage of our congregation. The desire of these converts for baptism by immersion, prompted us to reach out to other churches that would let us use their baptismal facilities on Sunday afternoons. Not only did the walls with the community begin to come down, but walls between other churches became drawbridges for friendship, collaboration, and a witness of the unified Body of Christ in our area. God set a fire in my heart, but the Holy Spirit blew it into a contagious fire within our congregation and Christian community.

If God has given you a vision for your own life with God, for growing intimacy with Him, for a love for God and neighbor that sets your heart on fire, then you simply have to find a way to share it with your people. Hopefully, you have been able to do that with your spiritual leadership team and others close to you in the church. In my case, I had to ask my church to help ME live out the vision God had given me. I had to lead from weakness. My brief summary might seem to imply smooth sailing, but I can assure you that the enemy attacked with a vengeance and our human frailties caused us to stumble many times. But, God had a purpose for me personally and for our people that would last far beyond my tenure there. He only asked that we let Him love us, help us to love Him, and let His love flow through us to others. When we said, "Yes," He created a contagious fire! Strange—it's just what the Bible said would happen.

Invite Others to Vision.

My vision unfolded more fully as I began to discover the visions that God was already planting within the hearts of His people. At first, my vision centered on me and God; later my vision transitioned into the future of a community of which I was a part—fantastically more exciting and far-reaching than I could ever have guessed. We share our visions not as banners to follow, but as urgent pleas to help us discover the fuller picture. "Would you vision with me? Would you listen to God with me? Would you help me understand God's dream?"

We need to let God tell us where to start in this invitation process. Maybe He'll direct you to a dear and trusted friend. Maybe your leadership community needs to hear what God is doing in you and receive your invitation. Wherever He leads you, you have to share it; you have to invite others to help you understand what God is saying to you. Then you have to invite them to discover what God is saying to them. Your vision is God's gift to you; God has a unique visional gift for each of them as well. "What if God's vision for them isn't consistent with His vision for me?" we may ask. It's a risk we have to take.

Chris Lyons comments about the ownership of vision.

I specifically remembered when a sophomore girl named Tailor verbalized the phrase that was summarizing a season filled with dialogue and conversation when she said, "Connecting as a family focused on Jesus." You could almost hear a gasp in the room as everyone simultaneously thought "THAT'S IT! That's what God has been stirring up in us!"

Since that experience, there is now an expectation (a new habit) that our ongoing community discernment will remain an "us" thing, an "all together" kind of thing. Chris the youth pastor doesn't head off into his office (or up on the mountain) and bring the tablets down from God to the people. God is in the midst of all of us.... speaking and giving vision.

I've heard it said that "people own what they help to create." And we've found this to be true. We've even gone so far in our youth ministry to believe that "student-owned ministry=student-owned faith."

When God gave me the vision of *Imago Christi*, I tucked it neatly into the hidden places of my diary and my heart. I didn't understand what it meant, so how could I share it with others, particularly my staff? When I stuffed

God's vision away, I almost destroyed my church and put myself through the most painful season of my life! I should have learned from Jonah, but I hadn't. Share your vision and invite others to discover theirs! It's the way that a flicker becomes a flame and a flame becomes a fire, and a fire blazes forth in Contagious Love.

In the next Chapter, we will discuss the process of letting God lead us forward. We'll explore developing mission and strategy that invites our ministries into the same kind of transformation. Amidst all the complexity of the Church, we'll see how Jesus leads us with knowledge and wisdom way beyond our abilities. Jesus will propel the love-fire of His Cross, bursting into our hearts and through our community of faith, into our world—to those desperately longing for Light and Warmth. Don't get ahead of Jesus, though. Wait in living prayer until He says, "Go!" and shows you the way forward.

CHAPTER 6

HOW TO SPREAD THE FIRE -
DISCOVERING THE WAY FORWARD

Are you ready to hear Jesus say, "Go for it! Help me ignite the fires of love in your congregation"? When we begin to discuss spreading contagious fire into the congregation, two frustrating memories come to mind. Too many years ago to admit, our family took its one vacation from Oklahoma City to Anaheim to see Disneyland. We traveled by car, exploring the wonders of Highway 66. By the end of every day, the car filled with loud complaints from the back seat where my sister and I would loudly chant, "Are we there yet? When are we going to get there? I'm bored!" For us kids, a journey was only intended to get us places, as quickly as possible. Early in the trip, my folks would respond patiently, inviting us to enjoy the scenery. Later, they'd make threats to never take us on a trip again. Our persistent bickering and my parent's exasperation brought firm demands that we just keep quiet. None of us quietly enjoyed the late afternoon scenery and we never took another vacation. I had a lot to learn about patience and enjoying the journey.

Some years ago, Bill O'Byrne, Endi Kovacs, and I spent a week in a cold, damp, and empty-except-for-us, Franciscan Monastery near Budapest to pray, discuss, and hammer out the foundational documents for a new order that came to be called *Imago Christi*. Three months later, we met for another week with about two dozen people interested in spiritual formation at Mt. Angel Abbey, south of Portland, Oregon. Beautiful weather, great food, and wonderful people of God made the time together a delight. Every day we shared ideas about forming a community to support our First Order Calling love relationship with God, out of which our Second Order Calling could emerge—to encourage Christian leaders to minister from a growing love relationship with the Lord. Each of us agreed that those who joined this Order would need to actually live out the intimacy with Jesus that we would be calling other leaders to explore. In the last afternoon of our Gathering, I suggested that we consider how to move forward with *Imago Christi's* Second Order Calling. "What can we be doing to start encouraging leaders?" The room grew quiet, as people figuratively pushed their chairs back from the table. Responses went something like, "Isn't it too early for that question? We're not ready to minister together; we're just getting to know each other. We just want to enjoy the journey and not worry about where we're going or how we're getting there." I'd learned some patience since my first story experience but felt just as frustrated in this one.

When we now raise the question, "Where do we go from here?" some of you may be thinking "When will we ever get going? Let's spread the fire!" You or others in your spiritual leadership community may not be so ready to launch, asking, "Have we learned enough to be able to invite others to journey with us? Is the congregation ready?" In Chapter 6, therefore, we're asking, "How do we know when we're ready to move from focusing primarily on our First Order Call to our Second Order Call—helping the people in our church/ministry discover their First and Second Order Calls?" Fortunately, God knows where we are in process and the extent to which the congregation is ready for us to move forward. Let's explore how we discern His timing and direction. First, let's recall the progress of our journey together thus far.

Where Have We Been?

We've seen that spiritual formation and missional momentum form the very foundations for ministry and cannot simply be made programmatic options in the life of the church. The Holy Spirit rarely seems to empower our attempts to "tack on Jesus" to well-oiled secular machinery. The Holy Spirit DOES, however, challenge us to ask the fundamental questions about who we are, personally and as a church, and how we're called to follow Jesus. Clarity about our identity and calling in Jesus form the basic building blocks for everything God wants to accomplish in and through us.

In Chapter 1, we dared to believe that Jesus still has a plan for His Church. We chose to stand in the hope of His shepherding power and wisdom to not only redeem the Church, but to take us into a dimension of boldness we haven't seen before. We envisioned a church so filled with lovers of God that the fire of that love propels people along a journey of personal transformation into the likeness of Christ. This journey of love naturally connects us to the lives of others for the sole purpose of sharing God's life-giving love in ways that illuminates the reality of the presence of the Kingdom of God. The flames of love that flow between us increase in brightness and power—a contagious fire. We desperately want to live out our Lord's command to love Him with our whole being and to love our neighbors as ourselves—taking the Gospel to all people. That's what we want for our own lives and for those we're called to lead.

Chapter 2 addressed how all that happens. We explored the spiritual formation process and the journey of transformation that turns us into lovers—for God's sake. The fire of God's love motivates us to reach out to family, friends, associates, and to the poor and needy both materially and spiritually. We looked at the lifelong process in which Jesus guides us through green pastures, clear water, valleys, and death-like experiences, so that we might learn to abide with Him forever. When we understand the path on which Jesus leads us, we're able to cooperate with His glorious work in and through us, in our particular season of the journey.

In Chapter 3, we recognized that leaders, themselves, must travel this new terrain before they can lead others to explore it. While we don't have to become spiritual formation and missional experts, our ability to lead comes from a spiritual authority that emerges from our own experience with Jesus, as evidenced in our lives. When God's love truly abides within us, the Holy Spirit leaps like glowing sparks into the hearts of others, inviting them into a new and deeper relationship with God and others. The Holy Spirit uses the fruit of our journeys, as leaders, to surface the longing in hearts of other people for intimacy with Jesus and the adventurous life to which He calls us..

Chapter 4 emphasized the vital importance of living the journey together. We meet God in personal prayer and we meet Him in others; both dimensions of encounter prove essential for our growth. We suggested that you invite your leadership team to join your journey with Jesus and to discover theirs. This bold and sometimes risky invitation may test your resolve for your own spiritual growth, but it will become a door-opener for the spiritual growth of your ministry.

We discussed Love's impact on our leadership style. Contagious Leadership puts God's love into action in ways that do not negate or undermine the leader's organizational responsibility. But, it emboldens others to hear their own call and step into God's plan with commitment and ownership.

Chapter 5 discussed the importance of discovering the longing and vision God has placed within us for our own lives. We looked at the difference between personal vision and institutional vision. Personal vision motivates people; institutional vision seldom does. As we share the personal vision God has laid on our hearts as leaders, we can then invite others to look to Jesus for His vision for them. Our personal vision, shared in humility and interdependence, will become contagious to those whom the Lord has chosen. Their vision and passion then become contagious to others. Contagious fire builds and grows as we discover God's destiny for our lives and experience the joy of loving Him and loving with Him.

In Chapter 6, we want to explore the question about where to go from here—how and when to move forward in our churches. Hopefully, we've begun to see the fire of God's loving intimacy bringing spiritual growth and healing in the members of our spiritual leadership community. We're learning to love one another in meaningful ways, and we've become impassioned about God's desire to set our churches ablaze. Maybe it's time to ask God how to invite the whole church into a deeper journey of love with God. Maybe our people stand ready to become healing agents to the needs of the world.

Ready? Set? Go!! ...or not.

While I'd love to be able to provide a simple "blueprint," guaranteed to work in every situation, you and I know that change never turns out to be that easy. The fire of the Holy Spirit doesn't work best from a "blueprint" perspective—Jesus tells us that He's more like the wind that swirls from all directions at once! Fire, by its very nature, takes into consideration all the environmental elements present; and it wants to grow and spread in a more organic and relational way than a blueprint's straight lines and precise angles type approach could ever do. Each ministry setting contains unique challenges and opportunities. Each leader follows Jesus with unique wiring and experience. We'll find that our way forward will be dynamic, filled with unexpected turns and discoveries—fanned by the winds of the Holy Spirit.

Our plan for the way forward may look much more like a spiritual "computer game" than the fixed ink-on-paper that we're used to. Every church belongs to Jesus—the Father has made Him Head of the Church. Jesus founded it; He empowers it; He understands all its individual and group foibles and difficulties. Only Jesus can lead us through the complexities of the journey ahead. Therefore, our next steps must simply follow Jesus. Conversely, any attempt to make Jesus an "assistant" for our plan creates a design for disaster.

Hopefully, your experience of watching Jesus lead in your spiritual leadership community has prepared you to lead. You've seen the ways that Jesus has guided and shepherded your group. The group's exploration of spiritual growth has nourished humility and the other fruits of the Spirit within you and has provided profound lessons about how Jesus leads the Church.

Most Christian leaders openly affirm Scripture's assertion that the Church forms the Body of Christ, with Jesus as its Head. The difficulty comes, for many, in our inability to know how that practically works—just how does He exercise that leadership? Without the ability to "intuit God's heart," and recognize how He's leading, we can be left to speculate about "What would Jesus do?" or resort to our own devices. Most churches, therefore, have adopted secular organization and leadership models. Our spiritual leadership teams, however, can help our churches discover how to follow Jesus.

In this chapter, we're going to raise some fundamental questions about following Jesus in ways that cooperate with His desire to set our people's hearts aflame with His love. We'll explore how the Holy Spirit inspires His followers to live out that love within the church and world until the warmth and light of their love-in-action demonstrates the presence of our Savior. We'll see how Jesus uses our love to call others into that same loving relationship. To follow Jesus' contagious fire initiative into our congregations and ministries, we need to gain knowledge and wisdom in three dimensions.

We need knowledge about the terrain to recognize Jesus' perspectives.

We need to understand how to hear the voice of our Shepherd—to discern His specific direction.

We need to consider how the fire of God's love moves from leader, then to spiritual leadership community, and then to congregational members so that we know what questions to ask the Lord.

Let's consider these three areas of understanding needed to follow Jesus as He leads us forward to ignite contagious fire within our members. We can trust Him to guide us.

> But if any of you lacks wisdom, let him ask of God, who gives to all generously and without reproach, and it will be given to him. But he must ask in faith without any doubting, for the one who doubts is like the surf of the sea, driven and tossed by the wind. For that man ought not to expect that he will receive anything from the Lord, being a double-minded man, unstable in all his ways. James 1:5-8

Your journey with Jesus thus far and your life in spiritual community has prepared you to ask in faith, listen, and follow.

Knowledge About the Terrain

What does leadership in the Kingdom of God require of us? By looking at the biblical stories of three great leaders whom God called and empowered to further His Kingdom agenda, we can identify some of God's methods in order to recognize how Jesus may be working with us in our situations.

Let's use Moses, David, and Paul as examples and try to draw some conclusions. While God instilled a great vision and call within each of these leaders, He did not simply lay out a prescribed path. He led them in a step-by-step discovery that enabled them not only to accomplish His plan, but to grow in their faith and intimacy with God. Rather than providing a simple blueprint, He helped them see their situation—the terrain of their journey from His perspective, and in ways that enabled them to trust Him for the next step. God's guidance helped them discover four areas of knowledge that proved essential in their ability to grasp where God wanted to lead and how He planned to move forward.

First, each leader came to know himself.

Second, he grew to understand those he led directly—the leaders who followed him.

Third, he discovered the character of his followers.

139

Fourth, each leader came to understand the culture in which he was called to lead.

Let's look at a few examples in each category.

Knowing Yourself

Long before God called Moses to "set my people free," He helped Moses to understand his strengths and weaknesses. Even prior to the burning bush, Moses had already learned that he could be rash and impulsive, even to the point of murder. Years tending sheep, submitting to a simple God-fearing leader, and discovering tender love for his wife, all created a humility within Moses that enabled him to follow the Lord faithfully.

David grew up in a simple and possibly taken-for-granted intimacy with God. His talent and spiritual strength seemed adequate to address any need that presented itself. But before God could launch David into his destiny as King, David had to confront the evil of Saul with no simple stone to protect himself. David developed his leadership skill by hiding in caves with untrained outcasts. He tasted God's lovesick pain over His people in his own agony of losing Johnathan. He realized his own sinfulness and learned to walk in humility through adultery and public humiliation. Living continually among adversaries and seemingly always on the edge of disaster, David learned that only God's love, wisdom, and power could sustain him.

The apostle Paul's privileged upbringing and "Harvard" education made him an easy target for pride and blindness. His zeal for tradition and doctrine had hardened his heart. Arrest, torture, and murder became the tools of his trade instead of the love and truth taught in the Torah. Before Jesus could call Paul as His Apostle and theologian and give him a vision for worldwide salvation, He had to blind him, render him helpless, and send him home to discover who he really was. Paul had to learn to surrender his reputation and discover how to follow Jesus, rather than the letter of the law. Only by sharing the sufferings of Jesus could his heart become softened and enabled to love and shepherd others. In weakness, the "Great Lion of God" discovered true power and the destiny of his apostleship. In knowing himself, Paul could lead with compassion and wisdom and truly glorify God rather than himself.

JD Ward comments about the important role pain can play in our transformation, as God often uses our very struggle to formulate our call to serve Him.

> Moses was a man without a people and created a new nation, David was the left-out kid in the family that became the "head" of the family, and Paul was the suppressor of the Church that became the promoter of the Church. This one single act—looking at our pain to discover our call, may be the most important direction tip we can give people.

Discovering the way forward begins in knowing ourselves so that we can recognize and cooperate with God's transformation within us personally. God has called you to lead and planted within you the truths necessary to discern His heart. As you gaze into the vision that God has laid upon your heart, about your own relationship with Him and a contagious fire within your people, ask yourself what God has taught you about yourself. Who has God chosen to use? What makes you a hard nut to crack? What evil lurks in your darkest shadows? What wounds threaten to disable you? How has God increased your capacity to love and be loved? Does intimacy invite you or threaten you? How are you wired? What strengths and weaknesses describe you? What gives you joy and what frightens you? Does God's greatness humble you or humiliate you? What will it take to make you a man or woman after God's own heart, ready for the calling that lies before you? In summary, how well do you know yourself?

How many people do we each know who have never had the opportunity to explore these questions and lived into old age, blind to their own weaknesses? We know many who die still separated from the people they love because no one has had the courage to show them the wounds they caused, and opened to them the opportunity to ask forgiveness and seek reconciliation. How many people do we know who underestimate how God can bless and use them because no one has ever affirmed them or encouraged them to step out in the safety of loving relationships? Blind women and men don't make good leaders—even with the best of intentions. Jesus spoke about our need to see.

> And He also spoke a parable to them: "A blind man cannot guide a blind man, can he? Will they not both fall into a pit? "A pupil is not above his teacher; but everyone, after he has been fully trained, will be like his teacher. Luke 6:39-40

The Church Fathers and Mothers continually point out that we can only know God to the extent we know ourselves. Self-knowledge represents a circular experience of discovery. The more we respond to God's love, the more we come to know Him. The more we come to know Him, the more He reveals our true selves to us. The more we know ourselves, the more easily we recognize God's active hand of love in our circumstances and in our hearts. That's the way that any truly meaningful relationship works, at some level. With our Lord, light is His dwelling place and truth is His nature. Mutual discovery paves the way to mutual love in our journey with Jesus.

God also reveals our true selves to us through community—people who love us enough to tell us the truth and then stay around to help us learn to live into it. Jesus, incarnate in others, can lovingly reflect back what they observe in us—both by encouraging our strengths and supporting us in our weaknesses. As we discussed in Chapter 3, seldom do we find ourselves simply plopped into that kind of community; instead, we need to invite others to join us in forming relationship of openness and trust. We give permission to others to be authentic and real as we model vulnerability and a willingness to listen. Still, it can be hard for others to tell us the truth, particularly when we're the boss or their pastor. Honest feedback can be hard to give and receive. However, if we honestly want to know the truth about our strengths and weaknesses and our progress in discovering the person

God has called us to become, God will lead us to the one or two or a few who we can trust and who will receive our invitation to journey together. In our case, we have called these men and women our spiritual leadership community.

Sharing our past with trusted friends can help us see ourselves more clearly. For example, *Imago Christi* uses a spiritual timeline as one method for framing our past and capturing the lessons learned. During our Spiritual Formation Discovery for Leaders retreat, we invite participants to look back over their lives and experiences with God and others, both pleasant and difficult, and begin to look for the patterns that emerge. In my own timeline discovery, I became amazed at how God used spiritual friendships, at key places in my own history, to help me grow and live as God's beloved. In my growing up experiences, I had found it more than difficult to trust love from others. Over time, God sent me friends who loved me enough to call me out when I rejected their loving gestures. I would never have risked becoming a leader until a loving mentor showed me that I could learn and that those I led would help me follow Jesus. Accepting God's forgiveness, and forgiving myself for the sins of my past, only began when I was able to confess them to trusted brothers and sisters and receive their words of absolution. I would never have learned how to abide with God in prayer if I hadn't had someone close enough to see how stubborn and driven I was, and who patiently encouraged me to take time with my Lord. God intends that we support one another in our self-discovery.

> Blessed be the God and Father of our Lord Jesus Christ, the Father of mercies and God of all comfort, who comforts us in all our affliction so that we will be able to comfort those who are in any affliction with the comfort with which we ourselves are comforted by God. 2 Corinthians 1:3-4

> Therefore, confess your sins to one another, and pray for one another so that you may be healed. James 5:16

In addition to a community of trust, truth, and love, we have access to many tools that can help us discover more about ourselves. Assessments such as the Myers-Briggs Temperament Analysis, the DISC, Strength Finders, the Grip Birkman Leadership Assessment, etc. have really helped me better understand myself and others. I am better able to love others when I recognize my own wiring and how to honor the wiring of others. With the knowledge of my own strengths and weaknesses, I am better able to build a ministry team that can accomplish what I could never do alone. In any great endeavor, God starts by transforming us, and only when we become ready does He call us to lead others. Bill O'Byrne explains our readiness from his own experience.

Our example of personal transformation forms the doorway for others to follow our lead. The point at which others notice a change (not because we broadcast it), they become inspired to want more.

To lead well, however, we need to understand the others called to lead with us We need to know the people we expect to follow our leadership; and we must understand the culture of the group we lead and the cultural context in which we live.

Knowing Our Leaders

Moses, David, and Paul each discovered the few people they could trust and formed an inner leadership circle. This circle changed with time and circumstances, but always included men and women who could share their visions and speak the truth as they saw it. Moses relied upon Aaron and Joshua. David listened to Nathan. Paul relied on Timothy, Barnabas, and Priscilla.

Hopefully, you have formed such a leadership community and through the process of sharing your spiritual formation journeys, and in working together, you have come to know and trust them. You recognize and honor God's call on each of their lives, affirm their strengths and giftings, and encourage them in their needs for growth. You and your leadership community model the kind of relationships you desire for the church community as a whole.

The leader's first responsibility must be the support and empowerment of the members of this leadership community. Believing that God has brought this group together for His own purposes, you can begin to recognize His strategy for moving forward within the dynamics of the group. The differing gifts of group's relationships and abilities to listen to the Holy Spirit will begin to paint the mural of God's direction as their leadership becomes empowered and released to follow Jesus together.

Therefore, to consider the readiness of the spiritual leadership community to move forward, they must ask whether or not they recognize, within themselves, the quality of spiritual growth that they want for the congregation. Has the fire of God's love become contagious in their own hearts and in their community? When they look at their experiences within their community as a "test case," can they say that the experiment has been "successful?" To what extent will the congregation see, within the leadership community, a quality of life that attracts them? Are the members of the leadership community ready to verbalize their vision for their own life with God? Can they describe the journey of faith and their own place along the way? If each one visited a small group or Bible study class within the church, could they share their own story about the way God's love has ignited in their own lives and how God motivates them to actively extend the love of God into the world around them? Would their stories reflect "success," or authentic ups and downs of learning, struggle, and growth? Would the group that they visited recognize God's love being extended to them?

If you can answer "yes" to these questions, then it's possible that your team is ready to be sent out "two-by-two" into the congregation. If you recognize that some members of the community aren't yet ready, then it might be wise to invite the group to reflect on these same questions. The group can assess their own readiness, and plan what it would look like to "move forward" in the spiritual leadership community, in preparation for moving forward in the congregation. One of the "troubling" phenomena of spiritual growth is one's

increasing awareness of his or her own personal imperfection. We begin to
get what Jesus meant when He said that "only God is good" (cf. Luke 18:19).
Our readiness can never be measured by our degree of perfection, but by our
authentic pursuit of God and our willingness and ability to vulnerably share
our experience of the journey.

Knowing Our Followers

Every congregation or ministry group has its own history, values,
traditions, and skeletons. Moses, David, and Paul all had to learn their
community cultures, meet people where they were in process, and only
then could they lead them forward into new realities. Many of these lessons
were learned through hardship and failure, but God used each experience to
provide greater knowledge and wisdom to His chosen leaders.

Given that no two people in our churches live in exactly the same place
in their journey with God, we need to discover, as much as possible, their
felt needs, hopes, fears, priorities and values. Not only can we make false
assumptions about our people, but some of them may also misunderstand
the perspectives of the congregation as a whole. We can easily assume that
the thoughts and feelings of our friends represent those of people we don't
know as well. A number of church surveys have been developed to help both
leadership and congregation gain greater self-knowledge. For example, Steve
Macchia's Church Assessment tool, "CHAT: Church Health Assessment
Tool," can be a wonderful resource and is available from LTI Resources.[1]

Ted Wueste comments about the importance of knowing our congregation.

It would seem best to use multiple avenues toward self-knowledge.
Assessments of temperament, place on the journey, and overall
congregational growth/maturity will prove important. For many
congregations, cultural values could potentially derail significant
movement toward a corporate vision. Assessing where a congregation
is in terms of history, patterns, and values is important. If there is a

---

1. Leadership Transformation Institute, www.leadershiptransformations.org

shared history of pain and hurt that remains unresolved, it needs to be explored and healed before a shared shift in vision can happen. Often, churches have DNA that is not observable at the personal level but is embedded in the shared life of the congregation. It is possible that individuals might not identify with this cultural DNA at the conscious level but asking about church history can uncover potential areas of exploration. So, like the personal timeline, a church timeline could be helpful. Outside "consultants," [like CRM's ReFocusing Team], can help walk us through these kinds of assessments.

Debbie Swindoll, Founder and President of Grafted Life Ministries also consults with churches about spiritual formation. She comments about the importance of recognizing the internal cultural changes implied in our contagious fire endeavor.

If I were consulting with a church at this stage, I would want to help them better understand and name the ideas, practices, theological truths, and misconceptions that were a part of their awakening and transformation. ...This information can be helpful as a beginning place of formulating a plan.... For example, I think the most common and foundational misconception that evangelicals face is their misunderstanding of the Gospel. Most of us were presented with the gospel in a very truncated way that goes something like this (very simplified version): Bad news–you are a sinner and you are going to hell when you die. Good news: Jesus died to pay the price for your sin and if you accept his sacrifice then you can go to heaven when you die instead of hell. You can't earn heaven on your own. Nothing you can do will ever be good enough. Jesus is the only answer to your sin problem and your eternal destiny.

While there is some truth in this narrative, it sets the stage for a number of misconceptions as one journeys forward in their faith. The first is that there is nothing more one has to do than believe in Jesus. Now that eternal destiny is settled by the cross one may go about their life in whatever manner they please. Some take it as far as saying that if one does anything else, for example practices spiritual disciplines, then they are nullifying the unmerited favor that is theirs in Christ...A second misconception is that sanctification...is now a responsibility of the saved person, usually motivated by gratitude in the best case and guilt and shame in the worst case. You get a lot of preaching that emphasizes our obligation to live morally because of what Jesus did for us. ...Being able to identify any of these types of roadblocks from the leadership team's experience could help address common cultural resistances in their broader church environment.

While we recognize multiple perspectives on the atonement, for "Good News" to be good news, our understanding must be based on the understanding of God's love. We easily quote John 3:16, "For God so loved the world...." But when we witness to others, we can easily paint God in unloving ways. As Debbie points out, relationship with our Lord, based on fear, presumption, or guilt misses the freeing foundation of love and the power of abundant life. Chapter 2 discussed the key biblical foundations that undergird our understanding of spiritual growth. The spiritual leadership community might use that chapter to assess misconceptions that may exist in their own church culture.

To assess the church's readiness to focus more deeply on loving relationship with Jesus and participation in His love for the world, we need to ask questions about congregational health. No credible coach would call a sick athlete into the game. Therefore, we have to discern the existence of unresolved issues and conflicts within the congregation. To what extent do factions or groups within the church exist that would oppose or misunderstand leadership's call to spiritual formation and missional momentum? Is the spiritual leadership community unified in their vision for their own lives and for the congregation? Is their leadership trusted to the extent that members can receive their personal testimonies and encouragement? Negative answers to these questions indicate that further groundwork may be needed to prepare the way.

Knowing Our Surrounding Culture

Moses, David, and Paul each had to assess the cultural context into which their people of faith would have to live and prosper. Moses waited an entire generation before his people were ready to move forward into the promised land; David had to draw God's people around a strong theocracy to keep them from straying into the multiple pagan religions around them; Paul had to navigate the complex intersections between Jew and Gentile, Greek and Roman to be able to proclaim an inclusive gospel that could embrace the whole world.

Jesus calls us first to love our neighbor as we love ourselves and later raises the bar by asking us to love our neighbors as Christ loves us. Even our enemies must become objects of our love. Scripture tells us that we can love only because God first loved us; His love flows through us naturally as the fruit of our loving relationship with Him. However, it's hard to love our neighbor, or enemy, when we don't really know them. We often come to erroneous conclusions based on limited personal experiences, false assumptions or projections in the media. We can falsely assume, for example, that the greatest concerns of people in lower income brackets relate to financial and material needs.

Jesus sent His disciples out two-by-two, to stay in the homes of local people, to meet them personally, and learn about their deepest longings. Only then could they share the Good News in ways that truly felt like good news to their hearers. We can learn about our neighborhoods and cities through data and discover some major community needs that we might address. But we can only truly "love" our neighbor when we come to know them personally, at least to some degree. In our increasingly isolated urban societies, we can befriend those around us and listen for the Holy Spirit's nudging to develop relationships when and where He directs.

JD Ward suggests, however, that we need to understand "loving our neighbor" in a greater context than we may be used to doing.

There is more to God's mission than building loving relationships with people. God reigns in the world as well as in the heart. Therefore, we need to address the world's need for systemic healing and for community healing. If we don't see this kind of work for social good as a chore, but rather see it as a gift, we can understand it in formation terms. God calls us to heal the world's pain in such a way that our own soul is healed. [See Isaiah 58:6-12]

JD's important emphasis highlights the truth that our personal transformation in Christ's likeness and our witness to God's love for others must be understood in the context of Jesus' mission to bring the Kingdom/ Rule of God to earth. Jesus told His disciples to proclaim that "the Kingdom of God has come near you" (cf. Matthew 12: 28 and Luke 10:9-11). The action of God's love in our own hearts must embrace the whole of the Gospel. Only when followers of Jesus meet people, with the same love that we've received, and in the context of their need, will people believe that the Kingdom of God has, in fact, come near them and look to the King.

A congregation can also work together to extend God's love in a wider reach, with programs that address the needs of our cities and world. From the perspective of a single individual, the needs of the homeless, for example, may feel too great and frightening even to consider becoming involved. However, together with others in our church and in our city, God's love can be shared in practical ways with significant impact. Knowing our leaders, our congregation and our surroundings enable us to help discern where God may be calling us to love in practical ways.

Steve Thulson's congregation, Centennial Covenant Church, resides in the upscale community of Littleton, Colorado. Researching their community through regular "prayer walks," they discovered that growing numbers of "inner-city poor," especially immigrant families, were moving into the north side of Littleton. These poor people didn't make themselves visible by begging on the streets, but were hidden away in small apartments, often housing several families. Once realizing the needs of part of their community, Centennial Covenant collaborated with other churches in the area, called North Littleton Promise, to create a significant outreach to these immigrant families. This ministry offers multiple opportunities for people to become involved, ranging from an afterschool Kids Club, mentoring, tutoring, ESL (English as a Second Language), and legal advocacy. In the last decade, city leaders have credited North Littleton Promise for a decrease in neighborhood crime and an increase in High School graduations.

Centennial Covenant's story illustrates the principle we stated above— Only as we come to know Jesus, ourselves, our leaders, our followers, and our church and city cultures will we be able to discern the possible ways that our Lord may want to lead the church. Hopefully your experiences together in your spiritual leadership community have helped to grow this awareness.

When we consider "moving forward," the spiritual leadership team must discern their own readiness to lead spiritual formation and missional momentum and the congregation's readiness to receive that leadership. Charlie Dodrill offers an important caution as we consider our own readiness to lead the congregation into spiritual formation.

> I think the transformation that is happening amongst the leadership team must be lived for a period of time to ensure that it is not, in fact, the next fad to come along and also to begin to attain at least the beginnings of wisdom when it comes to walking out this deeper life of contagious fire. For example, have the people on the leadership team begun to deal with the times of darkness, the epochs of despair, the feelings of unquenched hunger, etc. or are the majority still on the front end, living in near constant consolation? We need to be careful not to paint the picture of the initial "easy" part of the journey without having entered into the desert.

If, after addressing these three areas of knowledge and wisdom we need, the spiritual leadership team feels that they and the congregation demonstrate adequate readiness, we're ready to begin formulating our plan to follow Jesus as He leads us forward. I would like to flag the word **DANGER** at this point, however. When we move from the First Order dimension of our community into its Second Order considerations, we can easily slip back into secular approaches to strategic planning. Strategic planning takes on new dimensions in the Kingdom of God. We have to recall our fire analogy, continually checking our process against what we know about the ways that

God ignites fire in the hearts of our people. We've agreed that Jesus shepherds and empowers our spiritual growth, not we ourselves or a church leader. Jesus ignites the fires of love within our hearts, and the Holy Spirit fans the flames until we become contagious. No program, no matter how ingenious, can accomplish transformation in the hearts of people—at least not life-giving transformation. Jesus' work in our hearts doesn't happen in our sleep or in some invisible way; He invites our cooperation. He leads in and through our personal and group experiences. Through our mutual discoveries of spiritual growth, we learn to become attentive to God's leading. When the congregation, as a whole and within its groups, learns trust and vulnerability, they begin to discern God's "voice" more clearly. Yet, we can benefit from a process that helps us to discern together.

Discerning the Voice of Our Shepherd

While understanding principles that describe Jesus' leadership can be helpful, ultimately, principles won't cut it. Asking "What would Jesus do?" may be a place to start, but Jesus explains how He moves beyond principles to leadership that He knows will work. He said, "I do what I see the Father doing." (cf. John 5:19) Similarly, we're called to do what we see Jesus doing. I'll agree that's easier said than done; yet Jesus and the Apostles taught about how He reveals what He is doing and how He shows us how to follow.

God sent the Holy Spirit to each of us, providing various spiritual gifts for the common good. God reveals His leading and will as these gifts work together in a confirming way. Paul calls it "unity of the Spirit in the bond of peace" (cf. Ephesians 4:3). Father Terry Fulham, an Episcopalian rector, one of my mentors, and author of *Miracle in Darien*, often said, "If two of us disagree, at least one of us doesn't know the mind of God." Unity in the bond of peace flies in the face of the West's devotion to individualism. "I have a RIGHT to my opinion!" When the condition necessitates that we come to some group decision, we protect our rights of dissent through mechanisms like *Robert's Rules of Order* and voting. While we may resort to majority rule as the standard way to keep the peace or avoid going wrong, Scripture shows us that the "majority" has been consistently wrong. How do we follow Jesus together?

Experiments With Group Discernment

Many church leadership teams around the country are experimenting with prayer and consensus as a way of discerning God's leading. Steve Thulson describes his experience using a leadership team to follow Jesus together.

> *A need, sensed by some leaders, to pursue typical long-range strategic planning was channeled into intentional "discernment" about where the Head of the church wanted to take our church. One thing not necessarily planned or expected was how early on the appointed Team sensed the importance of being a community of mutual trust and shared hearts. As one member put it early on: "If we're going to lead the church, we need to BE church." The "process" of shared discernment became as important as any "product" we discerned." This discernment process impacted the whole church...clarifying our vision and deepening our formational practices.*

My own first real experiment with group discernment came while I pastored a church in Sandy, Utah. Our leadership team had retreated to a nearby monastery to ask God to show us how to engage more fully with the ministry of the Holy Spirit. Our group of four returned from the monastery with a list of thirty-four instructions we felt that the Lord had given us. One of those instructions seemed impossible. Jesus wanted the leadership of our church to make decisions by consensus, coming to complete agreement on both small and large issues, through prayer and honest discussion. I will never forget the evening meeting when we shared what we felt was the Lord's request. Our Church Council looked at us with absolute horror.

The Church Council had been schooled in *Robert's Rules of Order* and

153

accepted our national belief that the majority should get their way. It's not that they actually believed that the majority always had the right answer; it's just that the majority had the "right" to get their way. As to the "right" decision, our leaders would judge that by what ultimately worked. Of course, we prayed about decisions, but at some level doubted that we could actually "know" God's answer. The congregation accepted these secular assumptions but were greatly encouraged when a "strong majority" put forth a recommendation that affected the church. Even then, we voted and the majority, strong or weak, got their way. Some really important decisions even required a majority of two-thirds.

Despite the Council's horror at the thought of having to arrive at consensus, our leadership did agree to pray about it—really pray about it. They also agreed to relook at the New Testament's teaching about decision making. Over the coming weeks, we studied and discussed Romans, Corinthians, and Ephesians. We found "unity in the bonds of peace" a clear principle. However, the group expressed concerned that we were still obligated to follow the dictates of our Church Constitution. We found that the Constitution certainly did not forbid consensus or prayer and that "voting" could be used to determine the level of consensus we'd reached. Constitutionally, it could be done.

However, the group also recognized that, like all churches, we had some strong personalities in our Council and in the congregation: men and women who formed strong opinions and articulated their arguments with great skill. We also had some more passive members who hated conflict and were known to give in pretty easily. We realized that authentic consensus would require real honesty, and in many cases, a change of heart, not just mind. While our group got along well, an expectation of complete honesty from every member felt threatening. The most difficult barrier for us to admit was that many times we weren't really concerned with what God wanted; we simply wanted our own way. Could we really get past all these barriers and learn to hear from God together? We agreed to try. God honored our courage and changed the course of the congregation.

Of course, we had problems that arose out of all the issues I've just mentioned. One man resigned from the Council—one of the strongly opinionated ones. He told us that he thought we had made the right decision to seek consensus, but that it was driving him crazy. He didn't mind not getting his way as long as he could simply vote against it. He liked things black and white and the agonizing process of continuing to pray and wait on God kept him up at night. On a whole, however, the group learned to pray, talk things out, and pray again. We did give ourselves an out, however. If consensus seemed to be impossible on an important issue that demanded a decision, we could still agree to vote. I don't remember that it ever happened.

As Steve Thulson commented, the process of discernment often produces more fruit than the final decision. One time in my own experiments with discernment, we came to consensus on a decision, that we saw later, had clearly bounced. In our next meeting, we discussed our mistake, totally mystified, looking for where we had gone wrong. Finally, one of our quieter members asked for the floor. He confessed that he had lied. He had become so frustrated with the discussion that, when a straw vote was called, he consented. He shared that he had felt like an odd man out, the only one who felt reservations. The courage to stand alone, for no "undeniable" reason, proved too much for him. He confessed with tears, "I lied to you. I never did feel a peace about that direction." It now appeared that his reservation had come from the Lord. Had he expressed his distress, we could all have gone to prayer again and possibly have come to a different decision.

However, our brother's confession changed us. We realized that each one of us had a responsibility before God to tell the truth about what we experienced in the discerning process. The leadership team also realized our responsibility to provide a safe place for honesty—a place without judgment or impatience with those who couldn't yet honestly agree with the majority. God gave us each a sacred trust that we had to honor—to honestly follow

Jesus, despite the cost.

Hearing Jesus Through a Formal Discernment Process

Some years later I learned about the Rules of Discernment, compiled by Ignatius of Loyola for potential Jesuit recruits to discern their calling. Ignatius described two conditions of our heart that can be used to discern our alignment with God's will: consolation and desolation. Consolation consists of an inner peace and sense of faith and trust in God. Consolation refers to the "peace which passes understanding," described by the apostle Paul and the "peace I give you" promised by Jesus (cf. Philippians 4:4-7 and John 14:27). Consolation comes from the peace of being aligned with God's will. Desolation, on the other hand, represents the opposite experience— lack of peace, a feeling of agitation, dis-ease, even foreboding. Desolation does not come from God, but from our own spirit or the harassment of the enemy. While consolation and desolation may express themselves in feelings, they're spiritual conditions of the heart rather than purely emotions. When we pray for God's direction, we discern His "yes" within the experience of consolation and His "no" in the experience of desolation.

Ignatius teaches us that God's will can be recognized in our awareness of inner consolation—in the heart. He describes a process that uses both the mind and heart to discern God's leading through a multi-step process:

1) Identify alternative solutions to the problem or question at hand.

2) Identify the pros and cons for each potential solution.

3) Choose one of those solutions to take to God in the form of a single question which can be answered yes or no. For example, rather than asking, "Should we build a new church or remodel the existing one," we would ask, "Should we build a new church?"

4) Relinquish our own preferences and personally surrender to God's choice in the matter. We can't help forming personal opinions during the analysis phase. It's vital, however, that we fully seek God's will rather than

our preference. Therefore, we recognize our preference, surrender it to God, and ask Him to show us His will, whether or not it agrees with the answer we might choose.

5) Retire into personal prayer, first imagining a "yes" answer to our question, each one discerning either consolation or desolation as they picture that alternative. We then prayerfully picture a "no" answer. During prayer, we ask God to identify personal preferences or opinions that might get in the way of hearing His voice and freely choosing His decision.

6) When each one has had time for personal prayer and discernment, the discerners return to the group and share their results. If each member of the group identifies consolation with the same decision, then the chances are good that they have discerned God's mind.

7) If consensus does not appear, they return to prayer. If the group all feels desolation about both yes and no answers, it may mean that they have asked the wrong question. They then return to their alternatives in prayer, and ask the Lord to show them the right question to bring before Him.

8) The process continues until the decision-making group experiences consensus—unity in the bonds of peace.

Thomas Green, in *Weeds Among the Wheat*, beautifully unpacks this discernment method.[2] *Imago Christi* has simplified and described this process through a "Discernment Journal," available through their website.

Among the benefits of this discernment process, the "right decision" may turn out to be the least important—God has a reputation for redeeming wrong decisions. In the process of discerning, as we wrestle to hear God, we learn to recognize what Ignatius calls our "attachments," the things that keep us from fully relinquishing ourselves to God. For example, one elder realized that he had a strong aversion to debt. He confessed later to the group that if God wanted the church to go into debt, he unconsciously felt that God

2. Thomas Green, *Weeds Among the Wheat,* (Notre Dame, ID, 1984)

had to be wrong. As we consider a course of action, we may well identify attachments such as our fear of failure or rejection, our need to please certain people, etc. As we surrender the attachments God reveals to us, we become freer to follow Jesus, not only in this situation, but in our whole life.

The discernment process also provides a context in which we can learn to listen to one another and discern God's voice in someone who may disagree with us. We discover how to ask questions that help our brothers and sisters realize the truth which lies within them. We learn to trust God with the group, with our lives, and with the destiny of the church or ministry.

Imago Christi adopted this discernment process in our founding process and built it into our foundational documents. We use it informally in our Leadership Triad for decisions that do not require the consensus of the whole group. We use it informally when we make minor decisions like what book we want to study together or where we will meet for our next Gathering. When we find that we cannot agree upon some significant decision, however, we set aside days for the formal process. In one instance, we had to set aside years.

When a congregation knows that its leaders not only want to do God's will, but wait until they feel they have really heard God's voice before they move ahead, trust and courage emerge. A fellowship that knows that their leaders interacted in love and respect will be much more apt to interact with one another in the same way. People who experience God's love in action among their leaders, will gladly follow Jesus into the mystery of spiritual maturity. Only when they see Jesus' headship actively lived out among the spiritual leadership community will our people believe that a spiritual growth and missional outreach adventure is possible, and that Jesus will lead them.

Bill O'Byrne shares our experience working with a spiritual leadership team in *Imago Christi* and its impact on the whole community.

Imago Christi was founded as a community, and in community. Three of the original four members became its "leadership triad." Though there was organizationally one "team leader" for the ministry team, as a community we were intentional about leading "as community." It was not always easy, but time and time again the Lord led us and the community in a much more powerful way out of the consensus and diversity represented in a leadership team. We knew that it wouldn't have been possible with just one person leading the community according to a single set of gifts, or temperament, preferences, and style.... The unity that the Leadership Triad demonstrated became an example for the whole community to seek together. Conversely, where consensus was difficult to find in the leadership community, we knew it would be even harder to find in the larger community. The lack of unity, then, drove us to seek the Lord afresh individually, and wait on Him collectively, for His solution in His time.

Likewise, a leadership team demonstrates to a given congregation that a variety of perspectives, learning styles, growth stages and temperaments have contributed to the vision of Christian spirituality. This also provides an essentially inclusive and expansive model of spiritual community for the congregation to emulate moving forward.

Once we have come to understand ourselves as leaders, our congregations, our surrounding culture, and the process of discerning the voice of our Shepherd, we're ready to begin to ask our Lord specific questions about moving forward.

Questions to Ask Jesus About the Movement of Contagious Fire

Let's consider some categories of questions which can help us seek our Shepherd's directions so that we can better recognize how He may be leading.

Corporate Vision: First, the spiritual leadership team must discern, form, and articulate a clear vision for personal transformation into Christ-likeness and a life lived as an expression of God's love for all people. Our vision must not only reflect our biblical imperatives but the unique contexts of our lives and community as well as our church heritage and culture. Recall our discussion in Chapter 5 about vision. Our corporate vision should emerge from the collective visions of the community—in this case, the spiritual leadership team. For example, "What would it look like if everything we did in our personal lives, and in our church, were reduced to expressions of loving God and loving our neighbor?"

Chuck Orwiler comments about the importance of this vision.

> *The statement of vision needs to be descriptive of a cultural shift that captures the imagination of the congregation. From there, objectives and strategies flow within the particular church construct. The point, however, is not to "get things done", but to create a particular culture. That is the difference that sets Contagious Fire apart and sets this endeavor apart from typical strategic planning.*

Rather than imposing a vision upon our people, corporate vision should invite us to seek Jesus to discover the vision He has implanted within us.

Personal Vision: With our initial corporate vision in place, we have to discern which individuals and groups seem most ready to receive these personal vision invitations. With these people in mind, how might we craft our visional invitation? Who seems ready to form their personal vision for their own deepening love relationship with Jesus and participation in His Kingdom initiatives of love? In what language and settings might these people best receive our invitation and process it with the Lord.

Extending the Leadership Circle: While a number of congregational leaders may participate in the spiritual leadership team, many other leaders eventually need to be included. Whether leaders of major ministries in the church or leaders who teach or serve in less influential ways, their "leadership" demonstrates both their sense of God's calling as well as their influence with others. We honor and encourage their servant leadership by including them early in new initiatives, asking their input, inviting their participation, and valuing their support. Leaders who first hear about new vision through the grapevine or on the screen in the worship service rightly feel devalued and will probably oppose change. Chris Lyons underscores the importance of inviting leaders into the process early. He paraphrases a quote attributed to Patrick Lencioni: "If you want people to BUY in, you have to give them the opportunity to WEIGH in...."[3] How might the initial spiritual leadership community invite other leaders to join their journey and speak into the way God might be leading us forward?

Discovering Existing Fire: What do we already see Jesus doing? Where might we find evidence that the Lord has already gone ahead of us and prepared the way? Where do we smell smoke and discern the fire of the Holy Spirit? What groups or individuals seem to be exhibiting new life and vitality? People feel honored when leadership recognizes and affirms their zeal for the Lord and invites them to build on what God is already doing within them. For example, the youth ministry in the church I served blazed with enthusiasm, participation of lay leaders, and outreach into our community. Our Youth and Family Pastor, part of our spiritual leadership team, could easily cast his own vision for loving Jesus and invite his lay leaders to explore their own vision. In this situation, our Youth Ministry proved to be a great place to start. As it turned out, the increasing fire that the Holy Spirit birthed in our lay leadership and kids became a beacon both to the rest of the congregation and to the city. In another church, the small group ministry provided a wonderful place to begin.

Discovering People of Peace: Jesus sent His disciples out to look for households where peace would be received (cf. Matthew 10:13). In their proclamation of the Good News of the coming Kingdom of God, they were to start with the people most apt to receive the message. In addition to working with existing ministries where we already spot flames of love, we can also seek out individuals in

3. Patrick Lencioni is an American writer of books on business management, particularly in relation to team management. He is best known as the author of The Five Dysfunctions of a Team.

whom we sense the glow of God's presence. These people might not be the most active or influential members, but believers whose spiritual maturity focuses their church participation and personal lives. Many of these people of peace may be among the older members of the congregation. While not eager to join some exciting new program, they may well become thrilled to explore their own vision for intimacy with Jesus and love for neighbor, and become prayer warriors for this new focus in the life of the church. We may also learn more about how to craft and communicate our visional invitation.

Plan Organically: We must continually remind ourselves that the church isn't an institution or organization: it's the Body of Christ, a living organism. Therefore, it's important that we plan relationally. We're about people rather than programs, slogans, or performance goals. While we may well use teaching curriculums, retreats, devotionals, and other tools, God's fire becomes contagious only in the hearts of people. Jesus ignites the fire of His love through personal encounters and meaningful relationships. He grows us personally, and as a church, at His own rate, honoring the pace at which we are able to follow Him. It's easier to develop a flashy PowerPoint presentation than spend time with people. The presentation will be forgotten within months; the people, however, will live with Jesus into eternity. Only personal visions result in personal growth and fire our incentive to love.

Follow Jesus: We can research and learn. We can identify alternatives and even speculate on best odds of success. Only Jesus, however, really knows the way forward. Only Jesus knows, for sure, where to start and when. Our Good Shepherd has given us the discernment process we discussed above to help us hear His voice, together. Letting the "leader" decide or taking a vote might seem easier, but our shortcuts usually lead us the wrong way. Jesus never will.

Following Jesus always starts in the prayer closet. It then moves to community prayer. Only then do our attempts at obedience burst into flames of glory to God.

Terry Tarleton discusses the use of these discernment categories by his church as they moved forward toward contagious fire.

What we have found helpful in our church is to identify those who are "hungry" for intimacy with Jesus [people of peace], and integrate them into small groups that are geared more that way. In that way we've developed leaders who understand the need to "be with Jesus" over and above "doing for Jesus." We teach that "doing should flow out of being." Slowly our church culture is changing. Over 10% of our adults are now trained spiritual directors, and we have a number of small groups that have some sort of contemplative leaning, and/or a study that helps us to understand spiritual formation. We have taken the "turn the ship slowly" approach to formation. It has taken us about four years to get where we are, and still, we have a fair number of people who are not quite ready for formation. We trust that there is still a place for them to come along at their own pace.

Ultimately, we'll develop a plan that describes a clear path forward at a personal and corporate level, at least as far forward as the Lord has given us clarity. I'd suggest we always mark the plan with a "Rough Draft Date," however. No matter how well we use the discernment process to try to follow Jesus to the letter, we'll always make mistakes. Fortunately, however, Jesus excels at redeeming our missteps and teaching us through our mistakes.

In the following chapters, we'll discuss more specific approaches to the way forward. We'll discuss teaching and providing experiential opportunities to facilitate spiritual growth and missional outreach. We have to remember, however, that both our growth and our outreach result from fire—contagious fire birthed in the heart of Jesus and spread through the winds of the Holy Spirit. All we need to do is cooperate!

CHAPTER 7

REVEALING THE FLAME AND DISPELLING THE FEAR - TEACHING ABOUT SPIRITUAL FORMATION

Ah, teaching!!! Most of us preachers and teachers probably feel that we have finally—finally—arrived at the real deal! We love to teach. Our Contributors echoed the importance we place on teaching by submitting more thoughts and reflections about this chapter than in any of the other thirteen! It's probable that sermon series and class outlines have been forming in our heads since we began *Contagious Fire*, busting at the seams of our brains, waiting to enlighten the minds of everyone around! Once they get our vision of "Up and Down/In and Out" and the fourteen key Bible passages.... If only our people could fully understand, they would naturally respond with new devotion to Jesus, sacrificial love for neighbor and the world, and ultimately embrace our new vision for the church. Alas, if only it were that easy.

Having poked fun at us left-brain teachers and preachers, like me, we have to admit that teaching will play a major role to help our communities of faith grasp a new Kingdom vision for their lives and discover new ways to live out a deepening relationship with God. We'll need to provide the necessary "head" knowledge about God, love, spiritual growth, community, and our call to set the captives free. While some knowledge starts in the heart and rises to the head, most people need to understand before they can integrate experience with information at a heart level.

There's a lot of new insights to be grasped. Most of our flock has grown up, as we have, thinking that the Third Mansion's "working for God" represents discipleship's pinnacle and the ultimate life with Jesus in this world. They may have yearned for more experience of the Lord but feared that "more" would only mean harder work. Therefore, they've settled for the status quo, or considered bailing, because they either don't know what work might be needed or just aren't up for more work of any kind. For these stalled-out believers, we have fantastic news to share about this marvelous, liberating, and life-giving adventure with God that truly makes life abundant—contagious fire! So, let's talk about teaching.

To set the context for teaching spiritual formation, we'll return to our fire analogy. As you remember, the fire represents Divine Love—originating within God and spreading to His followers—the logs. We saw that our living "logs" have to become ignited. Sometimes we logs hold onto the old "sap" which we thought would sustain us. It takes time for us to become dry kindling, to come to the end of ourselves to a point where our "dryness" for God creates such an ache and longing that we can't help but burn! God so values our freedom that He would never force His love/fire upon us, even to save our lives. Recalling how we might build a campfire, we recognized that our logs would have to be placed near enough to the Flame to become hot enough to combust. At the same time, they need to be placed just far enough apart to provide air and oxygen—the Holy Spirit—to allow their flame to grow.

Our analogy struggles, however, when we start talking about "living logs." The logs must WANT to burn! Not only must they want to burn, but they have to PLACE THEMSELVES near enough to God to catch fire and near enough to one another to maintain the flame. How does that happen?

To try to entice our "logs" to want to catch fire, we began by showing them a leader, then a leadership community that had caught fire to the point they radiated God's love and had become contagious. Abundant life began attracting people! Hopefully, a good number of our members—our logs— decided they wanted to become more alive with the love of God, as well.

To fan the flames of that desire, we encouraged our logs to dream dreams and see visions, letting the Holy Spirit reveal their personal vision for a more meaningful walk with Jesus. They pictured what it might be like to become so in love with God that they feel free to express that love in ways that seem meaningful to them. Their personal vision contains a First Order component that continually increases the blaze of their love relationship with God. Their vision also includes a Second Order dimension—loving others for whom they feel a particular compassion and in ways that fit their particular gifting and wiring. Now, if we've been successful in our spiritual witness and in our vision casting, we've gathered a great bunch of logs eager to jump into the fire! To make that leap and become fire themselves, however, they need to be taught how to cooperate with God and with one another—how to become contagious fire.

We still have a problem, however. How do you teach spiritual formation and missional outreach to logs who constantly move around—always on their way to somewhere else? It's not like they're lying on a woodpile waiting for us to teach them about the fire of God and position them nicely to receive it. Some of our logs already know most of what they need, and others find themselves clueless. We see a few logs already jumping on the fire and others traveling in the opposite direction. Maybe that difficulty exists with any kind of teaching, but I think it's especially true in matters of the heart. Therefore, we have to think creatively as we consider the teaching aspect of leading a group into the spiritually forming journey of deepening intimacy with Jesus.

Before we start working on a teaching curriculum for spiritual formation, let's discuss some more basic considerations about teaching spiritual formation. Where in the world do we start? When we stop to think about it, the whole of Scripture and all the categories of theology speak in some way to the subject of spiritual formation. Biblical history tells the stories of God's transforming power in the lives of great saints and dark villains. Trinitarian theology, Christology, Ecclesiology, Soteriology, Eschatology, Spiritual Theology, etc., all provide important foundational understandings upon which we peer into what it means to live in relationship with God—to love and serve Him, and to become conformed to His Image. Let's explore some of the important dimensions of any curriculum we might choose within the following categories.

Teaching Meat, Not Just Milk

Teaching into the Questions Being Asked

Teaching Biblically in the Context of Our Church Tradition

Connecting Our Love Relationship With God and Love For Neighbor

Connecting Intellectual Learning and Experiential Learning

Finding the Settings Where People Learn Best

Teaching Meat, Not Just Milk

To help our people live into the magnificent relationship that Jesus offers, we must provide good foundational teaching—meat, not just milk. Every leader and leadership team will have to assess, for their own situations, the quality of the existing foundation. Some churches may be known for the warm vitality of their fellowship, but will readily admit that most of their people find themselves biblically illiterate. Other churches may boast about their congregation's biblical knowledge, but may wonder how many actually "know" Jesus in a relational way. Some congregants focus on what they oppose, socially and theologically, while others pride themselves for being "nonjudgmental," cautious to stand for anything, fearful of offending someone. The following sections will discuss what we might consider "meat" relative to spiritual formation—meat that addresses the whole of the gospel message.

We can identify foundational teaching, however, that needs to undergird our journey of spiritual growth. Bill O'Byrne suggests some essential foundations upon which our teaching of spiritual formation should be based.

The BEST of theology has to be the explicit foundation from which we speak, as well as the implicit content that we communicate between the lines of every message. So certain key theological positions need to be consistently in place in our teaching and preaching for "spiritual formation" to make sense, and be the natural conclusion of all our doctrine!

View of Good and Evil: Many people's "knee jerk" feeling about God is that of an angry, unpredictable, sin-punisher, no matter their professed theology of God. We must make every attempt we can make to demonstrate from Scripture, nature, and life, that God is truly loving and good. For people to even begin to want to trust God, let alone believe that He personally loves them, they have to reevaluate their negative views about God. Evil also must have a real place in our teaching to break down some of the inappropriate blame that gets thrown God's way.

ImagoDei and Vocation: Humanity often gets a bad rap in our preaching. However, God created us in His image for His pleasure and the good of all creation! What is the purpose of man? To love God and enjoy Him forever is a great start, but how do we do that? .... We were created to be God's partners in bringing His order and creativity into His creation.... We need to understand the nature of our calling, despite our struggles with sin and the reality of evil in the world.

Sin and Salvation: Humankind, though fallen, is still worthy of God's love, or Christ would not have come to express the full extent of God's self-giving, self-sacrificing love on the cross. We must teach that the Gospel proclaims good news about a loving relationship with God, not just a transactional gospel that simply gets us to heaven.

Spiritual Journey: Hidden in most of us is an expectation that we should get everything right. Or we've been so disappointed by failures and shaming that we don't even try. Scripture teaches that we cannot be perfect; something in us needs to be undone and remade through Jesus Christ, and by His Spirit. This critical element of the difference between the testaments must be clear! The centrality of love in the Christian journey focuses on intimacy with God rather than simply 'doing good,' serving more, or trying harder. ...Spiritual disciplines can't be understood as "works sanctification," but as opportunities for intimacy and love in our growing capacity to receive, to experience, and to express and communicate/give His love.

Spiritual Experience: ...We must approach all of church ministry from the perspective of a spiritual director! To do this, we need to teach the validity and proper focus of spiritual experience. How to know God's explicit will, to hear God's voice and discern it from our own or others', etc. Spiritual experience concepts need to become part of our preaching/teaching. Otherwise, spiritual formation ministry or emphasis will feel disjunct from the rest of what is communicated at church.

Bill shares from his years of experience working with Russian Christians and, through *Imago Christi*, with leaders in the US and several other countries.

Debbie Swindoll reminds us that we may also need to "unlearn" relational dispositions which don't match the truths of the Gospel.

It is always valuable to talk about what has to be put off amidst our teachings about what can be put on in our relationships with God and others. Since we are presenting a relationship premise for formation, it would be good for teachers to help their flock understand that their family-formed relational patterns (self-protection, self-reliance, self-promotion, etc.) get in the way of becoming a person who can freely enter into love and dependence. Many of us have a formative relationship (usually one of our parents) that travels inside of us for a lifetime and in which we occasionally get caught in those dynamics either with God or someone else. It generally takes a long time to heal our issues of trust and the wounds of our relational brokenness.

No matter where we minister, the focus of our teaching must address both the basic foundations of the Gospel message and correct the misconceptions that we spot in our own context. Each leadership team will have to decide what entrées need to be added to the existing menu.

Teaching Into the Questions Being Asked

Most church leaders have been trained in academic institutions that use a linear model of education—one that each of us has found helpful and necessary. In my undergraduate studies, I "wanted to know" how to design and build airplanes. Before I could tackle advanced calculus, however, I had to digest the milk of basic arithmetic and algebra. (I even had to learn to use a slide rule!) Our seminary education followed a similar model. We started with Greek and Hebrew, followed by biblical studies, and on to theology. Only then were we considered fit to tackle practical matters like preaching, teaching, pastoral counseling, etc. Most of us attended seminary to learn to preach and teach and counsel but recognized the need to survive all the rest to get there. Many of us have tried to repeat those linear models in our congregations, only to discover that our congregants are not willing to make the same sacrifices to learn what they really want to know. They rightfully expect us to address their questions, not ours.

When we consider teaching spiritual formation and missional momentum, therefore, we must recall our own line of discovery and the discussions in the previous chapters. We have agreed not to try to drive people where we think they should go, using the law of "should" and "must." Rather, we want to invite them to experience God's grace in new ways that generate a new vision of life with God—living abundantly in His love and incarnating that love into the world. We have challenged people to let the Holy Spirit create a new picture for their future: a relational picture—one that excites and motivates them. Because one's personal vision motivates their desire to learn, our teaching must address the questions that emerge from those visions— "How does this work? What does that mean? What went wrong?" Therefore, in what may seem like a backwards curriculum, we must discover the questions before we can teach the answers.

When we teach into the questions that emerge from visions of a love relationship with God and neighbor, we discover that the questions all circle around the words, "how" and "who." How do we get from here to there? How do we move from knowing about God to knowing Him? How do we know whether we're moving forward, backward, or falling off the map? How does one live in a way faithful to God and still be able to function in today's world? Surprisingly, the "Who" questions often follow the 'How" ones. How can I experience abundant life? How can I know what God expects of me? Who is this God who wants me to know Him personally? Who is Jesus in today's scheme? Who is the Holy Spirit? Who am I to get such attention from God? Who is my neighbor? Admittedly, the order may be reversed for some of us. For example, Melanie Saint James' questions started with "who."

> *I began by asking the question, "Who is this God that is so relentlessly pursuing me? Who is this God that loves me unconditionally and calls me His beloved?" It was only after asking "who" that I could begin to ask, "How can I show my love and adoration for the one who already loves me? How can I know this God or hear His voice?"*

Wherever our questions start, we must try to provide meaningful answers in ways that invite further questioning and discovery.

Soon after my conversion, I could easily tell you "who" God was—in a few sentences. Now, while I can still affirm those few sentences, the word "Mystery" says way more about Who God is for me. The more we know, the more we realize that we don't know very much at all. For example, we could easily say that the Earth is the third planet from the Sun. The more we explore it, however, the less help that definition provides. We realize that we could spend our whole life in places like the Grand Canyon and never come to fully know it, much less the whole earth. It works the same way with our growing relationship with God—the more we come to know Him, the more we realize that the Creator of the Universe lives way beyond our ability to know Him fully. When He gives us glimpses into His person, He opens up amazing vistas that have no language to describe them, no reference points from which to compare them, and only inadequate analogies with which to discuss them. We could only say that God is more wonderful, more holy, more pure, more beautiful, more Love than we could ever imagine (cf. Psalm 139). People, with even a glimpse of a vision for new life with God, need to understand both Love's invitation and the landscape for falling in love. Our teaching must truthfully paint the most beautiful and contagious picture through which the Holy Spirit draws our people into an amazing adventure with Jesus.

Teaching Biblically in the Context of Our Church Tradition

In their book, *Renovation of the Church: What Happens When a Seeker Church Discovers Spiritual Formation*, Ken Carlson and Mike Lueken describe their experiences in attempting to move their church members toward a deeper personal relationship with Jesus.[1] Unlike the title suggests, however, it was not the "church" that initially discovered spiritual formation, but the staff—in a life-changing retreat with Dallas Willard. Ken and Mike have shared, in a number of conferences, that they had inadvertently communicated to their congregation that much of what the church had previously been doing had been wrong, and they now had to move in a new direction, called spiritual formation. Like most of our churches, their people had never even heard the term, much less understood what it meant. The courageous vulnerability of these authors has helped many of us avoid trying to get our congregations to suddenly make right-angle turns that appear to criticize and confuse their members and their history. We can affirm and encourage our members by building on our traditions and expanding our horizons in ways that feel congruent with the reasons members joined the church in the first place.

When we try to import spiritual formation truths from other traditions, new terms, or new meanings for familiar terms can easily cause

---

1. Kent Carlson and Mike Lueken *Renovation of the Church: What Happens When a Seeker Church Discovers Spiritual Formation,* (Downers Grove, IL, IVP Books, 2011)

misunderstanding, confusion, and resistance. Phrases like Lectio Divina, silence, solitude, contemplation, inward journey, being versus doing, etc., can confuse and frighten people unfamiliar with their meaning. Members may wonder if the leader has strayed from the scriptural and doctrinal traditions with which the church has become identified. Renaming and reframing can avoid unnecessary knee-jerk reactions. For example, Imago Christi adopted the phrase "abiding prayer," with reference to John 15, to include subjects like meditation, contemplation, centering prayer, wordless prayer, and silence. Without initially introducing a new vocabulary, we talk about the dimensions of prayer in the context of abiding in Christ, where we can understand prayer as the exchange of life as well as information. Once people become accustomed to the concepts, we can begin to introduce new terms that can help them connect to discussions about prayer in other Christian traditions—terms which may prove helpful in their own discussion of their experiences of prayer.

In retrospect, we recognize that the same kinds of difficulties were experienced in the Charismatic Movement. Frequently, "traditional churches" tried to help their people become more acquainted with Holy Spirit by using "Pentecostal" language and practices. Confused and threatened, many people left their "churches in renewal," trying to find another church that fit the traditions with which they had been accustomed. Sometimes they stayed, but tried to get their pastor fired.

We don't have to step outside our church tradition and vocabulary to move toward the spiritual formation of our members. I'd guess that you have always encouraged a personal love relationship with Jesus and the call to live that love out with others. While you may want to become more intentional or focused on that message, you can affirm where your people have been, where they've journeyed so far, and encourage them forward—forward in the church that feels like home. For example, if your people can handle a Catholic author, like Basil Pennington, to study prayer, then go for it. If that's too threatening, then it might be better to start with the devotional life of Martin Luther, John Wesley, A.W. Tozer, D.L. Moody, or some other well-known and respected leader in your tradition. Then, newer voices like Richard Foster's works on prayer which describe prayer in various Christian traditions can be introduced. Someday, your people might feel delighted to study Thomas Merton or Thomas Keating, but maybe not initially. The goal, therefore, isn't to move people to some ecumenical understanding of the spiritual life, but to give them permission and avenues for their journey forward, using accepted and reputable guides.

Connecting Our Love Relationship With God and Love For Neighbor

As we discussed in our opening chapters, many churches have focused more heavily on either the missional outreach or the spiritual formation ends of the contagious fire spectrum. Our thesis, in *Contagious Fire*, intertwines both dimensions of the Christian life, insisting that we come to know and love God in both: without knowing and loving God we cannot fully know and love our neighbor; without coming to know and love our neighbor we cannot fully come to know and love God. However, many of our people associate the "Gospel" with one or the other. Our love relationship with God and our loving ministry to the world both proclaim the Gospel of the Kingdom where Jesus lives as King. Therefore, our teaching must continually make that connection so that eventually our people grasp and embrace the whole of the Gospel.

Connecting Intellectual Learning and Experiential Learning

Some fields of study depend upon "data" to build knowledge and then use experience only to validate that data. In our study of our relationship with God, however, experience builds the central portion of our relational knowledge base, and data informs that experience. For example, the study of relativistic physics depends on mathematical principles. We then use experimental experience, gained through linear accelerators and other procedures, to demonstrate whether or not we got our math right. Our faith, however, emerges from our experience of God and the working of the

Holy Spirit in our hearts. Our biblical and theological knowledge helps us understand and interpret our faith experience. Seminaries, for example, have often understood their purpose to teach information, leaving faith experience to the purview of churches. Churches then wonder why their new pastor's faith seems so shaky under stress.

Melanie Saint James investigated this problem as part of her doctoral research.

In my D.Min. thesis (2000), I addressed the role of the seminary to adequately prepare students spiritually for the rigors and demands of ministry as well as help them grow and flourish in their relationship with Jesus. The party line from the seminary and its faculty was, "This is a seminary; it is not the church. It is the role of the church, and not the seminary, to adequately help students grow in their relationship with Jesus and prepare them for the spiritual rigors and demands they will face in ministry."

Consequently, when I spoke with local pastors about spiritual formation in the church, ... they responded by saying that they were so horribly overworked already that they just didn't have the time it would take to spiritually form and prepare students for ministry. They concluded, therefore, that it was the role of the seminary.

While *Contagious Fire* doesn't focus on seminary students specifically, the teaching/learning gap can be the same. We can teach information from the pulpit and then assume that the individual will successfully integrate that information within their faith relationship with God. Like the pastors Melanie interviewed, many of us don't feel like we have the time to devote to our faith formation. Hopefully, you have personally responded affirmatively to Jesus' words spoken to you and to Peter, "Do you love me? Tend my Sheep" (cf. John 21:15-17). As Christian leaders, we're committed to intentionally grow in our love for Jesus and to teach His beloveds how to live in His love as well.

We must continually connect the two aspects of learning—information and experience, knowing about and knowing personally. The following chapter will focus primarily on the experiential aspect of spiritual formation. However, we cannot keep them separated in the life of the church. While we may "teach" about prayer in one setting, we must always provide opportunities to "experience" prayer in another. The questions that emerge from our learners' experience will inform what we teach.

We can tell people that they will encounter Jesus by extending loving care for the poor and needy, but when the connection really happens to them personally, the scriptural truth, "When you have done it to the least of these, you have done it to me," fully comes alive (cf. Matthew 25:40-45).

Tammy Long describes her integration of information and formation at South Bay Community Church in Fremont, California.

> When we focus on the "how" and "who" rather than the "what," the curriculum becomes secondary to the formational facilitation of the teacher. Therefore, teachers need to know how to intentionally listen to the Holy Spirit. ...Now, even in a "regular" Sunday school class, I am more interested in what God may be saying in the group and how I can create the space for personal and community reflection, than I am concerned about making sure I get through all the course material.
>
> I feel practices such as holy listening and spiritual discernment are important for teachers to understand, learn, and incorporate to be able to balance the head and heart. I typically have explained this as dual consciousness, listening to the students and the Spirit. I also like JD's comment below about listening to what is alive in me as I teach.

Finding the Settings Where People Learn Best

Where do adults, in your congregation, receive teaching? For most of our churches, gone are the days of the age-focused Sunday School class for adults. In most of our churches, only a small percentage of adults attend any type of formal Christian education opportunities. More typically, adults go to worship and take their kids to a simultaneous Children's Sunday School. Or, they drop them off for Sunday School and go out for coffee. For most congregations, "teaching adults" happens through the weekly monologue sermon. Too many times, for example, we expect to impact congregational life through an adult class when less than five percent of our people attend adult classes. Some churches provide learning opportunities in small groups, Bible Studies, or other settings. Community and spiritual friendships also provide essential contexts for discovering the truths about relationship with God. In relationships of vulnerability and honesty, we learn to recognize God's presence in one another and to see that He meets each one of us uniquely and personally.

When we start planning to teach, we must consider the venues in which our people can actually receive the teaching they need. Probably, you will need a variety of settings to reach a significant percentage of your membership. For example, sermons might be designed to teach enough to fan the flames, as well as provide invitations to deeper learning opportunities. In Chapter 6, we discussed the importance of identifying areas of congregational life where we're already seeing life, energy, and fire as places to start. For some of our ministries, like youth, men's, women's, and small groups, the venue may have to change for each ministry focus. Once personal vision becomes embedded, members may become willing to adjust their schedules to attend special retreats and classes.

Chris Schutte comments about the importance of Sunday morning to model our journey of spiritual formation.

> *How do you get the basic contours of spiritual formation into the minds and hearts of the congregation? Hopefully Sunday morning worship, whatever your liturgy, can be used along these lines as well. The rhythm of song, silence, prayer, scripture, creed, confession, Eucharist, and dismissal is deeply formative in both intellectual and experiential ways.*

As a point of contrast, JD Ward worries about depending too much on Sunday morning and formal classes.

> *The invitation language for Christian Education is also so important. I have found so few people are willing to commit to classes, let alone*

the kind of time it takes to do real formation. The idea that this can happen in a worship service is not something I strongly believe in. That might be hard to hear, but I think most people come prepared to serve with certain expectations, and it is really hard to get past those expectations most of the time for most of the people. The consumer mentality runs strong. So, the idea of doing formation in less formal settings is an important strategy.

Designing a Spiritual Formation Training Center in the Church

With these general considerations in mind, let's explore how we might design a "spiritual formation training center" within our church life. Lets use an image of a pilgrim torchbearer to consider what our people need to learn to successfully grow in their love for God and for their neighbor. This helps us picture our spiritual formation teaching ministry in the "journey" analogy we've been using for spiritual growth. Imagine our members, our living, moving, adventurous logs, setting off on their journey of spiritual discovery and growth. Not only have they been dressed in the right clothing, equipped with a backpack and the necessary gear, but they're each carrying a fire—maybe only a flickering match, maybe a candle, maybe even a torch. They're on a lifelong adventure with Jesus as their Shepherd. Probably most of our journeyers won't like being called "logs," or sheep, for that matter, so let's call them "pilgrims"—contagious fire pilgrims!

Therefore, when we ask ourselves what we need to teach these fiery pilgrims, to help them successfully navigate their spiritual formation journey, we might use this trek imagery and the support our pilgrims need to know in each aspect. Let's explore these five elements and discuss each in turn.

In Shape and Dressed for The Journey: What heart readiness toward God and what knowledge do our people need to have to become suitably dressed for the journey?

Equipped with a Map and GPS: How can we teach our travelers about the destination, the trails, their companions, and the terrain?

Backpacks and Gear: What resources do we need for the trek ahead?

Cross Trainers for Long-Range Journeys: How do we teach in ways that both provide information and further equips people for discovery as they experience more of God?

Base Camps for Renewal: How do we provide teaching opportunities to address new questions birthed in new experiences on the journey?

In Shape and Dressed for the Journey: -What heart readiness toward God and what knowledge do our people need to have to become suitably dressed for the journey? Two passages come to mind that speak of being "in shape" and "outfitted."

> But whatever things were gain to me, those things I have counted as a loss for the sake of Christ. More than that, I count all things to be loss in view of the surpassing value of knowing Christ Jesus my Lord, for whom I have suffered the loss of all things, and count them but rubbish so that I may gain Christ, and may be found in Him, not having a righteousness of my own derived from the Law, but that which is through faith in Christ, the righteousness which comes from God on the basis of faith, that I may know Him and the power of His resurrection and the fellowship of His sufferings, being conformed to His death; in order that I may attain to the resurrection from the dead. Not that I have already obtained it or have already become perfect, but I press on so that I may lay hold of that for which also I was laid hold of by Jesus Christ. Brethren, I do not regard myself as having laid hold of it yet; but one thing I do: forgetting what lies behind and reaching forward to what lies ahead, I press on toward the goal for the prize of the upward call of God in Christ Jesus. Philippians 3:7-14

> Finally, be strong in the Lord and in the strength of His might. Put on the full armor of God, so that you will be able to stand firm against the schemes of the devil.... Therefore, take up the full armor of God, so that you will be able to resist in the evil day, and having done everything, to stand firm. Stand firm therefore, having girded your loins with truth, and having put on the breastplate of

righteousness, and having shod your feet with the underline preparation of the gospel of peace; in addition to all, taking up the shield of faith with which you will be able to extinguish all the flaming arrows of the evil one. And take the helmet or salvation, and the sword of the Spirit, which is the word of God. Ephesians 6:10-11, 13-17

I've underlined key words in these two passages which could provide a core curriculum which might be adapted for sermons, classes, small groups, etc. As the apostle Paul says, although we haven't attained perfection, we do need to understand the basics about the nature of God, His call of love on our lives, grace, our responsibility to respond in faith and obedience, with the help of the Holy Spirit, etc. Without these basics, we will misinterpret the leading of our Good Shepherd and respond inappropriately to our experiences along the way.

These passages, and many others, address the foundational preparation and covering needed by every Christian. Their truths become particularly important for those of us who have caught fire with the desire to know our Lord more intimately and launch onto a journey into the abundant life of the Kingdom. We'll find every member of our church in a different place regarding these fundamentals of their faith. Some of our people may already be "in shape," "ready to run the race," and "dressed for the journey" through many years of listening to sermons, attending classes, prayer, and personal Bible Study. Others may only understand these profound truths at a surface level, yet may not feel the need for a class in Basic Christianity. As we discussed earlier, it may take the fire of God's touch and a new personal vision for the contagious fire journey to enable this latter group to realize what they don't know and now want to learn. We have to look for opportunities to teach into the questions that people have begun to ask, and meet them in the settings in which they can ask them.

Terry Tarleton commented on this level of teaching in his own congregation.

Certainly, there are no easy answers nor a "one-size-fits-all" approach that will work for every congregation! While we don't use a specific curriculum in our church, we have used a number of really good books as introductions for various aspects of formation. I have taught Teresa's material via "Mansions of the Heart," and found it to be invaluable as a starting place. When people find themselves in Mansion Two, they know what to expect next. Personally, I was blown away when I read about more of the "being stages" (4-7). I remember telling my wife—even though we had been saved all of our lives (both saved as young children), "Why didn't we know there's so much more?" Just the ability to have something to hang my hat on when I tell our people "there's more" was amazing. I have had many people come to me with tears in their eyes and thank me for giving them hope that an intimate relationship with Jesus is really possible. Just knowing what to expect next and that there is so much more was freeing for Janice and me, and we are so excited to help others find their place on the journey.

Equipped with a Map and GPS: How can we teach our travelers about the destination, the trails, and the terrain? Where are we going? What does the terrain look like? What obstacles might we face along the way? Who will be accompanying us on the journey? Will we meet "bad guys" in our travels, and what defenses do we have? What do we need to know about our Good Shepherd who guides us?

In light of those questions, most of us must admit that we, like Terry, have failed to teach a biblically faithful description of our lifelong journey with God. We may have taught about the initial stages of discipleship, presented the Four Spiritual Laws, provided biblical overviews, and in a few cases, encouraged our people to discover their spiritual gifts. Even our seekers have journeyed with God to some degree, and many of our pilgrims will have journeyed into a deep and loving relationship with the Lord. To what extent, however, have they been prepared for their journey with Jesus?

The Willow Creek "Reveal" studies show that those who have journeyed the furthest—the "Christ-Centered Believers" tend to express the greatest dissatisfaction with church programs and their relevance to their personal spiritual growth.[2] When people don't understand the journey and become confused, they generally become unhappy and tend to blame others. We all need to know what to expect in our lifelong relationship with God and feel that we are growing and making progress.

Therefore, we want to choose a paradigm for spiritual growth and missional outreach that makes sense to our pilgrims—one that describes a journey of hope, joy, meaning, and personal fulfillment. Remember that we want to address people's personal vision for life with God, not an institutional vision—no matter what journey model we use. We might choose the ancient model of purgation, illumination, and union. We may prefer something that sounds more contemporary such as Seeker, New Believer, Disciple, and Christ-centered. From our earlier chapters, you already know my bias. We need a model that emerges from the long history of the Church; one that has been validated over the centuries. The model should represent the clear teaching of Scripture and contain markers that relate to our experiences of God along the way. In our increasingly global culture, our paradigm for spiritual formation must describe our fundamental growth in relationship with God, independent of individual cultural norms and assumptions such as levels of education, access to literature, availability of retreat centers, luxury of free time, etc. Teresa's seven stages of growth use the analogies of growing up and maturing as a person (the first three Mansions), followed by falling in love and becoming married (Mansions four through seven). I find that the Seven Mansions described by Teresa of Avila best fits these criteria.

Having made a case for Teresa's model, I recognize we each must use a model with which our pilgrims can relate. After studying the Mansions paradigm, you might feel that seven phases of growth contain more detail than your people need. Conversely, a three-word model may prove too simplistic to be helpful. *Imago Christi* originally used the Teresian model, as it's described in *Mansions of the Heart*, in our Spiritual Formation Discovery

---

2. Willow Creek Association, *Reveal: Where are You*. Available from www. willowcreek.com

for Leaders retreats, designed for Christian leaders—men and women well along in their spiritual maturing process. Soon we began to receive requests from these leaders to provide the Discoveries in congregational settings. Initially, we were concerned that the Teresian model might be too complex or deal with experience too far beyond less mature believers. We have found, however, after hundreds of Discoveries in many countries, that the model has been well received by virtually all of our participants. We've been careful, however, to present the Mansions primarily using testimony narratives rather than downloading all the detail that's available.

Imago Christi has also experienced that people appreciate a model based upon historical roots, even if we decide to use a simplified version. For example, a Study Group of the Spiritual Formation Partners in Denver, Colorado, identified four stages based on Teresa's paradigm. Each of the four stages of growth correlate to the Teresian mansions, so that both teachers and learners can draw upon the considerable material available to describe their spiritual journey. They felt the following stages would be helpful for modern congregations.

Seekers – Pre-Christians

New Christians – Mansions 1-2

Workers with Jesus – Mansion 3

Falling in Love with Jesus and Loving God – Mansion 4-7

Centennial Covenant, in Littleton, Colorado, has also adapted the seven stages described by Teresa into four stages. Their Journey Team felt that keeping the transitional Mansion 4 stage would prove helpful. They settled on the following stages:

Seeking and <u>Following</u> Jesus – Mansions 1-2

<u>Growing</u> through Learning and Serving – Mansion 3

Abiding with Jesus – Mansion 4

Deepening Intimacy of Love – Mansions 5-7

Both groups listed curriculum topics for each of their stages. I have included both curriculum outlines in Appendix B. However, most congregations that we've worked with have simply used the Teresian Mansions paradigm, using easily understood language and examples to describe it.

Now that you've selected a Journey Map that adequately describes stages of spiritual growth and the accompanying experiences within each stage, we may want to teach our pilgrims to use their spiritual "GPS," enabling our pilgrims to locate themselves generally on the map. *Imago Christi's* Teresian Mapping Tool may prove helpful in addition to reading and studying the descriptions of the stages of growth. The Mapping Tool, with personal coaching, can be found on the *Imago Christi* website.

Backpacks and Gear: Now that we've selected our Map and helped our pilgrims locate their place on it, we can consider other questions our pilgrims may want addressed along the way. What do we need in our backpacks—what resources will help us journey with Jesus and have fun? Because the meat of this material has been covered in Chapter 2's discussion about the nature of spiritual formation, I'll only say a few words here. When we think of the "Backpack," we want to think "resources" rather than upfront teaching. While we can address these topics in a traditional class, these topics lend themselves more to "just-in-time" learning. While we may orient our pilgrims to the topics before they head out, the real answers to their questions lies in their backpacks.

I'd suggest that the minimum load for pilgrim backpack should include:

Self- Knowledge – Trekking Style

Abiding Prayer – Time in the Tent

Spiritual Community – Companions on Our Journey

Spiritual Disciplines – Trekking Principles

Spiritual Warfare – Fending Off the Bad Guys, Inside and Out

Spiritual Direction and Coaching – Just-In-Time Help

Guide Books – Insights From Those Who've Gone Before Us

Let's discuss each one, in turn.

Self- Knowledge – Trekking Style

While we can describe a "standard" spiritual growth journey, each person will experience it somewhat differently and find some practices more or less helpful than others. Personal reflection about temperament, learning style, view of God, past wounding, etc., can prove invaluable in our ability to understand our own experience and recognize God's leading voice. We discussed Self-Knowledge at some length in Chapter 2.

Abiding Prayer – Time in the Tent

Because this is a relational journey—deepening intimacy with God, communication with God lies at its heart. Like any relationship, as intimacy deepens the nature of our communication changes. While not wanting to force a pilgrim into some new form of prayer, we do want them to understand how prayer progresses as intimacy increases. In the early stages of our growth, our prayer focuses on information. We communicate with God primarily through talking to Him and asking for information and help. Gradually, our prayer focuses on relationship, knowing and being known. "Listening to God" becomes more important than speaking what God already knows.

As intimacy grows further, we discover that language can actually impede heart communication between Lover and Beloved. We need to learn to commune in silence and intuit spiritually. Knowing the general progression of prayer can help us realize when God changes the band on our GPS and how to "wait upon the Lord" in ways consistent with our relationship with

Him. Our fire must have a safe place to burn and grow. *Imago Christi's Spiritual Formation Coaching Manual* contains some excellent resources on Abiding Prayer.

Spiritual Community – Companions on Our Journey

Many of our pilgrims may have seen their spiritual life to be largely a private matter. Trekking with God, together with other believers, may not feel natural and even threatening. The principles of Christian community that we've discussed in Chapter 2 and Chapter 3 and the experience of some of those basic practices will prove vital for the successful journey of our pilgrims. While some people have developed spiritual friendships that can support their journey, most of us need help to identify fellow travelers and contexts for interaction. Our personal love for God burns brighter in the company of others who share their fire with us and encourage us when our flames seem to falter. In this company of fellow pilgrims, we learn to let our fire burn for God in others and to receive His flames through them.

Spiritual Disciplines – Trekking Principles

Dozens of spiritual practices have been identified that can help us become available to God in our growing relationship with Him. God can use disciplines such as prayer, Scripture study and meditation, solitude, rest and Sabbath, spiritual reading, rule of life, spiritual friendship, etc., to make our pilgrimage an amazing discovery. Their appropriate use, however, will depend on one's place in the journey, temperament, etc. Familiarity with spiritual disciplines and access to more information about them will further prepare our pilgrims for a wonderful adventure. Our fire becomes strong as we lean close to Jesus. Spiritual disciplines help us lean into the flames of God's love. Richard Foster's *Celebration of Discipline* and Adel Calhoun's *Spiritual Disciplines Handbook* provide some excellent resources.[3]

Spiritual Warfare – Fending Off the Bad Guys, Inside and Out

3. Richard Foster, *Celebration of Discipline: The Path to Spiritual Growth.* (San Francisco, Harper Collins, 1978). Adel Calhoun, *Spiritual Disciplines Handbook: Practices that Transform Us* (Downers Grove, IL, InterVarsity Press, 2005)

Scripture, particularly the New Testament, clearly teaches that spiritual warfare will be part of our experience in this world. Despite warfare's presence in the Gospels and Acts, and teaching about it in the Epistles, most modern Christians have never received biblical teaching about our enemy and his tactics, or take the devil seriously. I cannot count the number of times I have heard believers say something like, "I never gave the devil a second thought until I became intentional about my spiritual growth and began recognizing his temptations." While Scripture teaches us that our enemy, Satan, need never have power over us, we continually see the "Father of Lies" tempt and confuse our people. Some believers have become so accustomed to those lies they have come to confuse the lies with what they really believe. Worse, still, some mistake the enemy's lies with the voice of God.

The gift of discerning spirits has been given to every believer, but what good does it do if we've never been taught to use it? The apostles James and Peter both teach us that, in Christ, we simply have to resist the devil. How can we do that if we haven't learned to recognize him? Sending our pilgrims out without an understanding of the spiritual warfare they will encounter will certainly set them up for disaster. While darkness will never ultimately overcome the Light of Christ, our enemy will certainly try to douse our flames and, if possible, extinguish our torch. Proactive teaching and community support can help us journey in Christ's victory. While a number of books have been written about spiritual warfare, I prefer to simply teach from the Scriptures and bypass much of the speculation that seems to be added to the biblical teachings.

Spiritual Direction and Coaching – Just in Time Help

We've discussed the importance of spiritual direction and coaching many times in the previous chapters and will discuss it in greater detail in Chapter 11. While some of our pilgrims may have spiritual communities adequate to provide the support they need, many more will benefit from a listening and discerning relationship of spiritual direction and coaching. We've said that increasing intimacy with the Lord brings greater self-knowledge and the awareness of wounds and blocks to growth that have inhibited our journey. Finding these skilled helpers with whom our pilgrims can share honestly about their wounds and blocks, and receive guidance and healing, often opens the door to further spiritual growth. We need others to see and affirm the fire within us and help us discern how our Lord reaches out to us with the fire of His love.

> For this reason, I remind you to fan into flame the gift of God, which is in you through the laying on of my hands. For God did not give us a spirit of timidity, but a spirit of power, of love and of self-discipline. 2 Timothy 1:6-7 NIV

Grafted Life Ministries provides an excellent inventory of trained spiritual directors. See www.graftedlife.org.

Guide Books – Insights from Those Who've Gone Before Us

Most of our traveling pilgrims continue to benefit from direct teaching and coaching. Many times, however, new vistas can be discovered, and questions answered through the experiences of the countless women and men who have traveled the journey before us. For example, authors like Richard Foster, have provided wonderful overviews of the journey of prayer that might be perfectly adequate for a pilgrim in the early phases of their journey. Later on, this same traveler may benefit from the writings of the Desert Fathers and the Church Fathers and Mothers on the mysteries of infused prayer. For those early in their prayer development, devotional guides may provide a vital resource. Stories of people who have journeyed before us can encourage and instruct us. The Bible, of course, stands as our basic text. The more we get to know Jesus, the more that the Scriptures come alive to us and our reading moves from learning to personal discovery—of God Himself! Many spiritual formation books provide excellent bibliographies. *Imago Christi's Spiritual Formation Coaching Manual* and the *Spiritual Formation Discovery*

Workbook provide annotated bibliographies, organized by Mansion.[4] James M. Houston's *Classics of Faith and Devotion Series* gives us access to some of Christianity's great men and women of God.[5] Christian history records countless numbers of believers set on fire through the stories and teaching of women and men ablaze with the glory of God.

Cross Trainers for Long-Range Journeys Appropriate teaching methods for a Journey Perspective

The most important "teaching" we can do might be to "teach our teachers." As we mentioned earlier, most pastors and teachers have been wired as "left-brain" learners. We learn through information and concepts. Many, if not most, of our congregants learn more effectively through story and experience—visually, with the right side of their brains. While each of us has some inborn learning "preference," we all learn best using all of our gray matter. Furthermore, many truths about the spiritual life can only become real to us through experience. For example, we can <u>say</u> that God answers prayer and quote numerous Scripture verses as proof. We only <u>believe</u> that God answers prayer, however, when He actually answers OUR prayers.

While books and prepared curriculum can provide very helpful sources from which to teach, we must also develop the kinds of teaching skills which facilitate spiritual learning. If we teachers hope to cooperate with the Holy Spirit's work within our pilgrims, we need to become intentional about developing the way we teach. As we respond to questions that emerge during the journey, we must not only provide helpful information, but facilitate guided experiences in which our pilgrims can discover God's answer for themselves. We've already discussed the following list of teaching attributes, so I will simply list them here. Then we'll look at some significant insights from one of our Contributors about putting them into practice.

---

4. The Spiritual Formation Coaching Manual can be purchased from www. imagochristi.org and Amazon.
5. Houston, James M, *Classics of Faith and Devotion.* Bethany House Publishers, Minneapolis Minnesota, 1984, 1996

Responding to questions rather than simply giving information

Personal vulnerability which encourages openness and honesty

Facilitating personal discovery through reflective questions and experience

Connecting the experience of loving God and caring for neighbor

Starting our teaching from a biblical and local tradition

Using language that our people understand

Finding the settings where people learn best

Connecting intellectual and experiential learning

JD Ward shares some examples from his ministry about integrating these eight teaching attributes, using his five categories.

Two things we have found helpful is to define how transformation might happen and what are some good teaching principles for formation teachers. ReWire has used both of these in our teaching of pastors and found them very helpful to reshape the pastor's training. For our transformational teaching, we talk about the balance of time, God's Presence, guidance, reflection, community and exposure in every formation process we begin. We use the following Five Principles of A Rewire Teacher as a guide.

1. SPEAK TO THE HEART
It is important to understand that the curriculum is only the vehicle through which transformation happens. The curriculum is designed to open people up to the work of the Spirit in their lives. Often, it is necessary to veer from the curriculum content to deal with what the Spirit is doing in the members of the class. Therefore, teachers must be aware of three voices at once. Teachers attempt to listen to the Spirit, listen to the heart questions of the participants, and listen to what is alive in themselves as they teach. If we are to speak to the heart, it is important to keep this order.

2. BRING PEOPLE TO THE UNKNOWN
The ReWire curriculum, especially in Beyond, is designed to create angst in people so that the disequilibrium moves participants to make the commitments necessary to resolve this internal crisis.

It is not a curriculum to create mastery over some scriptural text or theological truth. It will often provoke people and challenge long-held assumptions. This is intentional. For if we don't move people past their known knowledge and into a new, unknown land, transformation is impossible. Therefore, we teach to create this angst. Most teachers have been trained to resolve this tension. In ReWire, we do not feel the need to resolve tension. We let people live with it and encourage them to resolve the tension for themselves. Therefore, we do not feel the need to answer questions when they are asked. We assess if the tension would better serve the participant than receiving an answer, and then act accordingly.

*3. JOIN PEOPLE IN THE HARD PLACES OF THE JOURNEY
People do not need experts, they need fellow sojourners. We expose our own vulnerabilities, questions, and needs. In this way, we move the class setting, that has classically been understood as teacher/ student, to one that embraces more of a midwife motif. We are to coach people through the process that gives birth to something new in their lives. Vulnerability and struggle are hallmarks of a well-taught course. Helping carve out the nature of a real question is essential in teaching ReWire. In essence, we teach to the question that is worthy of a pondering for a significant amount of time.*

*4. SPIRITUAL APPRENTICESHIP VERSUS SPIRITUAL DIRECTOR
In classic spiritual direction, a director reflects back to participants questions that help people see God in a new way, in the context of their lives. This is highly valuable. However, for the ReWire classes we choose an apprentice approach. We walk with people, but perhaps just a slight bit ahead of them, in the journey. We may not know the destination, but we know the questions that will get us all to a new understanding. We unapologetically come into the spiritual relationship with a new agenda, a new idea, or a new path to discovery. Then, in the midst of offering this new data, we carry out spiritual direction with the participant on how they are responding to that data.*

*5. MAXIMIZE THE POWER OF REFLECTIVE COMMUNITY
People enter community when they have a common journey. ReWire classes are designed to create a community that is on a journey of discovery. In community, people find they have commonness with others, even while their own voice is affirmed and developed. Even*

more so, community takes root in people's lives when personal reflection deepens each person's sharing. It is the teacher, then, that holds this communal learning sacred as well as helps give voice to the cooperative learning ethos. The teacher should learn ways to maximize this process in the structure of the class as well as be adept at intuitively fostering communal learning in less formal teaching times. (You can discover more about ReWire and its resources at www.crmleaders.org/teams/rewire.)

Carrying a flame through life may seem pretty straightforward, but we're talking about Holy Fire—Consuming Fire. God's fire always seems clouded in mystery; it bursts into a blaze just when it seems to be going out, it shines the way forward when all we see is total darkness; it goes underground in the hearts of seekers who seem to be traveling in the wrong direction; Holy Fire always confuses us. We'll never be able to carry the torch of God's glorious love alone. We'll always need brothers and sisters who can encourage and teach us along the way and pick us up when we fall.

Base Camps for Renewal: How to teach into new questions birthed in new experiences of the journey? How can we provide opportunities for rest, growth, and encouragement along the way?

I remember drooling over a friend's story about his raft trip down the Colorado River and through the Grand Canyon. He'd signed up some years before his turn came to join a raft trip company and several other rafters on this two-week whitewater adventure. Months before their departure, he received literature about his pre-trip exercise program and the equipment he needed to bring. To be fit enough to travel safely on this trip, he would have to be able to swim against the current, lift himself or another rafter from the water into the raft, and help carry the raft and the gear. His suggested gym workout plan would prepare him for the physical fitness test that he would have to pass to board the raft.

The day finally came when he met the river guides upstream of their departure point. He said that he was so excited that he'd almost forgotten everything he'd learned in preparation. He barely passed his fitness test, and they set off down the beautiful blue Colorado River. After hours of thrilling, but exhausting, rowing and holding on for dear life, they finally arrived at their nighttime camp. To his surprise, tents had already been set up, his gear neatly stowed in a tent with his name on it. Dinner wafted in the air with a delicious intoxication that floated to the hungriest stomach he'd ever experienced. After an amazing supper and before an early bedtime, his guides told jokes and taught the real lessons of river rafting and the skills they would need for the coming day's adventure. While the rest of my friend's story expounded mountainous waves and endless canyon walls, the heart of his adventure often recalled the base camps—the lessons he learned and the friends he made in those adventure retreats. What might "Base Camps" look like for our spiritual formation pilgrims?

Let's reflect a bit about the purpose of a "Base Camp(s)" in a hiking or mountain climbing situation. Because we're talking about a long-distance journey, I'd like to think of multiple Base Camps rather than the one often used for mountain climbers. Base Camps provide:

Pre-prepared safe places to stop

Professionals available to care for the needs of the travelers

Provisions and supplies for the travelers, both for their time in camp and for the coming journey

Opportunity for rest and renewal

Training about the coming phase of the journey, new equipment and methods, etc.

While we'll be discussing spiritual formation experiential opportunities in the following chapter, let's reflect here about Base Camp style teaching opportunities. Base Camps, by definition, provide "just off the trail" opportunities. Therefore, we need to imagine some stop, rest, and learn events positioned outside our pilgrims' regular life and ministry experience. Therefore, Base Camps wouldn't fit as part of the regular Sunday School program or simply a unique evening in a small group or Bible Study group, or part of a home study program. To get our pilgrims "off the scene" in a restful learning environment, we might consider a retreat experience, a banquet with a special speaker, an outing or trip, or a conference, etc. There might be value in arranging Base Camps for a fixed group of pilgrims that would gather together periodically. Alternatively, our pilgrims might enjoy getting to know other people in a more come-as-you-can arrangement. Base Camps could be designed around topics, such as abiding prayer, Scripture meditation, mercy missions, worship, discovering God in the arts, etc. Base Camps might focus simply on rest and renewal, like guided or unguided silent retreats. Base Camps designed for particular phases of spiritual growth could explore participants' personal experiences and the changes that accompany those stages.

One might imagine Base Camps scheduled a year in advance with a variety of settings and topics from which people could choose to fit their schedule and interest. Assuming that our pilgrims have been taught about the spiritual formation journey and have had opportunity to locate themselves within that paradigm, they should be able to select the Base Camps which best fit their needs. We have discussed the kind of teaching style that best facilitates spiritual formation, but our focus on addressing questions rather than dumping information will be particularly important for our Base Camps. "Answering questions" doesn't mean we have to limit our teaching to responding to specific questions posed by participants, but addressing issues that may arise experientially related to the topic of the Base Camp.

For example, a Base Camp on Abiding Prayer might invite participants to participate in a process that would help them surface issues they face or their concerns about how to proceed. Followed by a time of silence and personal prayer, participants would meet in small groups and share their experiences of prayer at the Base Camp, in comparison with their regular daily devotional times. Groups might then identify two or three questions or topics of concern that surfaced in their discussion. The group leader would collect these topics and give them to the Base Camp leaders to help guide the following teaching and discussion time.

We might imagine a Mercy Base Camp where participants meet at a downtown hotel. They might visit a homeless shelter, help serve a meal, and talk with the residents. The evening and night could be designated as a silent solitude time to reflect on their experience, pray, and surface issues which emerged within them. The next day's teaching and sharing time could focus on those issues as well as material that prepares the participants to explore their own role in loving their neighbor as Jesus has loved them.

In every case, Base Camp must be made a "sacred place" where safety, vulnerability, honesty, and confidentiality provide an opportunity to learn without being judged.

We know that teaching about spiritual formation forms a critical building block in our vision for contagious fire. Returning to our analogies, fire can be a wonderful and beautiful thing, if one knows how to use it. It can also burn and destroy when misused. Likewise, hiking can provide an exhilarating adventure when hikers understand their own capability and the rigors of the trail ahead. Poor judgment and missed trails can prove painful and discouraging. For our journey of spiritual growth—our deepening intimacy of love with our Lord Jesus, we need to understand a wide range of information from the basics of the Gospel. We need to understand the clear teaching of Scripture about our spiritual growth, self-knowledge, Kingdom worldview, and healing; then we can progress to spiritual disciplines and the mysteries of intimacy with God.

We've also agreed that information alone doesn't often change hearts. Beyond "knowing about" God, we're called to "know God" personally. This personal and relational knowing involves both understanding the truth about God and experiencing its reality in everyday life. Our teaching becomes most effective when tied directly to opportunities to experience God personally, in new ways and depths.

> Prescribe and teach these things. Let no one look down on your youthfulness, but rather in speech, conduct, love, faith and purity, show yourself an example of those who believe. Until I come, give attention to the public reading of Scripture, to exhortation and teaching. Do not neglect the spiritual gift within you, which was bestowed on you through prophetic utterance with the laying on of hands by the presbytery. Take pains with these things; be absorbed in them, so that your progress will be evident to all. Pay close attention to yourself and to your teaching; persevere in these things, for as you do this you will ensure salvation both for yourself and for those who hear you. 1 Timothy 4:11-16

Remember the story of the two disciples who met Jesus on the road to Emmaus?

> Then their eyes were opened, and they recognized Him; and He vanished from their sight. They said to one another, 'Were not our hearts burning within us while He was speaking to us on the road, while He was explaining the Scriptures to us?" Luke 24:31-32

That's what we want to happen to our pilgrims as they receive our teaching—opened eyes, recognition of Jesus, and burning hearts!

CHAPTER 8

TOUCHING THE FIRE - OPPORTUNITIES FOR EXPERIENTIAL DISCOVERY

Eons ago, my wife and I served as volunteer high school youth workers in our small church in Southern California. One weekend we took our twenty kids on a retreat in the mountains to reflect on some profound book which I have long since forgotten. What I have never forgotten, and never will, came out of a surprise discussion started by one of the students who, like most of the rest of the group, had grown up in the church. She interrupted the study and stated that she seriously doubted that God existed. She hypothesized that religions were invented by people just to give themselves some hope beyond the current mess that humankind experienced. To our surprise, several of the other kids shared common doubts. The discussion ran late into the evening with various speculations about God, the Bible, heaven and hell, and the Church. This retreat wasn't turning out like I had planned at all.

Finally, in exasperation and exhaustion, I asked the group whether they just wanted to philosophize or find out the truth. What could they say? They all voted for the truth. I suggested a thirty-day Christian experiment: Each taker would commit as much of themselves as they could to as much of God as they could understand, no strings attached, and see what happened. The only condition would be that they would agree to say one honest prayer a day, even if it went something like, "I don't believe in you, God." We would reconvene in a month and see what happened. Whether through peer pressure or the work of the Holy Spirit, every one of the students took me up on the experiment. To my knowledge, every one of them became committed Christians and a few of them pastors. Our Lord sparked fires of love within their hearts—they experienced God. Their contagious testimonies changed our church into a beacon of light which shines to this day. Those students not only experienced God, they became contagious fires that ignited hundreds, if not thousands, of fires of love around the world.

In Chapter 7, we considered the "teaching" components necessary to introduce spiritual formation and missional outreach to a congregation. We discussed how to help our "logs"—we decided to call them "pilgrims," understand that it is God who ignites His love within them. He then keeps their fragile flames alive by inviting them into community where they'll live with other pilgrims. By journeying together, each person experiences the support of one another's flame so that they can grow up to full maturity in love. We have to find ways to help them respond to their call to become torchbearers to the world as they journey with Jesus. As in each of our chapters, we stressed that no "one-size-fits-all" curriculum exists. Each leadership team must assess the needs of their own congregation and start by addressing the questions people long to understand. As we discussed in Chapter 6, that means that we must know the history of our congregations, as well as the perceived needs currently sitting in the pews.

We also agreed that intellectual understanding addresses only a part, maybe a small part actually, of what we need to "know" in our relationship with God. While "knowledge about" God provides vital foundations, "knowledge of God" provides the essence of our relationship with Him. Learning everything there is to know about fire doesn't set us on fire. Now, in Chapter 8, we're ready to take the next step, and it's really simple. If we want to grow in a loving relationship with God, we must actually experience God—enter His fire of love. Let's explore, therefore, how to help people experience the flames of God's love for themselves.

Bill O'Byrne reflects about the vital importance of actually experiencing God in our spiritual growth.

> It is the experience of God that breaks through all of the walls we've set up to God, or boxes we've put Him in. The experience of God outside of our neatly constructed concepts and presuppositions allows us, even forces us, to abandon our defenses and cooperate and engage with what we now know is true about Him. Our faith grows, not because someone told us, but because we know the truth and reality of God experientially. It is this confrontation with a Reality beyond ourselves that truly transforms us! Experience is not merely ancillary to belief, but an essential aspect of it.

Would it be an exaggeration to say that the vast majority of Christians go to their graves unable to recall a single time that they actually experienced God? I'm not saying that God has not acted in their lives, just that they haven't recognized it. One can have a transactional relationship with God but miss the glorious gift of knowing Him personally. We know that human relationships build through interpersonal experience and interaction. Our relationship with God develops and grows in the same way. While it is true that "in Him we live, move, and have our being,"—living every moment in God—most of us have never learned to discern God's presence in an ongoing way (cf. Acts 17:28). While the Holy Spirit constantly tries to reveal the Trinity to us, we must learn to become attentive and aware. Then we can become receptive and responsive, as well.

For example, if we decide to experience the stars that surround our planet by occasionally gazing past the streetlights while we walk the dog in the evening, we might conclude that the few stars that exist aren't all that interesting. Hopefully, someone would tell us that we must find a time and place where all the local light does not obscure the most magnificent lights we could imagine. So, on a dark night, away from the city and highway lights, maybe near Pagosa Springs, Colorado—at 8,000 feet where I live, we might look up and become astounded by the beauty that had beamed at us all the time—we just never saw it.

In the same way, we must find times alone when we can become still and perceive, with our hearts, our Lord who never leaves us. Recognizing our Lord can be as hard as seeing the stars through light and air pollution. Our Lord whispers words of love in a language with which we are not yet familiar. In time, we may learn to discern His presence in the stillness of our prayer closets, in others, and in the seemingly unimportant events of the day. Eventually, we get to know Him so well that we fall in love, and learn to intentionally cooperate with His courtship. Ultimately, God becomes more real to us than anything we could ever know with our senses—a Consuming Fire!

For this kind of deep loving relationship to develop, however, we need to engage in the kinds of experiential opportunities that correspond with our current place in the journey. Dozens of "spiritual disciplines" can potentially provide ways for us to become attentive to God's presence. However, like any other activity, practices which prove appropriate and helpful for some leave others flat. While certain experiences become doorways to receiving God's light early in our journeys, these very same methods can become impediments as we grow in intimacy with Jesus. For example, devotional guides with daily scriptures may significantly facilitate prayer for people journeying through Mansions 1-4. However, that same tool might only distract those drawn to contemplation, journeying in Mansions 5-7. The Movements of Growth sections of Mansions of the Heart describe spiritual disciplines appropriate for each stage of spiritual development.

The problem, however, is that "spiritual" disciplines work differently than human ones; things just work differently in the Kingdom of God than they do in the kingdom of this world. We can work out regularly in the gym in ways that will consistently build body muscle. Conversely, only God can build spiritual muscle—our spiritual exercise only provides an opportunity for us to cooperate with Him in the process. Let's explore some of the important ways we enter into this cooperative process and how our church community might facilitate spiritual experience for our pilgrims and help them touch the Fire. We'll discuss ten vital aspects of spiritual experience:

1. **Discovering the Nature of Prayer**

2. **Experiencing God Through Experiments in Prayer**

3. **Encountering God in Scripture**

4. **The Necessity of the Prayer Closet**

5. **Meeting God in Guided and Silent Retreats**

6. **Experiencing God in Beauty**

7. **Sitting With God in Spiritual Direction**

8. **Meeting God in Spiritual Community**

9. **Meeting God Through Serving the "Poor"**

10. **Walking With God in a Rule of Life**

Discovering the Nature of Prayer

Before launching our pilgrims off into the appropriate disciplines for each stage of growth, we must first consider the uniqueness of communion and communication in the Kingdom of God. We need to help our people understand something of the nature of spiritual relationship and experience unique to our life with God. Misconceptions can discourage believers who long to "hang out with God," but don't know what to expect, or expect the wrong things. For example, we often hear people talk about "hearing God's voice." However, if we expect to hear audible statements from God in our prayer times, we'll be very disappointed. While God certainly can speak out loud to us, He more often whispers to the heart. How do we relate to the

Trinity when we can't use our senses to help us?

Sometimes, we must unlearn old patterns. My early disciplers taught me that I could talk to God. The communication formula went something like this. God lives "up there," I live "down here," and messages can be sent back and forth. When my message contains a request, it will take some time for the "answer" to come down. If something happens in the following days that seems associated with a "yes" answer to my question, I should assume that God has answered my request favorably. If "nothing" happens, I can guess the answer to be "no," or at least "not now." I can send up as much information as I like; God never tires of listening. However, Scripture's insistence that God already knows all that information confused me. Why would I talk on and on If He already knew what I was going to say? Occasionally, people would say that they'd "heard" something from God; but when questioned, the way that they "heard" usually seemed pretty vague to me. Although the Bible describes audible voices from heaven, appearances of angels, and signs and wonders, I soon learned that I should not expect these experiences today. Nevertheless, I took the formula at face value.

Most Christians that I knew spent their prayer time waiting for some "word" from the Lord. This waiting, however, had to be done with a Bible in hand because God only really "spoke" though the words printed in the Bible. I was told that if a passage I happened to read seemed related to my circumstance, then God was surely attempting to communicate with me.

Gradually, my frustration with the slow and unpredictable heavenly mail system grew. I finally I discovered a "better way." I could do all the "talking," but not have to wait for answers. Rather than waiting for the mail, I could make some great substitutions. My discovery of Oswald Chamber's *My Utmost for His Highest* became a great blessing.[1] Whether or not God was speaking to me, Oswald's insights proved profound. I often wondered how

---

1. Oswald Chambers, *My Utmost for His Highest, Grand Rapids Michigan, Dodd, Mead, & Company; Discovery House, 1935, 1992*

he got so smart. Reading Oswald made me smarter, too. Fortunately, God didn't leave me in this faulty prayer routine. He did enlighten me through Oswald's insights. Even though I might not be "hearing" from God, some inner prompting caused me to return again and again to that place of talking ~~and listening~~—called prayer.

Experiencing love in prayer also confused me. I was taught that God loved me, but His love would not be discernible through the normal channels with which I usually recognized love—words, touch, facial expression, etc. I would just have to take it on faith. Feelings were also to be held with suspicion—many factors could affect my emotions. Warm emotions couldn't be trusted to reveal God's love. Sometimes, however, people reported emotions of joy or peace to validate some contact with God. How would I know the real deal from my own inventions?

As I read more about prayer, I learned about solitude and silence. Solitude made some sense for the purpose of reducing distractions, although I found that no matter where I went, I brought plenty of distractions with me in my head. Silence, however, seemed pointless. People told me that I couldn't "hear" God if I did all the talking, but if one doesn't usually "hear" God audibly, then why the silence? The fact that I continued in regular prayer at all can only be attributed to God's profound mercy and loving persistence—something—Someone drew me nearer to the flame I could not see or feel.

Many years later, I learned that communication with God happens mostly in the "heart," rather than the brain or ears or eyes or mouth. Men and women who've spent their whole lives in prayer explained that I was born with a damaged, maybe dead, spiritual communication faculty that God built into me for the purposes of relating with Him. They went on to explain that when Jesus became my Lord and Savior, the Holy Spirit enlivened this faculty within me. My spirit, now made alive, could engage in two-way communication with God beyond the words, thoughts, touch, or feelings with which I learned to communicate with my fellow human beings.

Learning to use that God-given faculty, however, turned out to be no easy matter. While I wanted a predicable formula, prayer seemed frustratingly subjective. God continued to woo me, touching my heart with His healing flames of love—teaching it to recognize His heart and to listen with mine. Finally, the prayer of silence became for me more than the absence of speech or thoughts, but the very nature of communion with my Beloved. Love no longer referred to some emotion, or affection, but the very life of God in which I am invited to live—in Christ and with those around me.

We need to tell people about the nature of communion with God before we set them off on a journey of frustration and disillusionment. We also need to meet them in the frustration and disillusion they may already experience, and lead them into new opportunities to experience communion with God—the way He intended. Even though it takes a lifetime to fully live into communion with God, we can at least start the journey in the right direction, looking for the right signs, expecting the Holy Spirit to teach us.

Prayer speaks of relationship. The quality, depth, and frequency of communication indicates one's level of intimacy in any relationship. If you wanted to gauge the depth of relationship in my marriage, you'd ask how Charlotte and I spend time together and how we share what's on our minds and in our hearts. Communication, in our relationship with God, goes by the name "prayer." The nature of our prayer experience changes over time, similar to the way our communication with one another changes. As infants, we don't understand anything being said to us, but quite skillfully make our needs known. Without language, we use tone, volume, expressions, and movement to communicate. As we grow, we learn to understand language and to use it. Much of our school training focuses on developing our ability to communicate and to use language effectively. Maturing further, we communicate both in language and in more subtle body language with people close to us. Boys slap backs, hit, and wrestle. Girls hold hands, whisper, and giggle. As love enters our experience, communication grows, both in depth of information and in quantity. Eventually, "just being together" can express love and commitment more profoundly than language ever could. Long-married couples find that they've learned to intuit one another's thoughts and predict their next words. Sometimes in elder years, verbal communication can become difficult or impossible, but facial expressions, touches, and simple presence can communicate more than long letters or verbal sharing ever could. From the day we're born until the day we die, relationships revolve around communication. The nature of that communication, however, can radically change. Transitions also happen in our communication with God—prayer.

While Christians insist that relationship with God sustains us above all other relationships, it seems incredible that many believers spend little or no effort learning to communicate with God. Our Christian education programs focus more on the biblical history of other people's relationship with God than helping us experience ours. We may be given some beginner's model for our use of words such as ACTS, but we eventually learn that putting endless words to Adoration, Confession, Thanksgiving, and Supplication (ACTS) feels like leaving messages on an answering machine that never calls us back. Never mind that no one has taught us to learn God's language so that we could discern His communication to us. Imagine how few human love affairs we would have if the couple's communication became limited to a one-way "ACTS" monologue. How might we coach a couple who came to us pleading for help, saying, "We really want to get to know one another, maybe even fall in love, but how?" Believers who have been touched by God's love ask the same question—how! People need to learn how to have a conversation with God. While teaching about prayer can be helpful, nothing can substitute for practice, discovery, and coaching.

Experiencing God Through Experiments in Prayer

How might we encourage and help our pilgrims to travel a journey of prayer discovery, consistent with their life situation, personal wiring, and stage of spiritual growth? A spiritual mentor once suggested that I "experiment" with prayer and let God show me how He wanted us to communicate. The thought of experimentation felt freeing; some experiments worked, and some didn't. Discovery became the focus rather than success or failure. I felt affirmed that God would help me find a pattern for prayer that would be suited uniquely for me. I'd need someone to help me know where to start relative to my general space in my spiritual journey. I would have to explore what times and places seemed to help me become still and focus. Various tools, such as Scripture, devotionals, music, etc., could help me look beyond my busy activities to my relationship with God. Prayer partners and accountability relationships could help me stay with it and provide a place for me to debrief what I was learning.

Many resources have been written to help our pilgrims experiment with prayer. It's important to choose prayer and devotional resources that provide the right amount of structure and content for the individual person, as a function of their own preferences and stage of spiritual growth. Pilgrims who are relatively new to prayer will appreciate a structured prayer process, meaningful content, and even written prayers. The more experienced our pilgrim becomes in their conversation with God, structure may become a hindrance and Scriptural or devotional content less helpful. *Mansions of the Heart* addresses specific types of prayer appropriate to each stage of growth and lists helpful books and resources. The *Mansions Study Guide* provides Scripture and prayer exercises to help one explore each type of prayer.

Encountering God in Scripture

Learning about God and our ancestral history with Him occupies most of what we have traditionally called discipleship. Thankfully, the Canon of Scripture provides the boundaries, theological and historical, within which we understand God, ourselves as children of God, and the world. Our spiritual growth, as followers of Jesus, must align with the clear teaching of Scripture. Our "experiences" of God must be tested against Scripture's revelations about the ways God interacts with us in His New Covenant grace.

Without that foundation, we'll be left to our own speculations, affinities, and personal biases from which to interpret our relationship with God and our experience of His active presence in our lives. In the previous chapter, we discussed the possibility that teaching about spiritual formation begins by correcting misconceptions about God and His Kingdom that may have resulted from faulty teaching or the lack of biblical teaching at all. In any case, for our pilgrims to use Scripture as a place to meet God, they must understand the meaning of what they read, in the context of the particular text, and in the context of the central teaching of the New Testament.

We identify the Bible as Canon because we believe that the Holy Spirit inspired its writing and assembly. We also believe that the Holy Spirit inspires its reading and reflection. We can read Scripture for "information." We want to know about God and how to relate to Him, in the particulars of our lives. Less commonly, however, do believers meditate on Scripture as a context in which God communicates Himself—not just about Himself, personally, contextually, and relationally. Sometimes the information can actually distract us—we may focus on the history or theology and miss the "still small voice" of God speaking to us personally. Many of us "professional" Christians can recall how the rigors of Seminary or Bible College all but ruined our devotional use of the Bible. We became so focused on WHAT the passages said that we forgot about WHO wanted to speak to us personally in the text. Scripture itself, however, invites us to meet God within its words. For example:

I rise before dawn and cry for help;

I wait for Your words.

My eyes anticipate the night watches,

That I may meditate on Your word. Psalms 119:147-148

I remember the days of old;

I meditate on all Your doings;

I muse on the work of Your hands.

I stretch out my hands to You;

My soul longs for You, as a parched land. Selah. Psalms 143:5-6

God invites us to meditate on His Word, to personally meet Him in the context of Scripture. This meeting with God requires that we form new ways of addressing Scripture—more with our hearts than our heads—"listening" for God's word to us personally, at a new level. While Bible studies that focused on WHAT God was saying in a text have been vital to our development, now we must learn to become attentive to His "still small voice" within the text more intuitively. The Desert Fathers (the earliest Christian monks who inhabited the desert of the Middle East, starting at the end of the second century AD) teach that God "speaks" to us spiritually, to the heart rather than the head. While God can project His thoughts audibly through sound waves through our ears, His "voice" profoundly transcends verbal communication. For example, Genesis shows us that God's words not only communicate, but actually accomplish what they say.

For example:

In the beginning God created the heavens and the earth. The earth was formless and void, and darkness was over the surface of the deep, and the Spirit of God was moving over the surface of the waters. Then God said, "Let there be light"; and there was light. Genesis 1:1-3

When God speaks to us, He actually creates the truth within our hearts. The Desert Fathers tell us that once God places His message within our hearts, our minds spot it and surfaces that word to our conscious attention. Our mind or "intellect" then decides whether or not to recognize it and pay attention to it as God's word to us. While this sounds simple, we usually struggle initially with the process. We're used to communication—words—

coming to us externally, either audibly through spoken words or visually through written words. In both cases, we easily recognize that those thoughts did not come from us. However, God's personal word does emerge like a thought from within us. The "thought" feels/sounds just like any other thought that we might have. There's no "sound" or "feeling" that shows us clearly that it has come from God. The apostle Paul teaches that we're not left helpless, however, but that the Holy Spirit gifts us with the spiritual gift of "discerning spirits." God enables us to discern the difference between our own spirit, the Holy Spirit, and demonic spirits. It's this gift that enables us to "hear" the voice of our shepherd (cf. John 10:27; 1 Corinthians 12:4-11).

Chuck Orwiler shares how he learned to let the Scriptures speak to him.

When I was an undergraduate student, our class was given an assignment to write a commentary on the book of James. We were, of course, eminently unqualified for such an endeavor. Somewhere toward the beginning of that task I laid aside my reference books. I began to chew on little bits of the text at a time, asking myself only how God might be speaking to me through that text. I continued through the book recording my thoughts. In the process I learned how to let the Bible "read me." It was an experience of the Living Word teaching me through the written Word. I don't remember what grade I received. Since then, I have learned a great many academic skills in studying the text. Those are wonderful tools that I cherish and practice. However, on a personal level I have continued a simple discipline of letting the text read me and then responding in obedience. Nothing has been more forming and intimate in fellowship with my Lord.

While we're given this ability to recognize God's voice to us, we're not forced to use it. Like all other spiritual gifts, we must intentionally use the gift. We must also learn to use our gifts in concert with the rest of the Christian community. This all takes time, coaching, and practice. Let's use Matthew 19:21 as an example of letting the text read us. "If you wish to be complete, go and sell your possessions and give to the poor, and you will have treasure in heaven; and come, follow Me." As I meditate on this passage, listening for God's specific word to me, I recognize a number of possibilities within its words and phrases: complete, sell your possessions, give to the poor, treasure in heaven, come follow Me. I consider each one, asking God which part I should meditate on with the possibility that there is something He wants me to recognize for my own life. Is He calling me to become complete? Do I want to become more complete? Does God want me to sell all my possessions and give them to the poor? Or I might focus on the whole passage and see if one of those possibilities seems to grab my attention. In each case, I make a subtle judgment whether or not to consider it personally and to what extent to take it literally for my situation. I would probably pass pretty quickly over the "sell my possessions" part, assuming that God does not want me to make my family destitute. Without really asking Him about it, I may assume that He isn't speaking to me in that phrase or, if He is, that it's not literal, but more figurative, like becoming more generous. Only through the gift of discerning spirits can we make out God's particular word to us.

Abba Anthony of Alexandria Egypt heard God's specific word to him in Scripture. He managed a large business in the city. He read this Matthew passage and felt that God was actually telling him to sell everything, give it to the poor, and follow Jesus in some new way. He did sell everything and gave the money away. Asking God to clarify how he was to follow Him specifically, Anthony felt God directing him to walk into the Sahara Desert without any supplies. Anthony did just that and started a movement that ultimately resulted in the conversion of the Egyptian nation to Christianity for many years.

How did Anthony know that God was actually directing him in that passage? He had come to love God to the point that no word lay beyond his willingness to be obedient. Anthony had learned to use the gift of discerning spirits, and recognized that the thought of selling everything was not motivated by any self-desire to impress his Christian friends. He recognized that the devil was not tempting him to test God or deceive him into some foolish action. Anthony recognized the voice of his Shepherd and obeyed.

In a much less dramatic way, Jesus spoke to me about my reluctance to set consistent quality time apart for abiding prayer. One day, I was reading Luke 9:59-60.

> And He said to another, "Follow Me." But he said, "Lord, permit me first to go and bury my father." But He said to him, "Allow the dead to bury their own dead; but as for you, go and proclaim everywhere the kingdom of God."

While the passage doesn't discuss prayer, I immediately realized that although Jesus had been calling me onto the mountain to pray with Him consistently and daily, I had been putting Him off until I could get other things done. In some way, I realized that "go bury my father" referred to my obsession with having everything done and everyone pleased. Abiding prayer changed from trying to practice a spiritual discipline to a direct response to my Lord and Savior—Follow Me. My decision could only be, "Yes, Lord." God used that passage to change my life, making an hour of prayer each morning my first priority.

We can see that "hearing from God" contains many levels of attentiveness and discernment. We may not want to hear what God is saying to us and dismiss it without even seriously considering it. Or, we may want to hear some verse because it validates what we already want to hear and readily assume that God has spoken to us. Therefore, we must "test the spirits" by measuring what we think we hear against the clear teaching of the rest of Scripture and with the Christian community God has given to us. Therefore, we approach prayer in the Scriptures experimentally, just as we engage prayer in other forms. In the process, we learn attentiveness, we grow in self-knowledge, and we begin to "recognize" God's voice through the discerning of spirits. Eventually, we learn to obey what God says to us.

Experiencing God in the Journey of Prayer

Prayer "practices" can help us become attentive to God's initiative toward us in Scripture. Methods like Lectio Divina, Ignatian meditation, etc., can provide wonderful opportunities for us to actually experience God. The spiritual formation movement has produced a number of wonderful resources that help us slow down, listen, reflect, and dialogue with our Lord. Early on in our Scripture meditation process, coaching, guidance, and group prayer can help us experiment with these prayer practices. As we grow in our ability to become attentive to God, one verse may profoundly serve as a diving board into the magnificent pool of prayer.

To help us get past the idea of prayer as simply "information exchange," *Imago Christi* uses the term "abiding prayer," taken from Jesus' invitation to abide in Him, as branches abide in the vine (cf. John 15:1-5). The "communication" between the vine and branches—and between us and our Lord, involves much more than information. It contains life and sustenance—Love. Prayer consists not only of talking and listening, but of sensing and living in God's loving presence in stillness and peace.

Terry Tarleton shares his exposure to these new dimensions of prayer.

My wife and I went to a pastors' Sabbath retreat for 10 days where we were introduced to contemplative prayer. That felt weird for folks raised as Southern Baptists, but we were desperate to know more of God. We learned how to slow down and listen. In the listening we learned to hear the still, small voice of God. We discovered that God really does have something to say when we stilled ourselves and shut up. To this day, Janice and I do way more listening in prayer than speaking. Through that process, combined with spiritual direction, we have both encountered the living Jesus who desires to spend time with us. This has been the single most transforming aspect of our faith.

Within the process of abiding prayer, we can briefly describe some simple and progressive practices that help us commune with our Lord. When introducing people to these practices, I sometimes ask them, "How will you know that your prayer time has been successful?" Some respond about their ability to express their concerns to God, while others hope to hear a word from Him in the form of information, direction, answers to questions, or blessing. I suggest that we're "successful" in prayer when we simply show up; the rest is up to God. I often explain that it's helpful to decide before we start our prayer time how long we plan to spend and then spend that time with God, no matter what. We too easily and quickly assume that God isn't communicating with us—that our prayer time isn't successful because we don't yet discern what's happening. Demotivated that God has not adequately met our expectations, we move on to something more "productive." With that qualifier, let's explore the progressive methods of prayer that comprise the journey of abiding prayer. While we'll discuss them separately, a given prayer time may include several of these forms.

Conversational Prayer: Like any conversation with another person, we talk and listen. Because this conversation takes place with the Creator of the Universe, we want to focus on listening and responsiveness. Therefore, start the conversation by becoming still in a listening posture. While we may have entered our prayer time with some specific things we would like to discuss with God and questions or requests, we should wait to see if the Lord has something else He would like to discuss first. Imagine Isaiah in the Isaiah 6:4 passage, where he sees God on His throne, surrounded by all the angels. Could we imagine Isaiah rushing up to the throne with a lengthy monologue of thoughts, questions, and requests? No, he waited, sensed the magnitude of the scene, and then responded. Like Isaiah, when we sense the Lord initiating a line of discussion, we respond and interact with His leading. When, it feels appropriate, we then introduce our desires. Realizing that God already understands our situation and our feelings, we can either briefly express our thoughts or sit silently letting our thoughts and concerns simply be present to the Lord.

Lectio Divina (Divine/Spiritual Reading): In this form of meditation on Scripture, we slowly read or listen to a short passage several times. During the reading, we become attentive to the words of the text that seem to "jump out at us" or capture our attention. At the same time, we become attentive to our own feelings and responses to those words. Once we feel that God desires to speak to us in a particular word or phrase, we become still and intentionally present to God. We let Him focus our attention and expand on the word in our own context. We respond to His promptings and seek His direction. After several minutes of silence, we may journal the experience, trying to capture the essence of our interaction with God.

Ignatian Prayer: In this form of Scriptural meditation, we use Lectio Divina, adding our imagination. We choose a short passage of Scripture, one with a story or visual scene. After multiple readings, we ask the Holy Spirit to guide us as we place ourselves imaginatively in the story. We might become one of the characters in the story or a bystander observing the event. We imaginatively use our senses to see, hear, smell, and feel the scene. We observe our own reactions and feelings. As we did in Lectio, we focus on that aspect of the story that stood out to us, asking the Lord what He wants us to notice that speaks to our own circumstances. Because we already understand the "truth" or "principle" that the story illustrates, we listen beyond the story or its theology. We discern the Lord's word to us personally, letting Him guide our thoughts from the story into our own feelings, relationships, and situations. Moving from this time of active thought and reflection, we move to silence—just being with the Lord in the midst of our reflections. We respond to the Lord as insights come. The formal Ignatian Exercises suggest a journaling process that helps capture the prayer experience.

Chris Lyons describes his experience of imaginative prayer and the way that God spoke to him.

I attended a seminary class on spiritual direction held at a church camp. After some informal sharing and personal quiet time, we were led through a prayer exercise. The facilitator told us to imagine ourselves walking on a beach all alone, reflecting on the state of our lives. We were then told that we were about to personally meet Jesus on this beach. Jesus was going to have a word for us, a word about the state of our lives. Soft music and beach sounds played from the stereo in the background. Something about being away from the bustle of the city and out in nature made it pretty easy to lose myself in this exercise. The facilitator continued: "Now you see Jesus in the distance on this beach, walking toward you.... but first you look down and discover an object. Pick it up. It represents your life right now and Jesus wants to talk to you about it." Within my imagination I looked down in the sand and saw a glass mason jar, abandoned in the surf. A wave of shame hit me as I picked it up and imagined the reaction of Jesus. "Empty? Jesus is going to say that I am empty!" Funny as it is to say, I wanted to run away from my own imagination, to escape that coming encounter with Jesus on the beach. The facilitator spoke softly, "Jesus is face to face with you. What does He say?" Cringing, I did look up from the jar in my hands to find myself in the presence of the Lord. I don't remember what he looked like, but I could tell it was Jesus and I heard His voice. "You are open." His tone was affirming, loving. "You are open." My own brokenness and history had led me to a natural default of shame, but Jesus wanted to lead me forward with grace.

Wordless Prayer: In Wordless Prayer, we may start with any of the forms we've discussed above. At some point, we become still and attentive to the thoughts passing through our minds. Without verbalizing—wordlessly, we let the thoughts or the questions that may have surfaced come before the Lord as payers. Passively allowing the process to continue, we attempt not to guide the conversation, but to become quietly attentive to our own feelings and the promptings from the Lord. Following the prayer time, journaling can help us capture what we feel the Lord has said to us and to explore the implications further.

Bill O'Byrne shares a dimension of wordless prayer that he finds meaningful.

I find that my wordless prayer experiences began primarily with music as I'd let God carry me along on the melodies, silently allowing my heart respond to Him—without verbalizing or discussing my reactions, but with emotional and heart responses too deep for words. I often experience that same wordless prayer response to God in nature and in art.

Contemplation and Centering Prayer: Like wordless prayer, contemplation often follows one of the forms of prayer we have just discussed. In this form of prayer, we focus our attention upon the Lord directly, attempting to exclude other thoughts. (In "Meditation," conversely, we focus on God THROUGH other words and thoughts such as a biblical passage, a song, or some object such as a cross.) In contemplation, we present ourselves to Him, trusting His love and presence, for the sole purpose of responding to Him in love and intimacy. Without thoughts, words, or mental images, we remain silent and present, loving and being loved. When distractions come, we gently push them to the sidelines, to be dealt with later. When prayer concerns, questions, or requests come to our minds, we similarly let them wait until this "just being with God" concludes. Although we have not expressed our thoughts or needs, or even praise and adoration, we trust that the Lord has been present to our whole being, loving and transforming us. If He chooses to speak to us, we continue to hold His words in stillness to be pondered later. In contemplation, we have come to God, not for information, answers, help, or consolation, but to simply express our love for Him through our intentional presence.

Silence: We use the word "silence" to refer, not simply to the absence of sound, but to a God-given time of absorption in God that He gives to us during contemplation. While abiding in Jesus, we find, to our surprise, that thoughts, feelings, insights, questions, and distractions seem to disappear while we become aware only of God, lost in His beauty, mystery, and love. Experiences of silence usually last only seconds or minutes, but can become extended as God may choose.

We need to warn people that the journey of Abiding Prayer contains some steep terrain and barriers to be overcome in the early stages of our journey, as well as dry deserts as we proceed. The productivity values of our culture and our churches, added to our own addiction to information, always threatens to derail us. We have become so accustomed to seeking God as a means to our own ends that it often takes the Holy Spirit some real work to bring us to the point where our "life of prayer" becomes satisfied with God Himself.

So many times, God has responded to my frustrations about not "getting anything" in prayer by saying, "Tom, you mean that I am not enough for you?" It broke my heart to admit that was exactly how I felt and to call out to Him again, "Create in me a clean heart, oh God...." Although I felt frustrated with myself, Jesus knew that I was still learning, and He was delighted to continue to change my heart so that I could enjoy His love. That's the nature of prayer—abiding in, enjoying, exploring, becoming alive in Love.

The Necessity of the Prayer Closet

In the famous Sermon on the Mountain, Jesus instructed His disciples and the crowds about prayer. "But you, when you pray, go into your inner room, close your door and pray to your Father who is in secret, and your Father who sees what is done in secret will reward you." Matthew 6:6 While public prayer and prayer in groups will always play important roles in our lives, personal, private, consistent prayer lies at the center of our relationship with God. Jesus modeled this "inner room" prayer life by his frequent visits to the mountains to pray (cf. Matthew 14:23, 17:1, 28:16, Mark 6:46, Luke 6:12, 9:28). Great women and men, remembered for their faith and impact on the Christian movement, consistently follow Jesus' injunctions about private personal prayer. Martin Luther consistently spent two hours in the morning for prayer. Historical accounts of Luther's life report that, when faced with a particularly busy day, He would say he had so much to do that day that he must spend three hours in prayer in order to be able to get it all done.

Our culture, however, so values productivity that many, if not most, Christian leaders admit that they seldom take prayer-closet time with God, but pray-on-the-run. It may be easy to ask God for things, "on-the-run," but it's almost impossible to listen that way. In earlier chapters, I have shared that forming a consistent time for abiding prayer was the most difficult "spiritual discipline" of my Christian life. When it came down to the bare truth, serving God won out over being with Him. His power and blessing were more important to me than His love. Through relationships with many Christian leaders, I've found that my struggle wasn't unique—but common. Jesus' call to the prayer-closet diagnoses our priorities, provides the training ground for our discernment, bathes us in God's healing love, teaches us to hear His voice, builds our love and intimacy with God, and transforms us into Christ's likeness. I've found that my prayer-closet times have become the place where I sit at the hearth of God's love, where He warms my heart until it glows and burns with love that becomes contagious. As I recognize and receive God's love for me, I also recognize His love for others I have met. Then it becomes a great honor and joy to love them with the fire Jesus has placed within me. The fire that really becomes contagious always emerges from the prayer closet.

Our prayer-closet becomes for us the Garden for Adam and Eve, the Mountain for Abraham, the Burning Bush for Moses, the Jordan for Joshua, the Cave for Elijah, the Temple for Isaiah, the Desert for John the Baptist, the Womb for Jesus, the Mount of Transfiguration for Peter, James, and John, the Road to Emmaus for the two disciples, the Upper Room of the Last Supper and Pentecost, and Patmos for the Apostle John. If they'd been too busy, our lives would be much different! Without your consistent abiding presence in your prayer closet, abundant life will always allude you. As leaders, we must discover its fire for ourselves, model it for others, and invite everyone to experiment and find God's hearth in their own lives.

Meeting God in Guided and Silent Retreats

Brother Boniface, my spiritual formation mentor, addressed my Type-A-driven personality with the comment, "There is a monk in all of us, Tom, but sometimes we have to get off the scene to discover him." Over time, I developed a regular morning "prayer-closet" routine that proved really significant in my growing relationship with the Lord. However, when I recall the profound encounters that God has used to teach and transform me, most of them occurred when I was "off the scene." My monastery trips usually lasted four days. The seven daily worship Offices provided the framework in which I could rest, read, worship, hike—all in prayer. My days in an attentive and listening mode provided a rich space in which God could get through to me in ways that didn't happen in my one-hour prayer-closet times.

Charlie Dodrill and Chuck Orwiler agree that in times away, we can become more easily immersed in the Holy Spirit and filled with His light and power.

> *Charlie: After having been a Christian, called to ministry, and having worked on the mission field, etc., I had an encounter with the Holy Spirit that I could not have orchestrated, but which literally gave me an entirely new life. My theology was so very bad at the time and I didn't believe more than I believed about the Bible and the whole Christianity thing. I had one encounter with God in a way that my brain had no chance of explaining, and afterwards, I realized that God knew who I was and cared enough about me to tell/show me. That experience turned my faith, my calling, my relationship from something I saw as a job into a living organism that would lead to Love. This proved to be my most notable "cementing" experience.*

> *Chuck: I've had a few major Spirit encounters as well as what seems like a mostly continual washing of the Holy Spirit that have been fundamental to my experience of God.*

Often, the Holy Spirit has to get us "off the scene" to fully get our attention.

I am not the only one who gets so caught up in the crazy pace of life, particularly the life of the church, that regular focused time with God can feel almost impossible. "Off the scene" doesn't take a monastery, but times in a quiet, restful, and worshipful setting can enable us to become still and attentive to our presence with the Lord. For those of us relatively new to our relationship with the Lord, a structured and biblically focused retreat with short opportunities to just "be" with God can become life-changing. Extended times alone with God, unstructured and unmanaged, may enable the more spiritually mature to commune with God in ways impossible in the midst of multitudes of demands all attacking at the same time. Few of us, in any stage of our journeys, will actually "get off the scene" without an invitation, encouragement, and an appropriate place to get away. At any stage of the journey, time alone and time in community to debrief can enable significant strides in our relationship with God.

Ted Wueste discusses his encounter with God in an extended retreat.

Several years ago, I was coming to the end of a 5-day silent retreat that was the concluding part of a three-month sabbatical from pastoral ministry. I was feeling a bit of pressure about what I was bringing back to our congregation. This was the content of much of my listening during the final day of the retreat. I'd ask, "Lord, what do I bring back?" Very clearly, I heard the Lord say, "Bring Me back, I'm enough." This was profound for me on so many levels, but it cemented into my heart that He is truly enough and the answer to the longing in my heart personally as well as vocationally.

Conferences can also provide focused time to learn and grow. *Imago Christi* provides three-day events called Spiritual Formation Discovery for Leaders. These Discoveries provide topical spaces where participants can interact with God and debrief with fellow retreatants about key aspects of their growing relationship with God. In each module, presenters share a short teaching and personal story about the topic. Participants then engage the topic personally in prayer combined with some activity, followed by a debrief time with other participants to help summarize and clarify their experience. Within the Discovery process, we explore four movements of our spiritual journey: 1) Discovering lessons learned from our history with God; 2) Discovering where we're going in our relationship with Him; 3) Discovering where we find ourselves in the journey; and 4) Discovering how to cooperate with God in the ongoing process. I'll share this movement in more detail, as it describes the general movement that we find necessary, at some level, in the journey of spiritual growth.

The following brief overview will give you a feel for this progressive experiential process.

Introduction:

> Discovering the nature of spiritual formation and its relationship with discipleship
>
> Discovering the biblical foundations for spiritual formation (Often done in Prework)

Discovering Lessons Learned From Our History With God

> Discovering Spiritual History Timeline
>
> Recognizing key life experiences and interactions with God
>
> Identifying how God works in good and difficult times
>
> Discover insights, changing views of God
>
> Recognizing how God has been leading them into deeper relationship and love.

Discovering Where We're Going in Our Relationship With God

> Discovering Longing for Intimacy with God
>
> Explore what their ideal relationship with God might be like
>
> Ask God to reveal an image of deep mutual love and interaction
>
> Write a short paragraph to describe this ultimate First Order relationship.

Discovering Where We Currently Find Ourselves in the Journey

Exploring the Teresian Mansions, discovering our current journey range

> Identifying the key movements of growth associated with one's journey place

Discovering blocks and barriers to our own spiritual growth

Discovering How to Cooperate With God in the Ongoing Process

Discovering how to cooperate with God in abiding prayer

Discovering how to cooperate with God in spiritual community

Discovering the way forward with a spiritual formation plan

Discovering Post-Discovery group follow up

Imago Christi's Discovery events can be found on their website, at www. imagochristi.org/discovery, and are often scheduled at the invitation of one or more local churches or ministries.

Progressive retreats, like the Discovery, can provide retreatants with a sense of growth and continuity that motivates continued participation. One congregation uses trips to other countries, combined with interactive experiences to provide opportunities for spiritual community development and personal growth. The ways that we can help our members "get off the scene" can be varied and fun, designed to fit the needs and preferences of each congregational setting. God simply awaits the opportunity to accompany us on the adventure.

Experiencing God in Beauty

Gary Thomas opened up new doors for many of us in his book, *Sacred Pathways*, where he describes various ways that people connect with God related to their personal wiring and preferences.[2] For example, some naturally feel God's presence in nature, while others feel drawn to God in art or liturgy, or…. Key to each of these pathways lies the perception of beauty for the individual person. As Designer and Creator of the universe, God reveals His nature to us in ways that we discern as beautiful. Each of us perceives beauty in different ways, but we may not be aware of the settings in which beauty

---

2. Gary Thomas. *Sacred Pathways: Discover Your Soul's Path to God*, Zondervan, 1996

connects us with God. Myra Perrine helps us take Gary Thomas' work further through identifying our most meaningful ways to connect with God in His beauty. Her book, *What's Your God Language?* and her companion workbook of spiritual exercises provide some excellent resources to help people of various "spiritual temperaments" engage in a more experiential relationship with God.[3]

JD Ward recalls how God touched and changed his life through an encounter with beauty.

> *While I was on a silent retreat, I was praying quite intensely. I was feeling convicted about the sin in my life and being rather condemning of my condition. Then at that moment God gave me a vision of a painting. And I was looking at this beautiful painting and critiquing the painting colors and texture. Then I felt God over my shoulder in the vision. He asked me, "When I critique this painting so hard how do I think it makes the artist feel?" I said not very good. Then God said, "Well you are the painting and I am the painter. I have made you beautiful, but you continue to criticize my work." This was a life-altering vision and changed my understanding of God. A deep understanding of belovedness overtook me that day.*

Sitting with God in Spiritual Direction

We've discussed the importance of aligning our cooperation with God's inviting presence in ways that correspond to each person's general place in the spiritual formation journey. One way to gain this kind of insight can come through a spiritual direction relationship. Not only do few churches provide teaching about how to relate to God in prayer, fewer still provide meaningful places to discuss our prayer experiences and help us discern God's leading in our everyday lives. Spiritual directors can help us interpret our prayer experiences and discover appropriate ways to commune with

3. Myra Perrine. *What's Your God Language? Connecting with God through Your Unique Spiritual Temperament (Nine Spiritual Temperaments--How Knowing Yours Can Help You)*, Salt River Publishing, 2007 and *What's Your God Language? Coaching Guide*, Amazon, 2011

God. Spiritual directors have been trained to listen with us to God, and invite us to recognize God's word to us in various situations. Rather than "directing" us about what to do, they ask questions which help us discover what the Lord may be telling us. Spiritual directors have also been trained in the use of spiritual disciplines and can help us find practices in which we can become more attentive to our Lord's presence and leading. By listening to us and to the Lord, they can help us find spiritual disciplines which match both our temperaments and our relative place in our growing relationship with the Lord.

Fortunately, more and more spiritual direction training programs now include training about the process of spiritual growth. Both "Selah", provided by Leadership Transformation Institute and "Sustainable Faith," associated with the Vineyard Movement, use Teresa's Seven Mansions as described in *Mansions of the Heart* as a spiritual formation paradigm, and provide excellent and qualified spiritual direction. Many other schools and programs now provide spiritual direction training. Debbie Swindoll's "Grafted Life Ministry" provides a web-based resource to help identify trained spiritual directors in various parts of the world. While face-to-face spiritual direction meetings provide the best settings, internet video conferencing such as Skype and Zoom can also provide excellent settings for spiritual direction. Ultimately, however, God intends that our primary support for our spiritual journey come through our local brothers and sisters in Christ.

Meeting God in Spiritual Community

In Chapter 11, we'll discuss "Spiritually Forming Community" in detail. The majority of spiritual formation experiences we provide for our pilgrims will involve "community" to some degree. This section, therefore, will focus on our need to provide experiences in community. We may find spiritual community a scarce commodity, however, in many of our churches. Our "meetings" often focus on the business of the church or a particular ministry rather than on one another. Even though we open and close those meetings with prayer, *Robert's Rules of Order* often governs our interactions instead of the loving movement of the Holy Spirit. The church gatherings that may be available to us may not be safe places to share our hearts.

Many of us have experienced betrayal of our confidentiality through the rumor mill or the "prayer chain." Unfortunately, our Bible studies can often focus on biblical facts and principles rather than the persons in the room— leaving us lonely, confused about our experience or lack of experience, and afraid to speak honestly about our struggles for fear of being judged. Prayer in our small groups often focus on participants' physical circumstances rather than matters of the heart. Therefore, we need to ask ourselves the extent to which we actually provide opportunities for our members to really share their spiritual journeys together. If your church provides small groups, you may want to look at both the topics and the focus of the groups, as well as the depth of interaction within them.

If we're to provide spiritual community for our members, we may have to do more than provide a new curriculum for our groups; we probably need to coach and train people how to live together spiritually. One church developed a Group Covenant which set forth expectations of any group that met within the life of the church. The Covenant specified qualities of group interaction such as confidentiality, honesty, listening without interrupting or judging, sharing about life at both a physical and spiritual level, prayer both within the group meetings and for group members between meetings, etc. Our discussion in Chapter 4, "Internal Leadership Community," can provide further insights into what elements we might include in a Group Covenant. The Covenant applied to Bible study groups, sharing and discussion groups, as well as ministry teams. Group leaders received training about how to facilitate group meetings in ways that facilitated spiritual depth and support as well as accomplishing other goals of the group.

Chris Lyons expressed his experience with the vital role of relationships in spiritual growth.

*I've been meeting with a pastor friend for over 20 years and have seen
how God has used this experience as a way that God could speak and
challenge us to grow. This intentionality around other relationships
nudged me into spaces/situations where the expectation was set – God
is on the MOVE and is going to MOVE in and through you, Chris.
It seems to me that most significant faith steps I've observed are ones
ACCOMPANIED by a fellow traveler that God uses profoundly. This
isn't just relational, but it seems INCARNATIONAL – that I meet
Jesus in my brothers/sisters as we seek to follow Jesus together.*

Fundamentally, spiritual community happens within personal
relationships. While church leadership cannot establish those relationships
for people, we can provide intentional opportunities, geared to the needs of our
members. Didactic Bible studies, topical small groups, potluck fellowships,
ministry teams, mentoring relationships, and spiritual friendships can,
with the right process, provide wonderful opportunities for our pilgrims to
process their lives with God and receive the support and encouragement to
really enjoy the journey. When our church culture teaches, encourages, and
facilitates meaningful spiritual community, embers will burst into flame and
campfires will enlighten the church community with a contagious brilliance!

Meeting God Through Serving the "Poor"

It has always amazed me that Jesus shared the most profound spiritual
truths in conversations with people who didn't accept Him or believe in Him.
The disciples learned how to follow Jesus by accompanying Him into the
lives of the sick, the poor, the antagonists, and the sinners. They experienced
the Father's love in action and grew in their own faith as they watched Jesus
loving others. Jesus has called us to follow Him in the same way. "As the
Father has sent Me, I send you" (cf. John 20:21).

When we enter into relationship, no matter how seemingly trivial, with
people who need God—Jesus calls them the poor, we experience God in
profound ways. Jesus works from within us to reach out to others. When we
really engage with others for the sole reason that God directed us to help, we

encounter God and His life-giving love in multiple ways. We feel His love motivating us beyond our normal inclinations; we taste His love for those to whom we minister; we discover God's love for us in the midst of our own struggles to love freely and without judgment or reward; we see Jesus in the other person even though they may not yet know Him. While we may feel that nothing of significance happens in some caring event, Jesus never loves through us passively—He ignites sparks of love in dark corners of people's lives, corners that may never have experienced light before. As we care for others, Jesus says that we literally care for Him (cf. Matthew 25:35-40).

My daughter serves as the directing social worker in a homeless day shelter. Occasionally I get to visit the Trinity Center and have coffee with the "neighbors." I sit at the tables and listen to their amazing stories. Jesus sits there, within me, listening, loving, radiating life, forgiveness, hope, and healing. I get to watch and sometimes, at His bidding, add a word or two. The neighbor then moves on, maybe to get something to eat or take a shower, often without any sign that the encounter had meaning. But I know the truth! I know that the Creator of the Universe has just met personally with a man or woman whom He deeply loves and longs to bring into His abundant life. I know that Jesus reached out and touched that person's heart in some way that would someday forever change her. The Holy Spirit whispered His invitation to love and life and deposited in some inner place the embers of hope. Without any visible sign, I know that miracles are happening—in that neighbor and in me. Even in the furtive glance of someone I would never be drawn to as a friend, I see the eyes of Jesus and hear His voice, "Thanks, Tom, for loving Me in this beautiful person." Talk about spiritual experience—two transformations!

Too often we trivialize missions, outreach, and evangelism simply as work we have to accomplish to please God or help people. When Jesus commands us to love our neighbor as He loves us, He doesn't simply mean that we do nice things for people. He invites us to enter into the same spiritual "space" with another person—the space of His presence—love, and enter into His redeeming work. We often think that the "good" we do for others is simply "for" others, when in fact Jesus offers us the most amazing invitation to know Him more deeply and discover ourselves more profoundly in the other. Scripture speaks clearly that we can never separate loving God and loving one another. In our ministry to others, the fire of our love for God becomes contagious—its flames fanned by our experience of Jesus in the encounter.

Within most of our churches, however, we need to help people connect the dots between loving God and loving neighbor, between experiencing God's love for us and experiencing His love for the other. Our mission teams return from an outreach and tell their stories to the congregation. Not only have people next door or across town or on the other side of the world been blessed, but always, always we see that these missionaries themselves have been profoundly touched and changed. I don't think that I am alone in having to admit that I have often failed to help those missionaries, in my care, unpack what God has done within them, to make explicit the implicit and subjective movements of the Holy Spirit as they joined Jesus in the act of loving. Too often the "high" of caring for others wanes when we return to the inertial flood of life because the miracles Jesus accomplished in our hearts were never really recognized and celebrated. We can, however, learn to become attentive to the work of the Holy Spirit in both the one who cares and in the one who receives—and celebrate!

Steve Thulson describes one of the ways his church works to connect the dots between their outreach ministry and God's work in their own hearts.

Our former Pastor to Students, Randy, took kids as well as adults on several mission trips to Kenya, South America, and urban Denver. Each day would begin with team members taking time to open themselves to God and listen for any promptings, and end with the team processing what God had been doing IN them, as well as through them. There seemed to be a good integration of First and Second Order loves.

Ultimately, of course, Jesus calls us to love Him in those closest to us—

our family, friends, coworkers, and neighbors. Sometimes we find it easier to "stand up for Jesus" with people we don't know and may never see again. Spot the persons nearest you, and hear Jesus saying from within them, "Come love me here; let Me love you here, too."

Walking With God in a Rule of Life

The fire of God's love won't become the life-fuel of our lives if our walk with Jesus consists only of random rendezvous prompted by church programs. When we experience God only in pleas of desperation or passing thoughts, our fire-tending teeters on the edge of forgetfulness. We continually need someone else to add kindling, fan our flames, and stir the fire. Our cooperation with the Lord in His work to draw us more deeply into His heart of love must become habitual—a new way of life, intentionally abiding in abundant life. Even monks and nuns, who live in cloistered communities designed to help them love God, find that they can easily become distracted and lose sight of why they live together at all. They need a pattern of life that continually brings them back to their purpose, to God and their common call to love Him and those they serve. How much more do we, called to live devotedly in love with God in the midst of this frantic world, also need a pattern, a rule, a guide to help us follow Jesus?

Using the categories we have been discussing above, we can develop rhythms that will help us meet God regularly in each way of experiencing God. We also need others to provide accountability, encouragement, and prayer. With a rhythm of life that supports us, we can resist the demands of our culture so that we can follow the longing to know and love our Lord with our whole hearts. We need a personal Rule of Life.

While historically, most "Rules of Life" were designed for those living in monastic communities, many contemporary models have been designed to provide great starting places for those of us who live in the marketplace. Steve Macchia's *Crafting A Rule of Life: An Invitation to the Well-Ordered*

Way provides an excellent resource. The *Imago Christi's* Covenant, found on www.imagochristi.org, gives another example. Peter Scazzero offers some excellent resources in his *Emotionally Healthy Spirituality* series.[4]

Our Rule of Life can help us become aware of our Lord's direction and enter into what Chuck Orwiler calls Holy Obedience.

> *In my tradition, John 15.14 has been emphasized, "You are my friend if you do what I command." So, I was trained from the beginning to do what I understood God wanted of me. Jesus repeatedly correlated love and obedience. He said that joy is the result. It works! I call it Holy Obedience. … When people risk acting on what they see through a glass darkly it consistently elevates them to a more intimate knowledge of the Holy. That begins with an initial step of faith, and those steps never diminish.*

Experiencing God

We've been discussing ways we can help our people experience God. Every person on the planet could describe their experience of God—for better or worse. Those who deny or misunderstand their experience travel a journey of loneliness, confusion, hopelessness, and ultimate despair. Those who follow Jesus intentionally experience Him at every turn in a journey of adventure, love, and joy. Our love relationship with God takes a lifetime and beyond to fully mature. The journey begins long before we come to affirm Jesus as our personal Lord and Savior and accelerates as the Holy Spirit brings us into a personal growing relationship. This relationship is intended to blaze with flames of love that brings us great joy in abundant life and sparks to life a fire of love in others.

The difficulty, however, remains that the Holy Spirit invites and empowers us, but never drives us forward—we can easily become stuck. Many of us, maybe most, don't realize that there is more—much more to the adventure than we have experienced. We can become discouraged and turn back. We

4. Peter Scazzero, *Emotionally Healthy Spirituality: It's Impossible to Be Spiritually Mature While Remaining Emotionally Immature.* Zondervan, Grand Rapids, 2006

all need help and encouragement to maintain the journey and discover the heights and wonders of God's love. So, God calls some of us as pastors and teachers and counselors and spiritual directors and friends to fan the flames of God's love and provide opportunities to learn and discover and grow—to experience God. That's what the Church is about.

In Chapter 9, we'll consider how our leadership, vision, teaching, and spiritual experiences become critical to our pilgrims' ability to deal with the dangers along the trail. Intentional and unintentional forces wait to splash water on our flames of love, head us off on the wrong path, and cause us to flounder and fail. I think you'll recognize some of these dragons in your own life.

CHAPTER 9

COMBATING THE FIRE EXTINGUISHERS - FACING THE DRAGON TOGETHER

Another Kind of Fire

We've been talking about the fire of God's love that warms our hearts until it becomes a beautiful and contagious flame of love for God and for all people. There exists, however, another kind of fire—one that blasts against our flame and tries to scorch us.

> And the great dragon was thrown down, the serpent of old who is called the devil and Satan, who deceives the whole world; he was thrown down to the earth, and his angels were thrown down with him. Revelation 12:9
>
> So, the dragon was enraged with the woman, and went off to make war with the rest of her children, who keep the commandments of God and hold to the testimony of Jesus. Revelation 12:17

In the hands of God, this dragon fire purifies us; without His hand of restraint, it can scorch, disfigure, and cripple us.

> Jesus, full of the Holy Spirit, returned from the Jordan and was led around by the Spirit in the wilderness for forty days, being tempted by the devil. Luke 4:1-2

This other kind of fire comes from our sin and the "flaming arrows of the evil one" aimed at our weakness (cf. Ephesians 6:16).

> For the wages of sin is death, but the free gift of God is eternal life in Christ Jesus our Lord. Romans 6:23

> If we say that we have no sin, we are deceiving ourselves and the truth is not in us. If we confess our sins, He is faithful and righteous to forgive us our sins and to cleanse us from all unrighteousness. 1 John 1:8-9

> Submit therefore to God. Resist the devil and he will flee from you. Draw near to God and He will draw near to you. James 4:7-8

> Put on the full armor of God, so that you will be able to stand firm against the schemes of the devil. For our struggle is not against flesh and blood, but against the rulers, against the powers, against the world forces of this darkness, against the spiritual forces of wickedness in the heavenly places. Ephesians 6:11-12

> Each man's work will become evident; for the day will show it because it is to be revealed with fire, and the fire itself will test the quality of each man's work. If any man's work which he has built on it remains, he will receive a reward. If any man's work is burned up, he will suffer loss; but he himself will be saved, yet so as through fire. 1 Corinthians 3:13-15

As we see, Scripture describes our encounter with this fiery dragon in dreadful detail.

I trust that you've read this Chapter before launching into a Contagious Fire project in your church or ministry. If you haven't, you probably already recognize the issues we'll address. Hopefully, too, you'll find some encouragement. Yes, our attempts to change the culture of our ministries will be fraught with difficulties; no, we can't eliminate the arrows and spears hurled at us by our friends or by the enemy. But, we can keep them from piercing our hearts and thwarting God's plan.

We could have addressed this push-back at the beginning of the book and again after each chapter. However, it makes sense to talk about it here because, in the flow of implementing change, trouble may well be brewing. Whenever we yield ourselves more fully to our King, seeking to become like Him and to advance His kingdom in the Church and the world, resistance will always come. Resistance comes from many sources, on many fronts. It comes from within us as our sinful dispositions claw to maintain their hold upon us. Resistance comes from the culture of our society, terrified of a new and unknown King. Resistance, retaliation, and attack blast at us from the enemy of our Lord, and of our souls, who desperately clings to his failing domination of the earth. Sometimes we encounter the dragon early in our contagious fire initiative, and other times it waits in the shadows for just the right opportunity to strike. In any case, it will come.

Resistance, pushback, and demonic attack don't necessarily mean that something has gone wrong or someone is messed up. We do mess up, but encountering the dragon is a normal and predictable part of any movement toward significant spiritual growth. We know something is very wrong when frustration and conflict don't happen. However, our King hasn't led us into the battle to be defeated. Jesus has prepared and equipped us so that the evil fire only refines and strengthens us to glorify our Lord.

To prepare ourselves, we'll discuss our battle with the dragon as he attempts to douse His contagious fire from three perspectives:

First, we'll consider how the dragon tries to drown our flames as leaders and pilgrims advancing in their intimacy with Jesus and commitment to His cause.

Second, we'll discuss the corporate push-backs, which often stem from these same personal attacks but often take a more hidden form from within the community of the church.

Third, and most importantly, we'll recall how God not only protects us in the battle, but redeems our struggles and turns them into opportunities for even more profound spiritual growth.

Warfare Aimed at "Leaders"

Any battle strategist knows that their enemy can be easily crippled if the leader is first taken out. We're using the term, "leader," in a general way in this discussion. Within the Kingdom of God, we "lead" because we follow Jesus into the lives of others. One's leadership may be associated with a defined role, such as pastor, worship leader, teacher, etc. Or, leadership may simply emerge from the presence of Jesus within us to influence others for good. The leaders we refer to here may be part of the spiritual leadership community, serve in some other ministry of the church, support other pilgrims in prayer, etc.

While the enemy constantly schemes about how he might use the weaknesses of our congregational members, his prime target will always be YOU, and the people who serve Him intentionally! Not only do we leaders share the same weaknesses that face all people, but our very role as "leaders" can actually make us more vulnerable, by hiding our disabilities, making us more susceptible to falling. The enemy will always attack us at our weakest links. However, when we know where those weaknesses exist, we can stay alert. When they're hidden from us we can become sitting ducks for the dragon's breath. God sometimes uses the enemy to inadvertently show us these weaknesses so that we can turn to our Lord for healing and strength.

Painful Light in Dark Places

Brother Boniface used to remind me, "When God shines His light on Himself, we become awed, mystified, delighted, and enwrapped with love. When He shines His light on us, we find ourselves shocked, mortified, embarrassed, humiliated, and ashamed." We had no idea! On more than one occasion, he repeated that saying to me because God's light had, in fact, fallen on me. Boniface would respond to my embarrassed reaction with, "Isn't that wonderful?" I didn't feel wonderful at all; I felt miserable. "Don't you see how you've grown? Don't you remember a time when you would have brushed off this revelation with some excuse? God has grown you to the point that you are able to see the truth and let Him transform you." It took a long time for me to begin to thank God for those revealing lights.

In each of the seven mansions of growth, God invites us into a deeper understanding of ourselves—both our belovedness and new insights into our fallen nature and the sin which still lurks within us. These insights aren't given to shame or to humiliate us. Rather, He shows us the dark places that need healing with His infusing love. Even though we may know that God doesn't condemn us, the knowledge can still feel painful, terribly painful. We may scream, "This walk with God isn't supposed to hurt. God is supposed to make me feel good about myself. Something's wrong here. Someone has led me astray!" That kind of reaction proves that "someone," in fact, HAS led us astray!

We live in a culture built on the "I'm OK—you're OK" fantasy, fully embracing the "pursuit of happiness" in any way that feels good to the individual. We go to church to make us feel happy—to feel OK about ourselves. That's the Gospel, isn't it? Many churches have given up talking about sin because we don't want to hear it. "Just give me information, reassurance that I am loved, and a friendly place to make friends (who will make me happy)." Eventually we learn that God's loving touch diagnoses the wounds that hold us back from the fullness of His love, blinding us to joy, and keeping us from a destiny that will change the world.

Eventually, we learn to seek these wounds of love—wounds that can become doorways into the heart of our Lord. Right now, however, we may not be happy campers at all. Without someone to explain how our misery comes from the presence of God's Love, we can turn in upon ourselves in shame, hiding from others in the church because we feel like hypocrites. We can even lash out at others as though they are the ones accusing us. Of course, we can't admit why we lash out; that would expose our darkness. The Bible calls the devil the accuser of men's souls for good reason. Therefore, rather than simply trying to manage sin, let's identify some of the opportunities that our woundedness has provided—for our failure and the enemy's attack. Hopefully, this discussion will help us recognize which ones have become danger zones for us personally, before the attack comes.

Enemy Fire

The Desert Fathers teach that most spiritual attack comes in three categories: gluttony, avarice, and self-esteem. These sin areas certainly aren't unique to leaders, but the enemy's associated strategies can be subtly disguised for Christian leaders. Let's discuss some of the arsenal that I've wrestled with personally and some I have seen in others. You be the judge if these targets hang on your back, used by the enemy to try to distract and discourage you from pursuing the Lord's contagious fire.

Attacks of Gluttony - habitual greed or excess in eating. While overeating and excess weight may be a problem for more leaders than we would like to admit, our "greed" temptations may lurk below the surface and may even appear quite "holy." I may appear to have my congregation's best interests in mind, but I may be more motivated by having a large congregation.

Bill O'Byrne comments about the wide spectrum that gluttony takes in our culture.

> *Our idolatry of comfort, ease, entitlement, and pleasure defines the extent of our gluttony. Gluttony has to do with our appetites, like food and sex, but extends to include all consumables and pleasures. "More is better" makes a vice out of God's good gifts through excess. Gluttony turns work into workaholism, which for Christians translates into a ministry addiction, where health and family are sacrificed. And whenever we "can't have enough," we find that gluttony also applies to self-esteem, because we can never have enough affirmation.*

There's one form of gluttony that I'd like to highlight; one that I've found particularly seductive and destructive for Christian leaders. You may be able to find many more. Whatever your appetite attack might be, the enemy may try to use it to disable you with strategies much like this one.

The Gluttony of Busyness: The enemy tries to head us off at the pass to deepening intimacy with our Lord by providing endless opportunities for ministry. These "opportunities" may include particularly

240

needy people or troubling situations. Often, however, our increasing time demands deal with good things. "The church seems to be growing; let's add a new service, pastor." "Pastor, I'd like to start a new mission outreach. Would you mentor me?" "We've just been invited to broadcast our services on the local television station! This will take more time and preparation, though, pastor." "The men's group can't agree on their next project, pastor. They really need your leadership." And so it goes—all good things, but just too many of them. First, to deal with our increased load, the enemy tempts us to slack on our prayer time (Who will notice? You can make it up later.) to provide the extra time. Simultaneously, we're tempted to take on more than we can handle, relying on adrenalin and the fragile patience of our families. Understandably, our sleep gets disturbed, exhausting us further. The "opportunities" just keep coming, but seemingly unassociated with our spiritual formation initiative. Now we're running on fumes. Yet, people praise us for our hard work and obvious commitment. What will it take for us to realize that our addiction to busyness hasn't been motivated by the Lord at all? The enemy has used our sin-based desires to suck us into what feels like a lose-lose situation. Debbie Swindoll describes another line of attack which exacerbates our busyness.

> Ironically, one thing that we have experienced often at Grafted Life is an attack against our practical functioning as an organization. For example, Satan seems to be particularly fond of attacking us through our website. We have had many problems with our website developers; we have been hacked by Islamic extremists; some of our web developers have even experienced attack in their personal lives when they worked on our site. We often find ourselves the target of these subtler practical derailments that cause discouragement, delays and distractions.

I can relate to Debbie's experience, having had to pray over Skype and phone connections when I'm cut off at the precise moment when a spiritual direction conversation became critical, or we're in the midst of warfare prayer. It's happened too many times to be brushed off as coincidence.

Once in overload, we're then tempted to gloss over other issues with a careless attitude. The enemy attempts to fill us with pride and the delusion that a little unfaithfulness from such a brilliant and spiritual leader won't be a problem. It's all targeted to make us fearful and careless, causing us to slight our relationship with God and power through ministry and relationships on our own. However, the roots of our gluttony may be "powered" by deeper issues within us.

I succumbed to this aspect of gluttony while serving my first church in rural Minnesota. Right out of seminary and filled with grand ideas for the Church, I tackled every opportunity to preach with power, enhance the worship service, recruit lay leadership, provide meaningful pastoral care, launch new mission initiatives, etc. Encouraged with this young and energetic pastor, the congregation responded wonderfully! I was having a blast. At the same time, the Lord began wooing me toward a deeper life of abiding prayer. I began reading about listening prayer, meditation, and contemplation. Soon, however, the "demands" of my young family and this vibrant church took all my time—more than all my time. Fortunately, within a year, I landed in the hospital with serious pneumonia—exhausted. The Lord used those days in isolation to get my attention and show me that I needed to follow Him—first in prayer. God didn't lead me to the end of my rope—my gluttony did that. As we spot our gluttony attachments, we can then surrender them and learn to let our Lord fill the needy spaces they have left.

Avarice - extreme greed for wealth or material gain:

Men and women don't usually go into the ministry for financial wealth or material gain—at least not most of us. Other kinds of "gain," however, fit quite well within our religious settings. Henri Nouwen, drawing on the temptations of Jesus, mentions areas of greed that can become snags for each of us: success, popularity, and power (cf. Luke 4:1-13).[1] Nouwen suggests that, when we doubt God's ability or willingness to provide all we need, we can easily turn to these false gods to help us feel like worthwhile leaders. Let's

1. Taken from an address to Erlam college. Written source unknown.

look at how these three may invite avarice attacks from the dragon, which identify attachments in our own hearts.

The Avarice of Success - I don't know anyone who doesn't want to be successful—at least successful in the things that person values. In each area of ministry, we define success in a unique way that seems reasonable and attainable. Some of us may want large ministries with a wide impact. Others fancy a unique, cutting edge venture. Still others may feel that success looks like peace and the absence of conflict. Personal "success" can easily become couched as God's calling—the Great Commandment and Great Commission, the Kingdom of God, etc. If I'm successful, then God will be glorified—right? Of course, our membership wants success too, so what's wrong with success?

The problem with success as our motivator comes with its difficulty to be measured, especially in the church. We have no legitimate standards by which to measure success in a local congregation. Others judge our level of success by their own standards. Someone is always ahead of us. Our members are always changing. Just about the time we have "peace on earth," some malcontent comes along. The "other shoe"—the unpredictable and uncontrollable lurks just around the corner of every evidence of success we seek. "The higher we climb, the further we might fall." To make matters worse, the leader's definition of success differs, to some degree, from others in the congregation. Just when we're feeling pretty good about the day or season, someone comes into our office and points out our failures. "Success" often represents a moving target, floating just outside our reach. Because success eludes us, our desires for success cast shadows of fear on everything we do.

The enemy wiggles into our success needs in various ways. He specifically targets the very things that we desire most. If he can't totally undermine our goal, he can worry us about failure and frustrate our efforts to succeed. He attempts to distract our focus on the Lord, hoping we will hurt others with whatever we do when we're worried and frustrated. Most of all, the enemy whispers fear messages about the potential for failure (the opposite of success, right?). He tempts us to evaluate everything we do in terms of its probability to succeed, rather than the Lord's calling and direction.

I can imagine myself reading this book and evaluating the chances that this Contagious Fire approach will work in my church. Maybe you've been doing that, too. It's the wrong question, of course. If success has become important to me, either because I think I possess it and want to hold on to it, or because it has alluded me and I want to take my best shot at it, my fears about success/failure always guide me—more than the Lord. Our "success" is simple obedience—the outcome is none of our business.

The Avarice of Popularity - Popularity may well be a category of success for many of us, particularly pastors and caregivers who value the feelings of others. Like success, I don't know anyone who wants to be "unpopular" with the people he/she values. Good relationships with our people and loving interactions provide doorways to ministry; they're also an important part of our spiritual formation.

We look for popularity in various ways. Some want to be known as a great preacher, while others look for popularity in their counseling or visionary leadership. Our popularity becomes attached to performance. Many of us seek to get our popularity needs met through affirmation from anyone for anything—by pleasing them. So, what's wrong with people-pleasing? Like success, popularity isn't necessarily a problem until it becomes an attachment—something really important to us—more important than our relationship with God—than pleasing God.

The problem with people-pleasing lies in its illusive posture just beyond our control. No matter how hard we work, how well we prepare, and how many people support us, the changing tides of opinion always threaten to snatch our popularity away. The enemy uses this attachment mercilessly against us, trying to make us flatterers with some and paranoid with others.

Unexpected emails and phone calls easily become threats of disaster. Like the avarice of success, we can become deceived that popularity must be what God really wants for us. I might long for a deeper relationship with God, for me and my people. However, if it might threaten my popularity, I may decide, "This may not be the right time to be spending more time in prayer." If I have already launched into the spiritual formation journey personally and with my ministry, the enemy will use my desire for popularity to try to get me to turn back or to proceed with such caution that nothing will ever come of it.

JD Ward comments about the subtle contract that our desire for popularity can form in a congregation.

> It can be tempting to accept the social contract pastors have with congregations. "As long as you don't ruffle the feathers, you can have that pension our church offers, and I will even throw in my condo in Hawaii once in a while." In other words, we like the benefits we get by maintaining the status quo. This can extend to our members too. Most people have bought into the American Dream of security, comfort, and pleasure with a little of the Jesus sprinkled on top. The fear that intimacy with God may lead them to a life that estranges them from the benefits of society, is a prime reason I believe people stay away from serious formation and discipleship. People (me too at times) believe the lie of culture over the words of Jesus, especially about lifestyle issues. Another way to say this is, we would rather experience the joy of consuming than experience the joy of being consumed. I think this can be a major hindrance for both formation and mission.
> These subtle "success contracts" can become attachments for both leaders and the congregational members. We become attached to popularity because we have come to believe that it will make us a worthwhile person. Meanwhile, God offers us daughtership and sonship.

The Avarice of Power - We've discussed the pitfalls of power-based leadership in earlier chapters. Suffice it to say here that our desire for power, either through control or influence, provides our enemy with one of his greatest avenues of attack. We know that only our Lord God possesses any real power; He doesn't need to wrestle power from us. Nor, does He give power to us. When we seek our own power, instead of God's, He lets us go for it—He's not a controlling parent. We then put ourselves in a powerless no-man's land that makes us easy pickings for the father of lies. We "ask wrongly" when we plead that God will protect our position of power. Only when we surrender completely to His Lordship, His direction, His control, and His responsibility for outcomes can we be of any use to Him. So, He lovingly lets the devil work us over until we've had enough. Unfortunately, that takes a long time for many of us—to surrender the illusion of our own power and surrender to God's. We become attached to the illusion of power because we have come to believe that power makes us a worthwhile person.

Self-esteem - confidence in one's own worth or abilities; self-respect

The Desert Fathers may list self-esteem last because wounds related to our identity and worth often lie within the roots of all the attachments. Every one of us grows up building a structure of self-identity. Our Creator placed this need within us as a special part of the image of God. We're designed to be loved, to be of worth and value, to have meaning in the world around us and beyond. God offers us all that through our relationship with Him. He offers us adoption as daughters and sons, heirs to the whole universe, His beloved, and fills us with His Spirit to bring in His Kingdom.

Unfortunately, most followers of Jesus formed their self-identity outside the wonderful Good News that's offered to us. We've used the building blocks of our family mirror, our appearance or abilities, and our early histories of perceived successes and failures. We drew conclusions based on worldly markers rather than on our identity in Jesus. Whether we came out of this process with relatively good feelings about ourselves or judgments of failure and inadequacy, the result remains the same—we live with conclusions based on faulty data. At some point after this developmental process, we received or recognized the Good News—Jesus and all that God gives us. The problem remains, however, that we receive Christ with our old identity. Even though we may learn the right theology, the little girl or boy within us "knows who we really are." Much of the work of the Holy Spirit in our spiritual formation focuses on enabling us to let go of the high or low self-esteem identity and live into the person we really are—God's beloved.

In the process of this transformation, however, we remain vulnerable to the enemy's self-esteem temptations—to pride or to shame. Either one, when taken in, renders us blind. Satan knows all about the structures we've built to try to support our self-esteem. Many have built their house on the approval of a mother or father, now long dead. Others' OK-ness may depend on their skill or ability to achieve certain goals, success, and popularity in all their varied forms. When these false structures seem to be holding up pretty well, the enemy tries to puff us up with pride and get us to judge others as less than ourselves. When we use caution to support our low self-esteem, the enemy praises our wisdom and shames us further in hopes of shutting us down altogether. He tries to blind us to the fragility of our self-esteem structure in hopes that we won't see the house built on sand beginning to crumble. When we become aware that our self-foundation feels shaky, the enemy attacks with memories of every dark failure or potential failure to convince us that hope lies beyond our reach.

JD Ward comments about the potential disasters of our blindness caused by our need to maintain the image of having it together.

> *Another way I have seen formation take a hit is attack by Satan to exploit a real weakness, in the leader, especially ones the leader felt they had already overcome. This can play out in many ways, marriage attack, financial trouble, failure of legacy longings such as a building campaign where a leader feels they need to establish their validity, or even the baser level of temptations (sexuality, alcohol, anger) resurfacing with a powerful force.*

Finding self-esteem only as beloveds of Jesus opens us to the light of Christ which enables us to turn to Him before disaster strikes.

Self-esteem's Fear of Intimacy - All of the attachments we've discussed above tend to isolate us—from God and from others. Consciously or unconsciously, we hide—terrified that others will discover our woundedness and shame us into worthlessness. So, we keep others at a safe distance. While we know, intellectually, that God knows all, we may feel safer at some distance—Jesus up in the sky at the right hand of the throne of the Father. We may find ourselves feeling quite comfortable with enough people to support us and enough of God to get us to heaven. Our enemy assures us that this safe distance feels just right.

The rub comes, however, when the Lord begins to knock in new ways at the door of our heart, asking to come in, to draw us closer so that we might know His love more profoundly. On the one hand, we may find His invitations attractive and part of us longs to let ourselves be fully seen and loved. Yet part of us may feel uncomfortable and uneasy—somehow this nearness feels threatening. Our enemy whispers, "If you get too close, He'll reveal all your faults and ask things of you that you can't do. You'll feel ashamed and miserable. Better stay busy at a safe distance." Terry Tarleton shares an example from his own experience.

> *I know another senior pastor who noticed that I was more peaceful than I had been in the past. When he asked me what was different, I explained how I had become open and honest with Jesus regarding my heart; and that my intimacy with Him had grown; and that Jesus was really becoming my best friend. He responded, "Yeah, but to do that I have to look at my junk, and I would rather focus on the external where I can measure things like attendance and finances." We want to operate out of black and white truth and not out of vague feelings that may betray what we know to be true. Many of our people have struggled with going deeper because of the fear of engaging feelings. I think the transition from head to heart (or at least addressing the disconnect between the two) is a scary one.*

The same kind of inner conversation goes on when our Lord invites us to love others as He loves us. As Jesus invites us to accompany Him into the lives of others in honesty and vulnerability, we may begin to feel claustrophobic—too close for comfort. The enemy again whispers, "If you get too close...."

Of course, we're not helpless against all of these attacks. The Lord stands ready to rescue us and wage war on our behalf more than we can ever see. It's hard for us to realize in the thick of battle, however, that only what feels like "defeat" can open our eyes to the door to victory—our real identity in Christ. As long as we think that we have what it takes, in our own strength, we'll always overestimate ourselves and underestimate the enemy. When, however, we recognize our own weakness we're able to stand in the power of our true identities as daughters and sons of God. "He who wishes to save his life will lose it; but whoever loses his life for My sake will find it" (cf. Matthew 16:25). "My grace is sufficient for you, for power is perfected in weakness" (cf. 2 Corinthians 12:9).

Now that we've touched on the dragons we face in our personal walk with Jesus, let's look at some of the attacks we encounter in the church.

Dragon Attacks in the Church

I've been surprised at the resistance to spiritual change in most congregations that I've pastored or consulted with. We might think, "Who could possibly be against spiritual growth—a more loving and vibrant relationship with Jesus, etc.?" However, for varieties of reasons some of our members will experience anywhere from cautious resistance to full-out rebellion. Resistance to change, misunderstanding, fear, and heightened spiritual warfare can all flare when the stakes become high. If painting the restrooms the "wrong" color can stir up a hornet's nest, just try messing with people's lifelong traditions, exposing their secret spiritual struggles, and asking them to take responsibility for responding to the Creator of the Universe.

One church that *Imago Christi* coached (We'll call it Jordan Community), moved largely unscathed into a deepening emphasis on spiritual formation ministry for several years. *Imago Christi* had provided several Spiritual

Formation Discovery retreats, first for staff and lay leaders, and then for the congregation. While a relatively small percentage of the members attended the Discoveries, the feedback reflected an overwhelmingly positive experience. With full support and participation of the pastors and several key leaders, a new ministry team formed to plan and implement spiritual formation at a congregational level. Sermon series cast a vision for personal spiritual growth. The ministry team met with small group leaders and other ministry teams, and made presentations to the church on Sunday mornings— all to communicate God's invitation to grow us all spiritually and enable us to experience His love more profoundly. In each case, the message seemed to be well received.

After a year or two, and seemingly out of nowhere, rumbles began to emerge about spiritual formation. A few members had checked anti-spiritual formation websites including ones attacking Renovaré. Believing what they read, these new "dissidents" passed unsubstantiated rumors among their friends in the congregation. Some people became concerned. Of course, no one took their concerns directly to leadership. Because the Senior Pastor had led the charge in the call to spiritual formation, he quickly became the target of that concern. Interestingly, the issues seemed both diverse and vague.

Some people challenged that the Bible provided all they (and others) needed; why talk about spiritual disciplines and special ways to pray? Others expressed concern that the spiritual formation emphasis felt like a departure from the denominational traditions—never mind that the denomination taught spiritual formation in its seminary and provided spiritual direction training for its pastors. A few members took the critical atmosphere as an opportunity to attack the Senior Pastor about his leadership style. Petitions requested that the Elder Board "review the staffing effectiveness." Some families, who had served as pillars of the church, threatened to leave; several did. Fortunately, the Elder Board supported the Senior Pastor and the spiritual formation initiative with an open and supportive posture. Congregational information meetings were held where people could ask questions and receive straightforward answers. The Senior Pastor survived and has recovered from the heart arrows he took from people in whom he'd invested so much.

However, congregational leadership became more cautious and spiritual formation initiatives slowed. Most of the people who left the church found new church homes, but both those who stayed and those who left experienced the wounds of accusation and rejection that come with any family breakup. That year proved to be a difficult one for most of the congregation. What went wrong at Jordan Community? What might go wrong in your ministry?

Hind-sighting, in the case of Jordan, didn't reveal major blunders. Jordan had always been a solid biblical church with meaningful mission and compassion ministries. No congregation nor its leadership team would ever claim perfection. Rather than some leadership blunder or congregational flaw, the "difficult year" can probably be attributed to a number of common human conditions that can arise in any congregation—commonalities which provide unfortunate opportunities for the enemy of the Lord and His Church.

While the list could be endless, several sore spots can become inadvertently poked when we take lifelong discipleship in the congregation seriously. Review the issues listed below. Which ones did you, as a leader, struggle with initially? Do you spot issues that have a "history" in your ministry setting? Do some of them particularly irritate you and make you impatient? Probably none of them can be totally avoided. Our church cultures embed assumptions about how we handle change, misunderstanding, criticism and the status quo. Knowing your church's culture and history and anticipating some of its corporate resistance patterns will be important in leading spiritual formation in the church effectively. While we can attempt to predict and defuse potential landmines, our success in dealing with the dragon will primarily reflect the depth of our spiritual leadership. It's from that well that we find strength, wisdom, and perseverance—and even the resolve to love people in the midst of their struggles. Let's consider some of the issues we and our members face.

Fear of Change

People usually join a given church for the way it is, not for how it should change. In the midst of a world seemingly out of control, most people like their church to be stable and a safe place—predictable, consistent, reliable. With our surroundings in such flux, many of us happily settle for spiritual milk or even boredom if it can offer us a sanctuary of peace and security. Some people like change and the resulting challenge. Others can tolerate change only as long as the promised payoffs justify the risk of the unknown. A few find change terrifying, speculating not only a glass half empty but draining, with the feared disastrous potential downsides taken as a direct personal assault.

With our danger antennas already buzzed by the media, many of us live on full alert—defenses up and anxiety heightened. For many, it may not take much to sound the alarm and spike the adrenalin. Fight or flight—the response can be surprising and hurtful, and often seemingly irrational. The frightened need someone to blame and something to fix. Scripture tells us that the devil uses fear (ultimately, fear of death) as the power of his assaults (cf. Hebrews 2:14-15). While most people struggling with changes in their church don't take fear that far intentionally, the enemy subtly whispers the chain of what-ifs that could spell death. "All I know is this really bothers me. It feels dangerous." Ted Wueste adds an important dimension in understanding our reaction to change.

Usually, no one is afraid of change itself—they fear loss. A significant question might be, "what are people afraid to lose?"

It's important, therefore, to ask ourselves that question, both for ourselves and for our congregation: "What might our people be afraid of losing when challenged to let Jesus draw nearer to them?" Some people might fear losing their appearance of spiritual eliteness. Others might fear the loss of predictability in congregational life. There may be fear of developing new programs can mean reallocation of budget dollars, leaving older programs underfunded. Many people fear deeper intimacy with God. It might mean

252

that I could lose precious time or have to give up some unhealthy habits. The list of "sacred cows" that people may be holding onto seems endless. We may rationalize that one day we will gladly get rid of the things the Lord asks us to surrender, but not now.

It's possible, however, that Jesus may not want to take something away, but to redeem it. For example, one couple from Jordan Church felt strongly that biblical literacy provided the church's most important foundation. They had worked hard over the years to establish and lead study groups that dug deeply into Scriptures. They feared that meditative approaches to the Bible would eventually undermine people's desire to really understand God's written word. Instead of verbalizing this fear to church leadership, however, they simply opposed meditative uses of Scripture, accusing them of being "New Age."

Eventually, their concerns came to light. Leadership affirmed the couple's desire for biblical literacy and took steps to make clear that we cannot presume to accurately hear God's word to us in a text if we don't know what it means. Eventually, many people who felt blessed by meditating on Scripture signed up for classes and groups which approached the Bible didactically. The couple and others like them learned that Bible study contains many depths in which we can meet God. God redeemed a feared loss by turning it into an advancement for the congregation. If we can recognize our people's feared losses, we may be able to assuage their fears in advance.

Misunderstanding

Any attempt at change usually provides opportunities for misunderstanding and confusion. When people don't understand or misunderstand, they often react negatively. One might think that people would simply ask for clarification and all would be well. While we might ask leadership for help if we realize we don't understand, most of us find it easier to guess or depend on someone else's take. More often, a person doesn't realize that they've misinterpreted a word or meaning and feel justified in their negative response. Leadership can assume that they have communicated clearly, but then months later, hear quotes which imply a totally different meaning than was intended. We need to be careful about the language we choose and the contexts in which we use it, but we have little control over what others hear.

A significant misunderstanding has to do with the nature of spiritual formation itself. While the Church has talked about "discipleship" for generations, language associated with spiritual formation can be unfamiliar to most believers. I am often asked about the difference between spiritual formation and discipleship as a way of asking, "What in the world is spiritual formation and why haven't I ever heard about it in my 49 years of church membership?" My "crystal-clear", and hopefully non-defensive, response explains that the term "discipleship" has been used primarily to describe the intentional instruction and coaching of new and young believers. Spiritual formation, on the other hand, refers to the process of spiritual growth throughout one's entire lifetime. While we could try to redefine discipleship, most people have found it helpful to use a different term. With all that said, their concern often remains. For one, they probably have not heard the word "spiritual" used apart from direct reference to the Holy Spirit (It's only used 30 times in the Bible, and only by the apostle Paul). More often, people have heard associated terms in non-Christian contexts, such as New Age, Native American Spiritism, or Eastern Religions. Even the word "spiritual" can cause suspicion.

"Formation" can be just as problematic, although not as negatively loaded. What does it mean for a person to be formed? What does it mean for one to be formed spiritually? We understand discipleship to include teaching, training, and character development, but this sounds different. If, then, into this cautious and confused mix we throw other words like Lectio Divina, silence, solitude, meditation, contemplation, mystic, Catholic, monk, monastery, vision, discernment…. Stop! We may find that we've brewed a soup that many consider inedible, if not poisonous. We can introduce new language, but we can't assume that people know what we mean or don't put other meanings to our terms. Whatever the cause, when people become confused they either withdraw or take the offensive. Either option usually results in hurt and provides an opportunity for the enemy to stir the water in negative ways. We've addressed some of these language and term issues in Chapter 7: Teaching About Spiritual Formation.

Criticism

OK, let's assume that we've managed to accurately define all our words and clarify any misunderstandings—with ample biblical references. We often face another unintended response to our intended message of "good news." We desire to communicate that God has provided a wonderful lifelong journey of deepening love, intimacy, and abundant life. We have extended a gracious invitation to envision a new future with God, filled with adventure. Our message casts great hope that God will redeem our faults and difficulties and turn them into victories for us and those around us. To help enable all this to happen, we offer a long list of spiritual practices and growth opportunities. Shouldn't that sound just like free ice cream on a sunny summer day?

However, good news can sound "not so good" when people think they hear implied criticism. When leadership suggests that I should grow spiritually, come to know God more deeply, and walk with Him more closely, I may well receive a message something like this:

Tom, you've failed as a Christian. Although you may be saved, you've missed the point. Those years of faith in Jesus, untold hours of church attendance and service, and your hard work at loving others just hasn't been enough. Don't feel too bad, though; most of your fellow church members find themselves in the same deplorable condition. Not all is lost, however; you still have a chance. Through a lot of hard work and a completely changed lifestyle you can get right with God and possibly, possibly, become one of the spiritually elite. When you finally arrive, you will be asked to take on even more responsibilities at church and in the community. Now repent and get to work.

To that message, unintended as it may be, I may just close my ears, walk away, or use language that can't be printed in this book. I probably won't, however, tell leaders around me what I think I've heard and how I feel. I won't say anything for fear they'll just try to prove how messed up I really am. Unless our people have access to safe and trusted relationships that can listen undefensively and help reframe the message, we may never know why some people turn a deaf ear, withdraw, or fight back.

Afraid of God

We discussed in our chapter on teaching spiritual formation that we may need to start teaching by addressing theological misconceptions that would certainly undermine any invitation to deepening intimacy with God. Probably the greatest misconception that blocks this invitation stems from negative views of God. Who wants to snuggle up to a God that's dangerous, hurtful, or uninterested?

Imago Christi sees these negative views of God quite often, even among leaders. We use a spiritual timeline exercise to launch our Spiritual Formation Discovery retreat. People are invited to depict their spiritual history over their lifetime through significant events in their lives. As part of this exercise, participants are asked to identify what we call their "Relational Baseline"— their changing view of God from childhood to the present. As an aid, we provide a list of possibilities such as Creator, Judge, Shepherd, Beloved, Grandfather, Parent, Truth, King, Helper, Friend, Mystery, etc. Depending on one's personal experience, each analogy or view of God can bring with it radically different emotional responses. It's one thing to want to grow in love with a "father" God if I have experienced a loving and reliable father, growing up. On the other hand, if one's father or mother relationship was abusive and painful, one might have a quite different reaction. It's quite natural to project one's experiences of parents and significant authority figures onto God.

I find that many people in our churches fear God, but not in the healthy respectful way that the Bible discusses—they're simply afraid of God. Whether this fear emerges from personal guilt and shame, bad theology, poor biblical teaching, unforgiveness, or… many people aren't so sure they want a closer relationship with God. As we discussed in our issues with intimacy, it can feel much safer for God to stay in the sky, for them to stay on the ground, to possibly check in occasionally, and perhaps ask for help for really big deals. These negative views of God develop over a lifetime, reinforced by wounding experiences, and ingrained in the person's identity. Their "God-view" becomes internalized into a "self-view."

The resulting self-talk may go something like this. "I'm not really a worthy person. God may love me because He has to, but He certainly doesn't like me; I don't even like myself. I am constantly disappointing God. He's just waiting to say, 'I told you so,' and put another black mark against my name. I believe in God and want to go to heaven, but don't ask me to get too close now." It's surprising that most fearful churchgoers don't realize that's how they feel at all. They think they believe the "Good News" message proclaimed by the preacher, never really wondering why "just occasional church attendance" feels quite adequate. These "God-fearing" folks, at best, ignore our invitations and, at worst, organize to make us stop torturing them. The enemy pokes and prods at these fears, assuring believers of the validity of the lies about God. He suggests that they are being asked to do the impossible and he prompts resentment for such unreasonable leadership.

These deep-seated fearful relationships with God can't be fixed by a sermon or the right Bible study. Like a husband and wife who have become afraid of each other, this fearfulness toward God will take inner healing, new experiences of trust, encouragement, and risk—in a community of brothers and sisters who truly live out the loving presence of Jesus. Restoration of relationship, trust, hope, and love may also take spiritual direction or counseling, and most certainly, healing prayer. That brings us to our next opportunity for the dragon to strike.

Challenged Complacency

Some years ago, I was invited to become a spiritual director for a ministry to high-powered Christian business and governmental leaders. These talented and influential men and women regularly attended Bible studies, filled meaningful roles in their churches, and gave generously to ministry ventures. In the course of my role there, we exposed these leaders to the top names in the spiritual formation world. At first, we saw lots of enthusiasm, but it didn't take long to realize that these seeds fell mostly on rocky soil—nothing grew. I discovered that these leaders felt that their Christianity was "good enough." Since then, I've run into "good enough Christianity" more often than I can recount. Why consider spiritual growth when one's current spiritual state is good enough?

Every church has its share of "cheap grace" members who take in a little and give the minimum. That's not what I am talking about here. What church wouldn't be delighted to be filled with the kind of men and women I described above? They're true believers, moral and upstanding members, who demonstrate their faith with skilled leadership, active participation, and big donations to the budget. Many of them, however, ignore, resist, or undermine a spiritual formation movement in the church. Why? Their faith is "good enough." "Spiritual growth may be needed for many others, but I'm just fine, thank you. Don't try to push something on me that I don't need."

When challenged, such a believer might respond, "Why might I think my faith is good enough? Consider it from my perspective. First, I have accepted Jesus as my Lord and Savior and am assured of my salvation. I am an active member of a successful church and generously donate my time and talents. I pray and study my Bible. I am a good husband/wife/father/mother. God has proven that my faith is good enough by blessing me with influence and wealth. I am a busy and important person with hardly any time to myself. You're telling me that God wants more? 'More' takes more work, and more work takes time. I don't have more time. Of course, I know I'm not perfect, but my relationship with God has been proven to be good enough. I resent that you can't see that."

Just like the other challenges that our people face, this person won't tell you this straight out, but their behavior will communicate their feelings—from indifference to counterattack. The enemy loves it.

Ted Wueste identifies another factor that may look like complacency, but which may require a different response.

> It feels to me that assessing "readiness" for both individuals and a congregation is important. I ran into some mistakes early on in my spiritual formation journey when I rushed people ahead – especially leadership. Some of my most "difficult" people were fellow pastors and elders. Specifically, I led a group of pastors/elders and spouses through a contemplative study. One of the leaders kept wanting to discuss things on the "head" level and really pushed back about talking about the heart. He just wasn't ready. Instead of doing "come one, come all" kinds of things, I've learned to opt for invitational offerings. I also try to talk people out of things at times. I've had many people who were willing to follow because they trusted me, but they just weren't ready. When I discover that certain people aren't ready, I try to normalize things for them and give them an "out" that isn't awkward for them.

Before we make judgments about our people we must come to know them well enough to understand their place in the journey and what next steps will be appropriate.

Mock Battles

I know, this list could go on forever, but I want to mention one more congregational lair from which dragons attack when we challenge our members to become mature in the Lord: hidden grumbles. In every congregation or ministry, some people have a seemingly minor grumble—a dislike for someone or something. While the issue niggles at them, its significance doesn't warrant a frontal attack. Or, maybe, they have tried addressing the issue with no success. So, the grumble smolders under the surface, and the devil blows softly on its coals.

Although the underground grumbler may not be personally opposed to the spiritual formation movement in the church, he or she, having become accustomed to fellowship with other grumblers, recognizes that a storm brews and people are being blamed. Sometimes, without even recognizing the source of their zeal, these grumblers can pick up the flag of discontent and use it to attack leadership or others in the church, joining the anti-spiritual formation ranks. The grumbler won't tell you what the real issue is; he/she may even have forgotten in the midst of the battle, but the arrows prove no less lethal.

The Dragons of Spiritual Warfare

I have to admit that spiritual warfare didn't rank high on my list of church renewal issues—until I became a pastor. My seminary training talked a lot about sin, but minimized the devil's role, if not ignoring it altogether. For months, I wrote off my dark thoughts and the subtle stumbles of some of my parishioners as coincidence or stupidity or.... Finally, the negative coincidences in people's lives became more than statistically probable. I had to relook at those passages in Scripture that talked about the devil and what to do about his constant harassment and deception. As God opened my eyes to the schemes of the enemy, I became totally amazed both at his subtle, and not so subtle, involvement with many in my congregation. More than that, I became amazed at God's power when I resisted and taught my people to do the same. Scripture remains absolutely clear about spiritual warfare, from the experiences and teachings of Jesus to the lessons learned and the clear instructions of the Apostles. I won't minimize the reality of spiritual warfare again; and I hope you won't either.

As you've hopefully noticed, I've mentioned the role of the enemy in each of the dragon conditions above. I've not gone so far as to "blame" those situations on demonic influence, but to miss his involvement would be foolish. Personally, I don't believe that the devil can make believers "do" anything, but Scripture clearly shows that he can lie, tempt, and deceive. The enemy uses our weaknesses as opportunities to con us into working for his purposes rather than God's. Therefore, as we face these reactions from our members, we must recognize that the battle is more complex than may be apparent. As we discussed in our chapter about spiritual formation teaching, for our sake and the welfare of our congregation, we must personally become knowledgeable about scriptural teaching regarding spiritual warfare and then teach our people. Within this category of dragon attack, like all the others above, our Lord has not left us helpless. Yet many ignore the obvious and get beat to a pulp before getting rescued.

Pathways to Victory - In Community

You may be thinking, "OK, Ashbrook, you've made your point. But you've made me wonder if I'm up for the battle! I'm not the only one who will have to face this warfare; even if I personally feel relatively confident in the Lord about all this, I'm not so sure about my people." Believe me when I say that I understand. I've described the battles I've faced and still fight; I have the scars to prove it. Having said that, I can also say that **God uses these battles as a vital part of our transformation. God uses the devil's schemes against the devil himself—for our good and for God's glory.**

> ... we also exult in our tribulations, knowing that tribulation brings about perseverance; and perseverance, proven character; and proven character, hope; and hope does not disappoint, because the love of God has been poured out within our hearts through the Holy Spirit who was given to us. Romans 5:3-5
>
> My grace is sufficient for you, for power is perfected in weakness. 2 Corinthians 12:9
>
> Consider it all joy, my brethren, when you encounter various trials, knowing that the testing of your faith produces endurance. And let endurance have its perfect result, so that you may be perfect and complete, lacking in nothing. James 1:2-4

The Desert Fathers similarly taught that the Lord uses the devil's temptations to help point out our vulnerabilities and cause us to come to Him for transformation. At just the right time, the Lord seems to withdraw

261

His light, His grace, ever so little from the believer. When the devil sees the disciple in a weakened state, he evaluates the best target and attacks, confident of victory. But in the midst of the aggression, the Lord restores His light and the disciple sees the place of weakness, resists in the power of the Holy Spirit, and turns to the Lord for strengthening and renewal.

I love the way Evagrios puts it, "When a demon is caught in the act of temptation by the believer, who immediately turns to the Lord for help and power, that demon, so scorned and ridiculed by his fellow demons for his blunder, flees to the pits of hell, never again to return to the scene of his demise."[2] Makes me smile just to write it! Jesus has won the victory for the Kingdom and for our faithfulness in His service.

Shepherding the Hearts of God's Beloved: There's probably no greater place than "facing the dragon" where we need to live into Jesus' invitation to Peter: "Do you love me… tend my lambs, shepherd my sheep, tend my sheep" (cf. John 21:15-16). Jesus had just been murdered; the disciples' lives were at risk; and the whole endeavor had fallen apart. Who could blame the disciples for running for cover? Yet Jesus told His followers not to run, but to walk into the flock and tend the hearts of His beloved. When we leaders have risked our livelihoods, stepped out in faith, done our best, and now face the devil's wrath and betrayal of members of our church family, everything in us tells us to run, fight back, or fix. But Jesus, who has led us all along—who knew full well the valley that lay ahead—calls us to love, to listen, to minister, to heal, and to stand our ground.

Jesus came in love to reconcile us to the Father, adopt us as His brothers and sisters into the fullness of abundant life, create within us a new heart and mind that can fellowship with God, and invite us into His Kingdom victory. It took the Cross. Should we be surprised or timid that we, too, experience that same battle? Said another way, can we say that we really follow Jesus if we don't?

---

2. The Philokalia, Vol 1, Faber and Faber Limited, London 1983.

Not that I have already obtained it or have already become perfect, but I press on so that I may lay hold of that for which also I was laid hold of by Christ Jesus. Brethren, I do not regard myself as having laid hold of it yet; but one thing I do: forgetting what lies behind and reaching forward to what lies ahead, I press on toward the goal for the prize of the upward call of God in Christ Jesus. Philippians 3:12-14

What does it mean to love Jesus and to tend and shepherd Jesus' lambs and sheep in the context of the dragon's attack? Jesus demonstrated just what He meant through modeling it in His own ministry. Jesus met the dragon Himself; He taught His disciples about the wolf that would come to steal their hearts; He showed them how to seek the Father for healing and strength. Let's look at all three in our own contexts.

Facing the Dragon Ourselves: One of the significant reasons that I and our Contributors have insisted that you begin this journey yourself, before casting a vision for spiritual formation and missional outreach in your congregation, has to do with gaining experience in facing your own dragons. One of the reasons we have implored you to gather around you a spiritual leadership community is to enable you to survive and grow in the midst of the dragon's attack. Just as Peter had to face his own cowardice and fear of growing intimacy with Jesus before he could tend and shepherd, we too must let Jesus take us into our own darkness and turn it into light. Within a community of trust, we can confess our attachments when we stumble over them, hear the voice that says lovingly, "Isn't that wonderful!" and grasp our Lord's hand for forgiveness, healing, and renewal. Peter must have done just that with the other Apostles or we would not have read of his discussion with Jesus. The apostle James describes this process in the context of healing.

Is anyone among you suffering? Then he must pray. Is anyone cheerful? He is to sing praises. Is anyone among you sick? Then he must call for the elders of the church and they are to pray over him, anointing him with oil in the name of the Lord; and the prayer offered in faith will restore the one who is sick, and the Lord will raise him up, and if he has committed sins, they will be forgiven him. Therefore, confess your sins to one another, and pray for one another so that you may be healed. The prayer of a righteous man can accomplish much. James 5:13-16

As we discussed above, we leaders share all the same foibles found in our congregations. But because we're leaders, the enemy will attack us first, trying to deceive us and then accuse us and try to shame us into hiding. Then if possible, he'll attempt to cause us to fall. Therefore, we must first tend and shepherd our own hearts in the company of other shepherds—elders who can pray with and for us. Only in the context of our own brokenness and redemption can we shepherd and tend our Lord's lambs and sheep. Only in the experience of the Lord's victory in our own lives can we ever bring hope to others.

Bringing Light Into Darkness: We can face our own weaknesses when we know that our Shepherd, through His loving Light, reveals our sins to us as stepping stones for transformation. However, many of us, live in darkness, believing that the journey should be easy, that sin really isn't that big of a deal, feeling shame when Jesus shows us where we need to grow, and hiding in self-condemnation or denial. We must, therefore, stand with the apostle Paul who proclaimed, "And He [Jesus] has said to me, 'My grace is sufficient for you, for power is perfected in weakness.' Most gladly, therefore, I will rather boast about my weaknesses, so that the power of Christ may dwell in me." 2 Corinthians 12:9 Not only must we learn to do spiritual warfare ourselves, but we must equip our members to experience victory in Christ. They, too, must learn how to put on the whole armor of God and to resist. For example, Debbie Swindoll suggests that we might set up a specific prayer team to deal with these dragon attacks launched against the congregation.

Our people will only believe that the battle is real, and that victory is possible when they see that reality in their leaders. We have to go further than teaching the Scriptures; we have to share the places where God's grace has been sufficient in our own lives. Our people need to see our battles and witness our Lord's victory in them. We have to "de-normalize" the old normal! People have believed that it's normal to have it altogether, or at least pretend to. In fact, the Kingdom's REAL normal can only be found in the ups and downs of our journey of spiritual growth, looking forward to recognizing our weaknesses so that we may become perfected in the power of Christ Who dwells in us! A significant part of igniting a congregation on contagious fire must include creating a journey climate where people remember that growth is healthy and growing pains are to be celebrated. Celebrating the personal testimonies, struggles, and victory in the congregation can help normalize spiritual growth. We can see, in the lives of those we respect, life's challenges, and the Lord's faithfulness and power in the face of the enemy's attempts to steal and destroy.

Chuck Orwiler also addresses the importance of ways to "normalize" life together as a church.

I'm convinced that the way we conduct the business of the church is perhaps our clearest insight into our life of faith. That is, the workings of the church "machinery" is an eminently practical laboratory revealing where we are placing our trust. Consequently, the sand the enemy throws into the gears, and our subsequent response is right before us. Since this realm always involves leadership, it may be the key area to address in terms of developing a communal kingdom response to our Lord and to the enemy.

Light in one area of our ministry and darkness in another debunks a leader's spiritual authority as well as the spiritual authenticity of the group. God's light must shine into every aspect of our ministry together, whether prayer group or church business.

Tending and Shepherding Jesus' Lambs and Sheep—in Love: It amazes me how many years I missed the Lord's connection of love with tending and shepherding. I'd always associated tending and shepherding with leading, teaching, organizing, etc., lovingly, of course. However, we've seen in our whole discussion of contagious fire that Love—Perfect Love casts out fear, ignites our hearts, motivates our followership, and empowers our love for others. We may be tempted to counterattack and defend ourselves from the enemy's darts and spears thrown at us by our congregation. We must remember, however, that only Perfect Love casts out fear. Fear forms the fundamental tool of the enemy and motivates hurtful behavior in God's lambs and sheep. So, we must love Jesus in ourselves and in one another.

> Blessed be the God and Father of our Lord Jesus Christ, the Father of mercies and God of all comfort, who comforts us in all our affliction so that we will be able to comfort those who are in any affliction with the comfort with which we ourselves are comforted by God. For just as the sufferings of Christ are ours in abundance, so also our comfort is abundant through Christ. 2 Corinthians 1:3-5

We comfort when we love. We love when we listen. We love when we affirm others, even when we don't agree with them. We love when we apologize and ask forgiveness. We love when we forgive those who hurt us. We love when we share our own struggle and ask for help. We love when we earn the right to be heard before explaining. We love by accepting people in their own struggle, just as Jesus does for us.

Steve Thulson comments on the importance of cooperating with God's redemptive work. He shares from his own experience of facing the dragon.

> *We need to see these battles as God's opportunity for transformation. That's been the case for our congregation and for me. Not only did God expose our vulnerabilities, but shed light on his formative work (e.g. clarifying our identity in Christ). God actually used our response to weaken the enemy's grip. Among other things, our leaders were reminded that "the critics are not the enemy. They're brothers and sisters." "Our struggle is not against flesh and blood." That opened doors for humble, honest and loving peacemaking efforts, as well as ongoing formation.*

Our King doesn't want to simply slay the dragon—that will happen soon enough, or to shape us up—that will happen on that day. Rather, He desires to use our difficulties to strengthen us and grow us into His likeness. Our willingness and ability to love in the midst of facing the dragon may ignite the contagious fire of love in our own hearts and in our congregation more than anything else we do.

Victory in the Army of Jesus

Our Commander in Chief has not intended that we fight alone, but uses our fellow soldiers in the service of our rescue and our victory. History has shown us that God allows these battles and their victories to enable significant changes in the Church as an integral part of movement of the Holy Spirit. Within these movements, God raises up many leaders, with the same passion, across different churches and cultures. We're greatly encouraged as we discover that God has called us to step into His will and advance the Kingdom—advance it with brothers and sisters who have also heard His call and been swept up in the winds of the Holy Spirit.

Statistics tell us, however, that pastors live as one of the most isolated professionals in the country. We tend to keep our heads down, plowing forward in our own settings. Competition and comparison make us uncomfortable with our peers, unless they live in some distant land. No matter how threatening it may feel, we must become intentional about reaching out, developing supportive relationships, inviting others by risking vulnerability, and bringing the church together in prayer.

While we've discussed the importance of a local spiritual leadership community, we also need to find spiritual formation community outside our group or congregation. Whether in local ministerial or mission associations or in personal trusted relationships, we need safe places where we can share our battles with the dragon and with our congregations. Another resource for us can be found in the spiritual formation groups formed in some regions for mutual learning, support and encouragement. The Spiritual Formation Society of Arizona, *Imago Christi*'s Affiliate Community in the Denver area, and Leadership Transformations are just a few examples. God continues to raise up spiritual formation and missional outreach communities all over the world. Seek and you will find.

It's possible that God may be calling you to develop an informal spiritual formation community in your area. The Contributors to *Contagious Fire* stand ready to assist you in their area of relationships. Other leaders and members of our ministries can benefit from these relationships, as well. Often a conference somewhere other than our own church or ministry can encourage our cautious followers that we're not totally off-the-wall or haven't joined the denominational enemy.

Now that we've joined Jesus in His sufferings, let's continue our discussion by looking at fanning the flames of contagious fire in our congregational worship experiences. We'll see that our community worship plays a key role in enabling the local church to become the kind of incubation center that births and matures vibrant followers of Jesus—followers on fire with His love and deployed with contagious fire into the world for which Jesus died. . Don't worry. You won't be asked to get rid of your pews, rearrange your chairs, change your music style, or fire your staff. Well...maybe.... Read on anyway.

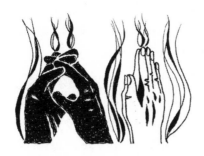

CHAPTER 10:

FANNING CONTAGIOUS FIRE - WORSHIP THAT MODELS ABIDING IN LOVE

I'm so glad that you survived Chapter 9! The whole warfare thing can make us wonder if this is all worth it or throw us into denial. When I find myself thinking that my shield of faith is buckling, I read some about Anthony of the Desert. Anthony became famous for both the intensity of the spiritual warfare he faced and for the humility that he embraced. His struggles and growth put my battle in perspective and reminds me how little power the enemy really has compared to our Commander in Chief! Fire can be refining as well as contagious. Building on the growth we're experiencing in warfare, let's return to our discussion of shepherding our flock and fanning the flames of love for God and neighbor—this time, through spiritually forming worship.

Some review can help put our discussion in context. Chapter 5 discussed how we might let the Lord show us how to invite our people to seek their own personal vision for a fantastic life with God that blazes with His love. Chapter 6 addressed another step in seeking the Lord's wisdom by identifying people and ministries where the Holy Spirit has already ignited sparks of love and hunger for more. Chapter 7 considered how we build the foundational coals that support a glowing relationship with God through teaching about spiritual formation in didactic settings. Chapter 8 explored the experience side of learning—ways we can provide opportunities for people to increase their fire through personally experiencing God's love and presence. Hopefully, you identified Sunday Morning Worship as one of the significant opportunities for both teaching and experience. We'll ask two questions, therefore. First, "What might our members' spiritual life look like if they imitated the process of Sunday Morning Worship?" Second, and to the point of this chapter, **"What might our worship services look like if they modeled the kind of contagious fire love relationship with the Lord that we're encouraging for our membership?"**

The Sunday morning worship service has become the place where most Christians experience "Church" and Christian community. It's where we shape our basic Christian beliefs and direct their impact on our lives. Our worship services, more than any other part of church life, therefore set a subtle but powerful model, for better or worse, for our daily lives with God. Look at your Sunday morning content and then compare it to what you want for your parishioners' daily walk with God. What does that tell you?

If one of our parishioners approached us and asked, "What should my walk with Jesus look like?" Let's list some of the key elements that we might share.

A daily personal experience of Jesus functioning as your Lord and Savior

Daily life lived in the peace and confidence of God's love, grace, and power toward you

A working knowledge of Scripture and its truths for your life

Prayer with God about your needs and the needs of others

Direction from Jesus as He shepherds you through daily life

Daily times of abiding prayer where you meditate on His word, attentive to His loving interaction

A rhythm of life in Jesus that balances work, play, rest, worship, and service

Spiritual friendships and community where you experience love and support

An understanding of God's calling to serve Him in the particular ways He has gifted you, and the experience of seeing God's hand in your care for others

While the list isn't exhaustive, we might use something like it to consider how our Sunday Morning Worship experience might model—not just teach about—these important elements of our life with God. Is it possible that, by participating in the church service, I might naturally learn a rhythm in my walk with Jesus that results in contagious fire?

During the development of *Contagious Fire*, I asked our Contributors to respond to the question, "What aspects of the Sunday Morning service do you find that you have "taken home" as a pattern for your walk with Jesus? Terry Tarleton, the senior pastor of a pioneering spiritual formation church, responded, "Honestly, very few, which REALLY makes me rethink some of what we are doing." Having personally attended Terry's Sunday Morning Worship service, I found more than a "few" take home models we'll be discussing. Terry goes on to discuss the things he brings to church "from home"—his personal spiritual journey. I think his response might typify how seldom we think about that question or think of Sunday Morning in that context.

Through participation in our worship service, it's possible for us to discover how to learn from God, let our hearts express our love and longing for Him in prayer and song, become still and listen, and minister to one another in practical ways—to experience Jesus. Our worship together can become a magnificent inspiration and encouragement for our members to connect with God personally outside church.

We want Sunday worship to use the same strategy adopted by ice cream stores around the country—taste a flavor for free—knowing that, once finding a flavor that the customer likes, a quart or gallon sale will likely follow. Wonder if they figured that out from the Bible? "O taste and see that the Lord is good" (cf. Psalms 34:8).

Unfortunately, many of our "worship" services focus on anything but "experiencing" God. Scripted from start to finish, we fill every second with entertainment, biblical teaching, challenges to shape up, an "efficient" Holy Communion, and a closing timed to get us out on schedule. (Did I forget the Prelude, offering, announcements, and Postlude?) Most of our worship services model what we DON'T WANT: little time to reflect, pray personally, relate to one another, or to intentionally worship God. Even unintentionally, our services model for our parishioners "that's how Christians should live." So, we go out and live at a frenetic pace, modeled in both church and society, and wonder why we never seem to connect with God.

While our churches come from different traditions and provide a variety of worship expressions, we all need to relook at what happens on Sunday mornings. We may teach one thing about spiritual formation and deepening intimacy with God but inadvertently model something entirely different. Many of us need to become more intentional about what we really want people to experience when they come to church. Do we hope that our people will encounter God or just learn about Him? We can't make God-encounters happen, but we can provide spaces in which worshipers can rendezvous with God, where they taste His love and they hunger for more, and where they can learn life patterns that cooperate with God's deep desire to give them more—much more. Let's discuss aspects of our worship services that can provide opportunities for God-encounters for our participants that model the kind of walk with Jesus that can result in contagious fire.

Preaching That Invites Discovery – Creating Second Generation Fire

As a preacher and teacher, I find that I've often been more concerned that people understand important information than that they become formed by what they learn. We sons and daughters of the Reformation realize the devastating consequences of biblical illiteracy. People can make terrible mistakes when they misunderstand God's revealed Word and the Gospel. Our life with our Creator needs the biblical foundation of our collective history with God. We need to understand who God is, who Jesus is, and why Christ came as a human being and died on the Cross. We need to understand God's offer of reconciling forgiveness and His offer of eternal life. To live as kids of the King, we must recognize the love and adoption provided for us through faith in Jesus, the power and wisdom to live in true peace, the abundance through the Holy Spirit, and the lifestyle of love lived in the absence of fear. Pastors accepted the responsibility to clearly teach and explain these truths to their congregations, and the ones I know take that calling very seriously.

Without minimizing the importance of clear biblical teaching, we cannot forget what Jesus says about "truth." "I am the way, and the truth, and the life; no one comes to the Father but through Me (cf. John 14:6). Ultimately, Truth, means way more than information—it's the very person of Jesus. Information, no matter how accurate, can never connect us to the Father; only Jesus can do that. However, we can get truth all turned around when we tell people four truths, suggesting that intellectual assent to these truths will result in eternal life. However, even the devil knows the truth of those four statements. We can inadvertently make the same mistake in our discipleship if we lead people to believe that the more they know ABOUT God the more they know God Himself. Again, the devil.... This information-based approach in our church gatherings can form or malform and truncate our experience of God and the Truth of the Gospel. Jesus calls us to Himself, not just to information about Him. Therefore, we can agree that our people need to understand the factual truths about the Gospel, and they must personally discover and enter into relationship with the One about Whom those truths refer.

For our preaching to actually ignite contagious fires within our hearers, it's important for us to express the contagious nature of our love relationship with God. Melanie Saint James shares her concern that preaching lead us into contagious intimacy with God.

> One thing that I have longed for on Sunday morning, is for someone to preach sermons utilizing the language of love, explaining how we can relate to God in love. Rarely, if ever, do I hear sermons using the language of intimacy as it relates to our relationship with God. We need to talk about the incompleteness we all feel and help our congregations get in touch with the longing that has been implanted in each one of them for a deeply personal, intimate, love relationship with Jesus. How do I experience that kind of relationship with God in my own life? How does the preacher experience that intimacy? How do I share with God my love for Him and what words can I use to express that love? I think people would love to hear their pastor share openly about his relationship with the Lord, how he expresses that love, what challenges he faces in developing intimacy and how those challenges are being addressed. What would it look like to preach on the Song of Songs where the language is very explicit in the language of love?

We have a plethora of love songs, poems, and stories to give us language for human love relationships. However, Melanie's questions address the reality that most believers haven't developed a language of love for God. Language provides the constructs for the ways we think and communicate. Without a language for our romance with God, we flounder and get stuck in frustration.

Dr. Gary Mayes, one of the divisional directors in Church Resource Ministries, made a profound comment that influenced my personal teaching and preaching, as well as the way *Imago Christi* leads our Spiritual Formation Discovery Retreats. Gary said, "What we say to people can prove helpful; what God says to them becomes life-changing. Therefore, don't steal the discovery." We describe "discovery" when we say, "The light bulb just came on! I think God spoke to me!" Jesus modeled leading people into personal discovery in His earthly ministry. He told stories and asked His hearers for their response. He entertained questions, often asking another question in reply. Then He taught into those responses in ways that invited personal discovery.

One courageous pastor who I know took Jesus' method to heart in a three-step sermon. First, he'd read aloud the portion of Scripture he planned to use, saying a few words about its context. Second, he gave parishioners several minutes of quiet to reflect on the passage and its personal application, asking the Lord to show them what key question emerged for them in the text and then write it on a 3x5 card provided in the bulletin. During the offering, the cards were collected and sorted, and several were chosen to give to the pastor. Thirdly, he used responses to the questions, in his sermon, to share how that text speaks to our experience of God in an everyday way. If the "brilliant insight" he'd previously planned to share didn't fit, he'd keep it for another week. My friend demonstrated the truth that the Holy Spirit works as much through the people as He does through the preacher. The congregation learned that they could expect the Lord to speak to them in the same way when they meditated on Scripture in the privacy of their own prayer closets.

Drama has been successfully used by many churches to communicate biblical truths in a way that invites us to use our imaginations and interact with the story. Dramas can be used to introduce the teaching time by raising some key questions that parishioners can relate to personally. Now, when the formal message begins, worshipers wait to see how God will use the message to address their personal connections with the topic. Can we trust God enough to believe that He can guide the preacher's message preparation and use a drama to simultaneously speak a multitude of messages that become to some degree unique to each worshiper? When that happens, people know that God is in the room; they know that God will be in the room wherever they go.

Bruce Larson, then pastor of University Presbyterian Church in the Seattle area and an early "preacher idol" of mine, would often place green, yellow, and red cards in the hymnal pew racks. During his message, he encouraged each listener to hold the cards. When they felt that the message was hitting home, they were to hold up the green card, just high enough that he could see it. You can guess what the yellow and red cards were used to communicate. Members of the congregation learned that the pastor trusted their responses as reflections of the Holy Spirit's guidance for his messages.

Every preacher has a particular style. Maybe 3x5 cards doesn't fit yours. There are many ways to enable our hearers to interact with the Lord, and with us, in the context of our messages. I invite you to take the Holy Spirit at His word—to let Him function as your counselor and guide so that the "teaching" part of your worship service can become life-changing discovery that's responsive to the questions on people's hearts. Invite other members of your church family to ask Him, too, and help you experiment. I have no idea what the Lord might reveal to you, but I do know that it will be fun—and transforming for you and your people.

Music and Song in Which We Can Express Love For God – Celebrating Our Fire Within

Music and song express the human heart in unique ways. From as far back as we have history, our hopes, dreams, longings, and our suffering emerge in melodies and songs that touch us in ways that no other form of communication can reach. Some music calms our spirits while another may excite and embolden our resolves. Music captures the heart's joyous celebrations and its memorials of tragedy. Love songs imprint their messages on the fabric of our souls when they express our longings for our beloved. The Psalms provide a wonderful example of the range of emotions and feelings that our worship music can communicate, from lament to the deepest expressions of faith and trust. Similarly, music has always formed a significant part of Christian worship. We sing to God; we sing about God;

we sing the message of the Gospel and the coming of the Kingdom. For many Christians, songs and hymns provide the most significant opportunity, particularly in church, to say out loud, "I love you, Lord."

As we grow in our love relationship with God, music and song become more and more important to our heart's ability to worship God with the heart. I recall my Fourth Mansion season when I "fell in love" with God in a new way. Singing songs "about" Jesus frustrated me. But harmonizing my love for and to my Beloved brought tears and waves of joy. Since becoming a follower of Jesus, I've always loved hymns and choruses, but for a season they became a vital link with Jesus. I became VERY opinionated about the kind of worship music that "nurtured me." I wonder if the "worship wars" we've experienced in churches all over the US in the last few decades, reflect the importance to our people of that musical link with Jesus. These days, of course, styles of music change almost before we have time to buy the latest CD, but the intensity of our feelings about music in the church reflects far more than our stylistic preferences. I'd guess that more people choose or leave a church over worship music than they do over sermon quality. The sermon can provide a "person-to-person" experience; our worship songs touch our hearts with God-experience—or at least it can. Charlie Dodrill reflects about the impact of music in his "takeaways" from church.

> I think the musical part of loving God is the biggest part of what I take away from a service and end up keeping with me. I can forget an entire sermon in minutes, but still have a tune knocking around in my head with words attached that, when I focus on them, help me connect with God. Also, if something turns out differently than I expected or requires something of me that I was not expecting, God will often bring to mind one of those songs.

Our worship songs also form our theology—for better or for worse. For generations, hymns have been used by the Church, not only to express our feelings toward God, but to teach us theology. Learning a good hymn can embed God's truth in our hearts sometimes more effectively than Scripture memorization, particularly for right-brain learners. In some of our recent attempts to enable worship music to relate to younger generations, Christian composers have written choruses with repetitive and predictable melodies that don't require the ability to read music. Unfortunately, some of these choruses focused more on simplicity than meaningful content. One friend calls them "Seven-Eleven Songs." She says that we sing seven words eleven times; she's not inspired.

Charlie Dodrill pushes back a bit about the use of "Seven-Eleven" choruses.

I might say, as someone who leads worship, that the 7-11 assessment, although it can be hard for some, can let others let go a little bit and just sing, connecting with God and their heart without having to read, consider, or second-guess....I see it like the early Desert Fathers weaving reeds or praying the Jesus Prayer....it allows your mind to be just occupied enough not to wander, but just "unoccupied" enough to connect with the heart.

JD Ward also emphasizes the importance of "simple" worship songs.

I think the point of simple worship songs is important. Many people view them as prayers in the same way Taizé can be prayer. Singing simple songs can help us align our hearts and not our heads to a truth. I felt that your approach seemed a little biased against the need for simple songs. It might be possible to redeem those songs by asking people to pray them.

Great insights, Charlie and JD. I will never forget the impact that the simple chorus, "I Love You Lord" has had on my worship of God!

Thankfully, more recent "contemporary" composers are looking more at the theology of the songs as well as their sing-ability. Terry Tarleton illustrates this important theological consideration.

Recently my wife and I attended a conference where we heard in several of the choruses, "come Lord, Jesus," or something similar. I have spent an enormous amount of pulpit time in our church reminding our people that we serve a God who lives "in us." One commentary says that Paul uses that phrase "Christ in us" 63 times in his letters.

> *Yet, for whatever reason, in worship we want to beg Jesus to come to us. So, at our church, no matter how popular a song is, we will not sing it if the theology does not line up with what we are teaching.*

Whatever the style of music a given church uses, we need to choose music that provides opportunity for hearts to connect—God's and the worshipers. This connection seems to happen best when the song expresses more than information about God, but actually prays the heart of the believer. Kevin Navarro, author of *The Complete Worship Service* and *The Complete Worship Leader*, and a member of the *Imago Christi* Community, likes to say, "Through lyrics we can pray.[1] I always tell worship leaders to pray their songs and sing their prayers. If we were to strip this song of its music, could we pray the lyrics?"

Bill O'Byrne suggests that we can adjust a song's pronouns to help us connect with the lyrics.

> *I have rearranged a number of worship songs from third-person into first and second person to help make a hymn or chorus feel more like prayer. Changing the words to "I-You" language, really helps direct our focus in worship. Sometimes it's powerful to start in the third-person "He" about God in general and then move into the "personal, direct speech" of first/second person during a repeat, or additional verse. Prayer before or after a third person song "about God" helps the worshipers transfer the direction of our worship directly to God.*
> *Singing about God can simply reiterate theological truth. Singing to God embraces the Truth.*
>
> *What might happen if, rather than simply singing three songs, we invited the congregation to pray as they sing and then provide a few moments of silence (that's silence, not background music) to listen for God's response? It's easy to call the musical portion of our church service, "worship," but worship means more than music—it's holy communication between God and His beloved.*

---

1. Kevin Navarro, *The Complete Worship Service* and *The Complete Worship Leader,* Baker Books, Grand Rapids, MI. 2005 and 2001

Bill O'Byrne comments about the use of instrumental music as a setting for contemplative prayer.

> *Instrumental music that has no familiar lyrics can also be used to introduce contemplation to a congregation! "Use this melody to commune with God!" J. S. Bach meant many of his pieces to be just such an opportunity for prayer as he penned the initials "SDG," or wrote out Soli Deo Gloria ("to God alone be the glory") on his works.*

Bill illustrates that some of our most profound prayer comes from the heart, without words. The apostle Paul describes this "prayer without words."

> *In the same way the Spirit also helps us in our weakness; for we do not know how to pray as we should, but the Spirit Himself intercedes for us with groanings too deep for words; and He who searches the hearts knows what the mind of the Spirit is, because He intercedes for the saints according to the will of God. Romans 8:26-27*

Instrumental music can help us focus and become attentive to this communion with God.

Special "contemplative" or meditative worship services can also provide wonderful opportunities for our people to experience a more reflective worship. Through the creative use of music, silence, Scripture reading, and Christian symbols, we can help worshipers become attentive to God's presence and wait upon the Lord. An example of such a service emerged from the Taizé monastic community in France. Over a 100,000 Protestant and Catholic youth travel to Taizé every year to spend time in a community of prayer, meditation, worship, and fellowship. While the monastic community contains only about 100 members, its worship style has spread all over the world. With thousands attending worship, from many different countries and languages, the service had to accommodate a variety of forms that crossed language and cultural differences. Worship leaders made use of art, symbol, various musical instruments, chant and choruses, Scripture readings in different languages, as well as movement and involvement by worshipers to create an experience with worldwide attraction. While a

Taizé service may be too technically difficult for a single church, groups of churches in most major cities around the world offer Taizé services monthly. Another example further illustrates the possibilities. St. Patrick's Episcopal Church, here in Pagosa Springs, Colorado, hosts a contemplative service once each month called "Sunday Night Unplugged." On the second Sunday evening, local guest musicians provide contemplative instrumental music. Scripture readings, poetry, and lots of silence for personal meditation make this 45-minute service a delight that attracts worshipers from various traditions from around the area. Whether on Sunday mornings or in other venues, music can provide a wonderful depth to our growing relationship with God—when that music invites worship that helps us encounter and connect deeply with God.

Terry Tarleton shared about a theme-focused Sunday morning worship that helped people address the difficult aspects of their relationship with God.

> *This summer as my wife and I were getting away for a whole month, at the beginning of that vacation I felt the Lord tell me we needed to have a service of lament. I felt surprised. Although we did have a couple of people with severe health issues, generally, things seemed good. By the end of our trip, members of our fellowship carried many very difficult and painful issues. So, we lamented. I started the service by teaching on lamenting, using some Psalms as examples. I explained why we need to lament, and encouraged those who had no reason to lament to love those who were suffering. At the end of the service, we formed groups of 4-5 and shared (as we felt comfortable) what the Lord brought up in us. All over the room people were crying as they found a safe place to be honest with their hearts. It was definitely the Lord.*

The historical church calendar provides many opportunities for special services, such as Advent and Lent. Terry's story illustrates the Lord's willingness to guide us to provide special worship opportunities that intersect where our people need to worship together. When that kind of spontaneity and vulnerable openness is modeled at church, members find it easier to follow the Lord as they feel personal needs to worship in ways that reflect what's going on in their lives.

Holy Communion – Consuming Fire

In the early years of my Lutheran pastorate, we celebrated Holy Communion once a month. Time constraints probably motivated the frequency rather than the importance we gave to the Lord's Supper. Communion takes time—time not only for the Words of Institution and other prayers, but more time for people to walk to the front, kneel, and personally receive the bread and wine from the pastor. It also takes time in churches which pass the elements down the rows. There's lots to do on Sunday mornings both with the regular service and with extra opportunities such as the children's choir, sharing by a returning missions group, etc. Churches with multiple services on Sunday morning have the same problem; prolong the service 10 minutes and we create chaos in the parking lot!

In more recent years, churches of many expressions have begun to offer Communion more regularly. Regardless of one's sacramental theology, we recognize that people experience something/Someone special in the Eucharist. Holy Communion provides us an opportunity to "do something" rather than just sit and watch. Much of our spiritual growth comes as we RESPOND to God's initiative in our daily lives. Holy Communion not only provides a blessing in the service, it models this responsive posture. The bread and wine are offered to us representing the love and sacrifice of Jesus; we must decide whether or not to respond to that invitation. In many churches, the congregation gets up and moves forward in responding mode and receives the spiritual in a physical way. This participation ties us historically and currently to the whole Body of Christian believers around the world and through time, and to Jesus and His disciples at the Last Supper.

Holy Communion and Baptism both represent opportunities for us to embrace the promises of Jesus, not only in faith, but in physical experience. Holy Communion and Baptism not only become encounters with Jesus in the worship service, but models our response to Jesus' offer to meet us in every situation in our lives—in real and practical ways. It's important, therefore, that we don't trivialize the Lord's Supper on Sunday morning by rushing through or multitasking it with other parts of the service. If Communion is "Holy", then we need to treat it that way. To do otherwise invites our people to multitask Jesus in daily life. We want people's full attention for the message; Jesus becomes no less present in the bread and wine?

Bill O'Byrne serves in the worship team of his church and comments about reconsidering the importance of Holy Communion as an integral part of the worship service.

> Celebrating Communion very directly draws our attention to God-in-Christ. Often, however, the sermon and invitations into ministry, focus on what WE should do, and overshadows what GOD has done and is doing. For that reason, we've considered doing Communion more often than our traditional once a month.

Spaces For Reflection – Sparks From The Fireplace

An important part of our spiritual formation message encourages believers to become attentive to the Lord's presence, to listen in prayer, and to meditate on Scripture rather than blast through as many chapters as we can. Listening to God takes time—a commodity scarcer to many people than money. While Scripture invites us to "wait upon the Lord," to "be still and know that I am God," our worship services often move so quickly from one thing to another that any attempt to reflect on what has just happened can be swept away by the next good thing. By the time a person gets home, the whole experience may be lost in a blur - obscured by the multitude of overlapping stimuli in the service and the day's coming activities.

One way to help people become reflective may be to add a few words of introduction that explain what we expect from God in each segment of the worship time. For example, simple introductory statements or simple prayers can help people tune in to the purpose for that time. Think about these examples: "Dear Lord, help us to hear your heart for us in these songs and express our hearts to you." "God has been speaking to you all week. Let's listen to the text planned for today to see how God will use it to continue the conversation you and He have been having." "Our offering today represents the gift of our whole selves to God in thanksgiving for all He has done for us. Use this time to surrender any burdens you may be carrying." "Father, you invite us to come to you in prayer, to seek your help and direction. We ask that the Holy Spirit express the desires of our hearts through the words of these prayers." You get the idea.

Terry Tarleton illustrates one way his nonliturgical congregation provides space for reflection.

> *We've introduced a "call to worship" before the song service. Our worship leader encourages our people to take about two minutes to review their week (in sort of Examen style). She suggests that they recognize what's in their hearts, and then to use that as a place from which to enter their worship time, hopefully connecting with the songs whether in consolation or desolation. The band plays quietly during that time. We feel this has helped our people connect more with what's in their hearts, honestly going to Jesus with their stuff.*

Another way to help our people interact with God in our worship services might be to add specific opportunities for interaction with God to happen. For example, what if we rearranged our worship service to add two minutes to its length? I doubt that any worship leader would find that hard to do. Imagine that we took our two minutes and divided it into four 30-second segments. What if, at the beginning or early in the service, we gave worshipers a 30-second time to think about how they would like God to meet them during the worship service? We might insert another segment after the message to reflect on the key take-home they felt the Holy Spirit highlighted for them, personally. Another segment could be added following a chorus or hymn, asking the Holy Spirit to inspire our hearts to continue to worship in silence. Following the prayer time of the service, time might be provided for people to silently express their own desires to the Lord and to listen for

His word to them. Because most of us have become so unaccustomed to real silence, it may take some explanation, instruction, and encouragement for people to become comfortable. I can assure you, however, that these reflective spaces will exponentially multiply the impact of the whole worship experience and model the kind of attentive lifestyle we want our people to live out in daily life.

"Space" represents more than time, but also physical places for special acts of worship. Most of the old cathedrals included not only the main sanctuary for worship, but small chapels along the side for personal and small group worship. Kneelers and communion rails provide space for prayers in a humble posture. Some churches use corners of the sanctuary for prayer ministry for specific needs. Altar calls to invite people to commit or recommit their lives to Christ often include an opportunity to "come forward," symbolizing our desire to be close to God. Special places soon become associated with special experiences and help us become focused on their intended use. We express this special connection in phrases like, "There's no place like home," Or "There's nothing like my own bed." We can provide holy ground both in the fabric of time and in the facility, for special opportunities to meet God. It just takes a little imagination, some planning, and explanation.

Symbol, Art, and Beauty That Reflect the Transcendent – The Wonder of Fire

You may remember that we discussed the different "love languages" people use to help them sense God's presence and respond to Him. Some see God most profoundly in nature, others in music, and still others in beauty, art, and symbol. We're told that while we learn with both sides of our brains, we all seem hardwired to learn most easily with one or the other. Left-brain learners connect best through concepts and ideas. Right-brained folks learn best through the physical world, rather than ideas. While most of us preachers and teachers—often left-brain learners, love ideas, facts and concepts, most of our congregation, and most of the population for that matter, learn best with the right side of their brain—the physical world. Experiences, stories, objects and sensations provide their best classroom for understanding.

We recognize the use of multiple sensory opportunities for worship when we study the history of our Christian tradition, filled with churches with high and vaulted ceilings, to remind us that the heavenly Kingdom of God has come to earth in our Lord Jesus. Beautiful mosaics, paintings, and statues communicated truths to a population that could hardly read and write, crossing linguistic and educational barriers. The Cross became the most famous symbol in human history and communicates volumes to anyone who sees it. Prayer gardens and labyrinths provided opportunities for believers to touch and smell and feel and walk in God's revelation of His very being. Beautiful music proclaimed the majesty and glory of God in sounds that moved the heart, often beyond words. Churches stood open all day, every day, so that people could take a few minutes to sit on "holy ground", to simply be with God in a place that felt safe and worshipful. Biblical history overflows with God's use of the physical to communicate the eternal—gardens, boats, fish, bread, blood, a burning bush, a mountain, a river, a stone in a sling shot, a city, a tabernacle, a lake, a tree, a star, a lamb, … a Cross.

The Reformation rightly emphasized the importance of correct theological and biblical literacy. In many traditions, however, words about God became more important than experience of God. We changed our focus from the aesthetic to the practical and judged our ancestors for excesses in Christian art that could have fed the hungry. In reaction, we (especially we Americans) designed churches as plainly and drably as possible to try to communicate our values of simplicity (and the importance of "saving money). While we may agree about past excesses, we must also agree that we have largely left behind right-brain learners. In many of today's churches, the ear has become the only sensory organ we rely upon and the primary sensory tool we value is music—loud music. Statistics tell us that many churches spend far more on their sound systems than on all their benevolence and missions combined.

Many spiritually maturing evangelicals find themselves attracted to liturgical churches which meet their needs to worship God with their whole beings—right and left brained.

We don't need to tear down our simply styled churches and build cathedrals to help people more fully experience God in worship. We can, however, take steps to make them beautiful. Banners, art, greenery, candles, symbols, and light can all help believers remember that they have entered a special place to worship the Most-High God. As we discussed related to worship "spaces", many churches are providing special physical areas, dedicated to prayer and reflection. Prayer Chapels, labyrinths, coffee nooks, gardens with beautiful plantings and benches, kneelers in a corner of the worship center, small rooms for spiritual conversations and spiritual direction, etc., can provide important opportunities for people to experience God, aided by their setting.

Early in my ministry, I served as associate pastor in a large bustling congregation in the Midwest. Every square inch of its campus served some useful purpose. My office felt like Grand Central Station. I longed for a place where I could get away to pray for short times throughout the day. No matter where I went, someone found me and asked me to do something or struck up a conversation.

One day, I was looking for something in the Sunday School area in the basement of the church. All the doors boasted clear signs indicating their intended use—all but one—a small locked corner door with no window and no sign. I found the custodian who, reluctantly, gave me the key. Opening the door, I discovered a dusty, 6x8-foot room packed with odds and ends and old furniture. Slowly, quietly, after everyone had left for the evening, I cleaned out the little room. I painted the walls, put a rug on the floor, hung a few of my favorite Christian pictures on the wall. I furnished the room with one comfortable chair, a side table and a small kneeler.

I'd created my own prayer closet!! I pounded a nail in the front of the door (Lutherans have become famous for driving nails in church doors.)

from which I hung a sign printed on both sides: One side said OCCUPIED; the other said VACANT. Most days I would tell my secretary that I had a short meeting and couldn't be disturbed (That was before cell phones and Google implants). Surreptitiously, I would slip down the hall and down the back stairs. Hopefully, no one would see me steal away to what had become the holiest place for me in the whole church—my prayer closet! Turning the sign to the "occupied side," I'd slip in and close the door. It felt wonderful! Solitude! Silence! I'm sure there had to have been an unseen but direct corridor from that little room directly to heaven itself! Occasionally I would retreat to the basement only to find the occupied sign already turned and the door closed. The nerve! After some months, I had to get there very early or very late—my prayer closet became occupied by staff and members almost all the time. The strangest part, however, was that no one ever spoke about it. For each one of us, the dusty closet had become our private Holy of Holies.

Prayer That's Personal and Practical – The Chariots of Fire

I find that one of the greatest learning curves for most of those for whom I provide spiritual direction has to do with prayer. Many maturing Christians simply have never learned how to have a conversation with God. I wonder if the trouble stems from the ways we pray in church. Prayer in church services varies greatly across the wide spectrum of our worship expressions. In some traditions, every prayer has been carefully crafted and then read by the congregation from its Order of Service. Other traditions, despising "canned" prayers, value spontaneous prayer which, almost always comes from the pastor or worship leader. In either extreme, the congregation only contributes by simply listening, possibly adding an Amen at the end. Many traditions limit prayers to opening prayers, a prayer following the sermon, and a closing benediction. A model presented in some expressions does not write out the words to prayers, but structure prayer to include certain categories. The ACTS model may be the most familiar: Adoration, Confession, Thanksgiving, and Supplication. Unfortunately, prayers of lament found in the Psalms don't easily fit. In some expressions, one must add Elizabethan pronouns and expressions, like Thee, Thou, Beseechest, ("est" on any verb makes it holy) to help God understand what we want to tell Him. (If I may kid Lutherans.... ☺)

Like other parts of our piety, our private prayer lives often reflect our church experience. Some of us can only pray from a devotional book or in categories that may have little to do with what we actually want to say. Worst of all, in all these examples, prayer has been reduced to talking to God. We dump our load of instructions for God and leave. Whatever happened to listening and waiting and knowing? We teach people how to study Scripture, but I can't remember one time since I became a pew-sitter that I've heard a sermon about how to pray. If communication forms the foundation for any growing relationship, sermons about how to pray should be among the most important.

While teaching about prayer can certainly help, modeling how to pray will have the most lasting impact. What if pastors and worship leaders publicly prayed honest and vulnerable prayers for themselves. Think what a prayer like, "Lord, you know how insecure I feel about this message and how unworthy I feel about giving it. I'm sorry for how grumpy I've been with my family this week, and I trust your forgiveness and your power to communicate what you want said," might mean to worshipers who seldom pray because they don't feel worthy. What if our congregational prayer time simply provided spaces for worshipers to fill in topical gaps—in everyday language. "Let's ask God for forgiveness where we've made mistakes." SPACE. "Talk to God about the ways you're tempted most." SPACE. "Pray for the issues in your family that trouble you." SPACE. "When you think of the world condition, ask God's mercy and help." SPACE. And so on. We define our level of friendship with others by our ability to simply be together and share. Our people desperately long to have that kind of friendship with God. How can we help them receive what God wants to give by modeling it in church?

Real Stories by Real People – Brightened by Contagious Fire

I kid my Lutheran colleagues that there are only two things we never discuss in public: our sex life and our spiritual life. Experience tells me that the Lutherans aren't the only ones. Many believers grow up in churches and serve in ministries having never, ever, heard anyone, except religious professionals, talk about God. Sometimes preachers tell stories about real people and God, but many people have never heard real people tell their own stories about their relationship with God. Most of us can talk about the Bible and about church, but feel totally inadequate to express our own experience of God. We have stressed the critical importance that spiritual community plays in our spiritual growth, but it's hard to form authentic community when we can't share what's going on with God. The stories by religious professionals can be easily discounted as inapplicable to "ordinary" people without theological degrees.

What if, instead of preaching for the full 30 to 45 minutes, we took 10 of those minutes and asked a member of the congregation to tell their story about that topic? What if those storytellers felt free to share their struggles as well as their victories? How might our people be blessed to realize that we're all in process, all on a journey—realize it, not just because the professional told us so, but because we see its truth in the lives of our friends? Of course, the witness talks can be helpful in themselves, but the real payoff comes when our members begin to share their journey with Jesus in their small groups, and with friends and working associates. When we experience the power of a simple story on our own lives, we might dare to believe that our own story may have meaning to others, and share it. So, we model that aspect of walking with Jesus—in church.

Ministry For The Needs of The People – Healing Fire

Thinking back on my own preaching ministry, I wonder sometimes if I simply picked the scabs off the wounds of my parishioners and then sent them home to deal with the consequences. To the degree that our messages and our worship prove to be prophetic, the Lord will always surface the issues He wants to deal with in our people, with the intention of setting them free. We have no record that Jesus preached and just sent people home. He ministered to their needs; He healed them. We need to follow His example.

We'll devote Chapter 12 to the topic of healing ministry in the church. Here, however, I'd simply like to suggest that we consider providing members an opportunity to pray with someone about what the Lord has surfaced—whether it's about something worrisome or a great joy. What's brought into the light becomes light; what stays in the darkness festers and becomes a target for the enemy. It's not all that hard to train a cadre of people to listen and pray without giving advice or judgment. These prayers can be available after church, at the altar rail, or at the side of the church or....

Charlie Dodrill shares experiences of church services that focused on the needs of people in unique ways.

I still remember a friend of mine who I would not have considered necessarily "deep" when it came to spiritual things. His church, one Sunday, decided to ask people who were willing to take their shoes off—the ones they wore to church—and leave them there to give to people in need. Almost the entire church walked out barefoot. My friend could not tell this story without weeping because of the impact that made on him. I think bold acts like that can really impact people in a way that they can take with them. Giving was probably never the same for him.

After a flood in Nashville, the church I was attending decided to take a spontaneous offering and give the whole thing to a small church devastated by water. I remember we raised well over $100,000, and we just all went and gave it to them right then. Things like this can be helpful–doing something unexpected from time to time.

We can model that turning to God and to one another with our cares and our generosity is the natural thing to do. We can demonstrate important ways we meet Jesus.

Accessible to "Outsiders" – The Hearth For Contagious Fire

Having grown up as an outsider to faith in Jesus for almost a quarter century of my life, I'm particularly sensitive to the ways we keep "outsiders" feeling like outsiders as they attend our churches. Insider code language can inadvertently tell visitors that "you don't belong here." When I first heard words like redemption, grace, gospel, liturgy, chancel, narthex, repentance, etc., I had no idea what people were talking about. Worse, I made wrong assumptions. While code language can be a problem throughout our worship services, it can cause real roadblocks when we talk about spiritual formation. In fact, our new spiritual code language can turn insiders into outsiders. Words like Lectio Divina, silence, solitude, inward journey, being vs. doing, meditation, contemplation, like the list above, describe important aspects of our spiritual journey.

However, if people don't know what we mean by them or misunderstand what we mean, we inadvertently, or intentionally, just let the words pass by. Worse, people may hang onto the code words and sling them back in another setting. It's like being with a group from another country who decide to speak their own language without thinking that we don't understand a word; we feel left out. In time, it's possible that we can teach our people some new vocabulary; but on Sunday morning, we'll always have outsiders looking for Jesus. As we discussed earlier, we want our people to be able to discuss their faith in everyday language—so we model that value in church.

A Taste of Spiritual Community – The Bonfire

So often people view their faith as a personal and private matter. Jesus, however, invites us into the family of God, adopting us as sons and daughters, brothers and sisters. He makes us the Body of Christ where our mutuality, interdependence, and love for one another reflect the very life and presence of the Trinity. All of the worship considerations that we've discussed above become finally formed in our experience in the context of true Christian community. While we will discuss the specifics of spiritual community more fully in Chapter 11, we must consider the impact of community in worship because visitors, seekers, and cautious followers of Jesus will discern the presence of Jesus, or at least confirm it—or not, through their experience of the presence or absence of God's love, felt in the Sunday morning community. Through conversations over coffee, greeters at the door, friendliness of people near us, invitations for further involvement, etc., we will either express the caring presence of Jesus or the aloof proof of His absence. People explore church because they believe, or at least hope, that Jesus cares for them. We need to be intentional about the way we show others that, in fact, He does.

A City Set Upon a Hill – Letting Our Light Shine

If, in this chapter, I've poked fun too close to home, please forgive me. Every pastor and worship leader works really hard to make Sunday morning a rich and meaningful experience. If, however, our Father has assigned us to nurture the growth of contagious fire among His beloved, we want to make that growth the top priority in every aspect of our ministry. Sunday morning, for most of our believers, provides the setting in which we minister and model the most. Therefore, our emphasis on spiritual formation—deepening intimacy in love with God and heart motivation to love neighbor must be kindled and fanned when we worship together. When we experience the contagious fire of God's love in worship, its brilliance and flames won't be easily hidden in the marketplace.

I walked up the stairs to the church door. Just inside, a smiling person handed me some paper. I asked where I might find Jesus. She responded that I should come in and see.

It's imperative that we see Jesus at church. When that experience provides models for our everyday walk with God, our contagious fire will enable many people to meet Him everywhere.

CHAPTER 11

BECOMING CONTAGIOUS BONFIRES - SPIRITUALLY FORMING COMMUNITY

Great to see you're still part of the Contagious Fire Community—filled with the Love that is God, filled with love for our world so desperately in need, filled with hope that the Lord is bringing the Church into its own. Jesus invites us to become a different kind of church—organically connected with Love, intimately related to the Trinity, set free to live fully as the children of God, eager to give away the gifts of God. The Head of the Church has sounded the trumpets to call us from the secular institutionalism that has dominated the Church for centuries to discover what it means to live as the very Body of Christ aflame with His love and deployed to bring His people home—with the contagious fire of His Amazing Love. It's great to know that you're on fire, too.

Jesus used this analogy of fire because it speaks to us about fundamental truths of His Kingdom. Not too many years ago, every person on the planet depended upon fire for their very livelihood. We used fire to cook our food and keep us warm and alive in freezing temperatures. Flaming beacons allowed us to communicate from mountain top to mountaintop, connecting us in communities of mutual support and protection far beyond our villages.

Fire made our engines run and provided transportation that hurled us along roads and rails, and through the sky to every corner of the world. We used fire to make implements and tools and the structures we live in. Fire, in all its various forms, has provided the means to create and build and become the global society we live in. Fire, in many ways, has accomplished in this world what Love is accomplishing in the Kingdom of God!

We can use what we've learned about fire to better understand how God uses Love to transform us and build His Kingdom. We know that fire cannot exist by itself. Fire needs matter, substance we call fuel, as its host. Combustion must be started from some external source of energy greater than that of the substance that is to be burned. The fire we're familiar with can only burn in the presence of oxygen, the life-giving substance for all living things. Fire can only be sustained when fuel is arranged close enough that the parts of the flaming fuel support the heat and flames of other parts, and far enough away to let oxygen flow between the parts. Fire spreads when its heat energizes other material to its combustion temperature. Anyone who's built a fire in the fireplace or nursed a campfire either understands these principles or failed to achieve a lasting fire. It's simply the way God made fire to work.

In Chapter 11, we'll discuss the Spiritual Community aspect of contagious fire in the Kingdom of God. Using the analogy of fire and what we know about the Body of Christ, let's describe Christian Spiritual Community.

Christian Spiritual Community happens when followers of Jesus 1) receive the fire of God's love through faith in Jesus; 2) experience the Holy Spirit's work of transformation into Christ-likeness; 3) come together so that their experiences of God encourage and increase one another's faith; 4) causing the whole community's love for God and for one another to burn more intensely with the contagious fire of God's love for the world.

God established community as the foundational environment in which He intends creation to live and flourish. Genesis says that God created the sea and land creatures "after their kind" to show that they were to live together as individual species. Then, after creating Adam, God said, "It is not good for the man to be alone; I will make a helper suitable for him..." (cf. Genesis 1:20; 2:18). God established spiritual community through Abraham and his descendants, saying, "I will be their God" (cf. Genesis 17:1-9). God divided His people into tribes to provide closer levels of community support (cf. Genesis 49:28). He reiterated His covenant to Moses (cf. Exodus 3:1-15). Through the prophets, God promised to renew His community and expand it in a New Covenant (cf. Jeremiah 24:7; 31:33). This new community will include followers of Jesus from every nation, tribe, tongue, and people (cf. Revelation 14:6). Jesus calls this new and eternal community together as its Shepherd and King (cf. Isaiah 40 and 41), and shepherds each one of us within that community (cf. John 10:11, 14). Spiritual community constitutes the fabric of the Church and the key to our relationship with God.

Jesus demonstrated His commitment to community by calling together disciples and shepherding them to proclaim the Gospel and to perform signs and wonders to people in need. In His High Priestly Prayer, Jesus asks the Father that we might experience the Trinity in our unity as believers and He promised to be present in a special way when we gather in His name (cf. John 17:1-25). Jesus pours out His Holy Spirit upon us when we believe so that the Trinity can actually abide within each of us. When we come together in His name, we not only experience God personally, we also experience Him incarnationally—in one another.

Tragically, most Christians live in spiritual isolation rather than community. Increasing numbers of believers no longer attend church or only visit occasionally. The vast majority of churchgoers whip in on Sunday morning, greet the few people whom they know, sit through the service, and return to the secular world that almost forbids them to talk about faith. While God created us to live in close fellowship with other followers of Jesus where we can find support and encouragement, most of us never talk about our faith, have no one we can look to for help in faith struggles or mentoring in spiritual growth. Most believers believe that what they've experienced of their relationship with God is all there is, and feel like failures at being "good Christians." The fire of God's love is caught in community; flames of love are nurtured in community; and the flaming love of abundant life happens in spiritual community. No wonder we've been living in an age where the Church only seems to flicker here and there. Our Lord not only calls us to Himself—He calls us to join Him in spiritual community—the Body of Christ.

Within Chapter 11, we'll look at the role of spiritual community in the contagious fire process, from exposing us to the Gospel invitation of God, our spiritual maturation as followers of Jesus, and the proclamation of the Gospel to every tribe and nation—from a spark, to a warming fire, to a blazing passion for Jesus, to a sacrificial torch of love for neighbor, to the contagious fire storm that will cover the whole earth with God's love. Contagious fire! Let's explore spiritual community from the following perspectives:

The Nature of Spiritual Community

The Struggle of Spiritual Community in Today's Church

Learning to Live in Open and Vulnerable Relationships

Developing Language to Talk About the Experience of our Relationship With God

Understanding Everyone as Pilgrims on a Journey With God

Creating a Climate of Growth

Providing Individual Coaching and Mentoring – Spiritual Discipleship

Building Community Around First and Second Order Calling

Forming Core Communities and Invitational Communities Within The Church

Taking Spiritual Community Into The World

The Nature of Spiritual Community

What makes "community" a particularly spiritual community? Henri Nouwen uses the story about Jesus going onto the mountain to pray to describe the nature of spiritual community. First, Jesus spends the night communing with God. Then He chooses the twelve Apostles. Finally, He takes His Apostles down on the plain to minister to the people. Jesus started in communion with God, sharing the very life and love of His Father. He then formed community with others who could share and live out their communion with God together, in mutual love and support. He then led that community into ministry to offer, to all people, that very communion with God that made them a spiritual community (cf. Luke 6:12-19). It is that kind of community and its role in fanning the flames of contagious fire that we'll discuss in this chapter.

Spiritual community shares the unity with God and one another that Jesus asks for, recorded in John 17. Jesus dwells within the spiritual community in the same way that the Father and the Holy Spirit dwells within Him. Spiritual community embodies life-giving Love—Perfect Love which casts out fear and transforms us into the image of Christ. The Holy Spirit binds spiritual community together, providing multiple spiritual gifts that enable its members to accomplish the work of Jesus in proclaiming the Gospel and bringing the Kingdom of God on earth. Every member of a spiritual community focuses their love on God and expresses that love through obedience to Jesus as they hear the voice of their Good Shepherd and follow His leading.

You and I read these pages because God used a spiritual community to offer the Gospel to us and then nurture us when we accepted it. God continues to use spiritual community to invite us into Kingdom work and train and equip us to live in the world as sons and daughters of the Great King. Contagious fire can only be maintained in spiritual community.

Scripture shows us that God most often reveals Himself and speaks to us through other believers. While we certainly have seen examples of personal revelations and visions which God used to call and direct His prophets and leaders, those "words" were most often directed to the community. The history of the Church shows us that we come to know God most profoundly within the loving relationships of other believers. How do we come to know our God who is Spirit and lives beyond the ability of our senses to see, hear, smell, touch, and taste Him? In a community indwelt by the Spirit of God, God reveals Himself to us through human senses. We learn from the experiences of others, through their insights, as the Lord speaks to us through them. We experience God's love in practical ways in one another as we share openly, vulnerably, and honestly. We hear His words of forgiveness, encouragement, guidance, and hope through the care of those around us. Spiritual community encourages us back into the prayer closet where we now spiritually, "see, hear, smell, touch, and taste" God's presence. Ultimately and ideally, Spiritual community happens in the Church, the Body of Christ. Unfortunately, we don't always find it there.

The Struggle of Spiritual Community in Today's Church

It's easy to talk about the Church as the Body of Christ with Jesus as its Head, but we often experience our churches more like secular institutions. Operating a lot like businesses, churches can focus on results rather than relationships. We may talk about spiritual community, yet without expecting commitment to one another or to God. Rather, our "communities" often model social clubs, available when it's convenient, where personal independence stands as its core value. How might we compare most of our congregations to the twelve disciples who committed themselves to Jesus and to one another, risking everything to love and serve Him? No wonder the Lord has to call us back to our first love—to contagious fire!

We might ask, "Why is Christian community so essential to maintaining a burning love relationship with God and sharing His love with the world?" God chose incarnation as His strategy to bring the Kingdom. Authentic spiritual community exists as incarnational community—Christ in you, the hope of glory (cf. Colossians 1:27). We learn to relate to God the Father as we relate to Jesus—God in human form. We learn to know Jesus Himself as we come to know Jesus in one another. We experience God's love as members of our community love us even though they know about our imperfections. We learn to love our "neighbors" in the world by leaning to love the ones in the church. A church culture that reflects Jesus' presence both grows His disciples and attracts the world around it. While it may be easy for the world to dismiss one person who passionately loves Jesus and others, a whole community that lives in the love of God becomes a contagious fire!

Forming spiritual community in the church presents a bigger challenge than we might imagine. True spiritual community reflects the unity and love of the Trinity. It's formed around mutual interest, trust for one another, vulnerability, and dependence on the presence of God. Many of our church cultures, conversely, have become places where people, particularly leaders, feel they need to pretend that they have it all together, to hide from one another the way Adam and Eve hid from God in the Garden. Within this kind of environment, we protect our vulnerabilities by focusing somewhere else. We may be able to talk about Bible study or theology or church programs, but talking about our growing edges in our relationships with God can be the last thing people want to do, or even think necessary.

For all these reasons, our attempts to develop spiritual community can be premature for many, throwing them into the deep end of the pool before we've taught them to swim. It may seem easy enough to advertise a spiritual growth group opportunity and unintentionally put people in a situation where they feel unprepared and cornered. While we can "look up" a question about the Bible, a query about one's relationship with God can feel mortifying if one can't answer it. It only takes one such experience that ends in embarrassment or worse, judgment, and people will find it hard to try again.

Therefore, like every aspect of transformation that we've discussed, we need to start where people are. That makes forming a group challenging when few of us find ourselves in the same place. Teaching, modeling, experiential opportunities, and various levels of community need to be woven together in ways that allow people to explore and discover in the freedom NOT to have it altogether.

Even though the church culture may make it difficult to form spiritual community, we can make it easier by intentionally forming an environment where people can grow into trusting and vulnerable relationships.

Learning to Live in Open and Vulnerable Relationships

For authentic spiritually forming communities to form and survive, the church must become the safest place on earth. God messes with the heart; He pokes the most sensitive places in our lives; He challenges us to risk more than we could ever think possible; Jesus delights in exposing our darkness to His Light so that our wounds and struggles become light. Therefore, if you would be my brother or sister in Jesus and help me follow Him, I need to be able to trust you—to know that I can be open and vulnerable and that you will listen, love, and pray without judgment. If I am to share my heart with you, I have to know that you will keep my confidence, unless you really believe I may bring harm to myself or to others. Then, I need to trust you to tell me what you think and what you'll do to protect me.

Many Jesus followers I know would feel safer sharing their life story, and their mistakes, at the local pub, with strangers, than they would at church. We have ways, in the name of caring and concern, of betraying the confidence placed in us, and sharing the tender privacy of others. "Oh, would you pray with me for Sharon? What's the problem? Well...." How would you or I feel if we overheard our doctor discussing our case over dinner with friends? We'd be furious and ready to find another doctor! Should a doctor be considered more trustworthy than a disciple of Jesus Christ? Quite the opposite. In most cases, this "sharing about others" may come from good motives—we want to help. No matter the motives, however, the one betrayed will find it hard to trust a Christian friend again.

Chris Schutte comments about simple ways to begin to turn the tide of vulnerability and trust.

> *I think that sharing personal stories in sermons, and having regular testimonies from folks on the journey, help create a culture where it's not only OK, but actually important, to acknowledge and embrace our messiness, and emphasize that, when we do, we're met with radical love and friendship "in the Beloved."*

Christian friendship and spiritual community constitute a sacred relationship. Communities of faith must become intentional about the ways they provide safety for one another and honor their place on the journey with Jesus. *Imago Christi* faced this issue painfully, early in our life as an Order. From the beginning, we shared openly and deeply with one another, in our gatherings, in our prayer-partner calls, and in our work together. Most of us have been pastors, missionaries, and spiritual directors, so one would think that forming a safe community would be easy. We were raised in the "just let it happen" cultural values of our world and only when we hurt a dear brother or sister did we realize that we had violated our spiritual community. Through honest and painful discussions, repentance and forgiveness we realized that we had to become more intentional about how we lived in community together.

To live out our common communion with God, we decided to revise our Covenant to expressly commit to the sacred nature of our relationships. We committed to share honestly, to listen to one another fully, to respond without judgment, and to hold confidentially what was shared with us. In the following Gatherings, we gave members permission to interrupt the discussion when one of these values seemed to be slighted and we reviewed our progress at the end of the Gathering. Until these values become ingrained in the DNA of the church or ministry organization, real spiritual community can never develop. In the same way that we said we might have to precede spiritual formation teaching with the truths of the Gospel, we may also have to increase the safety levels of our church culture before we can make headway with spiritual formation community.

Charlie Dodrill commented about essential elements of spiritual community.

> Safety in a group is essential. I always have my groups agree to three covenants at their inception of the group: 1. Confidentiality, 2. Showing up fully, and 3. Not fixing one another when sharing occurs. Vulnerability usually happens more quickly when these things have been agreed upon.

> Hunger is a huge quality within the group. There has to be at least one person in the group who is hungry to know Jesus. Using the fire analogy, that person would be the spark. Sometimes, someone in the group who casts a vision, hopefully with stories from their own heart/ life, can incite that hunger. It seems to be essential to the group. The fire can catch simply by hearing the hungry person's questions.

> Willingness to try things proves essential for the group development. When a group decides to do experimental things together, I have found that closeness grows quickly within the group. However, if a couple of people in the group aren't willing to try something with the rest of the group, it can create an unsafe atmosphere. Willingness to fail or look foolish is a biggie in my opinion.

Debbie Swindoll shares an important consideration about developing spiritual community.

> There needs to be an awareness and some kind of structure for including and looking to God in the midst of the community. It's not true spiritual community without an awareness of God in the midst of it. Most of us are so habituated in giving advice and "spiritual" answers to one another that we fall back into our established practices all the time. One structure that group spiritual direction uses is intentional pauses for prayer–time to stop and be quiet after someone has shared and listen for God, make room for the Spirit. Practicing this discipline can make a big difference over time in the spiritual culture of a group.

> In our Life with God series we provide a developmental structure

to grow the community aspect of our groups. For example, the first semester we focus on listening without group members responding to what others have shared. Over time group members are invited to give feedback and mentored in discerning prayer before they give responses. We also require that every group develop a group covenant which represents what it looks like to love each other well. Each semester they have to revisit the covenant and make any changes they desire.

Leaders are so important in spiritual community. We train the leaders for our Life with God groups, but we also have a small group leader training study called The Art of Spiritual Leadership which helps leaders to practice good listening, to pay attention to their own relationship with God, to become aware of God as the true leader of the group, to encourage honest sharing and to recognize and encourage grace-filled and loving responses to one another.

You can find out more about these resources at www.graftedlife.com.

Developing Language to Talk About Our Relationship With God

In a conversation with a friend and leader of an international Christian ministry, I asked, "Tell me about how you experience love in your relationship with God." Her reply surprised me, "I'd have to think about that; I don't think anyone's ever asked me that question before." Her life centered around God, but she honestly didn't know how to express how she had been experiencing God. We've said that spiritual community provides the place where we can unpack our faith journey with Jesus, where we can share our hearts, be listened to and taken seriously without judgment, prayed for without sermonizing, and protected from gossip. Even if that kind of community exists, we may still have a problem.

Even when people realize that it might be helpful to talk about their journey with God, most don't have language to express what they feel or experience spiritually. If we were to ask a committed church member, at random, to tell us about their relationship with God or their faith, the chances are that the two or three sentences that might follow would address denominational background, church membership, and roles in the church institution. We've developed language for sharing our experience in almost every part of our lives—except our life with God. Where does one begin? My life with God is my whole life! It's an ever-moving relationship, subtle, nuanced, with more mystery than clarity. I can tell you about my church experience, for better or worse. I may even be able to tell you about my theology, but how do I tell you about my heart? "Well, I believe in God, at least most of the time. He helps me a lot when I remember to ask Him... well, most of the time. The Bible is OK, although a lot of it seems pretty harsh. I'm not sure if it all applies today. I pray some. God is like a father to me. I never really felt loved by my father, though, so I'm not sure what to expect of God. Does that answer your question?" Actually, it's not a bad start, but the response would probably feel frustrating to both parties.

In our church groups, I've learned to stop asking people "How can I pray for you?" I get everything from hangnails to distant aunts' medical maladies, but seldom anything about their walk with God. I have been experimenting with another question, "How can I pray for your relationship with God this week?" Long pause.... I'm amazed at how hard a question that is for many people to answer. Any answer, however, makes a good start!

Not only do most of us lack vocabulary to describe our relationship with God in any depth, but many even struggle with what categories to address. Hopefully, our teaching and witnessing about spiritual growth can begin to provide these categories and some of the terms to describe our experience within them. Categories might include prayer, trust, fear, worship, truth, temptation, struggle, and so on. *Imago Christi* has found that the key concepts we need to describe our spiritual formation experience are: journey, First and Second Order calling, spiritual longing, spiritual blocks and wounds, spiritual warfare, experiences of presence, consolation, desolation, dark nights, abiding prayer, and of course, spiritual community.

Sharing feelings can present another problem. We men have been known for our difficulty in expressing any emotion other than anger. I see this struggle often, as I coach the Ignatian Exercises. These exercises provide an excellent scriptural meditation method using one's Holy Spirit—inspired imagination to put oneself into the biblical story and become attentive to what God might be saying personally to the person. The fourth journaling question asks, "What feelings and emotions did you encounter in your prayer time and what do they tell you?" Journaling point #4 can yield some of the most powerful insights into one's interaction with God, but many struggle to recognize what they feel during their prayer time. For many of my directees, I have to provide an extensive list of "feeling words" for them to consider as they reflect. It helps! Maybe we could help spiritual formation discussions by providing a similar kind of list of categories for our relationship with God, descriptive terms, and possible emotional responses.

Accepting Everyone as Pilgrims on a Journey With God

"Birds of a feather flock together." It's true of birds; it's true of people in our cultures; it's especially true in our churches, particularly our larger churches. People tend to segregate into various affinity groups—by age, interest, church involvement, music preference, family makeup, etc. Many times, these groupings form for good reason. People of similar situation often have similar interests and may form deeper relationships more easily. The downside, however, can be that we deprive one group from the wisdom and perspectives of the others. For example, many children and youth never learn how to worship in a congregation setting because they never do it. Either initially or soon after the service starts, they're shuttled off to something more "suited" to their age and maturity level. Kids like being with their friends and adults like less distraction in church. Everyone's happy. But kids seldom see their parents worship God, and parents miss the opportunity to share holy ground discussions with their kids. We could make similar comparisons for every segregation we make.

We also tend to "flock together" to protect ourselves from people who may not understand us or accept us. We fear that those with different backgrounds or life experiences may judge us negatively for our differences. The rich may judge the poor for not working hard enough. The poor may judge the rich for hoarding their possessions and not caring about others. Of course, neither assumption is appropriate. The same kinds of assumptions and judgments can be made at a spiritual level, as well. For example, we may judge others' depth of faith based on how regularly they attend church. Genuine spiritual community must embrace people where they are in the spiritual growth process, trusting God to lead and guide at a pace that He desires. Accepting others as "pilgrims in process" enables us to learn from one another and support one another's journey.

> We've described seven stages of spiritual growth, (eight, if we include Pre-Christians), with some distinctly different needs across this spectrum. There may be great reasons to have special classes or groups for new Christians and for "mature" believers. Sending a "baby" Christian off on an unguided silent retreat designed for "adult" believers, for example, probably wouldn't be helpful for the baby or the adults. Having said that, how will the new believer discover what it looks like to actively serve God, fall in love with Him, and become like Jesus if they aren't exposed to people for whom that's happening? Conversely, more mature believers can be reminded by young believers about the basics of life with Jesus that helped them grow and mature. Spiritual pride can be more easily recognized, and hopefully repented of, when we're with others who haven't traveled as far as we have on the journey.

Charlie Dodrill shares ways that he helps people feel free to accept one another in the unique ways that God meets them.

> Starting a more experimental group has been good for us. The format I used, after a couple weeks of hearing people's SPIRITUAL journeys, is that we would spend about 20 minutes introducing a spiritual practice/gift/etc., then the next 20 minutes actually DOING the practice together, then leaving the rest for processing what just happened. I have found it important for people to try things together and afterwards to hear not only the glorious stories of what happened between the Lord and Amy, but also hear Rick say, "This didn't do

anything for me." This can take the sting out when we don't get out of it what others did. We recognize that different things work at different times for different people.

As we've said earlier, some things just can't be taught; they have to be experienced. We often first see God working in others and then we spot that same work of the Holy Spirit in our own lives. An important part of our spiritual experience can come in relationship with others who are living a bit further on the journey. I talk a lot about Brother Boniface and often quote him. I can't imagine how poorly my journey with God would have progressed with just books and people in my own stage of the journey.

Whether in similar groups or grouped with different experiences and perspectives, we need to affirm everyone as a pilgrim on the journey, valued and honored in the place where God has them. Adults have no more value and deserve no more respect than toddlers, for example. God values each of us on the journey of spiritual growth—we're all in process. Bon used to say, "Every person in the world is in search of Jesus; they may be searching in the wrong places or they may not know that Jesus is what their hearts long for. Nevertheless, their search is real and God woos them forward." How will seekers ever know what an authentic follower of Jesus is like until they hang out with one? We can inadvertently create a "spiritual cast system," whether we use a spiritual formation paradigm or not. Through prayer and discernment, we need to recognize when it will be helpful to group similar folks and when we need to mix them up. In either case, we must love and honor each person right where they are.

Creating a Climate of Growth

While we've discussed the "lifelong" nature of our journey of spiritual growth in previous chapters, its vital importance makes it worth mentioning again in the context of spiritual community. Intimacy with the Creator of the Universe can never be "mastered." Our whole lives on earth, and certainly heavenly eternity become adventures of discovery. Randy Alcorn, in his book *Deadline*, describes a conversation between a new arrival in heaven and his guardian angel.¹ The angel explained his responsibility to teach the man how to live in heaven. The man responded with surprise that he had assumed that he would arrive in heaven knowing everything. The even more surprised angel responded that only God knows everything. It's God's nature to create and we could never catch up with His marvelous work! The newly resurrected man realized that he had arrived in heaven as a beginner and that a beginner he would always be.

We get a glimpse of the lifelong process of growth even in our human relationships. While we may think that we have come to know another person fully, we could never fully understand the vast intricacy and complexity of even a close friend or loved one, no matter how close a relationship we may think we have developed. The apostle Paul describes our knowledge of God as "seeing through a mirror dimly" (cf. 1 Cor 13:12). God reveals Himself to us over time as we become willing and able to experience more of Him. On the infinite scale of this discovery, we all find ourselves beginners. We're all learning how to know God, how to discern His voice and leading, and how to make ourselves available to the amazing revelations of His majesty and glory. Every spiritually healthy Christian searches for the "pearl of great price" and the "treasure hidden in the field" (cf. Matt 13:46 and Matt 13:44). Only the foolish would fail to seek help in finding them.

While the experiences and advice of authors may help us, we need fellow explorers with whom we can process our experiences, people a bit further along to help us discern. Teresa of Avila believes that most serious Christians allow God to draw them into deepening intimacy, at least exploring the Fifth Mansion. She regrets, however, that most of these believers misunderstand this new territory with God and, lacking mentors to help them, flee back to more familiar levels of relationship and remain there. We all need mentors

---

1. Randy Alcorn, *Deadline – a Novel* (Sisters Oregon: Multnomah Press, 1994)

and coaches who can help us explore the new country into which our Lord leads us and help us interpret our new experiences.

Individual Coaching and Mentoring – Spiritual Discipleship

Spiritual mentoring, coaching, and personal spiritual friendships form another important part of spiritual community. The importance of mentors and coaches has long been recognized within the business and academic communities. These sectors have created many new training programs, varying from general "Life Coaching" to more focused mentoring and coaching for technical and leadership development. While certified and technically trained coaches could prove helpful to any of us, congregations can also provide some basic skill development for spiritual mentors and coaches, such as listening, asking open-ended questions, and helping others explore God's direction. Many excellent books can provide training to help people coach and mentor successfully. For example, "Stephen Ministries" has been used in thousands of congregations to equip members to provide pastoral care for needy parishioners.[2]

We've discussed the helpful role of spiritual direction in our own personal spiritual growth and as a resource to our leaders and congregation. Personally, I can testify that God has used professional spiritual direction in very special ways in my own journey with Jesus. In reviewing my own spiritual history, however, I realize that God primarily used ordinary men and women with no formal training to introduce me to Jesus and help me learn to follow Him. Dr. Lambert, a linguistics professor at Arizona State University, introduced me to God; PJ, a campus pastor, encouraged my early growth; Ray, a machine tool company owner, demonstrated how Jesus can transform our lives through meaningful relationships; George, a theology professor, showed me what Christian community looked like; Kevin, a retired businessman, showed me how to minister in the power of the Holy

2. To find out more about Stephen Ministries, see /www.stephenministries.org.

Spirit; Kathryn, a homemaker, encouraged me to pray beyond words; Boniface, a monk, introduced me to spiritual theology and the mystical life; Bill, a retired pastor, taught me how to minister healing. I could go on and on naming people who God brought into my life at just the right time to show me what I needed to know at the time. I have certainly learned a lot from teachers and professors in church and academic settings. Few of these people, however, had been specifically trained to come alongside me in ways that proved life-changing.

Teaching and "on-the-job" training have always formed an essential part of our Judeo-Christian tradition. We've never expected a person to come to know God without first learning about Him and the life into which one has been invited. In recent centuries, however, the church has tended to focus more on information about God rather than relationship with Him. We have used academic classroom models rather than the rabbinic relational discipling and coaching reflected in Scripture. While Sunday School classes for children and adults can have their places in elemental teaching (Scripture calls it milk), coaching, mentoring, personal discipleship, and spiritual direction become essential in helping growing believers interpret their experiences with God. This "advanced discipleship" may also become an important context for maturing Christians to participate with Jesus' shepherding of less mature believers. For this to become common place, we must create a church culture in which we all understand ourselves as lifelong learners, as well as mentors. *Imago Christi's* Discovery, Discovery Companions, Mapping Tool Training, and Spiritual Formation Coaching Manual form a course for spiritual formation coach/mentor training that is accessible and affordable for church members.

We may make assumptions about people's spiritual journeys based upon how long they have been Christians or their ability to verbalize their spiritual experiences. Mentors and coaches can spot these areas of difficulty and help pilgrims embrace God's work in their present circumstance.

Terry Tarleton shares a story about mentoring in community that illustrates our need to have people close enough to us to help us interpret our experiences.

> *We have found that a brand-new Christian can learn how to pray contemplatively. A few years ago, a gentleman in his early 60's came to faith in our church. He immediately joined a small formational men's group I lead. At one point I was talking about prayer and how it is defined and practiced in different ways. This guy chimed up and said, "You mean there's a different way to pray than spending time sitting and listening to Jesus?" Of course, we teach other methods, but this guy, maybe because he was older, had dived into contemplative prayer, and was developing a personal, intimate relationship with Jesus. I was deprived of this for decades because no one told me about contemplation.*

Terry was then able to coach this new believer consistent with where God had led him in prayer. Dark Nights provide another area of great misunderstanding. Some people, when they experience a perceived loss of connection with God often mistake their situation as a Dark Night caused by God. Others fail to recognize God's genuine gift of a Dark Night and blame themselves for not loving God adequately. Mentors and coaches, as part of spiritual community can help these pilgrims understand how to respond to what they are experiencing.

Building Community Around First and Second Order Calling

You'll remember our earlier discussion about First Order and Second Order Callings, also known as the Great Commandment and the Great Commission. God first calls us into personal relationship with Himself, inviting us to receive His life-giving love so that He can focus our whole being around living in His love. Within this abiding relationship of love, we gradually become transformed into Christ-likeness. God's Second Order Calling challenges us to share our life-love relationship with others—loving our neighbor as ourselves and loving one another as Jesus has loved us. The ability to love—share life—with one another and our neighbor becomes motivated and empowered as we live in our First Order Calling. "We love because He first loved us" (cf. 1 John 4:19). As we've discussed, we often get these Callings confused and reversed. Worse, most groups in the church have been structured to reverse them and thereby fail to form and experience authentic Christian spiritual community.

Within our task and performance driven society, most church groups form around task (Second Order Calling) and then develop the minimum community necessary to accomplish that task. Whether in a Bible study, missions committee, elder board, etc., we may open and close with prayer and take prayer requests, but the members' ongoing relationship with God often gets ignored. While people may feel good about serving God, they also often leave feeling inwardly frustrated and uncared for—pawns in some greater enterprise. The reverse can be just as detrimental. Small groups can form for the sole purpose of sharing and prayer, focusing entirely on the needs of its members. This kind of group can easily become ingrown, developing a "God for me" mentality. Without any outward purpose, we can lose focus and miss meeting Jesus in others and loving Him there. Scripture tells us that our ability to love others comes from the depth of God's love that we experience. It also tells us that we can't truly say we love God without demonstrating the fruit of loving our neighbor. Missional momentum or motivation emanates from within our spiritual formation (cf. 12 John 4:7-11). Therefore, each expression of spiritual community should have both First Order and Second Order aspects to its life.

Let's look at a few examples to suggest how we might introduce, emphasize and foster the First Order component within an existing ministry context. How might we use the First and Second Order concept in a Facilities Committee? Clearly, this group has been formed primarily as a Second Order Calling group; they're to love neighbor through ensuring the safety and functionality of the church buildings and equipment. The group probably meets monthly with a long list of ongoing needs and new requests. Often made up of men, its members have been gifted on the "doing" end of the relational spectrum. They probably felt called to this committee because they like the feeling of accomplishment when they get things done. Members of the Facilities Committee may not immediately understand why time spent on their spiritual life will enhance the "primary" purpose of their ministry. I'll use bullet points to suggest how we might add the First Order component. You can fill in the rest.

Train the group leader as part of a church-wide leadership training process which connects the spiritual health of Jesus followers to their ability to discern His leading and accomplish what He says. As always, the training should be experiential as well as informational. (This step and the following training would obviously need to be established as part of the teaching and training discussed in Chapter 4.)

Training for the group members which explains the purpose and process of including spiritual components within the monthly meeting, accompanied by a plea from senior leadership to give it a six-month try—an experiment.

Provide a simple and relational discussion tool, possibly using a biblical passage that provides opportunity for personal but limited check-in for each member, and appropriate prayer. The "spiritual check-in" could go something like, "On a scale of 1 to 10, how would you rate your relationship with God this week? What event demonstrates your choice?"

Group prayer over the task agenda for the meeting, asking for God's specific guidance and provision for each task and for unanimity in decisions.

Close the meeting on time with thanksgiving for what has been accomplished, wisdom for what still needs to be done, and recommitment to pray for each person regularly until the next meeting.

Ongoing group leader follow-up and training to deal with problems that arise.

Committee members may resist the "extra time" at first. However, they'll become encouraged that they are following the process used by all the ministry teams of their church. As they become faithful to both parts of God's calling, they realize that the group members are as important to God and the church as are the buildings. Finally, when they discover that they get more work done in less time, they'll become committed to the process. They may even find themselves looking forward to the next committee meeting!

A similar process could be used for a Bible Study Group, but this time adding the Second Order component.

Training for leaders

Training and plea for the group

Opening check-in, similar to the committee check in

Bible Study process, with emphasis on personal relationship with God in addition to the truths of the text

Selection and ongoing short discussion and prayer for a group project that fits the interests and abilities of the group. Because the "primary" purpose of the group is Bible Study, a simple and relatively easy project should be chosen. They might serve in the local homeless shelter once a month, or choose a needy person and clean their house.

Closing prayers related to the members' relationships with God and reaffirmation to pray for one another daily

We don't have to start spiritual formation communities from scratch. We can begin by helping the communities that exist become more spiritually forming. Just as Jesus sent His disciples to seek out "people of peace" in the villages they were to visit, it's good to start with groups and ministries where we already see the Holy Spirit moving.

Chris Schutte shares his insights about moving ministry teams to embrace a more spiritual dimension.

> *I like the idea of moving existing "groups" in the congregation toward formation group (If you can do it with the Facilities Committee, you can do it anywhere, right!). Starting with a few folks who are currently small group or ministry leaders and open to formation, seems wise. We can allow them to lead their groups or ministries in this way. Slowly inviting other key group / ministry leaders in, and working with them, we can then commission them to, "Go, and do likewise." In my experience, however, there are some ministry leaders who are simply not open to leading in this way.*

> *Finally, in our congregation, I find that, when done well, the "Fourth Day" groups encouraged by Cursillo can be structured in such a way that leads to good community. By sharing their lives of study, piety, and "apostolic action," they are able to embrace First and Second order Callings in the context of a loving community. These groups, like any group, however, can fall into "ruts," so constant accountability for leaders is essential.*

God taught me about starting where He already was producing fruit through the Men's Ministry in one of the churches I pastored. The Men's Ministry consisted of a monthly breakfast in a local restaurant with a half-dozen retired men who ate breakfast and talked about whatever. In addition, however, they hosted an annual men's retreat at the beach, with a speaker and lots of free time. I invited the team leader to participate in the kind of training process described above. He challenged the group to try something for their retreat—experimentally. They decided to start the retreat with a small group check-in, continue with the speaker, and add a small group discussion about the speaker's talk. They developed a Group Guide that outlined a process for prayer, discussion, application, and prayer for one another. The men who had been attending the retreat for years, as much for the free time as anything, grumbled a bit at the new structure, but went along. By the next year, the retreat had tripled in size and the monthly breakfast moved to the church to provide room for many new and younger men, and better space for check-n, fellowship, and prayer.

In time, new spiritual community groups can be formed around more tightly focused spiritual formation subjects like abiding prayer, healing, contemplative worship, practice of various spiritual disciplines, and neighborhood outreach. In each case, however, groups should plan for both their First Order and Second Order life.

JD Ward shares an approach that ReWire uses to combine the First and Second Order elements of groups.

> We have lead groups down a spiritual formation path into mission that encourages people to read, pray and journal about a particular topic. Then they share these journal reflections in safe communities we call "sacred circles." After doing this for some time, the members become ready to commit to a covenant to be in a new process called "Deep Waters." This process is a yearlong internship in growing in their inward, outward and together journey. This process breaks into three equal parts of discussion: 30 minutes about how their prayer life is going, 30 minutes about the nature of community and how to live prophetically in the world, and 30 minutes to address specific outreach with which the group is involved. This process has developed many people into the practices of "contemplative activist" committed to mission groups that have sustaining power.[3]

Forming Core Communities and Invitational Communities Within The Church

Most of the churches I've served could be categorized as "cell-based" churches. The depth of learning, pastoral care, fellowship, and support happened in these small groups. While a large majority of our members attended these small groups, many others weren't involved. Some traveled or held jobs that made attendance difficult. Others felt cautious about feeling like newcomers in a group that had been meeting for a long time. We found that our spiritual communities needed to take a variety of forms directed to

---

3. JD's "Contemplative Dialogue Covenant" May be found in Appendix C.

people in different situations.

As we form spiritual formation communities within our ministries, we must be sensitive to providing long-lasting deeply committed "core" communities, who hope to stay together over many years. We also needed to create "invitational" communities designed to provide spiritual formation community for a shorter time and open for people to come and go. These "taste and see" fellowships can provide all the qualities of the core communities, knowing that they provide only an introductory experience with a beginning and ending time. We hope, however, that those who have a good experience in the invitational group will discover the richness of spiritual community and be able to join a core group or form one, possibly with other members of the invitational group. The invitational group can feel safer for those checking out the experience and avoid the guilt when newcomers in a core group decide it's not for them.

Taking Spiritual Community Into The World

Our Savior's Church developed a "sister-church" relationship with a small Baptist congregation in southern Haiti. An adult team traveled to Haiti for a week or two every year, and a youth team would go every other year. Each team spent months in preparation, primarily developing team community. Some volunteered only for one trip and others served on Haiti teams for many years. The teams often received glowing feedback about the impact that their loving relationships made upon the Haitian villagers.

We also found that ministering together as a spiritual community produced profound spiritual growth in the group members. Our "returning short-term missionaries" joined the Haiti team to help others, but discovered that God's love always travels both ways. They witnessed the power of God's love among the poor and received God's love from the poor. Jesus always sent His disciples out in community.

Most of us feel inadequate about taking God's love into the world in personal encounters. We're often afraid of "doing it wrong" or of personal rejection. Encouragement and support from the community can help us follow Jesus into natural relationships that God has designed for us.

Terry Tarleton shares one of the ways his community brings that kind of encouragement.

> It seems that our people are more effective in sharing their good news with others than ever before, simply because they are more in love with Jesus! We do talk often about inviting others into the journey we are on with Jesus. One of the things we do on Sundays (as often as we can) is to do what we call "Salt Reports." When our people are out and about and have an opportunity to pray for someone, lead someone into relationship with Jesus, share where their peace comes from, or to just be kind in some way, they write these up and send them to me and I read them at the beginning of the service. It's a reminder to us to take Jesus with us everywhere we go, and be aware of what HE is doing, and join in.

This kind of sharing helps members of the community realize that God uses simple encounters and natural relationships in which we can simply follow our hearts and do what's natural. God takes care of the rest.

Bill O'Byrne shares about a devotional guide that he used to help a mission team embrace God's work in their hearts amidst the journey.

> I put together a "Trekker's Spiritual Preparation Companion Guide" designed for a missions trip in the Himalayas! The Spiritual Preparation part of the devotionals helped team members set the trip in the context of each one's spiritual journey, and set expectation and anticipation for the participants to meet God in the trek. It also invited the team members to observe how their faith might be challenged in the process, and reflect about how they will face their fears and challenges, along the way.
>
> Use of the Daily Devotionals during the trip provided opportunities to notice God's hand and presence in the day, and record and process their experience individually and together. They'll never forget recognizing their ministry and the spiritual life or journey as

We've seen that spiritual community becomes vital to our ongoing spiritual growth and that the "spiritual" dimension of community can be developed anywhere people gather together in the life of the church. When these First Order and Second Order dimensions of community life are brought together, God's love flourishes in the participants and through their ministries in profoundly increased ways.

Not only does spiritual community enhance our internal church ministries, it also makes our outreach significant. For example, "unchurched" people often carry stereotypes about "Christians"—usually negative. They may believe that we're judgmental, hypocritical, simply members of social clubs, irrational, etc. When one Christian shows up who doesn't fit the stereotype and positively impresses these "naysayers," they can easily dismiss the Christian as an "exception to the rule." "SHE may not be judgmental and holier-than-thou, but the rest of them are." When, however, we reach out in groups bound together in Jesus' love, we're not so easily dismissed. Our diversity within the group provides a richness that no one of us could give alone. Our community witnesses to the presence and love of Jesus through our spiritual relationships to others. Jesus invited pre-disciples to "come and see" and hang out with His community without strings attached. In the company of His beloved, they became beloveds, too.

The absence of authentic Christian community first delayed my salvation for years and later became critical to receiving it. I've shared earlier that I grew up outside the church. As a child, I don't remember even knowing any Christians. A few people who went to church would invite me and a few times I went. Unfortunately, all I saw was a religious service with language and customs that immediately told me that I did not belong. How could I have known what went on in small groups and classes or the love and care shared among the members? Only years later, when my life seemed hopeless, did a community of believers embrace me with the arms of Jesus.

In that community, I not only "heard" about Jesus, I experienced Him in its community members. Through their encouragement, I eventually experienced Him myself. We Christians need spiritual community so that we can grow in our relationship with our Lord; the world needs our spiritual communities, so they can experience Jesus among us. Once they experience Him, believing in Him becomes easy.

In summary, we know that God never designed our journey with Jesus to be traveled alone. The Gospel has been given to communities of men and women so that others could come to know the Lord. Those same men and women have also been given spiritual gifts to build up the Body of Christ so that we may become mature in our relationship of love with God. Both purposes of God become realized in spiritual community.

There have been times and places in the world where society supplied supportive community as an essential part of its fabric. In the individualistic culture of the west, however, we must become intentional about developing spiritual community in our churches and ministries. Without community, the embers of our faith grow weak. In a vibrant spiritual community, our flickers of love become fanned into a blazing fire that sets our hearts aglow with love for God and neighbor—love that becomes brilliantly contagious. May we emulate the community of the first disciples who radiated Jesus.

"Now there were some Greeks among those who were going up to worship at the feast; these then came to Philip, who was from Bethsaida of Galilee, and began to ask him, saying, "Sir, we wish to see Jesus." John 12:20-21

In our next chapter, we'll discuss how our spiritual communities become places of healing and restoration so that the flames of Jesus' love might flash forth with a brilliance that truly glorifies God.

CHAPTER 12:

HEALING MINISTRY – REMOVING THE BLOCKS TO LOVE

James attended one of *Imago Christi's* Spiritual Formation Discovery for Leader events. A pastor of a growing nondenominational church, he had sensed the desire to share a more intimate relationship with God and learn to follow Him more closely. Before the Discovery, he confided, "I think that my theology and pastoral skills have been well-formed, but it feels like I'm trying to follow Jesus in a fog. I know He's head of the Church, but I have no clue how to understand His directions other than the principles laid out in Scripture. My prayer life feels like sitting in an empty room with my thoughts bouncing back at me off the walls and ceiling. I've always talked about a personal relationship with Jesus, but I'm realizing that something's in the way of really experiencing His love. I just don't have the peace and confidence I long for. I feel stuck."

Some months later, James' spiritual director asked him about other "god" figures in his life—people he valued and looked up to such as parents, teachers, relatives, particularly ones in his childhood. "Ask the Holy Spirit to bring to mind the person He wants you to consider." While James would never have thought of his father as a "god figure," his dad had always played a very important role in James' life. His father always encouraged his oldest son to excel, to reach his potential. James responded well to his dad's "you can do it, son" relationship. Pleasing Dad became a major motivator as he went through his high school years. James would tell his friends that his dad was his hero. Below the surface, however, James struggled with feelings of not quite measuring up. His dad's "you can do it admonitions" never quite came true. While James excelled in sports and academics, he never became the "best" in either category. Although James' dad never scolded or shamed him for his lack of perfection, James came to believe that "second best" represented failure. Midway through James' Freshman year of college, his dad suffered a massive heart attack and died almost instantly. James felt lost without his cheerleader, maybe even abandoned.

Now, many years later, James' healing began with these words from his spiritual director: "James, how might you compare your relationship with your dad and your relationship with God?"

In *Contagious Fire*, we've been exploring how we might help our churches become intentional about igniting the fire of God's love within our congregation to the extent that they become torches of the Gospel to the world around us. We know that the flame within us grows in brilliance and strength as we let God draw us to Himself more and more closely and transform us into the image of Christ. This intimacy sets us free to live life abundantly in the reality of our new identity as sons and daughters of God, in all the uniqueness and beauty in which each of us were created. With the fullness of God's love burning within us and the freedom to live out that love in ways that are natural to us, God's love becomes contagious to others as we care for others in meaningful ways. As we grow in our relationship with Jesus, we become able to do more than tell people about Jesus—we're able to show them His presence here and now. This process of becoming free to set others free lies at the heart of the Kingdom strategy of God.

The Spirit of the Lord God is upon me,

Because the Lord has anointed me

To bring good news to the afflicted;

He has sent me to bind up the brokenhearted,

To proclaim liberty to captives

And freedom to prisoners;

To proclaim the favorable year of the Lord

And the day of vengeance of our God;

To comfort all who mourn,

To grant those who mourn in Zion,

Giving them a garland instead of ashes,

The oil of gladness instead of mourning,

The mantle of praise instead of a spirit of fainting.

So, they will be called oaks of righteousness,

The planting of the Lord, that He may be glorified. Is 61:1-3

In Luke 4:18, Jesus identifies Himself as this Anointed One and in John 20:21, we read that Jesus sends us in just the same way that He has been sent by the Father. Jesus called together a band of followers and did for them just what God promised. He brought them Good News; because they mourned under the burden of sin, He comforted them and set them free; now, by putting His life within them, they could live in gladness and praise; finally, instead of fainting like saplings blown in the wind, they would stand as strong oak trees, growing by streams of living water. Now, like Jesus, they could invite others, with the contagious fire of God's love, to receive the same healing and strength they had received to become oak trees themselves. Oak, one of the hardest woods, burns the brightest and hottest—with contagious fire!

While Jesus came to us already a mighty Oak, He finds us as withering saplings, afflicted, brokenhearted, prisoners wounded by sin who mourn and faint. To form us into oak trees, Jesus heals us in the process of our spiritual growth and teaches us how to become instruments of healing for others. In this chapter, we'll explore how we can become intentional about this healing process in the church, both for ourselves and for those we invite to know Jesus. Here's how we'll proceed:

We'll explore the nature of our woundedness in mind, body, and spirit.

We'll look at the ways that our woundedness disables our ability to live fully as children of God and serve as His messengers.

We'll consider how Jesus provides the healing we need.

We'll discuss ways that our Lord's healing ministry can be lived out in the church.

While an exhaustive discussion of all these topics would take a whole book, we can at least overview each area and provide some resources for further study and point out leaders already making advances in healing ministry who can help us.

Terry Tarleton, pastor of a Vineyard church in the Phoenix, Arizona, area discusses the importance of healing in his own church and shares an important resource.

Peter Scazzero, author of Emotionally Healthy Spirituality, *says that one cannot be spiritually mature unless he's emotionally mature; they go hand in hand.[1] Yet the Western Church, in my opinion, squashes emotions—especially the negative ones! We say things like, "Emotions will lie to you, so they can't be trusted." Yet, Scazzero says negative emotions act like the check engine light on a car dashboard. They warn you that something is not right. I used to buy into the "ignore your emotions" idea. But, I realized that deep down I was an*

---

1. Peter Scazzero, *Emotionally Healthy Spirituality: It's Impossible to Be Spiritually Mature, While Remaining Emotionally Immature*

angry person. It wasn't until I began to do spiritual direction and inner-healing prayer, that I really faced not only my anger, but also my fear, sorrow, grief, and pain. In many ways they were all interrelated. I began to find freedom through being honest with what I was feeling and then, with the help of Jesus, discovering the roots of some of those wounds. Over time I began to become emotionally healed from some of my past stuff. The sad thing is that for decades I allowed my forty-year-old wounds to leak out on every person around me; those who had nothing to do with my pain.

Terry illustrates both the need to recognize our blocks to growth, but to find the resources to deal with them spiritually as well as emotionally.

The Nature of Our Woundedness in Mind, Body, and Spirit.

Why would God see us as "afflicted, brokenhearted, captives and prisoners, mourning, and fainting"? Certainly, when Isaiah wrote this passage and when Jesus read it in the Synagogue, the Jewish people were in bondage to foreign powers. We know that most Jews at that time interpreted the prophecy to refer to this physical bondage. We see, however, Jesus doesn't address the political situation, but the conditions of people's hearts. He promises abundant life, peace, and joy for those who would believe in Him. Through His death and resurrection, Jesus did in fact destroy the power which held all humankind in bondage to sin, death, and the devil. However, we find that people weren't instantly delivered from the consequences of sin after the Cross or even after Pentecost.

Abiding in Christ, letting Perfect Love cast out all fear, and living in the fruits of the Holy Spirit develop within us over time and through the transforming process we call spiritual growth. While we have been delivered from the ultimate consequences of sin, we still struggle with a sinful nature. While the Kingdom of God has come to us in Jesus, we have been born and raised in the Kingdom of this world. While the prison doors have been unlocked, we have to be live from our new nature to be able to live fully outside the prison, in the freedom of God's Kingdom. Let's look at some of the ways that all of us have been deformed and imprisoned by the world we live in.

Deformed Development: God created us in His image to grow and develop in a world without sin, to have models and environments which reflect God's love and purity. Because of sin's presence in us and in the world, none of us have experienced that kind of development. No one has had perfect parents, families, or communities. Their imperfections have wounded us. Because of our own sin, we did not respond to those imperfections perfectly; we sinned back. In our sinful responses, we wounded ourselves and others. Over time, we became deformed in ways that imprisoned us, hurt us, and caused us to suffer. Jesus came to heal us and set us free to become who we were created to be—children of the Most High God, reflective of His loving nature. Our deformity lies in the depths of our spirit, expressing itself in the ways we think and act and in our physical health. We can learn and practice new ways of thinking and acting but can only be re-formed through becoming healed, first in our spirits, then in our minds and bodies. Only God can do that and fortunately for us, God very much wants to heal us.

Deformed Identity: Out of our developmental deformity, we learn to see ourselves—identify ourselves, as deformed. In the same way that persons with a physical deformity might identify themselves as crippled, we let our circumstances form our identities. Underneath our projections of health, happiness, wisdom, talent, etc. we all see ourselves in negative and judgmental ways—like ugly, unworthy, incapable, unlovable, not _____ enough, too _____, etc. We not only find ourselves in the prisons of our deformity, but we have come to believe that we are, in fact, prisoners. Therefore, we think and act like prisoners, even though the door to our cells have been opened by Jesus and His Cross.

Terry Tarleton discusses the role of shame and how it can imprison us in our wounding.

One of the negative emotions that distorts our identity, one that I

330

tend to see come up over and over, is shame. In Brené Brown's book, The Gifts of Imperfection, she defines shame as "not being enough."[2] That definition helped me come to grips with my supposed shortcomings and failures and call them what they really were: shame. I was not enough. I felt that I had not met my own expectations or, quite frankly, the expectations of almost everyone around me. Yet, that all stemmed from one person in my life who never affirmed me the way I needed. Jesus has brought a lot of healing to that place in my soul.

Terry's story illustrates how easily we can be wounded. When we own shame, it becomes part of our own identity. Recognizing where our shame comes from and realizing that it is not appropriate may help, but only Jesus can accomplish healing at the level of identity—in our new birth as God's children and in the truth of His cross that the Holy Spirit brings to specific wounding memories.

Deformed Relationships: Because sin still works within us and because we don't function in the ways we should or even want to because of our deformed nature and identity, we continue to hurt one another. Our deformed development and identity lead to deformed relationships, because of our deformed ability to love.

For example, if I have an arm that doesn't work correctly, I may hit you when I only meant to pat you on the back. When I see myself as a vulnerable victim, I may respond to your kind intentions with retreat or aggression. Because I have not yet learned how to forgive myself and see myself as God's beloved, I may find it impossible to forgive you, judging you negatively. I may learn how to relate to others in positive and loving ways, but will continually be hindered until my deformed nature and identity have been healed and transformed.

Deformed Ability to Love: Worst of all, our ability to love has been

2. Brené Brown, *The Gifts of Imperfection: Let Go of Who You Think You're Supposed to Be and Embrace Who You Are*, Center City, Minnesota. Hazelden, 2010, 2017

deformed. As much as we may understand that we are to love God and our neighbor, our attention has been locked on our own deformity and pain; our negative identities make us resent others, fear exposure, and protect ourselves. When the urge to love that God created within us tries to emerge, we bend it to meet our own needs. We can love God and others only for what they can do for us. When we perceive that they don't meet the needs of our deformity, we stop loving. As a result of our inability to love and receive love (unworthy people aren't lovable), we become isolated from God and others. This makes us easy pickings by the devil who wants to reinforce our disabilities and false identities and blind us to the open door of our prison cells. Only God's love can heal and transform us and set us free from our prisons.

How Our Wounds Disable Us as Lovers of God and Neighbor

All of these dynamics of our wounding in sin also affect our relationship with God. Jesus said that He came to save the lost and the sick (cf. Luke 19:10 and Matthew 9:12). That's just what He did with his first disciples. We often joke about how clueless the disciples were and make fun of Peter's foot-in-mouth disease that so often tripped him up. We're seeing in the honesty of Scripture that Jesus called deformed men with deformed identities—called them to be healed and become healers. While they had been forgiven and saved through faith in Jesus, the transformation of their new birth would develop over the span of their lifetimes. Similarly, Jesus has called us to follow Him, saving us through His grace received in faith. Yet, we don't have to look too far to find plenty of people who can speak of our deformities. Let's look briefly at the ways that our brokenness and deformity distort our relationship with God even as adopted sons and daughters of God. We become captured in our false self-images, chained to fear, and left vulnerable to the Enemy's attacks.

Distorts Relationship With God: The story of the Prodigal Son beautifully illustrates our difficulty (cf. Luke 15:11-32). Even though God has come to us as our Heavenly Father with love and forgiveness, we may initially respond with gratitude but then find that our own warped identity and attachments to this world begin to try to use God for our own purposes. If we're possessed with identities of inadequacy, we may hide from Him or keep our distance. If we see ourselves as victims, we may try to use God to make us successful, etc. While God wants to bathe us in living waters of love and heal our diseases, we may find ourselves playing games to hide our woundedness and protect our fractured self-image.

Captures Us in False Self-Images: Because none of us can tolerate seeing our deformities and accepting the negative images we have of ourselves, we develop coping mechanisms to help us survive. We project, to ourselves and others, images that reflect what we want to be or think we should be. We may cover up our sense of worthlessness by becoming highly educated or good at pleasing and entertaining people, etc. Many times, we actually come to believe that's who we really are, ignoring the real qualities that God has planted within us. We may get away with those projections to some degree with others, but our deceptions never work with God. He loves the REAL person and calls "the real" us to come alive, just as Jesus called Lazarus to come out of the tomb (cf. John 11:1-44). What if Lazarus had not recognized his name or felt such shame that he refused to come out in public because of the stench of decay? We can cling to our prisons for fear of surrendering our prisoner self-image, terrified about the awful person who might be exposed beneath. While God invites us into deepening intimacy, we feel much more comfortable at a safe distance. So, our fire—instead of becoming contagious, smolders below the surface never receiving the breath that bring it into full flame.

Chains Us to Fear: While Jesus came to set us free in His love and fill us with joy and peace, our woundedness and hiddenness will lock us to the chains of fear—fear of exposure and failure. We'll continually find ourselves like the rich young ruler, needing to find excuses for not fully following Jesus and finding treasure in the heavenly realms.

Provides Opportunities For Enemy Attack: Finally, because we have maintained a safe distance from the protection of our Lord, the enemy hammers away to reinforce our false self-image, increase our fear, and tempts us to try to meet our needs without God.

Fortunately, God doesn't just wait for us to figure all this out and get it right. Surprisingly to many, a significant part of spiritual growth involves the discovery of our own brokenness, sinful tendencies, spiritual wounds, and the often-painful realization of our need for heart level inner healing.

God uses relational analogies such as Father, Lord, King, Shepherd, and so on to help us relate to Him. The Holy Spirit tenderly helps us to see how we have projected our instinctive feelings about these kinds of authority figures, based upon our experiences with parents, people in authority, or those who were supposed to guide us but ended up hurting us rather than comforting and helping.

He shows us how we use these same defense mechanisms that we developed to protect ourselves from the pain of "love-lost" (whether intentionally or unintentionally) to "protect" us from God. God's revelation of more of Himself to us can create a kind of holy crisis of both attraction and fear of God. Our hearts long for the deepest love relationship with God, but some hidden barrier resists His love and employs the defense mechanisms we have developed. He waits for us to be ready to face the facts that we are so desperately hiding from, to "come to our senses" like the Prodigal.

Our Great Physician slowly diagnoses the manifestations of our deformity, not to condemn or judge us, but to open us to our need for healing. Only when we have grown sufficiently in His grace to be able to see the truth does He shine His light into the dark areas of our lives. As we've discussed in Chapter 9: Facing the Dragon Together, we often cringe at God's loving revelation and retreat in shame. We desperately need the fellowship of the church to encourage us to accept our condition and come to Jesus for healing and release.

How Jesus Heals Us

Jesus heals those who come to Him for healing. As we observe in the
Gospel stories, Jesus never waves His hands over the crowds and heals them
all. He responds to those who come to Him and ministers to them personally
and individually in the way that best suits them and the malady with which
they struggle. Fortunately, these people realized that they were deaf or blind
or lame or struggled with evil spirits. Today, we medicate our stress and fear
and consult doctors to help us with our pains, only going to Jesus as a last
resort.

Melanie Saint James, a Certified "Daring Way," facilitator, shares about
how the local church can inadvertently cause or exacerbate wounds that
keep us from God.

> So many of the people I work with describe spiritual wounds
> related to church and the messages of judgment and shame spoken
> by a Christian leader implying that they don't measure up. Shame
> is a sneaky foe, and all it needs is secrecy, silence and judgment to
> multiply exponentially — and if there is anything we are good at in
> the church, its secrecy, silence and judgment. Shame tells us that we
> aren't worthy - worthy of the Gospel, worthy of God's love, worthy of
> being in leadership, worthy of trying to lead others through their own
> journey of healing. Who am I to tackle healing when there is so much
> in my own life that is still a mess and hasn't been healed? So, we put
> on masks, suck it up, and rarely allow anyone to see the authentic,
> imperfect, and messy us.
>
> At West Side Church here in Richland, WA, I co-taught a class
> with a friend of mine a few years ago, called "Going Deeper'",which
> commenced right after we held an Imago Christi Discovery at our
> church. We spent six weeks trying to help people grasp and come
> to terms with what it means to be God's beloved. Week after week
> we hit a wall in people that we just couldn't penetrate. We used
> Henri Nouwen's book "Life of the Beloved;" we watched the movie
> the "Butterfly Circus;" we shared Baxter Kruger's book, "Parable of
> A Dancing God;" and we meditated on all the passages in Scripture

that talked about God loving us, delighting in us, and calling us His beloved. Still, nothing penetrated through the hearts and minds of those in our class. I eventually sat down and began to list all the things we were up against: Bad theology that made God primarily judgmental and scary, unhealed wounds from childhood, the church and other seasons in our life, a faulty belief that being vulnerable is a sign of weakness, messages and expectations preached on Sundays that talked about how we don't measure up, and shame, shame, and more shame.

Being trained in Dr. Brown's work "The Daring Way™" and "Rising Strong™" is one of the few things that have helped us penetrate through some of the blocks and wounds that were getting in the way of people being able to entrust themselves into the hands of the God who loves them, knows them by name, and calls them His beloved. And just as important, we found a process in community, that began to help people tell those defining stories of crippling messages and expectations that silenced them into believing that they were unworthy of love and belonging with God. Helping people identify shame, understand how it operates in their life, and then providing them the time and space to tell their story has been healing for many of the people with whom we have worked. It is almost a guarantee that in our Daring Way™/Rising Strong™ weekends we will hear the words, "I have never shared this story with anyone before now". I think sometimes we underestimate the healing power of inviting people to share their story with us, and for us to offer them empathy free of judgment as they do so.

What we can't provide in the Daring Way™/Rising Strong™ weekends is long-term counseling. However, for some in the group, three days with us will bring to the surface issues that need more intentional, focused counseling – and as such, we regularly hand out a list of Christian therapists we know and trust, and who have been through The Daring Way™ themselves.

While we must be honest about the destructive presence of sin in our lives, Melanie points out the importance of communicating from a grace, forgiveness, and hope perspective. I recently had a committed evangelical Christian visit a liturgical church with me. The Confession of Sin and the Absolution form a regular part of the liturgy. We admit publicly that each one of us struggles with sinful tendencies. The pastor, then, proclaims that we each have been forgiven through the Cross of Christ. My friend, however, commented after the service that she felt put off by the "negative" emphasis on sin. She said, "We don't need to be reminded how messed up we are." She had not yet learned to see her sins as simply her human condition, rather than a matter of shame. We need to try to help people hear the "Good News" in our preaching and teaching.

When we come to Jesus, He receives us in the love and forgiveness made available to us through the Cross, negating the power of sin and death that has enslaved us. He invites us to meet Him, not as terrible people who need fixing, but as beloved children of God who have come to their Father to remove a splinter that hurts and disables us. Jesus listens as we forgive and receive forgiveness in our memories of key scenes of our wounding, receiving the healing power of His resurrection into that area of our lives. He heals those places at the spiritual level and then helps us learn to think and feel the truth of His victory rather than the lies of fear and defeat we have believed. Ezekiel prophesied just what Jesus would do when we come to Him.

> Then I will sprinkle clean water on you, and you will be clean; I will cleanse you from all your filthiness and from all your idols. Moreover, I will give you a new heart and put a new spirit within you; and I will remove the heart of stone from your flesh and give you a heart of flesh. I will put My Spirit within you and cause you to walk in My statutes, and you will be careful to observe My ordinances. Ezekiel 36:25-27

Jesus brings us into community where we can take one another to Jesus, Who lives incarnate within us, and ministers the healing gifts of the Holy Spirit.

Chris Schutte has developed a well-integrated healing ministry. Chris shares his perspective about the place of healing ministry in the overall Kingdom mission of the church.

> *Theologically, the healing ministry is grounded in the new*

337

creation. We're headed for a renewed creation with new bodies and perfect relationships with God, our fellow image-bearing creatures, and all of the physical world. So, we can pray in confidence that God is in the process of renewing all of us–our bodies and our hearts. John Wimber encouraged his people to pray that the future would come into the present.

Jesus uses healings and other miracles as "signs" of the presence of His Kingdom. Healings, wine made from water, people raised from the dead, and ultimately His death and resurrection all became signposts to the new reality of Jesus' authority and victory over sin, death, and the devil—ultimate healing for all of creation. "And they went out and preached everywhere, while the Lord worked with them, and confirmed the word by the signs that followed." (Mark 16:20)

For us to continue to deepen in our relationship with God, these barrier wounds must be healed. This healing happens in community as we confess our sins and receive healing ministry. If people are to grow in their faith relationship with Jesus, receive His love, love Him in return, and let His love to flow through to those around them, availability of this healing ministry in the church becomes essential. The apostle James recognized this need when he instructed,

> Is anyone among you sick? Then he must call for the elders of the church and they are to pray over him, anointing him with oil in the name of the Lord; and the prayer offered in faith will restore the one who is sick, and the Lord will raise him up, and if he has committed sins, they will be forgiven him. Therefore, confess your sins to one another, and pray for one another so that you may be healed. James 5:14-16

It's strange that so many Christians feel comfortable sharing needs for physical healing, but feel shame about their needs for the healing of their faith obstacles. We all admit that we're sinful and imperfect and that everyone struggles with temptation at some level. However, when we come face-to-face with such an area in our lives, we often prefer to suffer in silence rather than take the apostle James' advice and seek out the elders (mature) in our church family. While no one enjoys hearing a doctor inform us of some malady, we're thankful to know it's there so that we can do something about it. The Good News that Jesus brought to us should enable us to respond to a new awareness of sin, weakness, or wounding in the same way. Jesus came to set us free, not to shame us. We must learn that the Holy Spirit reveals our needs for healing as a gift to us, just like the medical doctor diagnoses an illness that needs treatment. Both want to help us, and our responses can be ones of gratitude and receipt of the power that can be brought to bear for our healing.

In my experience of my own journey and those of the leaders I have coached, awareness of our needs for inner healing of spiritual blocks and wounds can come anywhere in the seven-mansion journey, but particularly in the second and fifth mansions. As new believers, we're often so overwhelmed with God's goodness and love that our lives feel totally transformed. Jesus' presence within us brings new light and hope to every facet of our lives. As time goes on, we try to conform our attitudes and behavior consistent with the love that Jesus shows us and instructs us to imitate. However, we realize that change isn't so easy. In God's loving and revealing light, we realize that all kinds of "fleshly desires" motivate our thoughts, feelings, and actions. Personally, I began to recognize that desires for control and approval motivated much of what I did. Only when the Lord gave me eyes to spot the times I attempted to control and manipulate others, instead of love them, my disappointment with myself and my desire to live in a way that honored the Lord motivated me to seek help. Gladly, my Christian community could reassure me of God's forgiveness and encourage me to seek the Holy Spirit's help in resisting my misguided urges. The Holy Spirit did help me, and I was somewhat able to stop condemning myself. Unfortunately, however, I would struggle for many years before I discovered that God could heal me of the wounds that energized these sinful motivations.

Surprisingly, in the Fifth Mansion, our deep desire for unity with the

Trinity often produces opportunities to recognize the wounds within us that need deeper healing. Our love for the Lord has increased to such an extent that we feel that we can no longer tolerate any impediment to completely loving God and neighbor. In my personal example, above, these lurking misguided motivations remained mostly "under control" through the help of the Holy Spirit. Dallas Willard describes our efforts at keeping our issues under control as "sin management." What my heart longed for, however, was transformation, not just constantly trying to manage sin.

It's not that I thought I could become fully sinless, but these barriers to living fully in love with my Beloved and living out His love for others became antithetical to my deepest desires, tantamount to adultery. The only way I could authentically live the life in which the Lord had immersed me would be to die to self—not the self of my true nature in Christ, but to the little boy in me that had decided, without God, that control and affirmation would make me a worthwhile person.

Dr. Larry Lighty, a dear friend and Christian psychologist, led me through what was called "healing of memories." We returned to a key memory during my growing up years, one where I particularly felt out of control and unloved. Larry helped me recognize Jesus in the scene, imagining Him physically present. In prayer, I forgave my parents for not being "perfect parents," and asked the Lord's forgiveness for the vows I made to myself to control my own destiny. Then, I asked Him to heal the wounds created in that season of my life and to set me free from their control. The results were truly amazing. While it took some time to get over the faulty "habit thinking" I had developed over the years, the power of those wounds disappeared. When I recognized the temptation to return to control or approval as a way of finding safety, I would quickly turn to Jesus—now with not only the knowledge of His redemption, but its experience in this part of my life.

What I had known theologically for many years now became a personal experience. Jesus wants far more for me than simple eradication of my blocks to His love; He wants to redeem them in a way that actually strengthens my relationship with Him. In the process of healing me in this aspect of my life, God showed me His love and power, gave me compassion toward others who struggle to make Him first in all things, and set me free to love and be loved in a far greater way. "God works all things together for good" (cf. Romans 8:28)! Slowly, I learned not to fear the discovery of weaknesses in my life. The weakness no longer spoke failure to me, but opportunity to experience God's love and power in a new way. Perhaps you have similar stories that you can share that will set people free to accept themselves where they are in their journey with Jesus and not fear the day when He points out a sliver that He wants to remove.

Providing Jesus' Healing in The Church

Providing this kind of "heart-healing," however, can be one of the most challenging aspects of spiritual formation in the church, but absolutely essential to the release of missional momentum in our people. Most of our churches have never experienced the ministry of healing. We may have asked others to pray for us for physical issues, but inner healing, or healing of memories remains still unknown to most. While our churches and their leadership would certainly affirm that God answers prayer, they may never have seen anyone healed or experienced healing themselves. Some simply don't believe that God heals miraculously anymore. If someone dared to ask the pastor or elders of most of our churches for help with seeking God for healing, chances are that the pastor or elder wouldn't have the slightest idea what to do with the request, other than to say a quick prayer and send them on their way.

Despite the challenges, however, Jesus has a way of bringing light and power to our darkest and weakest situations. As people discover spiritual community where they feel safe, accepted, and progressing in their journey with the Lord, they realize that recognition of our need for healing isn't back sliding but a sign of spiritual growth. People can seek God for what He wants to give. Many churches and ministries have pioneered ministries for healing of the wounds of our soul as well as those of our body. If healing isn't part of our own tradition and experience, we can learn from others. Either way, we simply cannot leave God's beloved stuck without the ability to receive God's healing in our communities of faith.

Unpacking the whole subject of the Holy Spirit's work of healing and how to develop a healing ministry in our churches could fill far more space than we can address in *Contagious Fire*. In addition, many excellent resources have been made available to us, both books and training programs. We can, however, consider some foundational topics relative to healing ministry that are important for each of us to understand, so that we might receive healing ministry for ourselves or to consider providing it for others. We need to understand the clear teaching of Scripture about the ministry of healing. We must be able to stand in the confidence that God wants us to seek, receive, and minister healing.

Healing Both Commanded and Demonstrated in Scripture: The ministry of healing cannot be relegated to Pentecostal, Charismatic, or Signs and Wonders churches. Jesus, the Apostles, and the Prophets command and demonstrate that God desires to set His people free from both the physical, emotional, and spiritual bonds that impair and threaten their lives. Let's review just a few examples.

Isaiah connects healing with the redemption of the Cross – Isaiah 53:4-6 (Reference Matthew 8:17)

Jesus reads from Isaiah 61 and applies it to himself - Luke 4:14-18

Blind man healed at Bethsaida - Mark 8:22-26

Jesus could not do any miracles in Nazareth because of unbelief – Mark 6:4,5

Jesus links healing of the heart through forgiveness and physical healing – Luke 5:15-26

The twelve sent out to heal – Mark 3:13-19

The seventy sent out to heal – Luke 10:1-24

Peter gives the healing gift within him - Acts 3:1-26.

Paul raises young man from the dead - Acts 20:7-12

Paul teaches that healing exists among the spiritual gifts given to all
believers and that some are called to the office or ministry of healing
– 1 Corinthians 12: 1-11;

James instructs early church to minister healing to its members – James
5:13-15

Mark's Great Commission includes healing ministry – Mark 16:17,18

The Prophets predict Jesus' healing ministry; Jesus heals physically,
emotionally, and spiritually as signs of His Messiahship and then commands
His followers to do the same. The Apostles follow Jesus' example and
instructions as tools of evangelism and blessing. James, probably the Bishop
of Jerusalem, extends the ministry of healing beyond signs and wonders to a
ministry of the church to bless the followers of Jesus.

Many Christian leaders find themselves hesitant to introduce a healing
ministry in their churches because they're personally unfamiliar with the
ministry of healing and have buried many people for whom they had prayed
for healing. Most of us have grown up in "Nazareth" churches—situations
where people simply didn't believe that God will heal our bodies, minds, or
spirits. It's not that we don't want to believe it; it's just that we have never seen
it happen. The best we might hope for would be that God would in some way
help the doctors. Scripture tells us that God's gifts, both salvation and help,
must be received in faith. What do we do when we find that we simply do not
have faith to give or receive healing? I think that two important steps must
be taken. First, we must clearly teach what the Scriptures say about healing.
Second, we must provide a place where our people become free to safely
"experiment" with healing ministry. While our "faith" must be empowered

by the Holy Spirit, it also comes as a product of our experience. The crowds that surrounded Jesus didn't yet have "saving" faith in Jesus as Lord and Savior, but they had heard about and even seen examples of people who were healed by Jesus. Their "faith" went something like, "If Jesus can heal that blind man, then He can heal me. I am going to ask; what do I have to lose?"

In addition to helping our pilgrims become comfortable with seeking healing, we must teach our people how to "minister" healing. While our Lord invites us to pray for everything we need, including healing, we find that healing must also be "given" through the gifts of the Holy Spirit. This truth became real to me as I studied the passages listed above, particularly, James 5:13-15. I focused on the part of the passage where James says that the prayers of a righteous person can accomplish much. That sent me on a scriptural search to find what kinds of prayers resulted in healing. To my surprise, and bewilderment, I found absolutely none!

In every case, healing happened as a result of the command of the person doing the healing. Jesus didn't tell His disciples to go out and pray for the sick to get well; He told them to HEAL the sick! I found the explanation in the apostle Paul's teachings about the gifts of the Holy Spirit. In 1 Corinthians 12:9, Paul lists "gifts of healing" among the other spiritual gifts, such as teaching, prophecy, etc. We can see, therefore, that God intends healing to be "exercised" as a spiritual gift like other spiritual gifts. For example, someone gifted with teaching not only prays that the students might learn the material, but stands in front of the individual or class and exercises or ministers that gift—he or she teaches, empowered by the Holy Spirit. Prayer and ministry must be combined to share the gifts God has given us and to provide healing.

Like other spiritual gifts, we must learn how to cooperate with God in their use. For example, we see that prophets didn't just suddenly start proclaiming God's word, they learned to hear God's word, to discern it from their own thoughts (the gift of discerning spirits), and then follow God's leading in how to share that word and to whom (the spiritual gifts of knowledge and wisdom). The spiritual gifts must work together among the community of the Body of Christ. Learning to cooperate with the Holy Spirit in the use of spiritual gifts leads us to the topic of training healing teams and establishing a healing ministry within the church.

Developing a Healing Ministry in The Church: While God can heal in a variety of circumstances and situations, many churches have found it helpful to establish an intentional healing ministry where "elders" are trained to minister the various gifts that come together to bring healing and restoration to our lives.

Terry Tarleton shares insights about some of the ways God has guided them to respond to the healing needs of his congregation.

> In our church we have about ten certified spiritual directors (trained through Sustainable Faith), and four inner-healing prayer teams using Immanuel Prayer. We devote more time, energy and resources to these tools than we do to counseling. We believe spiritual direction and inner-healing prayer usually go straight to the heart and to the place where Jesus wants to work. We have found these, more times than not, more effective, less labor-intensive, and quicker than traditional biblical counseling.

A number of great resources have been written to help congregations develop a healing ministry. Jasona Brown, has recently published a wonderful book called, *Stone by Stone*.[3] Jasona shares her own story of healing and insights into healing ministry in the church based on her experiences in a Greeley, Colorado congregation. Chris Schutte, another Contributor, supports a wonderful healing team in his Anglican congregation.

In my own experience, healing teams function best when they have developed true spiritual community for themselves and have come to know one another well enough to recognize the various spiritual gifts the Lord has given to the team members. Healing teams need specific training before

---

3   Jasona Brown, *Stone by Stone: Tear Down the Walls between God's Heart and Yours*, 2015

being deployed. Francis MacNutt's ministry, "Christian Healing Ministries" provides on-line and local conferences and extensive written resources to train healing ministry teams.

Melanie Saint James shares how she and her husband provide a home setting for her integration of Christian healing and The Daring Way ministry.

> *My husband and I regularly hold weekend sixteen-hour retreats in our home, which dive deep into the areas of shame, worthiness, vulnerability, and belonging, based on the research and work of Dr. Brené Brown. The retreat provides participants with a pathway for examining and overcoming failure, heartbreak, and tragedy in such a way that these incidents become the places of greatest growth. Almost everything we facilitate centers around the blocks and barriers in our lives that keep us from authentic, vulnerable relationships with God and those we love. We examine the messages and expectations that diminish our self-worth and lead us to believe that we are unworthy of love and belonging – especially in our relationship with God. One of the things we have learned is that while a physical malady like a broken bone may hurt, it isn't nearly as painful as the spiritual wounds we carry around within us, most of which others may not know or ever see.*

Melanie has used The Daring Way material in a number of healing settings around the country.

I've also found that it's important for the healing ministry to be available in public settings such as Sunday morning, following the service. The public offering of healing prayer authenticates its role as an important ministry of the congregation. Some healing situations, however, are best addressed in private and scheduled settings, both because of the time required and the sensitivity of the situation.

Chris Schutte explains some of the dynamics of the healing ministry in his church.

> *Practically, at Christ Church we do a handful of things related to healing ministry: First, we have testimonies of healing from time-to-time–both physical and emotional. Also, we have prayer*

*ministers near the communion rails, so each Sunday, after people take
communion, it is easy for them to receive prayer. We make a strong
connection between receiving the grace of Jesus' finished work on
our behalf in the Eucharist, and receiving prayer for healing, usually
with anointing of oil. We also have a team that has been trained by
the MacNutts that meets with people for 60-90 minutes at a time by
appointment, and we've seen great things happen in that context. It is
essential that the team be trained well and maintain spiritual unity–I
meet with the leader of this ministry regularly to check in. Finally, we
have a "healing weekend" each year. We invite a speaker to come to
share on healing, offer prayer for healing, and work with our healing
prayer team.*

*One last thing: it's been fun for us to collaborate with other
churches in Phoenix–some Roman Catholic, some Lutheran, some
Vineyard, and some independent Charismatic–in this area. Each of
our traditions has a lot to offer in the area of healing, and, inevitably,
how we "do" healing ministry will look slightly different based on our
theological tradition and the calling of the individual congregation–
there is a lot to learn!*

I've personally worked with the Healing Team at Christ Church and
have been so blessed by the loving way they care for the people God brings
to them. Not only are many people healed and delivered, but all of them
experience the active love of God in the process—contagious fire!

Collaborating with Other Churches: Chris Schutte commented
about the benefits of collaborating with other churches in the area. Just as
the Holy Spirit gifts individual Christians differently for the common good,
He also raises up ministries in different churches to serve as a resource
for other congregations. If you are unable to raise up leaders for a healing
ministry in your flock, then look for a neighboring church that can already
make that resource available to your people. The healing ministry of another
congregation can provide an excellent training ground for new ministry
teams formed in other congregations. Healing ministry teams in different
congregations can collaborate in ongoing training by sharing the cost of
bringing in a teacher or sharing a healing ministry conference among several

churches.

Mental health therapists also provide another important resource that lies beyond the resources of most of our churches. Debbie Swindoll comments about importance of these resources.

I know that there are many places in the church that don't support therapy as an option for their congregants. I fully support the need for healing ministry in our churches. However, when God opens deep places of the heart, some people unravel beyond the capacity of many lay people to handle. I just had one of my directees experience this in his life. Through life circumstances and some issues that came up through direction about his relationship with his mother, he struggled to function well in his daily life. He needed a place to unpack what God allowed to surface beyond a monthly direction session. Therapy provided a good place for that. I was able to bless him to move in that direction.

When we open up the discussion of healing I think we need to be sensitive to those who need acute care and our leaders need to be trained to identify those people and help refer them to the care they need–therapy, recovery programs etc. Some people in our congregations suffer from long-term issues like mental illness, clinical depression or substance abuse and others may need an expert to help them uncover the source of their pain and broken relationships. People who have been traumatized by repeated abuse either physically or sexually sit in our pews every Sunday. In a similar way that we would refer the physically sick to an MD we should be referring the most vulnerable of those in mental/emotional need to trained/licensed caregivers. I don't think this is an either/or proposition with healing prayer but rather a both/and with cooperation between the soul physicians and the medical and therapeutic professionals. We need to dispel some of the shame that Christians feel when they seek therapeutic help for these hurts.

We know that all truth comes from God, as a gift to his beloved. He uses science and the skills of caring people to bring us insight and relief from many of our disabilities. God can use these professionals as His hands and feet whether or not they know it. Even better, Christian Counseling and

Treatment Centers have been created to treat people with the integration of prayer, healing, and therapy.

Healing of mind, body, and spirit constitutes a significant part of the Holy Spirit's work of transformation in our lives into the image of Christ. While God can certainly use us as wounded warriors, He desires to redeem our wounds to both set us free from their disabling influences and to give us compassion and power for others who struggle with similar issues. We become free to face our brokenness if we know that God provides healing and release. The apostle James makes it clear that responsibility for this ministry of healing resides in the local church. Healing for the maturing believer allows the flames of God's love to burn brightly with a wonderful invitation to seekers and new believers to receive this tangible experience of God's amazing love.

In the following chapter, we'll discuss the ways that we can become intentional about letting the fire of God's love become contagious. Matthew, Mark, and Luke all record Jesus' admonitions to become intentional about sharing the light of contagious fire (cf. Matthew 5:14-16; Mark 4:21-24; Luke 11:33-36). Shedding the "baskets" that hide our fire, however can be challenging for most of us. We'll explore how to make it just the NATURAL THING TO DO.

CHAPTER 13

THE WINDS OF CONTAGIOUS FIRE - SPIRITUAL FORMATION AS MISSIONAL MOMENTUM

We've been discussing the fulfillment of our dreams for the Church. When we look at the condition of our world and the "just do what it takes to get through life" attitudes of so many people around us, we long for the kind of world that Jesus came to give us—peace on earth, good will to all people. We imagine a world where people love one another and use their talents to bless our society for the common good, where we accept others as the beloved of God and want to help them discover abundant life. Rather than accept the lethargy we see in the Church, we align our hearts with Jesus who wants to set our world on fire with His love that will bring all people into the Kingdom of real and eternal life.

Recognizing that this contagious fire must start with us, we cry out to God with the Psalmist for His cleansing and restoration and for the new heart promised to us through Ezekiel. Make the Psalm your prayer. Believe the prophesy for yourself and the world!

Create in me a clean heart, O God,

And renew a steadfast spirit within me.

Do not cast me away from Your presence

And do not take Your Holy Spirit from me.

Restore to me the joy of Your salvation

And sustain me with a willing spirit.

Then I will teach transgressors Your ways,

And sinners will be converted to You. Psalms 51:10-13

Moreover, I will give you a new heart and put a new spirit within you; and I will remove the heart of stone from your flesh and give you a heart of flesh. I will put My Spirit within you and cause you to walk in My statutes, and you will be careful to observe My ordinances. You will live in the land that I gave to your forefathers; so, you will be My people, and I will be your God. Ezek. 36:26-28

See the contagious fire of Love transforming the land that Jesus has claimed for us and thank our Lord for calling you into that transforming process, for your own heart, for the hearts of those traveling with you, and those to whom Jesus leads you.

Both these passages connect the Great Commandment and the Great Commission, our First Order Calling to a love relationship with the Lord, and our Second Order Calling, to serve Him in the coming of the Kingdom of God. When we receive a "clean heart," we then "teach transgressors Your ways [of love] and sinners [who God loves] will be converted to You." Once our new heart of flesh has taken root within us, we will be able to "walk in My statutes…, observe My ordinances…, live in the land I gave to your forefathers…, and be My people and I will be your God."

Our contagious fire analogy fits well with this understanding of a new heart and its ability to finally enable us to live authentically as lovers of God and neighbor. Through the revelation of the Holy Spirit, we discover that the "spark" that enables our heart to connect with God has all but gone out. Listless and weak, we find ourselves barely able to focus on our own needs, striving for some happiness which can add energy to our lives. We encounter a person—one of these pilgrims, whose life has been filled with energy and purpose. Not only does their heart beat with its intended radiant fire to keep the person alive, but its fire enables personal health, vibrancy, fulfillment, and joy. The pilgrim's "big heart" overflows with the light of God's love in caring and helpful ways for others. In the contagious light and love of our pilgrim, we begin to long for this kind of living heart and eventually cry out to God for this new "clean" heart—one with the chaff of sin disabled and washed off so that its heartbeat can create real life. God's contagious fire has sparked the longing that only God can provide and now this heart transplant becomes available to yet another beloved of our Lord. Now a new burning heart creates a new pilgrim who joins the journey with Jesus and His other beloveds to become fully alive and contagious as well. In this chapter, we want to explore the second half of God's transforming work—loving others. What does it mean to live contagiously?

God not only saves us from sin and death through faith in Jesus Christ, but He remakes us so that we are able to live fully as His sons and daughters in the Kingdom of God, participating with His redemption of the world. Through this transforming process, He replaces the center of our being, our heart—that was spiritually dead through sin, with a new heart, one eternally on fire with His love and the power of the Holy Spirit. As we are conformed to the very image of our Lord Jesus, we delight to share His invitation with everyone through the message of the Gospel and deeds of love that demonstrate its truth and His love.

Using this analogy of a heart transplant, we've been considering how we might provide a church environment that supports the Lord's amazing work within and through us. We've discussed the individual's "pre-op" preparation through teaching, coaching, and experience. We've considered the kind of spiritual community that provides the necessary environment for the Lord's surgical operating room. Now we want to further explore the "post-op" strengthening and development that enables us to live in our new Christ-likeness. Of course, our analogy falters at this point because, while a physical heart transplant takes place over a few hours, the Lord's work of turning our hearts from stone into true flesh takes a lifetime. Nevertheless, we can see the parallels through multiple levels of preparation, surgery, and post-op rehabilitation.

After a physical heart transplant, we strengthen our new hearts by using them to pump blood with increasing efficiency. Similarly, we strengthen our spiritual hearts by loving—loving God and loving others. While our ability to love always comes from the indwelling presence of God, we must learn to cooperate through continually discerning the Lord's instructions and intentionally exercising our growing ability to love. These "spiritual exercises" come through prayer and service. We love God through caring for others whom the Lord loves—participating in the flow of life-giving love that God extends to the other. Conversely, we love our neighbor by intentionally submitting ourselves to deepening intimacy with God where we learn to discern His heart and then follow His leading with action. In this dual intentionality, we develop a kind of "co-orientation" where we relate to Jesus the way He relates to the Father. "I do what I see the Father doing" (cf. John 5:19). Rather than choosing some "good work" to do and then asking God to bless it, we let God choose our ministry of love, enter it with Him, and then trust Him to bring about His intended purpose.

Therefore, in Chapter 13, we'll further explore letting the love out, letting God make us contagious. We'll look at our "pilgrims' progress" internally—their new hearts becoming fully functional. Then we'll discuss how to create an environment in the church that takes our pilgrims beyond physical therapy into the world with blazing love. Here's the line of thinking we'll pursue.

Focusing Our Hearts to Love God, Self, and Others

Providing Opportunities to Love Others Without Programming

It

Honoring The Passions For Love That The Holy Spirit Stirs Up
Within Each Person

Creating Community For Mutual Support and Ministry

Focusing Our Hearts to Love God, Self, and Others

Does loving neighbor just happen naturally? We've seen the insistence
Scripture's that loving God results in loving neighbor—as we love ourselves
and as Jesus loves us. We've recognized that this transformation of Perfect
Love's perfection within us takes time and correlates with our deepening
life with God. Love of God, parents, and neighbor had to be commanded
by God in the Ten Commandments (cf. Exodus 20:1-17; Deuteronomy 6:5).
Even though followers of Jesus had received the Holy Spirit that enabled
them to love, we still read the exhortations of Jesus and the Apostles to love
others intentionally (For example, cf. Luke 6:27-35, John 15:12, James 2:8, 1
John 3:10). Somehow love for neighbor can become "stuck" within us. While
God's love empowers love for neighbor, actively loving others also requires
an act of our will in the response of obedience. We must cooperate with God
to focus the love within us toward others. It's even harder to focus our love
toward people we aren't naturally inclined to relate to or to like.

The fundamental "stuckness" that clogs our hearts and keeps our fires
of love from becoming contagious comes from our struggles with sin. Even
with the blazing fire of God's love within us, we are tempted to hold that
fire inside, using it to warm our own hearts. We can become content with
the benefits of receiving God's love—personal comforts of self-esteem,
provision, loving relationships, and assurance of salvation. Who could want
more? Yet, we're only experiencing a small part of abundant life.

Beyond the influence of our sinful tendencies—which the Holy Spirit has
empowered us to overcome, we also struggle with a lack of understanding
about how God's love works. At least two misunderstandings have hampered
our ability to live out the biblical principle that receiving God's love naturally

results in love for neighbor. First, we have tended to trivialize the transforming power of God's love by interpreting it as a kindly emotion rather than the very life-giving essence of God. Recognizing only affection from God, we're left with only the law to motivate missional behavior—God expects us to love others. We may even want to love others as an expression of our gratitude to God, but find that we lack the power to get beyond ourselves. We tend to focus on the product rather than relationship. While we tell new believers that God loves them and has a plan for their lives, we move quickly past the love to the plan. Mission can become a dreaded word for most of us because it is so often driven by "shoulds" and "oughts", and ultimately by guilt. We might assume that some feel-good charitable experiences could transform a self-focused life into an "other-focused lover," but it rarely happens. The Perfect Love that truly motivates our hearts to love our neighbor, and even our enemies, comes from our abiding immersion in the very life of God—in Love.

The second misunderstanding that can shoot our mission emphasis in the foot portrays spiritual growth as simply an inward journey of self-discovery and satisfaction. Possibly in reaction to the performance-driven exhaustion we have been experiencing, we over react to our First Order Calling to intimacy with God. We place ourselves and our happiness at the center of our universe and hold God accountable to wrap us in riskless bliss. Basking in God's love for us we settle for the healing of our own hearts and new freedom, joy, and peace. Many of us need to spend some time focusing inwardly toward our relationship with God, but abundant life ultimately focuses on God at its center. Healing, freedom, joy, and peace come as we are swept up in God's love for us as His beloved and His love for the many beloveds all around us. As God's love increasingly transforms our hearts, that love becomes uncontainable. We long for others to experience the freedom and joy of His love.

There's no question about our need to put "First Order relationship first." Terry Tarleton comments about his need to refocus on his "inward journey."

My experience is that I was unable to love well (purely from the heart of Jesus) until I did spend time on the "inward journey" to discover who I truly am in Christ, and to receive healing from some of my wounds of the past. I think that time of "being with Jesus," in a very inward way, cleared the way for me to love well (or at least more purely than I was before). I may be splitting hairs here, but I see way too many believers who are unwilling to look at their own hearts, even to allow Jesus to see what's in there, and keep everything external. I believe an externally focused life leads to false self-living, while an open and transparent inward-looking season with Jesus leads one to living in his true-self, and opens him up to "doing what Jesus is doing." I constantly remind our people that "Doing (the works of Jesus) flows out of being (with Jesus)." It feels like maybe the "heart work" aspect of this journey that I would label as "inward" is being dismissed–like there's not a place for it.

Terry beautifully illustrates that First and Second Order Callings aren't just "consecutive" phases of our life with God; both need to be lived constantly. We can let our focus, however, get out of balance and need to refocus. For example, monastery times provided that refocusing for me. Daily life as a pastor in a large and active congregation could easily sweep me into "doing" mode to the extent that even my daily prayer time became filled with concerns about the work I needed to do. Getting off the scene in a house of prayer, organizing my daily routine around the worship offices, and spending extended times in rest and prayer "reset" my First and Second Order balance.

Authentic spiritual formation can only be seen missionally—in the context of the Kingdom of God. Scripture puts it simply: "We love because God first loved us." It's a simple equation. The apostle James tells us that if the second part of the equation isn't happening, then the first part hasn't happened either (cf. James 2:14-17 and 1John 4:8). We are able to freely love only because we have first received the free love of God. We're invited into a relationship with God at the center where He not only loves us unconditionally, but unconditionally loves every other person as well. Most, if not all, of us enter this relationship driven by our own needs, and God meets us in those needs and loves us there. He draws us into community where we learn to give and receive love, experiencing God in others. He transforms our hearts to be able to see others through His love until true love for God and neighbor becomes "perfected" in us. As God's relationship of love sets us free to be ourselves, as pilgrims on a Spirit-led journey, we're able to drop our self-fulfilling strategies. In this freedom, we're able to see the beauty of God's love for others. The fire of God's love in the believer's heart inspires and motivates and empowers love for others with a brilliance and warmth that attracts people to Jesus. People see Jesus in us when they feel loved unconditionally—as they are, with no expectations. That's contagious love.

Ultimately, First Order Calling and Second Order Calling must merge within us. While it can be helpful to look at these two Callings from God separately, to keep us from living in one and neglecting the other, we must always remember that they remain fundamentally connected—God has called us into His very Life of Love—Himself. Missional momentum simply cannot be sustained on sympathy, compassion, duty, or guilt. Similarly, God's love cannot be hoarded as a means to our own selfish happiness. Avoiding these two extremes, we must always connect God's love for us and His love for others. Yet we cannot program one's ability to receive love or to give it away. Our individual developmental life experiences can make either one a simple step or an almost impossible leap. For example:

Sharon grew up in a home environment of conditional love that stressed financial success as the marker of personal worth. While she felt happy enough that God loved her, love had never been her motivator, unless it was expressed as approval—a result of her success. Sharon tended to view the poor and marginalized critically as people who should just get to work. She never found time to accept a role on one of her church's mission trips; prayer shared the same low priority.

James was raised in a family whose love for one another took center stage. He felt accepted with both his abilities and his shortcomings. Success was defined as living lovingly and creatively. When James became a believer, it felt natural for him to embrace God's love and forgiveness. While busy with a challenging career and young family, James found time to take mission trips, care for his next-door neighbor, and volunteer at his church food pantry. Prayer became an increasingly important part of his life, as well.

Sharon and James grew up in the same church, heard the same sermons, and were encouraged with the same opportunities to grow spiritually and to actively love those around them. It's not that one of them represented poor soil and the other good. Each one simply needed to be encouraged and loved at different points in their lives. James simply needed encouragement and opportunity to extend God's love to others. Sharon needed not only encouragement, but experiences that would challenge the biases that became part of her world view, and give her a joyful taste of letting love flow through her. No matter what developmental biases were created, we all need gentle but insistent discipling and shepherding. Let's consider some perspectives important to connecting contagious love with missional momentum.

Connecting The Loving Dots

We've discussed the necessity of connecting the two movements of loving God and loving neighbor in several of the preceding chapters, but its importance warrants reiteration here. We find that people are often attracted to God's work from either pole of the love dimension. Some people, maybe most, yearn for God's love and power to meet personal needs and find a secure life. Receiving God's love and loving Him in return form a natural bridge. While they may find love and concern for others an emerging motivation, they may not realize its vital connection to their partnership with God. Others may come to God because they want to make a difference for good in the world. Motivated by sympathy and compassion, they may find it easy to identify with God's love for the poor, needy, and marginalized.

These caring people often identify their relationship with God as prayer for strength to serve and blessings for others. They may not as easily recognize the necessity of their own transformation and intimacy with God to fully live out God's mission of mercy.

Charlie Dodrill shares his own transitioning experience as he allowed Jesus to deepen their relationship.

> *As a younger man, I got swept up into the liberation theology movement wholeheartedly, moving to South America to learn Spanish and to be martyred, standing for the rights of the oppressed in Latin America like Oscar Romero. I had yet to really begin to have a deeper relationship with God, but this was where I saw the action. That is what drew me to it. People were giving their lives for something greater than themselves and that was what my young, fervent heart was longing for.*

> *As years have passed and life has changed, long hours spent with Jesus seem to be resulting in more subtle ways of being with others who are hurting, lost, poor, mentally-ill, strangers, refugees, etc. The outcome is becoming less my focus; the person is becoming the object of God's love and desire–placed there unbeknownst to me by the One who lives in my heart. The ministry of presence becomes more and more real as time passes–simply being with someone without judgment or agenda.*

Initially, Charlie felt called to the work of justice and advocacy, and later to a more intimate interpersonal focus. We cannot say, however, that the latter represents a more mature calling than the first. Jesus calls us into every aspect of human life—to the poverty of heart, materials, and to change the hurtful systems of our world.

Alan Graham, author of *Welcome Homeless: One Man's Journey of Discovering the Meaning of Home*, recently shared his story with me, as we sat on the front porch of the small trailer where he and his wife now live.[1] Alan grew up as a faithful Roman Catholic and became a successful businessman.

1. Alan Graham, *Welcome Homeless: One Man's Journey of Discovering the Meaning of Home*, Nashville, TN, Harper Collins, 2017

In the midst of a Cursillo retreat, he encountered the third person of the Trinity in a way that changed his life and perspective—he knew that he was loved by God personally and specifically. Alan shared that the Holy Spirit began to reveal God and His profound love to him in ways that enabled him to see past his business ventures to the materially poor and homeless. He told me, "I'd come to realize that my response to God always had to be 'yes.' One day, when I saw some hungry homeless people in Austin, Texas, I heard God say, 'Do something about it.'" Alan went on to found Mobile Loaves and Fishes in Austin. This fleet of food trucks takes food to the homeless all over town. Alan recently started an amazing housing project for the poor, called Community First! Village. This multi-acre, tiny-house village provides quality housing for the chronically homeless, gives them work to help them pay their own way, and enables opportunities for hundreds of volunteers to give of their time and resources in profound ways.

Whether moving from a contemplative focus toward outreach or the other way around, regardless of where people begin, they need to be able to connect the dots between loving God and loving neighbor. One person may realize they need a heart transplant because of the desire for greater physical strength. Another person may realize that increasing strength will enable their new heart to become healthy. When we understand the process from both perspectives, we are more apt to lean into our First and Second Order Callings with more vigor and intentionality.

Several of our Contributors shared concerns that we recognize the need to continually reassess our Second Order Calling in light of our journey through the Mansion phases. Charlie Dodrill asks:

> *Is there a place for waiting for the season to change in our hearts before reentering/entering the world of active mission? If we have been a person who gains our worth from what we do, could there be a time where we step back from the outward ministry? I keep thinking of "Mansions of the Heart" and the transition from Stage 3 serving to Stage 5-6 serving.*

When we look back at our own histories, we realize that God has been purifying our love. Along the way, our motives have changed, although they never get fully purified. Jesus said, "Only God is good" (cf. Luke 18:19). In Charlie's story, for example, one might be tempted to conclude that he "jumped in too soon." However, it seems to me that we must recognize God's "dot connecting" in this context of journey, as well. To the extent that God has really touched our hearts, we're called to ministry at some level. Our zeal and ability to love may still be immature, but God delights in serving with us and teaching us. As we mature, however, our focus slowly changes from ourselves and the impact of our ministry to God and our love for Him. We begin to meet Jesus in others and love Him there. When that happens, much of our former "I know and you don't," and "I can really help you," attitudes shift. Seeing Jesus within our brothers and sisters, we begin to do more listening, seeking what the Lord is doing, and asking, "How can I serve you?" Sometimes this maturing may cause us to re-evaluate our calling. We may need to step back, as Charlie suggests, and focus more on Jesus, Himself, learning how to discern His heart, letting Him realign our motives. One might say that we jumped the gun and should have done all that with Jesus before we blundered off into ministry. While living intentionally into our First and Second Order dimensions is always important, I feel that we need to respond to God's call in whatever stage we find ourselves and in whatever way we discern that call. If we're growing spiritually, we'll always look back at our immaturity. Brother Boniface used to remind me, when I would complain about my dysfunction, "Jesus is quite adept at using sinners to bring in His Kingdom." Mentors and coaches, however, can help us spot some of our blind spots along the way, before they become stumbling blocks.

Chris Schutte shares a reflection on his own maturing journey.

> *The deeper I get on the inward journey, the more I feel drawn to the most vulnerable, and the more time I spend with the most vulnerable, the more I long for God and His Kingdom. So, there is a beautiful, formational path in this work.*

362

Chris and Charlie show that these "love God" and "love neighbor" dots aren't usually connected through being taught; they're connected through personal discovery. One of my memories of this discovery happened in Haiti, where I accompanied our church's mission team to a very small town in the southern part of the country. As this was my first trip with the team, the team leader sternly instructed me not to give candy, food, or clothing to children who begged from us as we traveled across the four-wheel drive terrain. As soon as we departed the airport, we were besieged by dirty boys and girls, about six to twelve years old—hundreds of them. Intent on escaping from the sheer mass of kids, I avoided the temptation to put something into one of those outstretched hands. A couple of days later, we stopped to rest in a small village. A ragged and malnourished little boy stood looking at us from across the town square. I couldn't take my eyes off him. He wasn't one of the kids we came to minister to in the southern village, but one of the beggars I was told not to mess with.

You guessed it. I found it impossible to do nothing. I took my protein bar and water bottle, walked across the street, and past the boy. I motioned for him to follow me behind the building. We met, and I asked him, using gestures, if I could pray for him. He nodded, and I put my hands on his head and prayed. I gave him my bar and water and returned to the group. Later, I was "busted" by the team leader, but it didn't matter. I literally couldn't help myself. To withhold that food from the boy would have been the same as letting Jesus starve. God connected the dots within me.

Discovering Our Call to Love Others

In Chapter 5, we discussed the importance of personal vision for our new life with Christ rather than a corporate one. We encourage each person to let the Holy Spirit give them a picture of what living fully in God's love and radiating that love in action to others might look like for them personally. While we would hope that these love visions would include both poles of the love equation, one typically focuses on the pole that the Lord used to draw them to Himself. People may need further coaching and mentoring to help them explore the other pole. We've spent considerable time discussing the First Order Calling pole, so let's focus here on the Second Order Calling part of one's vision.

What does it mean for a person to love one's neighbor as oneself or as Jesus loved us? While God's love relationship with each of us has commonalities, each "love affair" reflects the nature of the lovers. Similarly, "working together in the vineyard" will reflect the uniqueness of the person working with Jesus. Our life experiences often predispose us to compassion for particular groups of people or people in certain situations.

Our personalities often predispose us to the ways that we interact best with those situations. For example, two believers may be deeply touched by the plight of the sick who suffer without adequate medical care. One believer might be drawn to provide personal care to those who suffer, while the other may enjoy building facilities or equipment to express that care. In this example, we cannot say that the caregiver loves more than the construction worker.

Missional motivation emerges most powerfully when the focus of our personal compassion and our giftedness come together with the Lord's calling. Discovering this convergence comes through prayer, self-knowledge, community, and experience. In prayer, we learn to recognize the Lord's leading. Through self-knowledge, we discover the correlation between our own growth and various opportunities for mission. Our community provides encouragement and feedback as we consider alternatives and opportunities. Experience exposes us to opportunities to love that we may not have considered before and confirms or challenges our perceptions of our own passion, gifting, and calling. While prayer, self-knowledge, community, and experience can provide a context for personal discovery, each person must choose based on their sense of God's direct call.

Chuck Orwiler shares a story about people in his church who discovered more about their call to love.

> *Janette was chronically ill and pathologically loquacious. She literally talked people to exhaustion. Consequentially, she suffered from a dearth of life-giving companionship because most all who knew her eventually avoided her. One wanted to lend a hand to this weak little lady, but she inevitably drained all who offered. Even her only family member, a sister, avoided her as much as she could. Four people in her church, two men and two women, could not be content with joining the fatigued legions who now only shared their stories of frustration. They determined together to love Janette despite the cost of tedium necessary to walk with this woman in what appeared to be a one-way relationship. The real presence of Christ lived in the tangle of Janette's personality. It was Christ in them that drew the five together.*
>
> *Over the next couple of years Janette did not fundamentally change, nor was the foursome expecting it. Their intent was to be her companions in ways they could manage by quietly sharing mundane tasks of life. The Lord closed Janette's life on earth sooner than anyone expected. Thankfully, she had not lived that last chapter alone. The signature outcome for the five was neither personal transformation nor heroic effort. Rather, the love of God reigned, and it was beautiful.*

As Chuck points out, we cannot control outcomes in our lives or in the lives to whom we minister. The real outcome comes in the process of loving. That really is both beautiful and contagious!

Ultimately, only in the congruence between our fit and calling to ministry will our hearts become fully enflamed and empower us to live out the sacrifices of love. Only God fully sees that congruence. Congregational and ministry leaders, therefore, must be careful not to "recruit" people to fill programmatic slots and violate this unique calling from our Lord. Recruiting sets believers up for discouragement and burnout, while patience, coaching, and prayer can free God's people for a life of adventure and love with their Lord.

JD Ward comments about the connection with discovering our call and our passion to love.

> Once people find their call there is little to stop them from living it out with passion. Especially as they find healing for their own soul. Call happens when we offer healing to a broken place in the world and our own souls are healed.

This correlation between a broken place in our hearts and in the world happened to me on a mission trip to Mexico. Jesus touched my heart for the poor in a surprising way. Having grown up relatively poor myself, I'd felt uncomfortable around people that suffered financially. Encounters brought back painful memories of the web of situations that seemed to lock me and many people into a series of bad decisions and relationships that kept them in poverty. As a pastor, I've had many opportunities to bring some level of help to people in financial difficulties, but I discovered that money seldom solved the problem for long. The help they needed, but often didn't really want, would take much more time and ability than I could give. I dreaded the visits or phone calls from a stranger, "Pastor, I only need…."

God spoke to my heart in a new way when Charlotte and I accepted an invitation from Northwest Medical Teams to travel to Mexico to look at some ministry opportunities among the poor there. I soon realized that I had never really seen poverty. Our bus left Mexico City and drove for a few miles to one of the major city dumps. The difference between this dump and ones we'd seen before shocked and sickened us. This refuse plantation hosted a resident population of skin-and-bones families who the mafia allowed to live there to scavenge plastics, metal, and other usable materials. For this privilege, they could eat the rotting food they found and make shelters from the scraps of wood and cardboard they found. We wandered among the people, witnessing the utter filth and deprivation. To this day, I cannot eat "tortilla soup." These people gleaned the garbage for discarded tortillas and boiled them in the dirty water they could get from the nearby canal. Tortilla soup fended off starvation, but only just.

Finally, we boarded our padded seat and air-conditioned bus and headed out of the dump. As we passed the gate, a small naked boy, maybe about six years old, stood and watched us go by. His dark brown eyes caught mine and called out to my heart with a familiar voice—Jesus'. No words, just the imprint on my heart and a face that I have never forgotten. "Love me in the poor." God awakened love within me that I had not been willing to recognize before. I remain so grateful for a ministry that simply let me "see" both Jesus and the poor.

Providing Opportunities For Service Without Programming It

As it turned out, God did not call me to focus my ministry on the materially poor, although I have been able to accompany a number of ministry teams to serve the poor. These opportunities, however, became critical in both awakening love's fire within me and causing me to ask God how He wanted me, personally, to direct it. I am so grateful that Northwest Medical Teams didn't try to recruit me into "their" calling, but to expose me to potential opportunities, both for me and for my congregation. It seems to me that's what Jesus calls congregational leaders to do. Rather than start a program for the "poor" and then try to "staff" it, we identify mission opportunities for our people designed simply to expose them to "the least of these," with the upfront understanding that no one would try to recruit them. It's hard enough for most of us to even agree to see the painful parts of life. We feel guilty for what we have and feel obligated to try to change situations beyond change. But when the Holy Spirit snags us, no recruiting is needed. A story about snagging....

One congregation that I served provided a wonderful food and clothing ministry to the poor in our area. One of our members donated an outbuilding at her home to store food and clothing. Members of the congregation manned the ministry several days a week. Some picked up food from local retailers, others boxed it up, and others gathered used clothing from our church members and friends in the community. Still others staffed distribution days, to meet with the people who came, to listen to their stories, pray with them, and recommend other sources of help in the area. In some cases, I received referrals. Sid, a single Jewish man stopped by the church every few months. A friendly and seemingly well-educated man, he would come to talk and even let me pray for him. He'd show up for a few months on and off, and then disappear for a few more months. I finally learned that his disappearances involved the local jail or county mental health facility. When Sid would stop coming around, I'd track him down and go for a visit. We'd talk, and I'd try to help, but things just didn't seem to change for Sid.

One day, I invited my daughter, Emily, to visit Sid with me. Now in high school, I felt that she could handle both Sid's confused states and his often-difficult situations. At first, I think Sid felt embarrassed by her presence. Within a few visits, however, he would beam when Emily accompanied me, often standing and greeting her formally.

I share the story because God used my relationship with Sid in a surprising way. I don't know what became of Sid--one time when he disappeared I couldn't find him. I never saw him again. Emily, on the other hand, earned a Master's degree in Social Work, focusing on mentally ill and chemically dependent homeless people. She recently received the 2016 Field Instructor of the year award from the University of Texas at Austin's School of Social Work. Certainly, no church could have developed a program designed for that outcome. In fact, I don't think God even designed the outcome. He loved Emily and showed her His love for others and let her discover the way that her contagious love could bring her joy. Me? Jesus lets me engage with a segment of the poor in spirit—pastors and missionaries who long for the depths of God's love and the ability to set wildfires of love around the world.

Our churches and ministries can provide multiple "taste and see" opportunities for people to discover the ways that love best flows through them. In addition, members who have already become involved in a ministry can invite people to come with them for a "one-time" help out, with no expectations to sign up. These discovery opportunities go way beyond discerning our spiritual gifts and our abilities to recognize what we "might" be good at. We're inviting people to meet Jesus in various people and situations and listen for His personal call— "Follow Me."

A powerful way of creating these kinds of ministry opportunities has been offered through ReWire, a ministry of Church Resource Ministries and headed by JD Ward, one of our Contributors. JD and his team have developed a process for forming covenant communities within congregations that focus on both First and Second Order Callings, but with a particularly missional focus toward the poor. Members of these small covenant communities meet regularly to work on their own spiritual formation, especially in light of their interaction with ministry opportunities built into their group experience.

JD says that an important part of formation involves discovering one's "cultural captivity"—the biases that have been implanted by our culture, biases that judge people in stereotypical ways and block our ability to love others in meaningful relationships. While most participants truly believe that they are unbiased when then enter the program, they come to realize that they have inadvertently taken on perspectives that marginalize people for ethnicity, economic condition, gender, etc. These self-discoveries then become opportunities to seek the Lord's grace to love freely in ways that aren't dependent on personal approval of the other's behavior or their receptivity to attempts to help. JD echoes the monastic creed that work is prayer and that prayer is work. ReWire teaches that prayer and loving others represent equivalent spiritual disciplines. Properly undertaken, we meet God in both places.

We discover that we can only really accept God's love for us, "as we are," when we learn to see others through God's eyes—as His beloved. JD had found that relationships with the poor and marginalized become vital links to self-knowledge, humility, and healing. When we can see ourselves and others through God's loving eyes, we can enter into relationship with others as brothers and sisters and love them there. Maybe we can be helpful, but help is not the point—Jesus has called us to live out the Good News of the Kingdom of God and His love. "If you love Me, You will keep my commandments" (cf. John 14:15).

Honoring The Passions For Love That The Holy Spirit Stirs Up Within Each Person

Love happens organically. Jesus uses the analogy of the vine and branches in our relationship with God to illustrate how the fruit of love emerges. Our love flows to others when a relational link forms within us that connects us to another person, in light of who we are and how we've been formed. For example, I can easily relate to homeless men and women at the homeless shelter where my daughter serves as a social worker because I once shared such a place and situation with my alcoholic father. I saw the power of love to transform and heal as other broken men reached out to us with truth. Now, years later, I didn't necessarily need to form an ongoing relationship with these "neighbors," but could simply listen and care in the moment. The outcome of the encounter belonged to God, not to me. Love could flow through me organically, however, because of my own experience and passion.

We can do harm to others by trying to force fit them into some mechanistic system like, "God did this for you and now you're obligated to do this for Him." The apostle Paul tells us that the law kills, but the Holy Spirit brings life (cf. Romans 8:1). We bless the followers of Jesus when we help them respond to the Spirit's work within them. Often, however, people haven't yet spotted these places of connection and compassion within them.

We can incorrectly conclude that people not involved in outreach of some kind simply don't care. Some people have become preoccupied, even overwhelmed, with the responsibilities or concerns of their own lives. I shouldn't expect a young mother with three kids to accept my invitation for a month-long short-term mission trip to Africa, for example. She might, on the other hand, be open to volunteering one day a month in the daycare center where one of her children attends. Having said that, I shouldn't assume that her passion will become focused on kids just because she is a mom. So many times, we assume that professionals want to love others through use of their professional gifts. We invite financial folks to serve on the finance committee, teachers to work with our education program, etc. Many times, these invitations are accepted because the person feels obligated to use their talents for the church—a guilt motivation rather than love. How much better to expose a person to a variety of outreach opportunities and then watch to see where the Holy Spirit ignites sparks of love. Then we honor both the follower of Jesus and God by helping people discover how they might follow God's leading in ways that fit their life stage, abilities, and joy.

A dear friend, who earned a Ph.D. in International Economics, travels to the Dominican Republic each year to work with the poor in a medical clinic. He has no medical training, but delights in simply helping out in any way he can with a team of workers he has come to enjoy. Heath wants to love others through simple service rather than his expertise. Another person with his training and expertise might choose to serve on a committee for economic relief for the Dominican Republic. Both choices become powerful when the Holy Spirit connects the heart of the caring person with the need at hand. His story brings us to another important part of helping people find their place of loving—community.

Creating Community For Mutual Support and Ministry

In Chapter 11, we discussed Jesus' model of developing spiritual community based around each person's common commitment to commune with God. In communion with God, His love enlivens and transforms us. We call this spiritual formation. Our Good Shepherd then leads us into loving relationships with other believers where we continue to grow spiritually. In this community of love, we find the courage to follow Jesus into surprising places where love flows through us. Spiritual community becomes essential to support our ministry of love to others, particularly others with difficult needs. Spiritual community becomes essential to effective and sustainable ministry.

While we want to honor each person's desire to minister in a way that aligns with their passion and gives them joy, we cannot, however, send them off alone, without the support of a community that shares their calling. If someone wants to help the homeless, for example, but our church does not have a homeless ministry, we need to stop and seek the Lord further. It's possible that this one person's call to the homeless signals the Lord's desire to begin such a ministry within our church. To help us discern both the individual's call and God's call to the church, we can "send up trial balloons" about the opportunity and see who "grabs the strings." If others want to explore the possibility further, then give them the community support they need. However, if no one responds, we may need to help this person connect with a homeless ministry in another setting. If we simply send them out alone, we violate Jesus' way of leading and empowering, and set them up for a bad experience. We encourage this person's communion with God through continued prayer for God leading; we connect them with others who share that same passion; and then, and only then, we encourage them to launch into ministry.

We honor our brothers and sisters when we affirm Jesus as their Shepherd and seek to follow His leading in helping His beloved follow specifically and faithfully within the portion of the flock He leads to love in that particular way. To return to our previous illustration, Heath could not minister in the Dominican Republic alone. As part of a multi-skilled team, however, he can become the very touch of God.

JD Ward shares some story vignettes that illustrate what happens when God's love becomes contagious within us.

While working with homeless, I met a mentally ill woman named

Mary on the streets. I visited her every week in a drop-in center. When I got sick and was in the hospital for several weeks, she found out where I was, made a quilt for me, and took the bus to come give it to me. It was a sign of God's love and remembrance of me.

Enrique was a gang kid who came to my Young Life group every week to eat, learn about Jesus and meet girls. He never took anything I had to say seriously. At least, I thought he didn't. Now he has a wife and baby, is a committed school teacher and loves God. He taught me that God is working at all times even when we cannot see him

While in Ethiopia, we were driving where the women who were "fuel wood carriers" walk four miles up and down the mountain with 75-pounds loads. They were literally carrying their own death every day. One person suggested we help one of the ladies by loading her wood onto our van. In my mind I said, "Why? There are literally thousands of ladies and the gangs run this thing anyway. We don't know what would happen to her if we help her." As we passed another woman who had spilled her load all over the road, someone said, "We should help her!" And though it seemed like a drop in the bucket compared to the need all around us, we did help this one woman. When I tried to lift one of the logs up onto the van, I found it too heavy! I really don't know how she carried twenty or more on her back. We finally got all the logs on the van and she sheepishly got into the van. She felt embarrassed about her looks—even the poor love beauty. As we pulled up to the unloading station, everyone looked at us strangely. When they got what was happening, everyone at the loading station joined in to help. That day God showed me, through the woman and me, that He sees our pain. And He cares.

As JD points out, Jesus meets us in every encounter. He may use us to bless the other, but He always shows us some special dimension of His love. We just have to be attentive.

Connecting The Missional Call – Letting Love Out Intentionally

Love becomes contagious fire in the church when we nurture each person's personal relationship with God, trusting Him to ignite the fire of love within them, both for God and for neighbor. We fan the flames of love that God has created when we develop a community of love for God and neighbor, a community that understands that love for God and love for neighbor constitute a whole. We support the embers of love with our people as we help them discover the natural connections between their own stories and the needs of others. We enable love to become explosive when we help them discover relationships where their love can be shared in practical ways that brings them joy and helps others. We enable love to become a blazing light across the world as we release communities of lovers who follow Jesus into the unique places He has already prepared. "I have come to set a fire upon the earth and how I wish that it was already kindled" (cf. Luke 12:49). We live in a time when Jesus has, in fact, kindled that fire. What a wonderful joy we experience as we discover ourselves as His contagious fire!

CHAPTER 14

CONTAGIOUS FIRE – PULLING IT ALL TOGETHER

Wow! What an amazing journey we've been on! If you're reading *Contagious Fire* for the first time, I hope you're "on fire" with this vision of what God wants to do in our churches and ministries—Thy Kingdom come; Thy will be done. Let's do it; let's do it together! If you're working through this book for the second or third time, as you follow Jesus through *Contagious Fire* in your own setting, I want to honor you for your courage and faithfulness to our Lord Jesus. You're discovering, however, why churches aren't easily exploding into contagious fire all over the world.

My son, Marc, and I took my grandsons backpacking and camping last summer. In this monsoon season in Colorado, it naturally rained soon after we arrived in the high-country wilderness. The shower didn't last long and certainly didn't dampen our spirits. It did, however, dampen our potential firewood. Of course, we came prepared with fire starter to ensure a quick and roaring campfire. The boys gathered the firewood from downed branches in the forest and along the river where we set up camp; I masterfully set the fire starter, laid the twigs and branches, and struck the first match. Alas, no quick and roaring campfire. Propped on hands and knees, with eyebrows singed,

I huffed and puffed at the smoldering coals. Reeking with smoke and soot, I continued on into the evening. Finally, we had a fire respectable enough to roast marshmallows, but not much more. Our fire had not yet become contagious, despite my best efforts! God, where were you? Fortunately, Marc skillfully cooked our dehydrated food over a little butane stove—thank goodness we had an alternative. Because the fire in so many of our churches flickers so weakly, many church members and seekers are also looking for alternatives to the traditional "church."

Here's how we'll try to pull this all together. First, we'll review what we've discussed so far in *Contagious Fire.* We must hold onto the line of thinking we've been tracking, lest we lose the focus and direction of our course. I'll include a few reflective questions to consider for each chapter, to try to help you personalize that step in the progression. Second, I'll share some stories from our Contributors that give examples of ways they have approached various elements of the process. Third, we'll look at some of the resources available to you from within our Contributors, and the wider spiritual formation community, to assist you in the process. Finally, we'll celebrate what Jesus has been doing in each of us and in His Church—the winds of Contagious Fire!

The Progression of Contagious Fire

Chapter 1: Embers Can Be Fanned Into Flame - Hope For The Church

We imagined a community of followers of Jesus so filled with the fire of God's love that each one becomes motivated to love others dynamically and practically. Those set free by God's love begin to care for people, both near and far, as Gods beloved for whom their Lord died. This caring and loving will attract people to a personal relationship with God in Jesus and the abundant eternal life He offers. The Church would become a city set upon a hill whose inhabitants would set a forest fire of Love that spreads across the whole earth.

How About You?

What has God used most significantly to give you a personal desire to grow spiritually?

What has God used most significantly to create within you a desire to see contagious fire within the Church?

We've suggested intentionally connecting two movements in the Church: spiritual formation and missional church. Which movement has caught your attention most significantly? Which one represents the greatest area of discovery for you?

To what extent do you, personally, feel called by God to follow Him more intentionally to become contagious fire?

Chapter 2: The Nature of Divine Fire – Spiritual Formation from a Biblical Perspective:

We looked at key Scriptures, and examples of biblical leaders, that clarify God's desire for each of His followers to become like Jesus, both in nature and in mission. Introducing the concepts of First Order and Second Order Callings, we recognized that Jesus teaches us that He first calls us to a loving and interactive relationship with the Trinity. From the personal transformation that this love relationship provides, He secondly calls us to love one another as He loves us. I suggested that the seven mansions of Teresa of Avila provide a clear, biblical and relatable paradigm for understanding spiritual growth. We recognized that "love" is the very nature, presence, and power of God that transforms us into Christ's very likeness—His image. We connected Jesus' teachings about the interrelatedness of our relationship of love with God and our call and ability to allow His love to flow through us to others.

How About You?

Do you feel that the biblical case for contagious fire has been well-established in this chapter? What aspects challenge you? What do you find missing?

How do you respond to the discussion of First Order and Second Order Calling? In which area of calling do you find yourself most of the time, at this stage of your ministry? How might God be asking you to gain greater balance?

How do you respond to the discussion about a paradigm for understanding the process of spiritual growth? Can you relate to the Teresian paradigm discussed in *Mansions of the Heart*? Do you have a feel for your own season of growth within those Mansions?

What additional reading and study do you feel would help you provide leadership to a contagious fire movement in your setting?

Chapter 3: Becoming Contagious Fire - On The Journey Personally and Intentionally

Recalling that Contagious Fire addresses meaningful spiritual growth for an entire congregation or ministry, we recognized that a leader can only take people where they have already traveled. She or he must become immersed in this love relationship with God to the extent that they know the territory of spiritual growth from experience. Only when God's love in us becomes contagious to our followers will they become motivated to follow us at all. We asked ourselves about our own place on the journey paradigm and the extent to which we have been recognizing and embracing our own season of growth. Only a "leader in process" can help others believe that God will stoop to guide them in love's process as well. Through open vulnerability, we can draw others closer to the fire of God's love.

How About You?

What excites you about your experiential relationship with Jesus? What frustrates you about it?

To what extent can you put words to the LOVE dimension of your relationship with God? How do you experience God's love for you? How do you express your love for God?

Can you identify what you long for in your First Order relationship with God? What would "near perfect" intimacy with Jesus look like for you? What picture, image, or metaphor might describe it?

What action is God inviting you to take in your relationship with Him now? What excites you about the possibilities of going all in? What do you find frightening about saying YES to Jesus?

Chapter 4: Igniting The Spark Into Flame - Following Jesus Together In An Internal Leadership Community

We expanded our focus to explore Jesus' spiritual leadership style that both facilitates our own spiritual growth and paves the way for our spiritual leadership in our ministry setting. Jesus launched the Kingdom of God with a love-based, rather than a power-based, leadership approach. We urged you to call together key leaders within your ministry and invite them to enter more intentionally into their own relationship with God and to support you and one another in the process. Simply put, your personal glowing embers aren't hot enough or bright enough to be contagious; you need to become part of a real fire.

How About You?

Looking over your own spiritual growth history, do you find that you tend to keep your personal relationship with Jesus private, or have you tended to share your journey with others? Where in your history do you think you learned to live your faith that way? What kind of leadership style has emerged from that history?

How do you respond to the idea of inviting a spiritual leadership team to share your spiritual growth journey? What sounds attractive about the idea and what feels threatening or difficult?

When you think about forming a spiritual leadership community, who first comes to mind as someone with whom you would like to share your journey? When you think of the spiritual leadership team that will be most needed by your ministry setting, who do you think should be represented? Who should you invite first?

What help do you need to form a spiritual leadership community in your ministry setting, from God and from others? What will it take for you to lead in community, like Jesus?

Chapter 5: Sparking The Church - A Vision For Contagious Christians

Now we sense Jesus' call to invite others in our ministry setting to join us in this journey of love—love for God and for others. We explored the difference between casting an institutional vision and calling our people to explore their own hearts, letting the Holy Spirit create within each person their own vision of what a deepening love relationship with Jesus might look like. We refrained from imposing a vision—our vision, but extend an invitation to discover Jesus more deeply and His vision for them, personally. Once our people have begun to dream dreams and see visions, we're ready to move forward, to provide the teaching and experience that will help them meet Jesus in new ways and discover the love their hearts long for.

How About You?

Have you been able to formulate a personal contagious fire vision with First and Second Order dimensions in it? What will your preferable future look like in your relationship with God? What will loving your neighbor look like in broad focus? How will your personal contagious fire vision be contagious to others? (Remember that we are not talking about a corporate vision statement with which we expect others to align).

To what extent can each member of your spiritual leadership community answer the questions in number 1, above?

Can you and other members of your spiritual leadership community share your personal visions with humility and vulnerability? In what settings can that be done most effectively?

What process can you use to enable a significant percentage of the congregation to actively seek God for their own contagious fire vision? What help do your people need to formulate a vision statement that includes First and Second Order dimensions?

Chapter 6: How To Spread The Fire - Discovering The Way Forward

Now we're sensing God leading us to help our people fulfill their visions of contagious fire, rather than asking, "What would Jesus do?" We agreed to do what Jesus DID—engage with what we see the Father doing. After coming to know ourselves as leaders, we then must let the Lord show us the hearts of those we lead. We need to understand the church and community cultures in which we minister and the history out of which they come. Using the combined perspectives of our spiritual leadership community, we ask the Lord to show us how to address the subjects of the following chapters, identifying the best places to invite others into the process. The Lord leads each one of us in ways consistent with who we are and how we're wired. While our Lord does not expect others' journeys to look just like yours, He has nevertheless chosen you to lead in this situation and will direct you uniquely. When we start to lead change, we need to hear our Lord's voice, "Follow Me."

How About You?

How would you assess the readiness your ministry members to become serious about their own spiritual growth and ability to live out God's love in the world? What cultural and organizational DNA should be considered in planning the way forward? What is the best way to cultivate a culture that embraces personal growth?

What key leaders and "permission givers" need to receive your invitation and preparation to enter the contagious fire process? What settings will best facilitate this process?

Where do you already see the flames of spiritual life in your ministry? What people will be most receptive and ready to embrace deeper intimacy with God and intentional love of neighbor? Where do you need to start and where do you need to give plenty of time for folks to catch fire?

How might you envision a three-year plan for contagious fire in your ministry setting? Who should be part of this plan development? Who will oversee the process and make adjustments as you learn? Who will provide the primary prayer support for your ministry to come more alive with contagious fire? What ways might you stay abreast of who has actually embraced the contagious fire journey and who needs help? How might you provide congregational feedback that shows positive momentum and encourages others to join in?

Chapter 7: Revealing The Flame And Dispelling The Fear - Teaching About Spiritual Formation

After some kidding about how most of us feel like "teaching" forms the fundamental and most vital aspect of ministry, we took a serious look at the importance of helping our people understand both the biblical and practical foundations of spiritual growth in loving God and loving others. We agreed that clear biblical foundations for spiritual growth help our people understand their own journeys in Kingdom context. Whatever our situation, we need to assess the best places to teach and possibly innovate and create new opportunities. We considered teaching that should precede our pilgrims' launch into spiritual formation, teaching that responds to the questions that they begin to ask along the way, and mentor and coach type teaching that provides "just-in-time" help when our pilgrims encounter obstacles.

How About You?

Do you have a good feel for WHAT needs to be taught, based on your ministry setting? Can you identify what needs to be taught foundationally and what needs to be taught as a function of people's place on the journey?

What settings can best facilitate the teaching for those who need it the most? Can you identify existing settings and additional opportunities that need to be created? Have you been able to identify the resources that will be needed at both the foundational and journey levels?

What kinds of coaching and mentoring might be helpful for those who need it? What kinds of training will enable these coaches and mentors to minister effectively? What general leadership training for those in ministry leadership positions will help expand the spiritual depth in small groups and functional ministry groups? In what ways can you connect "teaching" and "experiential" opportunities to facilitate learning and growth?

How are you continuing to learn about what it means to become one with the Trinity and to express that unity in love to others?

Chapter 8: Touching The Fire - Opportunities For Experiential Discovery

Realizing that, just like we can't make people learn simply by providing information, we cannot make people experience God by telling them they should. We can, however, provide opportunities for people to make themselves available to God in new ways and trust God to connect with people and to transform them to the extent they make themselves open and available. Based upon the writings and experiences of classical and modern spiritual formation writers and our Contributors, we suggested that you find ways to provide spiritual experience opportunities in prayer, spiritual direction and coaching, retreats, beauty, Scripture, spiritual community, service, and a Rule of Life. Our encouragement to "know the Lord" needs to be accompanied by patience and gentle guidance to subject one's experience to the clear teaching of Scripture and to the wisdom of elders in our communities of faith. In the same way we must interact with our students in our teaching, we want to provide coaching, mentoring, and contexts where our pilgrims can debrief their experiences of God and receive insight about how to respond to God.

How About You?

Have you identified the ways you would like your people to experience God's love and love for neighbor? What spiritual disciplines need to be tasted before people may be ready to learn more about them or begin to practice them personally?

Can you identify the kinds of spiritual experience opportunities that will best fit your ministry setting and culture? Which ones already exist; which ones can be adapted; which ones need to be created?

Knowing that a small percentage of your people will participate in any one thing, what experiential resources and activities can be made available for people in a variety of settings?

In what ways can people share their God experiences to interest and encourage others?

Chapter 9: Combatting The Fire Extinguishers - Facing The Dragon Together

We recognized that resistance and counterattack form an important part of the journey. Our fallen human nature resists the deepening Lordship of Jesus. Clinging to our own attempts at control and our woundedness, we resist God's love and obstruct the flow of His love through us to others. God's gentle encouragement and challenge to live a new life surfaces painful realities in us, making us afraid. To make matters worse, our enemy the devil counterattacks. Armed with lies, accusations, and confusion, he pummels both the leaders and members of the congregation, attempting to cause us to turn from Jesus, fight each other, and stop our deepening love relationship with God. God, however, calls us to stand firm against the schemes of the enemy, put on the full armor of God, and resist in the name of Jesus. He uses this resistance and attack as opportunities to form and strengthen us as leaders, birthing patience, compassion, and perseverance in us. We must respond to these obstacles with love and patience, both within ourselves and within our ministry members, helping them stand firm in the Lord.

How About You?

In what ways have you experienced "push-back" in your own spiritual journey? How have you sensed the enemy trying to block your progress? Have you developed your own process of recognizing and countering these dragon challenges to your growth? What is the enemy's plan to take you down? To what extent do you feel ready to embrace these challenges as God's gift for you to grow?

Are you able to see the dragon's strategy against members of your ministry? How are the attacks similar and different? To what extent can you be open and vulnerable about the warfare you face? How can you help your people put on the full armor of God and resist?

At what levels do you see the enemy using hidden congregational dynamics to create mock battles which attempt to derail the contagious fire process? What "family systems" does God want to heal and recreate? What kinds of help do you need to enable your congregational culture deal with conflict in healthy ways?

How may community be rallied together in prayer, open discussion, and spiritual warfare to fend off the enemy, help one another grow, and to increase the spiritual depth of the community? What support do you need as a leader, outside your ministry community, to help you persevere and overcome?

Chapter 10: Fanning Contagious Fire - Worship That Models Abiding In Love

We explored how we might worship on Sunday in ways that model what we teach and the spiritual experiences we encourage. How might we make it easy for regular participation in Sunday morning worship to result in an everyday spiritual lifestyle that facilitates spiritual growth in love for God and neighbor? We explored how we might enable our worshipers to taste each aspect of the spiritual life. We looked at discovery-based teaching, music of love, Holy Communion, spaces for reflection, the use of symbol and beauty, prayer, story, ministry, and community. In each dimension of our community worship experience we want to give opportunity to taste, practice, and recall essential elements and practices that will enable daily life to become a journey with Jesus and a deepening experience of His love.

How About You?

How did you respond to the idea that Sunday worship services should model and equip your people to live out contagious fire lifestyles? Where did you find yourself saying, "Yes, of course"? Where did you shake your head and say, "No way"? To what extend do these reactions reflect your own biases? To what extent do they reflect barriers you see in the congregation?

Can you identify a process of change that would move your worship services more toward modeling a contagious fire lifestyle? Among the suggestions in this chapter, which ones do you feel might prove helpful in your setting? What adjustments do you see that I didn't mention?

To what extent could you cast a vision for a dynamic worship experience that invites participants to experience God at multiple levels in worship? While affirming the tradition of your worship style, can you invite your congregation to experiment and try new things, without an initial commitment to long-term change?

What leaders need to be part of the decision about what to change and how? To what extent do these changes need to be subtle and nuanced, and what changes need to be decided publicly in a way that explains the reasons? To what extent do you feel ready to humbly and vulnerably lead change?

Chapter 11: Becoming Contagious Bonfires - Spiritually Forming Community

We now turned our attention from kindling the fire and fanning its flames to the actual experience of contagious fire in Christian community as the Church. To provide opportunity for this increasing flame of love to burn brightly, we discussed ways of building and sustaining spiritual community that encourages and motivates our people to live in love and give it away. As we enable these dimensions of our life together, we will see our own faith grow, our love for God and neighbor increase, and our passion fully engage us to follow Jesus into the adventure of igniting the world on fire—with Love.

How About You?

To what extent do you feel that your church culture embraces and fosters meaningful spiritual relationships? Do you feel that honesty, openness, vulnerability, and personal growth have been embraced as part of your corporate culture? Where do you see God calling your ministry to grow in its depth of supportive community?

Do you see a congruence between your personal leadership style and level of openness and your assessment in question 1 above? What does this tell you about enabling the congregation to grow in its depth of community? Who can best model the kind of community that helps its members grow spiritually and serve God together?

What opportunities does your ministry provide for meaningful spiritual community to develop? In what ways are spiritual friendships modeled and encouraged? What new opportunities need to be provided and encouraged?

To what extent do you feel that you and your spiritual leadership community are able to vulnerably call for and facilitate deepening spiritual community in your ministry setting?

Chapter 12: Freed To Burn Brightly - Healing Ministry That Removes The Blocks To Love

We now affirmed that the recognition of our needs for healing represent significant spiritual growth rather than weakness or failure. Having tasted the freeing and life-giving love of God in greater measure and in the presence of a supportive spiritual community, we now long to love and be loved to the fullest. Our blocks become apparent as we attempt to live into our Lord's invitation, and we're grieved and saddened at our weakness. We, therefore, explored the nature of the life-giving ministry of healing in the Church. As we overcome our fears of the unknown and our attempts to control God, we discover how our Lord Jesus delights in taking us into the depths of our hearts, replacing darkness with His light. Now, as part of this dynamic community of life, we gain the courage to live out the vision that God plants within us—a vision of loving intimacy with God that flows so naturally through us to others that we flourish in our Lord's outreach to the world. We then explored various aspects of developing a healing ministry in the local church.

How About You?

As you review your spiritual history, can you identify spiritual wounds and blocks that God has healed? Did the Lord use other people to help you in a significant way? Have you come to a place where you recognize your needs for healing as a sign of spiritual growth? To what extent can you ask others to pray with and for you in support of your own spiritual growth? Do you feel that you can authentically encourage the ministry of healing in your ministry setting?

To what extent has your ministry setting been exposed to prayer ministry? Do people in your congregation seek out prayer for physical and spiritual needs? To what extent do you feel that the injunctions in James 5 are understood and practiced in your ministry setting?

Can you and your leadership team give public witness to both the need for and practice of healing prayer in your own lives? What other respected members might be able to share similar stories that would encourage people to consider healing more seriously?

What steps will help you, your leadership, and your members seek God for healing? What individuals and groups take prayer seriously and would be willing to learn more about the ministry of healing? Where would you start to develop or expand a healing ministry in your ministry setting?

Chapter 13: The Winds of Contagious Fire - Spiritual Formation as Missional Momentum

Imagining ourselves and our churches aflame with the love of God, passionate to take up our own crosses and follow Jesus, we close the loop in our discussion as we explore how our own spiritual formation fuels momentum for the Great Commission. As loving becomes natural for us, following Jesus becomes instinctive, and loving others—a great joy! We explored how we intentionally help people connect the dots, experientially, between God's love for us and the outflow of His love for others. Jesus has called us to join Him in bringing His Kingdom more fully in our time—He's setting an unquenchable fire upon the earth—a fire of love.

How About You?

To what extent have members of your ministry connected love for God and love for others? Do they see loving outreach to others as an opportunity to grow in their relationship with Jesus? To what extent have these connections been made in your own life and modeled in your ministry? Have you come to believe that abiding in God's love will naturally result in the desire to love one's neighbor?

To what extent is the missions outreach of your ministry based on recruitment or upon facilitating the individual callings of your members? If interviewed, would your members say that outreach represents an obligation or a privilege? To what extent have your people envisioned how they might love Jesus in others in ways congruent with their own gifts and calling? Has loving others in practical ways become part of the corporate culture of your ministry setting?

What ways does your ministry setting provide opportunities for people to experiment with mission outreach? Do mission teams actively invite others to "taste and see?" Are visitors and new members invited for short-term participation in ministry outreach opportunities?

How might God be inviting you to love Him and others more intentionally? How might you invite others to join you in becoming more contagious? In what ways can your ministry celebrate individual and group actions of loving care and advocacy?

STORIES ABOUT CHURCHES PURSUING CONTAGIOUS FIRE

Through the stories and resources of our Contributors we see real examples about how the Great Commandment and Great Commission come together in the Church of the twenty-first century. Some of these examples will illustrate certain aspects of the contagious fire process we have been discussing. Others will reflect a more integrated level. These stories represent attempts at faithfulness rather than flag-waiving success. Some of them might model approaches that could prove useful in your setting or they might spark other ideas that could. None of these stories can be held up as some sort of template to try to "plug and play." They simply illustrate a few places where followers of Jesus have caught fire in new ways and are exploring new depths of what it means to love God and neighbor, enabling their ministries to become a contagious fire.

You might begin by scanning their ministry websites to get a feel for the church, it's size, staff, etc. Then read the stories with an ear to Jesus. Our Contributors have participated in the Contagious Fire Project and share their stories here and in the previous chapters as an invitation to you—to dialogue and make supportive relationships. You can read the Contributor biographical sketches in the Appendices and contact them through their individual websites.

Bethany Bible Church, Phoenix, Arizona - http://www.bbcphx.org

Contact: Ted Wueste

Our goal in spiritual formation at Bethany Bible has been exposure to the masses and equipping with leaders. Because a spiritual formation paradigm for church life is often different from what people have experienced in the past, we've offered one-time classes, retreats, quiet prayer days, and other opportunities to stir desire and whet the appetite of those who are seeking Christ. Then, the deepest work is the work with leaders who will have an opportunity to live their life with God in a different way that can overflow into the lives of those being led. Finally, we've found that there are many who were hungry for a deeper life in Christ and the language of spiritual formation put words to their desires. Especially in a larger church, there are often a good number of people who have felt alone in their desire for intimacy with God and may have forever been confused with their experience of God.

A book like *Mansions of the Heart* has become a mainstay for exposing people to a different paradigm and giving confused seekers language for their experience. All in all, as a 60-year-old church, we've tried to go slowly and listen to the Holy Spirit for direction. Finally, rather than completely restructuring programs and settled patterns for church life, we introduced an annual "all church" study in which we asked the whole church (from children through adults, in their various groups) to engage in a spiritual formation study for 6-8 weeks. Each year, we produced a daily devotional and study guide that went along with the sermon and led to a small group experience. We found that most everyone has been willing to do something for a short period of time and many begin to engage in new ways of being with God.

Carefree Vineyard - http://www.carefreevineyard.com

Contact: Terry Tarleton

Our journey into a deeper more intimate relationship with Jesus, began when my wife, Janice, and I—Terry Tarleton, pastor Carefree Vineyard Church, hit the proverbial wall personally, relationally, and spiritually. One day we looked at each other and proclaimed, "The Church in America doesn't look much different from the world," and knew we needed to do life and church differently. We knew that there had to be more that Jesus had for us and our church.

We began to explore contemplative prayer, Lectio Divina, reading Scripture with imagination, Immanuel Healing Prayer, and many other formational forms of connecting with Jesus. Our journey led us to implementing these techniques into our church—they had become part of who we were.

To summarize how we operate now at Carefree Vineyard Church, I would characterize us as a formational church. We value the Word of God as much as ever, but now we teach people how to enter the biblical story via "reading with imagination," and asking Jesus, "What are you inviting me to in this story?" When we teach on Sunday mornings, the sermon almost always includes some version of inviting the congregation to allow the passage to penetrate their hearts and to reveal any area where Jesus wants to work personally. We end our messages with a time of silent prayer where the individuals are challenged to sit in silence and ask Jesus what He wants them to take away from their time that day.

We believe that the biggest key to spiritual formation is being willing to be honest with Jesus regarding what's in our hearts; to be open and honest before Him in our brokenness. Peter Scazzero writes in *Emotionally Healthy Spirituality*, that emotional maturity and spiritual maturity go hand in hand. We have used that book as well as many other formational books and series as texts for our small groups. We have studied *Mansions of the Heart*, the *Good and Beautiful God* series, and many others. We constantly challenge our leaders from children's ministry on up to ask themselves how they are helping their people to grow in intimacy with Jesus; to not just *know about it,* but also to *experience* the fact that they are indeed a dearly loved child of God.

At Carefree Vineyard Church we have always had a heart for outreach. In the past, we would plan regular outreaches to our community via service projects and the like. Somehow, though, the "planning" of these events seemed to take some of the Jesus factor out of the process. As we have collectively grown in intimacy with Jesus, and been more present to His presence, we have found that outreach, for most of the individuals in the church, has become more organic, spontaneous and fruitful! Instead of going out and feeling a need or obligation to tell someone about Jesus (without really checking with Jesus first), outreach has become more of a way of life; just doing what Jesus is doing *with* Jesus instead of *for* Jesus! We celebrate these individual stories on Sundays on a regular basis through what we call "Salt Reports."

Centennial Covenant Church – Littleton, Colorado -

www.centcov.org

Contact: Steve Thulson

Steve Thulson, Lead Pastor of Centennial, addresses several of the focuses of *Contagious Fire* in the following summaries.

LEADERSHIP COMMUNITY AND PLANNING STRATEGY

Centennial Covenant's two primary leadership teams (Council of Elders and Pastoral Staff), try to be together in what they attempt to develop in the church as a whole: a four-dimensional life with God that dwells in His presence as His children ("up"), connects as companions as His family ("with"), cultivates new life as His image-bearers ("in"), and activates love as his sent-ones ("out"). We call these our "Priority Callings."

These priorities also mean making sure our agendas include time a) to build honest and grace-giving relationships, and b) to place ourselves in Christ's presence to let His Spirit calm, focus and guide whatever we do. From time to time, a team member will remind us in our deliberations: "we need to be church." For example, when Tom Ashbrook led our Journey Team (to guide spiritual formation ministries), his common opening question as the team meeting began was "What do you each need to surrender to God to be fully present tonight?" He then would lead into some silence and/or personal sharing.

Through direct abiding prayer together, as well as trying to be aware of His constant presence, we try to take seriously that Jesus is the living *Head* of what is *His* church, *not* a remote *figurehead* of what is *our* church. This is "leading by following," i.e. giving priority to discernment of God's leading more than mere strategic planning. We don't presume we'll always get direct divine revelations, but at least we want to give the Spirit freedom to posture our hearts and instill his wisdom. Here's a recent example from January 2017: Our six Elders and five Pastors took a day retreat together as part of seeking fresh direction for the church's next few years. As "homework," an Elder suggested we each ask God for an image of what He desired for CCC. At the retreat, we took almost an hour for individual listening prayer, and then shared our hearts, including the images. The images and elaborations were strikingly similar, and fostered peace and expectation that Jesus was leading.

PROVIDING TEACHING, EXPERIENCES, AND COMMUNITY TO HELP MEMBERS DISCOVER VISION

Over the years, we've encouraged our Life Group leaders to remind members that they gather in Christ's presence, and so to let all be done "with" Him, not just "about" or "for" Him – whether socializing, discussing Scripture or a book, sharing needs, providing mutual prayer and encouragement, or engagement in shared ministry. This includes strongly recommended resources such as James Smith's *Apprenticeship Series*, Renovaré materials, Tom Ashbrook's *Mansions*, Ruth Haley Barton's videos/books, Peter Scazerro's books/videos on emotional health, etc.

In 2008, Tom Ashbrook invited me and a few other church leaders to experience a three-day *Imago Christi* "Discovery." The clear benefit led to encouraging others to do the same. An extraordinary Lilly grant for my 2010 Sabbatical supported about 50 of our leaders (Elders, staff and leaders of groups and teams), to participate in a Discovery. The positive experience was not only the occasion for personal growth, but also common language, vision and values. Forms of Discoveries have been among what we call "Equipping Pathway" experiences, workshops, classes – what we urge every adult to consider. Several years ago, a "Journey Team" was formed to guide our Life Groups, adult classes and individuals into more intentional and fruitful spiritual formation: clarifying a vision, providing equipping and resources, etc. One point of concentration has been to equip some members in peer mentoring, or as we later preferred to call it "Companions for the Journey." Several pairs or trios of members participated in a shortened Imago Christi

Discovery, processing their time lines, longings, blocks and plans together. Beyond occasional programmed events, our goal is to cultivate a culture of intentionally formational friendships – as one form of community alongside Life Groups and Ministry Teams.

MISSIONAL CALL

Here are two questions we try to keep raising: 1) How are formational and relational groups also serving in missional opportunities? and, 2) How are ministry teams also formational and relational opportunities? A major need for us is to integrate our four Priority Callings into holistic living – personally and with families, as a whole congregation, in worship gatherings, in Life Groups, in Ministry Teams, and in leadership.

In the Fall of 2016, about half of our adults worked through a "Bearings Inventory" for some self-examination of growth edges and obstacles in our Four Priority Callings. Though this was more for personal discovery than congregational assessment, leaders saw patterns of both strengths and needs. A majority of members reported two major obstacles: 1) In every dimension of life with Christ, most struggle with overwhelming busyness; and 2) For activating God's love outward in self-giving service, most cited a desire to do so, yet also a strong feeling of inadequacy and uncertainty about where exactly they fit in God's mission. This has led to a strong sense of God's leading to help our people discover their "every day, everywhere missional vocations" within a practice of His presence. The prayer is that more of us find ways to activate God's transforming outward love in what they're already doing day by day without necessarily adding yet more programmed activity to their more than full lives. The vision is that such "Focused Living" (as we're calling a two-part workshop facilitated by the Re-focusing arm of CRM in February 2018), will not only have missional impact, but be spiritually formational --- including some simplifying of life for our busy people.

Platt Park Church, Denver, Colorado - www.plattparkchurch.org

Contact: Charlie Dodrill

We are beginning to include moments of silent reflection at the end of our talk, on Sunday morning, to allow people to actually sit and connect with God instead of simply absorbing information, singing a song, then making small talk. By the time we reach the car, it is gone. Creating space for personal encounter with God right there in the service may be the only time some have throughout their week.   We now offer prayer for anyone who wants it (basic, but new to our church) during the service.

I, Charlie Dodrill, Pastor of Worship and Spiritual Formation, have started a group that has gone by several titles, but always remains focused on encountering God together and processing our experience. The basic format is that I, or another person from our community, shares an act/discipline/technique/thought/etc., that has helped us to encounter God in a tangible way. Usually we keep this part to about twenty minutes, and share how it came about in our lives, it's importance, the change we've seen as a result, etc. Then we all simply do it together–right then and there–making sure it isn't simply information, but something we all do together. This can last from 15-40 minutes. Then we always leave twenty minutes to process our experience. I think this is important because in my early years of trying these things, having only read the "highlights" of the saints and mystics, I was convinced that I was: 1. Doing it wrong, 2. Unworthy of the Lord's attention/gifts/affection, or 3. Just wasn't called to experience Him in that way. Allowing others to hear another say, "That didn't do anything for me" is very freeing and normalizing when the fireworks don't happen immediately.

We've focused on these subjects:

Lectio Divina

Silence

Listening on behalf of others (prophetically)

Discerning the different voices in our head/heart/spirit

Fasting

Mindsets in worship

Body postures in worship

Listening on behalf of self

Confession

Scanning our bodies and inviting the Lord to speak to us that way

Healing

Deliverance

Speaking in tongues (less actual practice in this one)

The Holy Spirit–Who He is and what He does

Breath prayer

Journaling

Imaginative contemplation

Scripture meditation, etc.

We have seen a big uptick in our small groups beginning formation practices as part of their curriculum. One of our women's groups spent an entire trimester doing meditative/imaginative Scripture reading every meeting.

South Bay Community Church, Fremont, CA – www.sobcc.org

Contact: Tammy Long

Our spiritual formation emphasis at SBCC began with classes in our Adult Christian Formation ministry during the "Sunday School Hour." Classes such as *Hearing God* by Dallas Willard, *Praying the Psalms* by Elmer L. Towns, and *Celebration of Discipline,* by Richard Foster attracted members who were hungry for experiences related to a deeper encounter with God. These were classes I taught, which spoke to my own hunger, and allowed us to journey together.

A friend gave me *Mansions of the Heart,* by Tom Ashbrook, which immediately spoke to my soul and gave me a framework by which to think about intentional spiritual formation and an understanding of the formation journey.

Again, from my own hunger, I started a small group called Sojourners. The pilot group was by invitation to those I suspected to have a hunger to grow in a deeper relationship with God and an interest to journey together as disciples. I planned to start the group if I had at least four people. Eight women wanted to be a part.

The group was intentionally designed to be different from our regular small groups in that it was not meant to be a Bible or book study, but an experience with God we shared together. God led me to James *Bryan's Smith's Good and Beautiful Apprentice* series as a support and guiding text. The premise of the books was exactly what I was looking for, and the inclusion of "Soul Training" exercises allowed us to keep the focus on encountering and experiencing God as we also learned about false narratives about God and the Kingdom of God. As Sojourners took root, it was like leaven, it became apparent that there were others who were hungry for a deeper experience with God.

I attended a Discovery from *Imago Christi* as part of my own continued formation and to glean what I could for our church. I was so moved by the experience that I decided to host a Discovery at South Bay. The Discovery was well attended and received, particularly by our leaders. From there we started offering a Mansions class during the Sunday School hour.

From my training as a spiritual director, I introduced what I was learning to the church. We introduced and began practicing Centering prayer, Lectio Divina, and the Examen in a variety of ways, including our annual prayer and fasting retreat, as a part of leadership meetings, and as brief guided practices during morning worship services.

Sojourners continued to grow with additional groups being started by those who had completed the one-year commitment, with others asking when the next one would begin. We also found those who had completed Sojourners exploring or expanding areas of leadership. Currently, two Elders, our Deacon chair, and another Deacon have experienced Sojourners. Other Sojourners are currently servant leaders. We see these leaders incorporating practices such as Lectio, Centering prayer, and a sensitivity to the movement of the Spirit in their leadership roles.

When we recently developed a 2020 Vision Strategic Plan, deeper intimacy with God was one of our goals. The strategy for this goal was to develop a tool that would allow people to discover where they are in their journey and craft an intentional plan to partner with what God is doing. The tool is based on the Mansions, even though we have used the imagery of ever-increasing light. The tool will be rolling out in 2018 and there is buzz about it. We are starting with church leaders with the expectation that all leaders will be engaged in intentional spiritual experiences with an accountability partner, to create space for the Holy Spirit to do His work.

Because we know the human tendency to be goal oriented and to think legalistically, we are also developing a new ministry called Spiritual Friends. Spiritual Friends will be trained and available to walk with people who have taken the tool and want to go deeper in understanding the spiritual formation journey. The training will include understanding the formation process in a way to convey the joy of the journey; an appreciation of where they have been, where they are now, and the invitation God is offering for deeper intimacy. It will also include an understanding of how we connect with God using *Sacred Pathways,* by Gary Thomas, to help people discover their unique way of connecting with God.

While we have found the pastor's support to be invaluable, we have also experienced that a contagious fire can come from the spark of just a few people. As individuals began to experience God in fresh ways, hunger was fanned and "the demand" for support, training and experience has grown. Still, to have church leadership and pastoral staff on the same page is extremely beneficial. Our pastoral staff attended the Discovery from *Imago Christi*. *Mansions of the Heart* is required reading, and they will go through the Spiritual Friends training as they also engage with the spiritual growth tool.

Key initiatives and strategies we have found impactful:

Christian education/formation classes to introduce formation practices and give people a safe place to learn, taste and explore formational experiences

Discovery by *Imago Christi*

Intentional small groups which focus on formation

>Shared resources and texts that allow the congregation to have common language and understanding – e.g.

>Mansions of the Heart

>Sacred Pathways

>Emotionally Healthy Spirituality

Spiritual growth tools for personal assessment and reflection

>Identification of core spiritual practices to be integrated into the life on a regular basis

>Centering prayer

>Lectio Divina

>Examen

>Silence and Holy Listening

An emphasis on prayer during and after worship services

Half day to full weekend retreats that allow people to encounter God and talk about the experience

>These retreats are 2-3 times a year and include prayer stations and spiritual practice experiences which allow time to "debrief" so participants can learn to recognize the movements of God. In addition to core practices mentioned above. We've done things like:

Parable walks

Prayer labyrinths

Journaling

Art as prayer

Spiritual Growth Reflection Tool and Spiritual Friends

Spiritual Direction

We offer spiritual direction to our congregation and community

Our denomination offers free spiritual direction to pastoral staff, and we strongly encourage and provide the funds as a benefit for any staff member to seek spiritual direction.

Missional outreach experiences that begin or end with spiritual practices above to link the formational process of head, heart and hand. Some may feel the focus on formation is not missional enough. Our perspective is discipleship, missions and evangelism are all deeply integrated. We believe as people draw closer to God's heart, they will also care about what God cares about. So, the link and connection are natural and can be easily nurtured, in both directions of "being" and "doing."

Longview Community Church, Longview WA/Bethany Community Church, Seattle, WA -

www.longviewcommunitychurch.org; www.churchbcc.org/

Contact: Chris Lyons

Our goal is family spiritual formation – intentionally connecting the generations in a "spiritual safety net" using family faith experiments. As a youth pastor serving students and families in local churches in the Pacific Northwest for almost twenty-five years, I am compelled to be part of a movement that offers a different spiritual script for students who often graduate from their faith when they graduate from our programs. We've been experimenting with congregationally connecting the dots in a way that inspires personal faith ownership anchored in community. We're striving to create a church culture that expects to send our graduates out into the world with a faith that keeps growing and reconnects with a new faith community.

Truly, our congregations are seeking to "lay a foundation that would last for the long haul" with our children—which I consider the goal of every Christian parent. Some have even called this the "bottom line" of youth ministry; not just the attendance of a student now, but their having an active faith-life, ten years from now.

Recently there has been a growing emphasis on creating and supporting "family ministry" within the Church. While various definitions exist to describe exactly what family ministry is about, one consistent element has to do with shifting the focus toward the parents and equipping them to better provide spiritual support for their children. (Some humorously describe trying to define "family ministry" as akin to "nailing Jell-O to a wall" - not an easy thing to do!). And while such a definition might be elusive for many congregations, at Longview Community Church, we are "sold out" for several key aspects of family-forming-faith.

We emphasize the partnership between parents and parish by intentionally passing on key resources to families to encourage greater opportunities for faith dialogue in their homes. We've found over the years that parents feel ill-equipped and reticent to discuss their personal faith with their youth, and therefore leave those discussions to the youth ministry. (Are we really "outsourcing the faith" of our children?) Our resources help parents learn to verbalize both the joys and difficulties of their walk with God. These conversations help our youth see faith in action, not just from ministry professionals, but from the adults closest to them. Obviously, the spiritual growth of our parents and other supporting adults profoundly affects the faith foundations of our youth.

In tandem with this family focus, our youth ministry is structured to create a type of "spiritual safety net" or "constellation of key relationships" around each young person in our midst. This structure for spiritual care is set up to reinforce the truth of Christian fellowship: true community is not an add-on bonus to our faith but goes hand-in-hand with our personal relationship with Jesus.

Building upon this relational model (highlighted in *Sustainable Youth Ministry* by Mark DeVries), the overall relational scheme anticipates "multiple adults pouring into" the life of each student, so that this young person lives at the center of the web, surrounded by a community following Jesus together. This picture ideally models our ministry for every student in our congregation. The adults in this network include Sunday School teachers, small group leaders, mission trip participants, the student's parents, other students in the youth group, and also a congregational Prayer Partner.

In the last five years of our Prayer Partner program, we have recruited adults (mostly from our fifty-year-and-older crowd) who make a commitment for one year to prayer daily for a student in our program. We supply the student's picture and contact information, insist that the Prayer Partner go through our background check process, and create an environment for the student and adult to connect at least quarterly at an open house over refreshments. Then we really trust the relationship to God. It's been incredible to see how these friendships have become more and more mutual in their prayer support and encouragement. Many of our senior adults have raved that their friendship with a student has been life-changing. And, our retention of Prayer Partners year to year has been over 90%.

The last programmatic piece of our approach is a Grad Prep Program. For our juniors and seniors in high school, we have designed a two-year discipleship process that equips our youth to truly prepare themselves for the faith transition after high school. These efforts must include an active partnership between families and the church to ensure that our students have been actually practicing critical community forming skills while they still live among us. Our monthly meetings provide significant training resources to safeguard a comprehensive sense of "being ready" to be sent as faithful followers of Christ into the world after graduation. Ultimately, it's about helping young people make their personal commitment to Christ a lifelong journey. A significant element of this training helps them be intentional about creating their own faith constellations in the season after graduation.

Our support for our young people continues after graduation as well. Within our intentional support of our families, we're providing ongoing support past the normally assumed "finish line" of high school graduation. Our Prayer Partners keep their relationships up with our graduates. We reach out with care packages and sharing prayer for our graduates, as well as intentionally including our young adults in mission trips in the summer. In all of these seasons of ministry, we continue to live out our vision of connecting as a family focused on Jesus.

West Side Church – Richland, Washington: www.westside1.org

Contact: Melanie Saint James

West Side Church in Richland, WA, is a moderate size (approx. 500 members) affiliated with the Evangelical Covenant of Presbyterians (ECO). Our Contagious Fire journey began when I attended an *Imago Christi* Discovery for leaders in Utah 2010, and then returned home to share my experience with the Christian Growth Committee who were, at that time, looking for a "road map" for Christian Growth. Upon reading *Mansions of the Heart,* by Tom Ashbrook, there was a collective "Aha moment" as we realized that God had provided us exactly what we needed -- a paradigm for spiritual growth from spiritual infancy to mature union with Christ. Soon after, West Side sent their pastoral staff to an *Imago Christi* Discovery in Portland.

Agreement among the staff was that the 3-day Discovery would be valuable for lay leaders, staff, and anyone else interested in growing in their faith, so in 2012 and 2013 West Side hosted two (one was all day, and the other evenings and Saturday) back-to-back three-day regional Discovery Events. Wanting to keep the conversation going after returned home from the *Imago Christi* Discovery, Rev. Dan Wodrich (the pastor for Christian Growth) and I began to develop a series of "Going Deeper" classes which we hoped would help our members find their "Next Step" on their spiritual journey whether they were in Mansion 3 or Mansion 5. While in all honesty, we tailored these Sunday morning and Wednesday evening classes to people in Mansion 4 and beyond, we were open to having anyone join these classes who were interested.

> In our first 10-week class we used Henri Nouwen's *Life of the Beloved*, Baxter Kruger's book *The Parable of the Dancing God*, watched and discussed the "Butterfly Circus," and read and meditated on Scripture passages that focused on God's deeply personal, unconditional love for us.

> For the first six weeks of this class, our main message was that God passionately loves each of us and calls us His beloved. While our class loved this "Contagious Fire" message, it was clear week after week that people were having trouble believing that *they themselves* were God's beloved.

> We realized that a love relationship with God was, in fact, the central message of the Gospel, and if people weren't getting it – then we shouldn't move on, instead, this was the very place we needed to camp until people did in fact get it. One of the phrases that we debated and sat on was, *"There is nothing you can do to make God love you more, and there is nothing you can do to make God love you less. You are just loved with all the love that an infinite God can offer."* We knew that one of the main issues we were bumping up against

was the issue of grace. How does grace work, who receives grace, and by what means does God communicate his grace to us.

As we've taught Going Deeper classes over the years, we've utilized such resources as:

Baxter Kruger's book: *The Shack Revisited – There is More Going On Here Than you Ever Dared to Dream*

Eugene Peterson's books: *Eat this Book – A Conversation in the Art of Spiritual Reading* and *Christ Plays In Ten Thousand Places – A Conversation on Spiritual Theology*

Alan Fadling's book, *The Unhurried Life – Following Jesus Rhythms of Work and Rest*

Mansions of the Heart by Tom Ashbrook and the study guide developed by Tom and Ted Wueste.

Brené Brown's videos on "The Power of Vulnerability" and "Understanding Shame"

No matter what we studied and debated together, we continually tried to help people grasp their belovedness. Week after week we prayed through Scripture together and we asked people to let the love in. Eventually, one of the men who most battled with us in the Discovery and then in our class for two years, came to us one unexpected Sunday and said "I got it! I got it! I got it! This truth about God's love for me is so amazing! It has completely changed my life and I want to thank you and Dan for the time you've spent walking with me as I wrestled with this truth about grace and God's love for me! As I've been thinking and praying about what to do with this good news, I've decided to start a Prison Fellowship Anticipate class at the State Prison for guys who are preparing to get out in a year's time. And I want you to know that at the beginning of every class I will invite the men to say with me *'There is nothing I can do to make God love me more, and there is nothing I can do to make God love me less. I am just loved with all the love an infinite God can offer.'* Once contagious love caught fire within this gentleman he couldn't help but pass that love along to others in need of the Good News.

One of the other things we did in our later Going Deeper classes was to begin our time with 30 minutes of meditation on a Scripture passage. For some, who had never been silent for 30 minutes, this exercise was hard, and I thought some might drop out. But they stayed for the entire course and one person asked me to mentor her.

As our congregation grew spiritually, we became ready to follow Jesus more closely. When our congregation made the decision to leave the PCUSA, the pastoral staff asked Tom Ashbrook to come and teach them the Rules of Ignatian Discernment. This process taught our Elders how to discern the correct question to ask God, and then walked them through a step-by-step process for discerning God's will regarding decision-making. After Tom's visit, the session agreed to adopt this process of decision making for important and possibly divisive decisions, like the decision about leaving the PCUSA and deciding about where to land denominationally after the fact. After their time of individual prayer and discernment, the session gathered again, and they went around the room asking where each person now stood. To the surprise of everyone in the room, they had now reached a unanimous decision to join ECO. What might have been a contentious and church-splitting debate became a unanimous decision. West Side has now agreed to utilize the Ignatian Rules for Discernment when facing other big issues, and has found the process invaluable. Our lead pastor has even begun to share the process with other Presbyterian churches in our area, as they too seek to make difficult decisions as a community.

Arumduri (Giant Tree) Presbyterian Church in Korea

Contact: Pastor Jaecheon Yee Through Tong Park Tong Park at CRM

Pastor Jaecheon Yee felt called by God, in 2009, to plant a new church centered specifically around the spiritual formation of the people God would bring him. He had become disillusioned with the stagnation and corruption in Korean churches and the growing apathy of Christians in their twenties and thirties. Even though the survival rate of new church plants in Korea was then only 2.1%, Pastor Yee gathered fifteen couples and their children on a retreat to pray and seek the Lord's guidance.

From that retreat, this small group decided to plant their new church based on the leadership style they saw in Jesus. They called it "Six Spirit" of Jesus way of spiritually forming His disciples:

1. Spontaneous Participation in Prayer

2. Personal Fellowship

3. Inculcation of Authentic Biblical Teaching, not like the Scribes

4. Retreat Empowering

5. Inside-Out Transforming Paradigm, Not Like the Scribes

6. Trips With His Disciples

In January, 2010, Pastor Yee took his flock on retreat to launch teaching on spiritual formation and formulating the other foundations of this new venture. Now, in 2017, Pastor Yee reports that his church has grown to about 350 members (many in the twenty and thirty ages ranges), with an average Sunday attendance of 250. About half of the congregation are actively involved in adult education that addresses intensive Bible knowledge combined with the stories of the great biblical heroes and their spiritual growth. A new Korean translation of *Mansions of the Heart* will enable Pastor Yee's church to adopt the Teresian spiritual growth paradigm to deepen their spiritual formation experience. Five full-time and three part-time pastors now serve the church community.

One of the exciting ways that Pastor Yee and his team encourage the spiritual growth of their members is through strategy number six—Spiritual Journey Trips. To date, he has taken six groups to such places as Cambodia, Malaysia, Kyrgyzstan, Eastern Europe, the Western Deserts of the USA,

Spain, and Banff, Canada. Participants on these trips practice spiritual disciplines and gain new perspectives from believers and their cultures in these adventures. Prayer, small group discussions, and ministry to the people they meet all combine to model the kinds of interactions that they saw in Jesus as He traveled with His disciples.

About 40% of his congregation have "graduated" from the Spiritual Formation Course. In the coming year, they will be sending a full time missionary family into Inner Mongolia, in China. Members of the church work together to care for disabled people in their area and reach out to lonely old men and malnourished children. They have adopted a church on one of the outer islands where they provide teaching and support.

Pastor Yee, and his wife, Seonmi, attended at one of *Imago Christi's* recent Gatherings to share their story and to seek opportunities for collaboration. We were thrilled to see how the Holy Spirit guided this church, in unique ways, to spread contagious fire in Korea and around the world.

LifeSpring Covenant Church - Loveland, Colorado –

www.lifespringchurch.org

Contact: Tim Musslewhite through *Imago Christi*

Many sitting in our pews, who had formerly been faithful servants, now seemed to have checked out or disengaged spiritually. We found that these people were actually frustrated that they were not experiencing more of the life of God. These people seemed convinced, however, that they had already experienced all that the church had to offer and that there was nothing more for them this side of heaven. Therefore, in 2004, LifeSpring began looking for processes and resources that would help people engage with God on a deeper level.

Our search led us to develop a spiritual formation ministry shaped largely around "The Journey," Year One of the materials created by VantagePoint[3] (www.vantagepoint3.org), a ministry based in Sioux Falls, South Dakota. VP³ has produced a three-year pathway of developing people for lifelong Christian discipleship and leadership.   "The Journey" is a seven-and-a-half-month process, which meets weekly, includes two retreats, a Personal Vision Workshop, mentored relationships, and other experiential learning experiences. It is designed to help people explore three questions:

1) Who is God?

2) Who am I?

3) What does God want to do through me?

A learning community of eight-to-twelve people is formed each year. Over nine years about eighty people have been through this process. "The Journey" is now offered every other year.

"The Alpha Course" is offered on the alternating years, as a basic introduction to the Christian faith for those who may be searching and for those relatively new to the faith.

To help individuals who have been through "The Journey" continue in a learning and growing posture, a second spiritual formation event is offered monthly, called "Journey II." Over the years, several resources have been used, including the two other processes offered by VantagePoint³. "A Way of Life" is designed to help people cultivate friendship with God through spiritual practices, develop community with others, and engage in mission on the way. "Walking with Others" helps people understand a strategy and practice of lifelong investment in the growth of others. The groups have read several books together, including Don Postema's *Space for God,* Helen Cepero's *Christ-Shaped Character,* Henri Nouwen's *Life of the Beloved,* and others.

Sunday morning Adult Growth classes have focused on spiritual discussion and experiential learning, believing that adults learn best what they actually have an opportunity to experience. Rather than lecturing, we give brief explanations and let people experience spiritual practices together in class, and then debrief the experiences together. Classes have been built around resources such as Gary Thomas' *Sacred Pathways*, Peter Scazerro's *Emotionally Healthy Spirituality*, and Mindy Caliguire's series of books, *Developing Soul Care*, *Simplicity*, *Spiritual Friendship*, and *Soul Searching*.

LifeSpring also occasionally offers *Imago Christi's* Spiritual Formation Discovery Events. This three-day experience dovetails beautifully with the VantagePoint[3] processes being used throughout the year.

As a pathway into many of these very intentional spiritual formation processes, LifeSpring periodically offers half-day retreat experiences, called "Wasting Time with God," designed to gently introduce people to practices with which they may not have been familiar.

Sunday worship allows time for people to experience and engage in practices such as *lectio divina*, imaginative prayer, use of the Examen, and other ancient practices of the Church, along with contemporary worship music and familiar hymns. The goal is to provide a worship experience, along with biblical teaching, that creates a space in which people can become enthralled with the person of God as manifested in Jesus Christ.

The central theme underlying of the spiritual formation ministries of LifeSpring is that Christians would come to understand and live more fully into their identity as deeply loved children of God.

RESOURCES FOR YOUR CONTAGIOUS FIRE

All of our Contributors lead ministries that attempt to be part of the contagious fire of God's love. Whether church pastors or resource ministry leaders, they struggle with each of the issues we have discussed in *Contagious Fire*. None of them have it made or reached perfection but have committed themselves to following Jesus as disciples—learners in the grand adventure of spreading the contagious fire of God's love across the earth. They are also committed to walking with you in this process.

In the following section, the Contributors that lead spiritual formation resource ministries share a brief overview of the ways God has called them to minister to the Body of Christ. Like the pastors who have shared above, these leaders don't pretend to be able to be resources for everyone. We all hope, however, that you will read these overviews with an ear to Jesus and contact us where you would like to check out a possible resource relationship.

The Order of Imago Christi - www.imagochristi.org

Contact: Bill O'Byrne

Imago Christi is a spiritual formation ministry team of Church Resource Ministries (CRM, Anaheim, CA) called to prophetically live out and invite Christian leaders into an intimate and transforming relationship of love with the Trinity so that the love of God will overflow through the Church into a world that desperately needs Him.

The spiritual formation missionaries of Imago Christi:

Minister to, mentor and train Christian leaders who are in a position to train and influence others, in order to intentionally multiply leaders in spiritual formation.

Foster spiritual community among Christian leaders in churches, mission agencies and "Christian professions" (counselors, coaches, spiritual directors, seminary instructors, etc.), *locally*, regionally and internationally.

Coach and mentor church leaders to help the Church (in all of its manifestations) become the place of spiritual formation that ministers to people, in every phase of the Christian journey.

Create resources and networks to train and support Christian leaders in each of these spheres and at various levels of the development of these aspects of spiritual formation ministry.

Help to foster a broad spiritual formation movement by reaching out to other spiritual formation entities and ministries and establish collaborative relationships with these goals in mind.

Resources:

Individual and group spiritual direction and coaching for Christian leaders.

Consulting with churches and ministries seeking to incorporate spiritual formation among their members and in their ministry focus.

The Imago Christi "Spiritual Formation Discovery for Leaders" event. A series of interactive spiritual formation modules, usually held over three days, leading participants to process five major themes essential to our holistic, spiritual growth.

Exercises for Discovery Companions by Imago Christi. Follow-up exercises from the Discovery event—8 weeks of exercises in each of the Spiritual Formation Discovery themes.

"Teresian Mapping Tool" Coaching and Training. The "Teresian Mapping Tool" is a coached, self-assessment test designed to help people identify their place in the spiritual formation paradigm, based on Teresa of Avila's *Interior Castle*.

Imago Christi Gatherings. The whole *Imago Christi* Core Community gathers three times a year to share our rhythms of transformation: Abiding, Gathering and Mission. Please feel free to register online and join us as a guest.

Spiritual Formation Coaching Manual & Training by *Imago Christi.* This Coaching Manual contains both a model for coaching spiritual formation as well as coaching guidelines in key spiritual growth areas. The Training process provides the skills and experience needed for you to coach others on their spiritual journey.

Spiritual Formation Discovery Facilitators Training by *Imago Christi* (coming later in 2018) will provide all training and materials needed for you to facilitate a Spiritual Formation Discovery event in an appropriate format for your ministry context.

Grafted Life Ministries - www.graftedlife.org

Contact: Debbie Swindoll

We partner with communities of believers to:
Prayerfully and intentionally seek to discern what God is doing.

Offer practical, real direction that begins with where people are.

Cultivate communities that offer safety, reconciliation, hope and belonging.

Create experiential opportunities for loving encounters with God, each other and the world.

Resources:

Consultation with church leaders, listening for where they currently find themselves and their congregants and helping them discern a developmental journey for deeper formation and relational growth.

Formation Studies that use Scripture as their foundation and are free from insider formation language. Each study provides a learning component, an experiential component and a small group component.

Our Life with God Study series is a three-year formation journey carefully designed to move people toward intimacy with God and others in everyday life. It is especially helpful for those in Mansions 2-4.

Our association of Spiritual directors provides on-line profiles for trained evangelical spiritual directors around the country who ascribe to a doctrinal statement and a code of ethics which can be viewed on our website. It also serves as a community for spiritual directors for companionship, further education and personal soul care.

Leadership Transformations, Inc. -

www.LeadershipTransformations.org

Contact: Steve Macchia

LTI endeavors to cultivate vibrant spirituality and attentive discernment among Christian leaders and teams. We believe "as the leader goes, so goes the organization, and as the soul of the leader goes, so goes the leader." Therefore, the needs of the soul must be the leaders #1 priority. May it be so in our generation!

Resources:

Equip spiritual directors through Selah, our Certificate Program in Spiritual Direction. We currently offer this in both in New England/Mid-Atlantic region and Phoenix, Arizona.

Train spiritual leaders through Emmaus—our Spiritual Leadership Communities. This quarterly, retreat-based cohort is on a three-year curriculum rotation with optional Certificate in Spiritual Leadership.

Provide spiritual health assessment for congregations through CHAT, our web-based Church Health Assessment Tool. It is currently offered through more than 50 denominational and regional networks.

Resource church and ministry leaders with the best spiritual formation books and on-line products through our Spiritual Formation Store.

Facilitate soul care retreats and conduct training events for leaders and teams on a wide range of spiritual formation topics, including church and team health, spiritual formation, leadership, discernment, etc.

Inward Journey Denver - www.inwardjourneydenver.com

Contact: Charlie Dodrill

Inward Journey Denver provides spiritual direction and soul care in group and personal settings. A team of spiritual directors seeks walks with seekers and believers as they discover deeper intimacy with Christ. Their ministry is hosted by Platt Park Church in Denver. Charlie Dodrill, founder of Inward Journey Denver and pastor at Platt Park Church, has started **"The Abbey."** The Abby provides a nine-month program for lead pastors and leaders of nonprofits called **PRAXIS** to introduce and guide leaders on a journey into a deeper intimacy with God. This consists of two 2-day retreats, one 1-day retreat, and six 4-hour evening gatherings throughout the year. PRAXIS involves guidance in prayer, spiritual direction, identity, and soaking in the love of God. PRAXIS is based on a similar program, in the San Francisco Bay Area, called soulCARE.

Church Resource Ministries (CRM) – www.crmleaders.org

CRM works to create movements of committed followers of Jesus by pioneering new ground among the unreached and unchurched, bringing lasting transformation among the poor, and mobilizing the Church for mission. Each one of our teams participates in accomplishing one or more of these initiatives in over 70 countries globally. By equipping pastors and lay leaders to take their congregations outside the walls of their church and authentically disciple people as followers of Jesus, we are mobilizing churches for effective mission. Three CRM teams, in addition to *Imago Christi*, particularly focus in the areas discussed in *Contagious Fire*.

ReWire

Contact: JD Ward though CRM

Endeavors to transform churches from the inside out by equipping members to impact their community, foster missional spiritual formation, and develop a sense of calling. ReWire offers churches the opportunity to move from "consumer," or church as a vendor of religious goods and services, to "missional," or church as a sent community to manifest God's Kingdom, celebrate God's work, and deepen their Spirit-led call. It's a move from missionary giving to missional living.

Resources:

Leadership Coaching — Step by step guidance to help prepare a congregation for the transition from consumer to missional

Workshops for Leadership Teams — 1- 3 Seminars on the theological and practical aspects of a missional shift

Missional Spiritual Formation — A discipleship journey for members to help them engage more deeply in the mission of God

Missional Sojourns — Trips (both local and global) to enlarge members' vision of the outward mission of God

Urban/Suburban Church Partnerships — Mutually beneficial partnerships with resourced and non-resourced communities

Prayer Retreats — Guided times of prayer and reflection designed to strengthen members' and leaders' inward experience of the transforming presence of God

ReNew

Contact: Ellen Burany at CRM

Our commitment is to walk alongside pastors, ministry leaders, and missionaries, as well as their spouses, to help them experience rest, renewal, and restoration of their souls in the midst of the ongoing demands of life and ministry. While we serve leaders who are experiencing burnout, pain, or emotional injury, we are also passionate to serve those who want to guard against these possibilities and grow in their effectiveness as leaders and ministers. Our team offers safe and confidential environments where leaders are able to grow in deeper relationship with God and in discernment and cooperation with the Holy Spirit as He forms and empowers their hearts, lives, and ministries.

Resources:

Individual Spiritual Direction

Group Spiritual Direction

Spiritual Retreats

Healing Prayer

Coaching to assist with discernment for life, ministry, and sabbaticals

reFocusing - www.refocusing.org

Contact: David Zimmerman at CRM

In a culture that proclaims that the Church is dying, we have hope because we believe that God has placed His calling on the lives of pastors and church leaders to lead the church beyond its walls and impact the community in undeniably powerful ways. In a culture that proclaims that the church is dying, we have hope. Because we believe that God has placed His calling on the lives of pastors and church leaders to lead the church beyond its walls and impact the community in undeniably powerful ways. Our calling is pastors.

Resources:

Awaken and Activate: Get trained in Steps 1 and 2 of our **Missional Pathway**. Find out how to equip every member of your church with perspective of God's unique shaping over their lifetime and how they can make a difference in the community.

Assess and Advance: Get trained in Steps 3 and 4 of our **Missional Pathway**. With this training, you will discover what God's heart is for your church in the specific city where you live, and also how God has wired your congregation to uniquely serve the unchurched.

Spiritual Formation Society of Arizona – www.sfsaz.org

Contact: Ted Wueste

Our mission is to engage learners and leaders in deepening intimacy with the Trinity. We realize that the world is a noisy place, both literally and metaphorically, and our churches often mirror the noise of the world. Leaders often find themselves stuck and frustrated because the desires of the world often shape church life more than God Himself shapes church life. Our desire is to provide safe places like Soul Care Days and prayer retreats where leaders can take a deep breath and remember who they are. Paying attention to their souls and living attentively to God's heart doesn't just happen, so we seek to equip leaders in these areas. We have a network of local spiritual directors and network with those who desire deep support for their life with God. In addition, we offer workshops and an annual conference designed to equip and encourage leaders in spiritual formation.

The Daring Way™ & Rising Strong™ - www.thedaringway.com

Contact: Melanie Saint James

Melanie Saint James shares her use of this ministry as part of her missionary work with *Imago* Christi. As a Christian leader who has struggled and fallen in ministry, shame has been one of those emotions that has nearly swallowed me whole. Yes, I prayed and repented, cried enough tears to fill a small lake, asked the Lord to forgive me, and still the issue of shame has followed me around like a gremlin whispering in my ear, "You are washed up. Used goods. No one wants someone like you around. Who do you think you are to teach classes on spiritual formation when you are so unworthy? Not even God can save you. You lost your spiritual authority when you fell, and now everyone knows you are a fraud."

These damaging lies from our enemy, along with the judgmental messages that rolled around in my head, left me emotionally and spiritually stuck. Eventually, I read Dr. Brown's book, *Daring Greatly*. It felt like she already knew me and was acquainted with the voices in my head. Her book gave me vocabulary that finally made sense of my experience, and even gave me a name for what I was feeling. The word was "shame." Shame, I discovered was that thing that, for some of us, stands between us and the source of love, and which blocks our ability to see, know, hear, and receive the gift of love. God's love is radiating all around us all the time, but my heart and emotions seemed unaware, blocked by shame and its ability to whisper lies of "never good enough." Like many others, the work and research of Dr. Brown changed my life. Learning how to become shame resilient and learn from my failure and falls, has taught me that failure is never the end of the journey. Instead, falls and failure become the compost out of which God is able to create something new and beautiful. It was through Brené's research and God's pursuit of me that I learned that God is able to create beauty out of the ashes of our lives.

I have since been professionally trained and certified in Brené's work and I currently offer two courses: The Daring Way™ and Rising Strong™.

The Daring Way™ is a 16-hour, highly experiential methodology, based on the research and work of Dr. Brené Brown, developed to help men, women, and adolescents learn how to show up, be seen, and live braver lives. During the process topics such as vulnerability, courage, shame, and worthiness are explored. The course focuses on developing shame resiliency skills and developing daily practices that transform the way we live, love, parent, and lead.

Rising Strong™ is a 16-hour curriculum based on the simple physics of vulnerability: if we are brave enough, often enough, we will fall. This curriculum is about what it takes to get back up and how owning our stories of struggle give us the power to write a daring new ending. Struggle can be our greatest call to courage and the clearest path to a wholehearted life. While neither of these curriculums are explicitly Christian per se, neither do they run counter to our faith. However, Dr. Brown refers to Scripture without quoting chapter and verse. Throughout her research Dr. Brown taps into the basic human experience and she invites people to trust that God means what He says and still believe that God loves us.

Together with my husband, Roy, we have led more than 20 Daring Way™ and Rising Strong™ groups or events to date. In addition to an art journaling course, I led as a Sunday School class at West Side church using Dr. Brown's book, *The Gift of Imperfection* as our text and our art journal as a way of exploring our own history. While some of these groups have been with all Christian participants, other times we have hosted Mormon couples, atheists, Buddhists, and those who have no specific beliefs at all. However, we believe that the Daring Way™ and Rising Strong™ curriculums are ways for Christians to grow emotionally, find healing for past or current hurts, and to practice telling our stories in a judgment free-zone, which for some may be their very first time. We believe that The Daring Way™ and Rising Strong™ events are one way a church or its staff can enable people to become Contagious Fire leaders in their church.

Flourish – Mid Columbia, – www.flourishmidcolumbia.com

Contact: Dan Wodrich

Flourish-Mid Columbia is a center for theological education for the **"everyday Christian"** in the Mid-Columbia region, to encourage, equip, and personally accompany followers of Jesus into thoughtful and wholehearted participation in His Life – in all of life – in our homes, the workplace, and in our community.

Resources:

Spiritual Formation Classes, Practices, Activities

Events and Forums

ReFrame Groups

Vocation Groups

Fellows Program

"Made to Flourish" Pastor's Network

OTHER SPIRITUAL FORMATION MINISTRIES RECOMMENDED BY OUR CONTRIBUTORS:

Renovare (Nate Foster) – www.renovare.org

SoulCare (Mindy Caliguire) - www.soulcare.com

Potters Inn (Steve and Gwen Smith) - www.pottersinn.com

Unhurried Living (Gem and Alan Fadling) –www.unhurriedliving.com

The Soul Care Project (Russell Courtney) –

www.thesoulcareproject.org

Gordon-Conwell Theological Seminary – Pierce Center; D.Min. Track "Spiritual Formation for Ministry Leaders" -

www.gordonconwell.edu/doctor-ministry/Spiritual-Formation-for-Ministry-Leaders.cfm

Denver Seminary's Soul Care Institute –

www.denverseminary.edu/academics/master-of-arts/christian-formation-soul-care

Talbot Seminary's Spiritual Formation Institute -

http://www.talbot.edu/isf

VantagePoint[3] (Rob Loane) – www.vantagepoint3.org

FOLLOWING JESUS INTO CONTAGIOUS FIRE

I think that you and I reside in a special time in history. Just when people feel that the world is going to hell in a handbasket, God breathes on His Church in new ways that bring new life. We could go on and on about society's condition and the weakening of the Church's influence. Yet, as you've seen in the stories above, many of us are experiencing an exciting new movement of the Holy Spirit—contagious fire.

Our Lord is calling the leaders of His Church to Himself at a new depth of love. He's calling His Church to proclaim the Kingdom through the contagious fire of Love. By transforming faithful leaders into His own image, through the fire of His love, God enables them to discern His voice, and love as He has loved them. He draws us together into a spiritual community, like a forest fire of love, to take His love into the world in a way never seen before. In the midst of what some feel are the darkest times in human history, the Father has stretched forth His hand and cast fire upon the earth—the fire of Love. His contagious fire will empower men and women of God and transform His Church. The fact that you are reading this book indicates that you, too, have heard His call. It tells me that your deepest heart's desire is to say YES—yes to your own transformation in Love and yes to the contagious fire that God wants for your ministry. You've become part of one of the great movements of God in the history of the Church, part of a great company of men and women who, with angels and archangels, proclaim:

Hallelujah! Salvation and glory and power belong to our God; give praise to our God, all you His bond-servants, you who fear Him, the small and the great. Hallelujah! For the Lord our God, the Almighty, reigns. Revelation 19:1-2,5-6

Let them give thanks to the Lord for His loving kindness, and for His wonders to the sons of men! For He has satisfied the thirsty soul, and the hungry soul He has filled with what is good. Psalm 107:8-9

425

This movement of God, however, demands more than any given leader can embrace alone. We desperately need you on the same journey—warriors with whom we can learn, bleed, pray, and gain courage. Our desire to follow Jesus more intentionally, at both heart and action levels, needs the support of a great army of the saints. We need them for courage as we begin, and later, when we discover that Jesus leads us beyond where we ever expected to go. Where? Into contagious fire, blown by the Holy Spirit, spreading throughout the Church! The Contributors and I encourage you to read and reread these themes in their progression, to pray through them, and then work through them with the leadership community in your ministry context. Using the reflection questions in this chapter, see how the Lord desires to ignite His contagious fire in your midst. Contact the churches and resources, mentioned above, as the Spirit guides you to learn from others who've responded to God's call to become contagious fire and travel in His way.

God is calling you into this movement of contagious fire! Listen to His voice to you; seek His face; follow Him the next step into the adventure of hearts so in love with God that they love the world—just as Jesus does!

APPENDIX A

SPIRITUAL FORMATION DEFINITION FROM TRUE NORTH PROJECT

(See Chapter 2)

Christian spiritual formation is the process of being shaped by the Spirit into the likeness of Christ, filled with love for God and the world.

God calls us all to become like Jesus. Jesus says, "I have come that they may have life, and have it abundantly." We experience this abundance of life – here and now – as our passions, character, understanding, and relationships are increasingly aligned with those of Christ. This lifelong transformation within and among us is the continual gift of God's Spirit. We are called to be renewed into the likeness of Jesus – but we do not always fully embrace this calling. Sometimes we seem content to be known as "Christians" without intentionally engaging with this work of the Holy Spirit in our lives. Other times we desperately long for a new way of life, wanting to grow in our walk with Jesus, but needing help and encouragement. We, therefore, commit to pursue passionately and to receive joyfully God's grace to be more fully transformed into the image of Jesus Christ.

John 7:37–39
*John 10:10
Romans 8:29
1 Corinthians 11:1
1 Corinthians 15:49
2 Corinthians 3:17–18
2 Corinthians 4:16–18
2 Corinthians 5:16–21
Galatians 4:19
Ephesians 1:3
Ephesians 3:16–19
1 John 3:2
1 John 4:17

As we are rooted in Jesus and in the kingdom, he proclaims, we are progressively transformed. Jesus is the center of all life and history, both the source and goal of all creation. God shaped this universe as a place where the love and life of Jesus Christ might flourish. Because we are formed in the divine image, we have the capacity to receive and express this life and love. Although human disobedience corrupts the divine image in us, God still forms a people able to love the Lord their God with all their heart, soul, mind, and strength, and love their neighbors as themselves. Jesus makes this possible through his life, death, and resurrection. In him we experience a restored relationship of love with God and one another, and continual transformation into his likeness. We are becoming a reconciled and renewed community – which is both the goal and the substance of life in God's kingdom. This is the good news we proclaim with joy to the whole world.

Genesis 1:26–28
Genesis 3:1–7
Proverbs 8:22–31
Isaiah 42:5–9
Jeremiah 31:33–34
Mark 12:28–34
John 1:1–18
John 13:34–35
Romans 5:9–11
Romans 8:1–11
Romans 8:19–23
Ephesians 2:11–22
Colossians 1:9–23
1 Thessalonians 5:23
1 John 2:7–11

Our engagement with God's transforming grace is vital. Renewal into the image of Christ is not a human attainment; it is a gift of grace. God mercifully uses all our experiences, including our suffering and trials, to teach and transform us. Even so, transformation requires our involvement and effort. We need to make ourselves available to the Holy Spirit's work in all our life experiences, particularly through intentional engagement with historical Christian disciplines, including Word and sacrament. These practices open us to the presence and grace of God. As a result, we become, through time and experience, the kind of persons who naturally express love, joy, peace, patience, kindness, goodness, faithfulness, gentleness, and self-control.

Matthew 5:43–48
Matthew 11:29–30
Luke 6:40
John 7:38
John 15:5–17
Romans 12:1–2
Galatians 5:16–25
Philippians 2:12–13
Philippians 3:12–16
Titus 2:11–14
Hebrews 5:13–6:1
Hebrews 12:7–13
James 4:7–8
1 Peter 2:2
1 Peter 4:1–2

Spiritual formation happens in community. As we long to know and follow Jesus and be formed into his likeness, we journey with those who share this longing. God is calling the church to be a place of transformation. Here we struggle to fulfill our calling to love. Here we learn to attend to the invitations of God's Spirit. Here we follow the presence of God in our midst. Spiritual community is the catalyst for our transformation and a sending base for our mission of love to the world.

Matthew 18:20
Luke 6:12–19
John 17:20–26
Acts 2:42–47
Romans 12:4–8
1 Corinthians 12:1–7
Galatians 6:1–2
Ephesians 4:1–16
Hebrews 10:23–25
1 Peter 2:4–10

Spiritual formation is, by its very nature, missional. As we are formed into the likeness of Christ, we increasingly share God's infinitely tender love for others. We deepen in our compassion for the poor, the broken, and the lost. We ache and pray and labor for others in a new way, a selfless way, a joy-filled way. Our hearts are enlarged toward all people and toward all of creation.

Isaiah 60:1–4
Matthew 5:14–16
Matthew 28:18–20
John 3:16–21
John 20:21–23
2 Corinthians 5:20
Galatians 6:10
1 John 4:7–21

We invite all people, everywhere, to embrace with us this calling to become like Jesus. By God's grace, we will seek to become lovers: lovers of God, lovers of people, and lovers of all creation. We will immerse ourselves in a lifestyle that is attentive and responsive to the gracious presence of God. We commit ourselves to the community of Christ's beloved, the church, so that we can learn this way of love together. We entreat you to join us.

Matthew 5:1–10
Matthew 13:44–46
Mark 1:15
Luke 9:23–24
Romans 12:1–2
2 Corinthians 6:1
1 Timothy 6:11–12
Revelation 21:2
Revelation 22:17

APPENDIX B:

SHORTENED MODELS BASED ON TERESA OF AVILA'S SEVEN MANSIONS WITH CURRICULUM SUGGESTIONS FOR EACH STAGE

Spiritual Formation Partners Model

Four Stages, based on Teresa's Seven Mansions:

> Stage 1: Seekers – Pre-Christians

> Stage 2: New Christians – Mansions 1&2

> Stage 3: Workers with Jesus – Mansion 3

> Stage 4: Falling in Love and Loving – Mansions 4-7

Stage 1: Seekers – Pre-Christians

Formal teaching at all stages (at a stage-appropriate level):

☐ Doctrine of the Gospel

☐ Biblical worldview

☐ Basic theology

☐ Deconstruct wrong theology

☐ How to share spiritually (language)

☐ Basic discipleship practices

☐ Rule of life

☐ Define church well; as a group in transformation

☐ Spiritual warfare

☐ Ending life well

- Prayer

- Spiritual disciplines

- Being and doing

- "Remembering" God's work in our lives, identifying issues in my own life

Stage 2 Teaching – Me Focus: Mansions 1&2

- Demonstrating the Journey with Jesus

- Doctrine of the Gospel

- Biblical world view

- Theology of God/Church, etc

- How to share spiritually – Sonship class

- Basic Discipleship

- Rule of Life

- Church = Transformational Journey together

- Spiritual Warfare

- Spiritual Disciplines

- Basic Balanced Life

- Community

Stage 3 Teaching – Me and You Focus: Mansion 3

- Spiritual gifts

- Ministry in community

- Discernment

- Vulnerability/Trust

- Accountability

- What is community

- Purpose of following Jesus

- Success radically redefined (cross)

- Symptoms of being called into a deeper walk

- Ministry prayer

- Sabbath rest

- Devotional life

- Ecclesiology

- Leadership

- Relational Bible Study

- Abiding Prayer/Listening Being and Doing

- Our personal blocks

- Fruits of the Spirit

Stage 4 Teaching – Thou Focus: Mansions 4-7

- Creating Experiences

- Ignatian Exercises

- Life & Person of Jesus – Friend

☐ Love of God – Books – Issues of Guilt & Shame

☐ Next Level of Surrender/Submission

☐ Identity in Christ vs Focus on being a Sinner

☐ Grace/Sin Balance

☐ Nature of God – Operative View

☐ New Levels of Longing for God

☐ Readings on Longing

☐ New Creation

☐ Prayer of Being

☐ Removal of False Idols / Attachments

☐ Emotional Healthy Spirituality

Centennial Covenant Model

Four Stages Based on the Teresian Mansions

Stage 1: Seekers – Seeking & <u>Following</u> Jesus

(Seekers, Mansions 1-2)

Stage 2: <u>Growing</u> Through Learning and Serving

(Mansion 3)

Stage 3: <u>Abiding</u> With Jesus

(Mansion 4)

Stage 4: <u>Deepening</u> Intimacy of Love

(Mansions 5-7)

Stage 1 Learning: Seeking & <u>Following</u> Jesus

Biblical Overview

- ☐ How to Study the Bible

- ☐ Basic Gospel Message

- ☐ Questions of the Faith

- ☐ Kingdom of God and Our Role

- ☐ Meaning of Sonship in Kingdom

- ☐ Worship

- ☐ Nature of Christian Community

- ☐ The Church and Its History

- God's Revelation in Nature

- First and Second Order Calling

- Nature of Christian Love

- Repentance and Forgiveness

- Grace and Justice

- Spiritual Growth

- Call to Discipleship – Service and Witness

- Rule of Life – Spiritual Practices

- Spiritual Warfare, Deliverance

- Addictions and Attachments

- Prayer – Conversation With God

- Knowing God's Will – Discernment

- Peacemaking/Conflict Resolution

Stage 1 Experience: Seeking & <u>Following</u> Jesus

- Small Group – Journey Specific

- Large Group Teaching and Worship

- Christian Community and Friendships

- Evangelism Events

- Mission Outreach Internship

- Mentor Relationship

- Opportunities for Repentance, Confession, And Absolution

- Vulnerable Witness of Maturing Christians

- Christian Friends in The Market Place

- Opportunity to Share Testimony

- Alpha Program

- Nurture the Wonder And Awe, Worship, Outdoors, Art, Music, Etc.

- Power Ministry--Seeing God Doing Things

- Recovery Groups

- Life Focus Groups

- Family Ministry

- Personal Devotional Life

- Conferences on Healing

- Intergenerational Ministry/Relationships

- Counseling

Stage 2 Learning: <u>Growing</u> Through Learning and Serving

- Relational Bible Study

- Missions – Home and Abroad

- Discerning Ministry Calling-Spiritual Gifts,

- Temperament, Passion, Life

- Stage, etc.

- Stewardship

☐   Discernment

☐   Fruits of the Spirit

☐   Consolation & Desolation

☐   Community Accountability and Support

☐   Worldview Implications

☐   Success Redefined

☐   Ministry Prayer

☐   Scripture Meditation/Abiding Prayer

☐   Christian Leadership

☐   Peace Keeping/Conflict Resolution

☐   Rule of Life & Sabbath

☐   Longing for More

☐   Wounds and Inner Healing

☐   Life Stage Discipleship

☐   Issues of Pride/Self

☐   Intercession

Stage 2 Experience: <u>Growing</u> Through Learning and Serving

☐   Applied Bible Study/Application Gp.

☐   Leadership/Ministry Training

☐   Opportunities for Service in The Church

☐   Ministry in The Workplace

- Conferences on Spiritual Gifts

- Mentor Relationships, Spiritually and Practice

- World Mission Opportunities

- Life Stage/Issue/Gender Conferences and Classes

- Discovery – SF Journey Overview

- Guided Prayer Retreats

- Spiritual Friendships

- Vision Casting Events

- Sacrificial Opportunities

- Participation in Sunday Worship Experience

- Healing and Deliverance Opportunities

- Cross-Cultural Christian Interaction

- Ignatian Exercises

- Spiritual Formation Conferences

- Counseling

Stage 3 Learning: <u>Abiding</u> With Jesus

- Discerning Jesus in Scripture

- Jesus as Friend

- Relational Bible Study

- Lectio & Ignatian Prayer

- Worship in Love

- Trinitarian Theology

- Our Personal History of Love

- Abiding Prayer – Silence, Waiting, Response

- Relinquishing Control

- Spiritual Disciplines of Devotion

- Sacred Pathways – Ways We Connect with God

- Service As A Response To Love/As Love

- Dealing With Guilt And Shame

- The Heart – Thinking, Feeling, Intuiting, Faith

- Spiritual Direction

- View of God As Love

- Dealing With Fear

- Community and Worship

- Spiritual Experience

- Dealing With Attachments

- Development of Longing

- New Levels of Devotion – Desert & Church Fathers And Mothers

Stage 3 Experience: <u>Abiding</u> With Jesus

- Relational Bible Studies

- Contemplative Worship

- Discovery – SF Journey Overview

☐   Shared Testimonies of This Season of Growth

☐   Devotional Prayer Retreats

☐   Mentor Relationships

☐   Spiritual Friendships

☐   Rule of Life - Time With God

☐   Spiritual Disciplines of Intimacy

☐   First Order Community

☐   Spiritual Direction

☐   Introduction to Mentoring

☐   Spiritual Formation Coaching

☐   Group Discernment

Stage 4 Learning: <u>Deepening</u> Intimacy of Love

☐   Scripture – Christ in You

☐   Scripture – In Christ

☐   Prayer – Language of Love

☐   Prayer of Contemplation and Silence

☐   Dark Nights

☐   Spiritual Experience Beyond the Senses

☐   Reconciling Mary and Martha

☐   Addiction, Inner Healing, Deliverance

☐   Spiritual Theology and Mystics

- ☐ Life in the Church

- ☐ Spiritual Direction

- ☐ Mentoring Others

- ☐ Spiritual Friendships

- ☐ Rule of Life – Solitude

- ☐ The Pain of Love – with God and Others

- ☐ Experiences of Union

- ☐ Surrender and Detachment

- ☐ Modeling Vulnerability

- ☐ Loving God in Others

- ☐ Discerning 2nd Order Calling

- ☐ God as Parent/Lover

- ☐ Leaving Well – Loss and Death

Stage 4 Experience: <u>Deepening</u> Intimacy of Love

- ☐ Advanced Study Opportunities

- ☐ Spiritual Direction

- ☐ Becoming A Mentor

- ☐ Contemplative/Silent Retreats

- ☐ Opportunities for Solitude

- ☐ Inner Healing and Deliverance

- ☐ Discovery – SF Journey Specific

- ☐ Spiritual Formation Conferences

     ☐   Spiritual Friendships

     ☐   Development of Longing

     ☐   Spiritual/Covenant Community

     ☐   Opportunity to Witness Publicly to New Season Of Growth

     ☐   Life Stage Issue Conferences

     ☐   Spiritual Creativity – Writing, Art, Music, Storytelling, Etc.

     ☐   Redefinition of Role In Church

     ☐   Discernment Relationships

APPENDIX C

CONTEMPLATIVE DIALOGUE COVENANT

Sacred Circles provide the space to share reflections that grow through the inward journey and provide an opportunity to learn from one another. It is important that we hold in common Contemplative Dialogue Rules in the journey together.

Overall Values: <u>Confidentiality</u>: Personal sharing within the small group is considered sacred therefore what is shared stays in the group when you leave the group. **<u>Being Comfortable With Silence:</u>** Silence provides time for reflection and hearing the Spirit and you should expect periods of silence during the dialogue. Be at peace with the silence and resist the urge to speak just because of the silence.

When Sharing:

<u>"I" statements:</u> Speak in the first person; talk personally from your own story.

<u>Root your sharing in your own experience:</u> Refrain from generalization and remarks that are overly abstract, philosophical, or theoretical.

<u>Equal time</u>: As you share and listen, be aware to provide time for each participant. Be concise. Make one point or relate one experience then stop and allow others to do the same.

When Listening:

Sharing is a gift: Receive the sharing with a spirit of thankfulness. There is no need to comment on the gift, simply receive it.

Active listening. Do not cross talk. Listen fully without thoughts of how you might respond or what you would want to share. Simply listen to and accept the thoughts of the person sharing without adding/changing or responding to them.

Reflective listening. Listen to what is God saying through the experience of the person sharing. Enter into their experience and their journey.

Response:

Silent Prayer: After each person shares, the others should sit in silence for 30 seconds to 1 minute, praying for the person who just shared, lifting them and their needs before the Lord. The person being prayed for – and only that person -- can add additional comments during this time of silence.

What Resonated: After all participants have shared and been prayed for you can respond by sharing what, if anything, resonated with you.

_____   _____

Signature   Date

CONTRIBUTORS TO CONTAGIOUS FIRE

The following men and women served as Contributors for the Contagious Fire Project. They assisted in the development of *Contagious Fire*, from its chapter outlines to suggestions on development of the book. They also allowed me to quote them based on comments they made online in Contributor Discussions. While I copied and edited their discussions, they have each approved the final drafts. Their comments are protected under the copyright of this book.

CHARLIE DODRILL

Charlie serves as the Pastor of Spiritual Formation and Worship at Platt Park Church in Denver, a "smallish" multi-denominational church in Denver, CO. In addition to regular pastoral duties, he helps train and recruit the congregation's small group leaders, leads the spiritual formation ministry, teaches, and leads the musical part their worship services. Charlie founded a small center for spiritual direction called Inward Journey Denver, where he serves as the Director, and spiritual direction to members of the congregation and community. The Inward Journey Denver ministry provides an opportunity for people to consider their journey with God in light of His love and desire for a deepening personal relationship. Charlie also serves as an adjunct professor at Denver Seminary in the Spiritual Formation department.

Charlie has received a Bachelor's Degree in Studio Art from West Virginia Wesleyan College, and a M.A. in Spiritual Formation from Denver Seminary.

As a musical composer and song writer, Charlie has produced a number of Christian CD's, including *Charlie Dodrill Prologue to This Drama*, and *Charlie Dodrill Eyes of the Exception*, published by Barnabas' Brother Publishing-ASCAP.

Charlie describes his passion for spiritual formation: "The passion of my heart is to see individuals and groups encounter Jesus in real ways. I believe the hunger that is sparked in such encounters ignites the fervent hunger that we all have inside of us. I want to help people experience this spark and journey with them as they grown more and more intimate with the Lover of their souls."

For more information about Charlie and his ministry, see

www.plattparkchurch.org

www.inwardjourneydenver.com

TAMMY LONG

Tammy Long serves as the Executive Pastor of South Bay Community Church in Fremont, CA. SBCC is a multi-ethnic congregation in the Bay Area whose mission is connecting with God, growing together and changing the world. Their vision is to excite spiritual transformation in Kingdom community and engage the broken world with the story of God's love. Tammy has hosted Imago Christi's Spiritual Formation Discovery for Leaders for SBCC and the region and continues to provide spiritual formation teaching and growth opportunities for the congregation. She is an ordained pastor, teacher, writer, trained spiritual director, wife, mother, and grandmother. Her joys away from the office include reading, movies, traveling, being in nature and spending time with her family.

She holds a Master's Degree in Education from Cal State East Bay, a Masters in Christian Formation from North Park Seminary, as well as ordination with the Evangelical Covenant Church.

Tammy is passionate about seeing people connect with God and grow deeper in love with the Trinity, both individually and in community. Whether through preaching, teaching, spiritual direction, facilitating a small group or leading a retreat, Tammy's deepest joy is walking alongside others as they draw closer to the heart of God and experience spiritual transformation.

For more information about Tammy and her ministry, see

www.sobcc.org

CHRIS LYONS

Chris serves as Pastor to Youth and Families at Longview Bethany Community Church, in West Seattle, WA. He is very involved in the youth ministry network in his area and loves engaging city-wide opportunities to serve the young people of his community. Chris' passion is to see youth grow in their personal relationship with Jesus Christ and to deepen that relationship in the midst of community, using music, sports, fun, friendships and youth programs. Another vital aspect of his ministry is to nurture and inspire family-based faith in the midst of inter-generational connections within the church. He has been doing ministry in the Northwest for over 20 years. He also teaches and consults with youth leaders and churches around the country. Chris' wife, Lisa, is a school nurse and amazing partner in ministry. They live in Longview, WA with their three children, Katie, Nikki,

Chris received his B.A. in History from Ohio State University, his M.Div. from George Fox Evangelical Seminary, and his Doctor of Ministry degree from Gordon Conwell Theological Seminary.

Chris' D.Min. Dissertation, *Connecting the Dots in Community: Investing in a Congregational Commitment to Prepare Students to Transition from High School without Graduating from their Faith - by Inspiring Personal Faith Ownership Anchored in Christian Fellowship*, builds on the need for parents and other adults to embrace intentional spiritual formation and be able to openly discuss their spiritual journeys.

Chris shares his passion for the Church relative to spiritual formation: "I believe that God is calling the wider church to receive young people as full-fledged partners in ministry. This partnership should be the mission of every church interested in vital ministry with the emerging generations."

For more information about Chris and his ministry see

http://www.churchbcc.org/

STEVE MACCHIA

Steve Macchia serves as the Founder and President of Leadership Transformations, Inc. (LTI). LTI is a ministry which focuses on the spiritual formation needs of leaders and the spiritual discernment processes of leadership teams in local church and parachurch ministry settings nationwide. He is also the Director of the Pierce Center for Disciple-Building at Gordon-Conwell Theological Seminary, where he also teaches the Spiritual Formation for Ministry Leaders track in the Doctor of Ministry program. Previously, he served as president of Vision New England, formerly known as The Evangelistic Association of New England. Steve has also served on the pastoral staff team at Grace Chapel in Lexington, MA. He is a spiritual director, mentor to young leaders, leadership coach, conference speaker, and author. He is the delighted husband of Ruth and the proud father of two grown children, Nathan and Rebekah.

Steve received his B.A. in Christian Education and Elementary Education at Northwestern College in Orange City, IA, and his Masters of Divinity and Doctor of Ministry degrees at Gordon-Conwell Theological Seminary in South Hamilton, MA.

Steve has authored several books, including *Broken and Whole, Outstretched Arms of Grace, Path of a Beloved Disciple, Wellspring, Crafting a Rule of Life: An Invitation to the Well-Ordered Way, Becoming a Healthy Church, Becoming A Healthy Church Workbook, Becoming A Healthy Disciple, Becoming A Healthy Disciple: Small Group Study and Workbook, Becoming A Healthy Team, and Exercises for Becoming A Healthy Team.* Steve has also written a number of articles and columns for various publications, including Conversations Journal, Outcomes Magazine, The Fellowship of Presbyterians, Focus on the Family, etc.

Steve describes his passion for spiritual formation: "I envision a Holy Spirit—empowered Church led by spiritual leaders who invite others to discover spiritual maturity together in a spiritual community where spiritual friendships practice spiritual conversations that uphold and affirm spiritual transformation for all, ultimately leading to spiritual renewal—the making of 'little Christs" to light up the world with the love of God, Father, Son and Holy Spirit — in our lives, communities, and throughout the world."

For more information about Steve and his ministry, see

www.leadershiptransformations.org/macchiabio.htm

www.gordonconwell.edu/piercecenter

BILL O'BYRNE

Bill serves as Co-Founder and Team Leader of *Imago Christi*. He served as a missionary with Church Resource Ministries in Saint Petersburg, Russia from 1993 to 2015 with his wife Priscilla, where they raised four children. He also taught Spiritual Formation and Biblical Studies at Saint Petersburg Christian University. Bill has served as a spiritual companion for pastors, ministry leaders and missionaries, primarily as a coach for the Ignatian Exercises. He also presents in Imago Christi's Spiritual Formation Discovery retreats. As team leader for *Imago Christi*, he coordinates the ministries of its full time spiritual formation missionaries. Bill now lives with his family in Denver, Colorado.

Bill has a BA degree in Theology and German from Wheaton College and an M.Div. and M.A. in Christian Education from Trinity Evangelical Divinity School.

He has published *A Lenten Journey: A Contemplative Devotional On the Passion and Resurrection of Christ, Fugitive Encounters: The Story of Luke, Gospel Writer*, "Longing for God at the Heart of Mission, co-authored with Tom Ashbrook in Global Mission Handbook: A Guide for Cross-cultural Service, "First and Second Order Calling," with Tom Ashbrook, http://www.imagochristi.org/Pages/FomativeTopics.aspx, and "Conversion in the Teresian Mansions," https://www.imagochristi.org/formative-topics/

Bill describes his passion for spiritual formation: "I have a vision to see the Community of Imago Christi serve as "an international order of spiritual formation missionaries," to foster the spiritual formation of Christian leaders, nurture spiritual formation communities, and help the Church embody spiritual formation ministry and become a place that ministers to people, in every phase of the Christian journey, towards deepening intimacy with Christ, by providing training opportunities, formational environments, curriculum, and relational networks for maturing Christians, as well as renewing existing structures of evangelism and discipleship with spiritually formational principles and goals."

For more information about Bill and his ministry, see

www.imagochristi.org

www.crmleaders.org

obyrnereport.blogspot.com

CHUCK ORWILER

It has been Chuck's joy to serve as pastor of a single congregation, Denver Friends Church (Colorado), for over 37 years. Retired from this position at the church, he continues to cultivate formative living through discipleship in his church and serving as somewhat of a pastor-at-large in the Denver area. In the latter role, he provides retreat leadership and spiritual direction, primarily with seasoned ministry leaders. He has been active in the organizational restructuring of the Friends Churches in the Rocky Mountain region with the intent of developing a spiritually forming emphasis in our governance. He also helped found the Rocky Mountain Spiritual Formation Partners: a group established to encourage the development of spiritual formation, especially in our churches. He has been active with the Spiritual Formation Alliance which sought to network spiritual formation resources and leaders nationally and locally.

Chuck received a BA in Christian Ministry from George Fox University, and a MA in Counseling from Denver Seminary. He also received a D.Min from George Fox Evangelical Seminary in Church Leadership and Spiritual Formation. He received training in spiritual direction at the Vincentian Center for Spirituality and Work which, he says, "changed the way I approached my pastoral role."

Chuck contributes to the *Fruit of The Vine* devotional guide (Barclay

Press), and occasionally writes adult Bible study lessons for *Illuminate* (Barclay Press).

Chuck shares his passion for spiritual formation: "I live to help people know and follow the real Christ in the real world. Christ is present. His invitation is always before us to come, take His yoke, and learn from Him. There is no better place to do so than in our ordinary congregations in which the clay of the jar and the glory of the Treasure are ever before us."

You may contact Chuck through Denver Friends Church, www. denverfriendschurch.com.

MELANIE SAINT JAMES

Melanie Saint James is a member of *Imago Christi*, an international spiritual formation ministry that develops spiritual formation resources and provides spiritual coaching and mentoring to Christian leaders and the churches they serve. Formerly a Presbyterian pastor, she now serves as a "spiritual formation missionary in residence" at West Side church, in Richland, WA, a medium sized faith community affiliated with the ECO denomination. Melanie teaches spiritual formation classes, provides spiritual direction and mentoring, and leads retreats for people yearning to develop a deeper, more intimate relationship with Jesus. Melanie is also a Certified Facilitator of The Daring Way™, that focuses on shame, vulnerability, courage and worthiness. Melanie also utilizes Dr. Brown's work to help retreat participants identify the "blocks and barriers" that keep them from fully experiencing God's unconditional, transforming love for them. Melanie now lives in Richland, WA with her husband, Roy.

Melanie received a B.S. in Biology from Pacific Lutheran University, an M.Div. Regent College, an MA Clinical Psychology from Fuller Theological Seminary, and a D.Min. in Spiritual Formation from Azusa Pacific University.

Melanie has published her D.Min. dissertation, *"The Place of Spiritual Formation In the Context of Theological Education: A Faculty Perspective"*

Melanie shares her passion for spiritual formation: "For me, spiritual formation is primarily about love - God's love for us, and our love for God. All too often, the heavy demands of programs, people, and the institutional needs of the church can draw pastors and leaders away from spending time abiding in the Father's love and allowing Him to mature them in the ways of Jesus. This lack of renewing, refreshing, and spiritual transformation can eventually lead to spiritual weariness, irritability, depression, growing isolation, and even burnout. My passion for spiritual formation in the church flows out of these truths. Thus, I believe we all need to hear Jesus calling our names and inviting us to "Come away with me to a quiet place to get some rest " so that we might grow in our capacity to love and be loved, for our own sake, and for the sake of a world desperately in need of being drawn into a community of love.

For more information about Melanie and her ministry, see

www.imagochristi.org

www.crmleaders.org

www.westside1.org

www.thedaringway.com

CHRIS SCHUTTE

Chris serves as Rector (Senior Pastor) of Christ Church Anglican, a medium-sized congregation in Phoenix, AZ. CCA sees its mission to, grow mature disciples of Jesus, in the power of the Holy Spirit, through the breadth and richness of Anglican worship and intentional, scriptural, and community-based Christian formation. They serve as a resource and actively partner with other Christ-centered churches and organizations, seeking to expand God's kingdom in their city. After ordination, Chis served in Prescott for three years, for two-and-a-half years in Paradise Valley before coming to CCA in 2007. Chris lives with his wife Tracy and their children, Owen, Anna, and Claire. In his free time, he loves to read, watch baseball, walk, run, and, occasionally, watch a movie.

Chris received his B.A. in History and Classics from the University of Arizona in Tucson, AZ, and his M.Div. from Gordon-Conwell Theological Seminary in South Hamilton, MA

Chris describes his passion for spiritual formation: "The church needs to be a place where people can learn to follow Jesus in community, experience God's love, God's heart, and God's mission for his people."

For more information about Chris and his ministry, see

www.christchurchphoenix.org

Twitter: @chrismschutte

DEBBIE SWINDOLL

Debbie is the founder and Executive Director of Grafted Life Ministries. Grafted Life serves the church in the area of spiritual formation through curricular resources and training for small group leaders and staff. GLM's small group studies are designed to transition participants from performance-based discipleship to a relational model which facilitates honest and intimate encounters with God and members of their community.

Since founding Grafted Life, Debbie has developed 10 studies with her writing partner, Monica Romig Green. She serves as a spiritual director with both individuals and groups and writes and speaks on what the Bible teaches about relationships with God and others. She gets a lot of relational practice in her family with a husband, three grown kids, two kids-in-law and five grandkids.

Debbie is profoundly grateful for her excellent training from Biola University. She received her M.A. in Spiritual Formation and Soul Care from Talbot's Institute for Spiritual Formation.

Debbie's passion for formation: "I am a bit of a theology nerd but good theology is wasted on us if we can't access its truth in our daily experience. I love helping people move beyond giving mental ascent to Biblical ideas to an actual experience of God in their day-to-day lives."

To learn more about Debbie and her ministry visit:

graftedlife.org

TERRY TARLETON

Terry Tarleton recently served as Senior Pastor of the non-denominational Carefree Vineyard Church in Phoenix, Arizona, a church of 100-plus he founded in 2001. He "planted" the church out of nearby Vineyard Church North Phoenix, where he served as executive pastor for eight years.

Terry received his B.A. from Excelsior College in Liberal Arts, earned an M.A. in Theological Studies from Liberty Theological Seminary, and received certification as a spiritual director through Sustainable Faith's School of Spiritual Direction.

Terry describes his passion for spiritual formation: A life-long follower of Jesus, I became passionate about spiritual formation in 2010 when ministry burnout and a personal crisis led to an "inward journey" with Jesus that noticeably transformed my way of doing life and church. I am excited about leading everyone from new believers to pastoral leaders to a fruit-filled life where serving flows out of an intimate, authentic relationship with Jesus. I believe that the Church in America is generally more committed to *doing* the works of Jesus than *being* with Jesus. One of my favorite sayings is "doing flows out of being."

For more information about Terry and his ministry, contact him at ttarleton@protonmail.com

STEVE THULSON

Steve has served as Lead Pastor of Centennial Covenant Church in Littleton, Colorado since 1987 when the congregation was just two years old. The congregation now averages about 300 participants in our Worship Gatherings. Their mission is to seek to follow the living Jesus on our "shared journey of transformation in his mission to our broken world." Steve has been intentional about enabling members grow in their faith and share God's love. He initiated a "Journey Team" in the congregation that has used Imago Christi's Spiritual Formation Discovery for Leaders events, as an introduction to spiritual formation, provided fomationally focused adult education classes, helped focus Life Groups, and implemented a "Companions for the Journey" ministry. He and his wife Darlene have three adult children and seven grandchildren, and live in Littleton, Colorado.

Steve has degrees from the University of Colorado and Wheaton College (B.A.), and Fuller Seminary (M.Div. and D.Min.). His doctoral dissertation explored a priority as a Pastor: "God Focused Discernment in Leading a Church to Health and Growth."

Steve's shares his passion for spiritual formation:

"A primary and constant question for our leaders is how we let Jesus be the living Head of his church, not a mere figurehead. The answer is grounded in the personal reality that I am a loved son of the Father, a servant and friend of his Son, and a dwelling of his Spirit. I long for such grace to take hold more deeply in more lives."

For more information about Steve and his ministry, see

JD WARD

JD leads the ReWire Team with Church Resource Ministries since 2009. ReWire offers spiritual formation materials and processes that help create missional hearts in lay people and offers training to pastors to learn an approach to discipleship called Missional Spiritual Formation. JD has served for 30 years mobilizing people into ministry with the poor. His call to serve the poor directly has led him to work with gang affiliated youth, juvenile detention centers, the homeless, low income seniors living in nursing homes, and managing projects in Ethiopia and Kenya. He has worked at University Presbyterian Church in Seattle Washington, Menlo Park Presbyterian Church, and Lakeside Presbyterian Church in San Francisco. JD served for 5 years with the Northwest Leadership Foundation running a large urban youth workers training program called Vision Youth. JD and his wife Tracy live in the Bay Area of California. They have 7 sons ranging in age from 15-25.

JD graduated from Seattle Pacific University in Business Management and received his M.DIV. from Fuller Theological Seminary.

Among a number of articles and training materials, JD has produced "Beyond," a curriculum to help church members discover and live out their God-given calling. This journal is meant to be used in tandem with their Call course material.

JD describes his passion for spiritual formation: "In 1997, I began to explore a more contemplative approach to life, reading contemplative authors and regularly visiting a monastery in B.C., Canada. Since that time, I have dedicated my life to the integration of mission and contemplation."

For more information about JD and his ministry, see

www.crmleaders.org

TED WUESTE

Ted directs the Spiritual Formation Society of Arizona, and also serves as a pastor in the local church. He practices spiritual direction as a part of his pastoral ministry as well as with those in the broader Christian community. Ted also teaches as adjunct faculty in the Spiritual Formation Program at Phoenix Seminary, and serves as Senior Faculty for Selah, a training program in spiritual direction. Having planted and served as lead pastor of a church in Texas for almost 10 years, he most recently has served as Executive Pastor of Spiritual Formation at Bethany Bible in Phoenix. Ted loves living in the desert of Arizona with his wife, Jenifer, and children, Trey and Claire.

Ted has degrees in D.Min. in Leadership, from Phoenix Seminary, a Master of Sacred Theology, from Dallas Seminary, a Master of Divinity, Western Seminary, in Portland, Oregon, a Certificate in Spiritual Direction: Selah, Leadership Transformations, and a Certificate in Spiritual Direction, New Way Ministries.

Ted has published *Mansions of the Heart Study Guide*, Co-authored with Tom Ashbrook, *Let Every Heart Prepare Him Room: Advent Reflections*, and *The Practice of the Presence of God Study Guide*.

Ted says about his passion for spiritual formation, "Having served as a pastor for the last twenty years, I have grown deeply passionate about seeing people become aware and intentional about their own spiritual formation. In addition, thinking about the ways that our churches are involved in spiritual formation is of deep interest to me. Finally, my deepest passion is for the formation of leaders because churches will only go as far as their leaders have gone."

For more information about Ted and his ministry, see

www.desertdirection.com

www.sfsaz.org

www.bbcphx.org

www.mansionsoftheheart.com

MARKUS HUGHES – COVER ARTIST

Markus Hughes is a modern artist who enjoys working with oil, acrylic, charcoal and more. Born in Illinois, he currently resides in Pagosa Springs, Colorado. Markus has been both an artist and Sports Massage Therapist for more than 20 years. Paintings can be purchased, and custom artwork can be created to your liking, by visiting his website, MarkusHughes.com. Custom signed prints of the book cover art "Contagious Fire" are available for purchase through his website.

For more information about Markus and his work, see:

www.MarkusHughes.com

SPIRITUAL FORMATION RESOURCES

BY R. THOMAS ASHBROOK

for

Individuals, Spiritual Directors

and Congregations

Presence

a

Novel

Presence tells the story about Jesus' physical appearance to three people in a small town , how their lives, church, and town become transformed. This amazing and down-to-earth story sparks the kind of contagious fire vision in its readers discussed in *Contagious Fire.*

Presence and its study guide, *Discovering Christ's* Presence, Provides a personal and group reflection on the Novel and the biblical

foundations underlying our experience of Jesus—Present.

Mansions of the Heart

and

Mansions Study Guide

 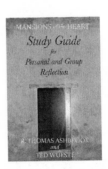

Mansions of the Heart: Exploring the Seven Stages of Spiritual Growth, uses Teresa of Avila's seven mansions to explore the life-long journey of spiritual growth. While *Mansions* has been used with great success by seminaries, spiritual formation programs, and Christian leaders, the Mansions Study Guide, by Tom Ashbrook and Ted Wueste now makes Mansions accessible to small groups and spiritual direction relationships. This interactive study for personal reflection and group discussion enables Jesus followers to discover where they are in their journey of spiritual growth and learn how to cooperate with the Holy Spirit's transformation work.

Made in the USA
San Bernardino, CA
15 June 2018